Dear Winston,
Merry Christmas 2020
with love from
Jo, Colin, Caitlin & Felicity

Warren Dockter is Research Fellow at Clare Hall, University of Cambridge. He received his PhD in History from the University of Nottingham.

OUR IMPERIAL No. 1.

[What with his pronouncement on Mesopotamia, and the opening of the Imperial Conference, this is a great week for Mr. Winston Churchill.]

This illustration by Frank Reynolds appeared in *Punch* on June 15, 1921.

CHURCHILL AND THE ISLAMIC WORLD

Orientalism, Empire and Diplomacy in the Middle East

WARREN DOCKTER

I.B. TAURIS
LONDON · NEW YORK

First published in 2015 by I.B.Tauris & Co. Ltd
Reprinted in 2015 and 2016
London • New York
www.ibtauris.com

ISBN: 978 1 78076 818 2
eISBN: 978 0 85773 714 4

A full CIP record for this book is available from the British Library
A full CIP record is available from the Library of Congress
Library of Congress Catalog Card Number: available

Typeset in Garamond Three by OKS Prepress Services, Chennai, India
Printed and bound by CPI Group (UK) Ltd, Croydon, CR0 4YY

For my Fathers,
Albert, Bill, and Doug
For your faith, love, and devotion.

CONTENTS

LIST OF ILLUSTRATIONS

Plate 11. Winston Churchill with King Abd al-'Aziz Ibn Saud of Saudi Arabia at Auberge due Lac, Fayoum, in February 1945. (Source: Churchill Archives Centre, The Broadwater Collection).

Plate 12. Winston Churchill's famous 'Let Us Go Forward Together' poster in Arabic. (Source: Australian War memorial, Canberra, Australia).

Plate 13. A Persian man gives the 'V' sign. This photo was sent to Winston Churchill by Major-General Robert Cotton Money, G.O.C. Balochistan. (Source: Churchill Archives Centre, The Broadwater Collection).

Plate 14. Winston Churchill inspecting the Guard of Honour in Tinerhir, Morocco, January 1951. (Source: Churchill Archives Centre, The Clementine Churchill Papers).

ACKNOWLEDGEMENTS

In many ways this book was a result of a discussion I had with Professor Chris Wrigley. Without his enthusiasm, interest, support, supervision, and friendship this book would have been impossible. This book and I are further indebted to his careful proofreading of my seemingly ceaseless grammar mistakes. I am also indebted to Dr Spencer Mawby for his encouragement and fine-tuning of my ideas and to Andrew Holt, Peter Stelfox, and Laura White. I would also like to thank my editor Tomasz Hoskins.

I am grateful to the School of History, especially Amanda Samuels, and the International Office at the University of Nottingham for their financial educational, and moral support. I am also grateful to T and T Signs, Inc. for its faith in me, my project, and for its generous contributions. I am further indebted to Marc Herzog, Stephen Mitchell and the British Institute at Ankara for their financial support as well as research assistance. I would also like to thank the Scouloudi Foundation in association with the Institute of Historical Research who generously contributed a grant towards the publication of this book.

I am very thankful for the support of the Churchill Archives at Churchill College in Cambridge, especially its director Allen Packwood, whose tireless help and interest has aided my research in numerous ways. In addition, I would like to show my appreciation for the support of the Fellows and Master of Churchill College and for the support from the Fellows and President of Clare Hall. I am also grateful to the Fitzwilliam Museum, the Bodleian Library, the British Library, the Hallward Library, the National Archives, and the Churchill Centre.

I would like to thank Sir Martin Gilbert who met with me to discuss my project and whose biography of Winston Churchill this book leans on heavily. I would also like to thank Dr Sue Townsend and Dr Paul Bracken for all their support, guidance, encouragement, and much needed laughter. Additionally, thanks to Christopher Catherwood, Vejas Liulevicius, Paul Addison, and Piers Brendon for their willingness to discuss my research and Richard Toye for all his help and his friendship.

I would like to thank my family for their love, faith, patience, and occasional financial assistance. Thank you so much Barbara, Doug, Bill, and Albert. I also want to thank my late stepmother Terry, who is greatly missed and whose memory has been warm and reassuring. Furthermore, I must thank my siblings Joseph Morgan, Kelli Dockter, Natalie Dockter, Madelyn Dockter, and Ben Dockter for always keeping a smile on my face and making me laugh when I needed it the most. I would also like to thank my extended family: the Georges, the McCurrys, the Morgans, the Roses, and the Wests. I must also thank my partner Lisa Stelfox who has been patient, loving, and supportive.

Many thanks must be offered to my friends and colleagues who helped to light my path during the course of this book. Katie McDade, Mark Storey, and Ceri Gorton deserve a special mention. Matt Phillips, Barry Phipps, Eamonn Tootile, Alan Kissane, Keith Nottle, Emily Buchnea, Paul Henshaw, Neil G. Howe, and Ben Wales have also been great friends and welcome distractions.

I must also thank those at home who left the light on for me. Chaz Cooper, Ben Mullins, and Alex Cameron have been great friends whose support, encouragement, and comradery have been greatly appreciated. Additionally, I must thank Justin Roddye, Jason Smith, Jeremy Watson, Kevin Buchmeier, Andrew Cooper, and the many others who have been very supportive.

INTRODUCTION

The effects of British imperial policy continue to resonate in the Islamic world and analyzing its origins is crucial in understanding the current geopolitical context of the 'Arab Spring', the 'War on Terror', and the rise of ISIS. Such an analysis must include the role played by Winston Churchill because, as the historian David Fromkin put it, 'No man played a more crucial role [...] in giving birth to the Middle East we live with today than did Winston Churchill.'[1] Yet relatively little attention in historical research has been paid to Churchill's relations with the Islamic world. This is a strange omission – as his military and political life often became intrinsically connected to it.

Churchill is, of course, a central figure in twentieth-century British history. He had a significant impact on the history of the British Empire from its zenith to its dissolution after World War II. His life was dedicated to serving the British Empire and its people, first as a journalist and junior officer with the 4th Queen's Own Hussars cavalry regiment, and later during an active political career that lasted from 1899 until the mid 1950s (though he technically remained an MP until 1964). Much has been written about his prolific political career, especially his roles in the two world wars, but his relationship with the Islamic world has not received major academic attention.

Churchill's career as a soldier and journalist brought him into contact with Islamic forces. In 1897 he served against Muslim tribes on the north-west frontier of India in what is now Afghanistan and Pakistan, as well as against the Dervish Empire in Sudan in 1898. Churchill's attitudes and perceptions about Islam developed during these early contacts and would later influence his policies regarding the Middle East and India throughout his political career.

However, the majority of non-biographical works on Churchill focus on his role as Prime Minister during World War II or on his period as a Liberal minister (1905–15). This approach overlooks periods of his early life, especially prior to World War I, and aspects of his policies concerning the Middle East and other Asiatic Muslim countries. This has created an historically inaccurate account of Churchill's role in the making of Britain's Middle Eastern policy, and its continuing influence on contemporary geopolitics. Historians generally misunderstand Churchill's unique perception of Islam by associating his views with those of his contemporaries in British leadership. For example, historian David French writes in his article 'The Origins of the Dardanelles Campaign Reconsidered' that 'the entire War Council (including Churchill) held the conviction that "the Turk was inherently inferior to the white man"', and, more specifically, he extrapolates from the minutes of the Dardanelles Commission that Churchill believed in 'the innate inferiority and poor fighting qualities of non-European troops'.[2] Other historians simply dismiss Churchill's experiences with Islam; for example, historian of the Middle East, David Fromkin asserts that Churchill was a 'rising but widely distrusted young politician with no particular interest in Moslem Asia'.[3] Clearly, these misunderstandings occur because historians do not fully consider Churchill's early military career and his subsequent books regarding the operations on the north-western frontier of India or in the Sudan.

This book addresses such misunderstandings by exploring Churchill's attitude towards the Islamic world between 1895 (shortly after he joined the military as a junior officer in the 4th Queen's Own Hussars cavalry regiment) and 1955 (when he resigned his position as premier). It examines how Churchill's perception of Muslims, Islam, and Islamic culture was shaped by his early experiences in the military and demonstrates that these encounters during the formative period of his life helped him develop a respect for and fascination with the Muslim world. This later shaped his policies as a political and military figure, especially during the world wars, as Colonial Secretary in the early 1920s, during his 'political wilderness' in the 1930s, and as a postwar premier in the 1950s. In addition, this book will reveal that Churchill's engagement with and understanding of the Muslim world stands in stark contrast to the purely imperialistic and orientalist perspectives of many of his contemporaries. In that regard, it becomes obvious that Churchill's attitude was not that of a typical British politician. His views of Islamic people and culture were an often paradoxical and complex combination of imperialist perceptions composed of typical orientalist ideals fused with the respect, understanding, and magnanimity he had gained from his experiences in his early military career, creating a perspective that was uniquely Churchillian.

This 'Churchillian perspective' is also useful in helping to illuminate the parameters of 'the Islamic world', in terms of religion, ethnicity, and culture. Clearly, such monolithic terms as 'Islamic world' are indictive of nineteenth-century thinking and are not particularly useful today due to the dynamic nature of Islamic identity. Islam is not an ethnicity, it is a religion and it is a multi-faceted religion with several practices and branches at that. However, Churchill's perception was deeply rooted in such Romantic Victorian constructions. For instance, Churchill undoubtedly connected the Islamic religion to peoples of the Middle East, specifically Arabs and, to be more specific, Bedouin Arabs. The facts that the majority of Muslims are not Arab and that not all Arabs are Muslim, did not dissuade Churchill. He was at least aware of this in some way, as he conceptualized much of British India as a component of the 'Islamic world'. However, for Churchill Indian Muslims were, culturally speaking, mere echoes of the Bedouin Arabs and were, therefore, in need of British supervision and leadership. In this way, Churchill believed that Islam and the British Empire might find a common purpose.

In geographic terms, Churchill typically referred to the 'Middle East' as the primary region of Islamic influence. However, the term 'Middle East' was itself a problematic and mercurial term that represented another Romantic, Victorian imagined geographic space.

In fact, Churchill often changed the geographic parameters of the Middle East to meet his immediate political needs. Recognizing this Churchillian perspective as a problematic and shifting definition of the 'Middle East' and 'Islamic world' this book adopts the notion that *Dar al-Islam*, or the Muslim regions of the world (literally, the House of Islam) geographically included the Middle East, North Africa, and parts of Central and South Asia. A notable exception, which is different to how we might conceptualize it today, is that the Islamic communities of Pacific Asian countries, such as Malaysia and Indonesia, are not included. The book does not include these communities because Churchill never really reflected on them as being a substantial part of the Islamic world. Despite this omission, the Islamic world in 1910 included around 20 million Muslims in Turkey. In British India there were approximately 62 million Muslims, 10 million Muslims in Egypt, plus the numbers of Muslims in the Ottoman Middle East, including nomadic Bedouin tribes.

Moreover, the 'Churchillian perspective' of the Islamic world might be understood to have three major features: the geopolitics of the aforementioned regions, their religious identity, and their ethnic identity. These features, combined with geographical considerations, come together to create a dynamic picture of the 'House of Islam', some of which lay outside the British Empire (Turkey and the Ottoman Middle East before 1918), some of which was contained within the British Empire (India), and some of which was contained in the informal British Empire (Egypt, Persia, the Middle East after 1918, and Pakistan after 1948).

In order to demonstrate Churchill's complex, often mercurial, and evolving relationship with the Islamic world, this book studies his life chronologically. Churchill's long life in British politics provided several instances when he left his mark on British–Islamic relations. These marks were so important, in part because of the dramatic changes that were ongoing in British–Islamic relations during Churchill's lifetime. Twenty-one years before Churchill's birth, British–Islamic relations (and in fact Britain's entire relationship with the East) changed as a result of the Indian Mutiny of 1857 (or the Indian Rebellion), which was believed in Britain to have been instigated by its Muslim subjects and centered on the Muslim Mughal Emperor. Once Britain regained control of India, its approach to Empire in India dramatically changed with the Government of India Act of 1858. This resulted in the end of the British East India Company's rule in India, with its holding being distributed to the British Crown, the establishment of a formal British government in India, and the creation of a new administrative, governmental department, the India Office. This formalization of British rule in India was fully consolidated in 1877 when Prime Minister Benjamin Disraeli formally presented Queen Victoria with the crown of India. But despite such extensions of British power an underlying tension persisted in British policy with its Muslim subjects, which would manifest itself as a deep fear of a pan-Islamic movement once again igniting the fury of the Islamic world.

This fear increasingly affected British relations with the Muslim Ottoman Empire, because British imperial experts expected any such pan-Islamic movements to be endorsed by the Caliph (who was also the Sultan of the Ottoman Empire), who represented the head of the Islamic religion. British expansionism combined with a desire to keep the Ottoman Empire as an ally resulted in increasingly complex relations during the latter half of the nineteenth century. The continued slow decline of the Ottoman Empire gave the British an opening to expand their influence in the region in places such as Egypt (which was ostensively under Ottoman control) in the early 1880s. However, Ottoman weakness also led Britain to repeatedly support the wayward empire against the expansionist Russian Empire in order to help insulate British India.

To further confuse British–Ottoman relations in the late nineteenth century, British diplomacy was held hostage by British politics. The Conservative Party, led by Benjamin Disraeli, typically held pro-Ottoman stances in imperial policy, owing largely to the notion that the Ottoman Empire would help check the advance of Britain's traditional enemy in the East, the Russian Empire. The Liberal Party, on the other hand, led by William E. Gladstone, held a very anti-Ottoman position in imperial policy, believing they could court Greece against the Ottomans and eventually throw the

Ottomans out of Europe. Meanwhile, the Ottoman Empire was struggling with its own internal problems. Arab proto-nationalist movements in the Levant, Mesopotamia, and in the Nejd began to gain momentum and would ultimately ally themselves with Britain in World War I, thus cementing the importance of British–Islamic relations while demonstrating that the Islamic world was itself undergoing substantial changes. This was most obvious after the close of World War I, when the caliphate was dissolved and the threat of pan-Islamism was no longer thought to be controlled by the Caliph, but rather by competing Arab nationalist causes. An additional layer of complexity with British–Islamic relations is best summed up as 'oil politics' and this played a major role in British diplomacy in the Middle East after World War I. In each of these major diplomatic issues Churchill's influence can be seen.

However, the importance of this context has been overlooked by scholars when considering Churchill's views on Islam and the Muslim community, and these issues are largely absent from the existing literature surrounding Winston Churchill. This is apparent in three key areas of the historiography. The first gap in the literature is evident in the huge historiography surrounding Churchill, which covers, in detail, most of his career but largely omits his relationship with the Islamic world. The second gap centres on British relations with the Middle East and the Islamic world as a whole. This considers British cultural assumptions and British policies concerning the Islamic world during the Victorian, Edwardian, and modern eras while providing a context to Churchill's particular views. While there is a plethora of literature here, none of it explicitly examines Churchill's personal opinions and attitudes towards the Islamic world. The third gap is in the historiography on Churchill and the Middle East, which typically only examines Churchill's relationship with Zionism or his notions of British imperialism. The literature on this topic often lacks an academic reappraisal of Churchill's polices in the Middle East from the paradigm of British–Islamic relations during his time as Colonial Secretary in the 1920s or later as Prime Minister. However, perhaps the most important contextual question concerns Churchill's view of Islam as a religion.

Churchill and Islam

Churchill's views on Islam were complex and helped to inform his unique 'Churchilllian perspective' on the Islamic world as a whole. In order to understand Churchill's opinion of Islam it is important to start with the larger picture of how he felt about religion in general. Clearly, like most of his contemporaries, Churchill was heavily influenced by monotheistic, Judeo-Christian traditions. The evidence for his preference can be seen in Churchill's anti-Hindu bias in the 1930s and his disdain for the lack of a coherent, if not more Westernized, religion in African pagan tribes in his reflections on his trip to Africa. It might be understood that Churchill equated Christianity with progress and civilization, whereas other monotheistic religions, while useful in helping to bring civilization to the regions where they were practised, were essentially retrograde forces when compared to Christianity.

However, despite Churchill's reverence for Christianity, he 'paid tribute to Christianity as an outsider'.[4] After reading Edward Gibbon's *Decline and Fall of the Roman Empire* (1776–89) and Winwood Reade's *The Martyrdom of Man* (1872), Churchill adopted a vaguely atheistic view of religion, and though he passed through an 'aggressive anti-religious phase', he basically became a deist who believed in something of a God who 'shaped the destinies of England and of Winston Churchill in particular'.[5] So, for Churchill, religion was intrinsically linked with civilization and progress. It is through this prism that Churchill's views on Islam can be appreciated.

Though Churchill rarely reflected on the tenants of Islam and its place in the world as something of a civilizing force in harsh lands, he did occasionally engage with it, especially in writing his accounts of frontier war on the north-west frontier in India and in Sudan. His most famous reflection on Islam comes from his book *The River War* (1899), which chronicled his time in Egypt and Sudan. The following passage is especially damning of Islam and has been used by amateur historians, journalists, bloggers, and those with a political agenda to colour Churchill's legacy with false perceptions of Islam, creating an impression that he was both Islamophobic and a bigot:[6]

> How dreadful are the curses which Mohammedanism lays on its votaries! Besides the fanatical frenzy, which is as dangerous in a man as hydrophobia in a dog, there is this fearful fatalistic apathy. The effects are apparent in many countries. Improvident habits, slovenly systems of agriculture, sluggish methods of commerce, and insecurity of property exist wherever the followers of the Prophet rule or live. A degraded sensualism deprives this life of its grace and refinement; the next of its dignity and sanctity. The fact that in Mohammedan law every woman must belong to some man as his absolute property, either as a child, a wife, or a concubine, must delay the final extinction of slavery until the faith of Islam has ceased to be a great power among men.
>
> Individual Moslems may show splendid qualities ***thousands have become brave and loyal soldiers of the queen: all know how to die***: but the influence of the religion paralyses the social development of those who follow it. No stronger retrograde force exists in the world. Far from being moribund, Mohammedanism is a militant and proselytizing faith. It has already spread throughout Central Africa, raising fearless warriors at every step; ***were it not that Christianity is sheltered in the strong arms of science – the science against which it had vainly struggled – the civilization of modern Europe might fall, as fell the civilization of ancient Rome.***[7]

However, the use of this quote to justify Churchill's position on Islam is very problematic and misleading. First, it must be understood that Churchill was going through a particularly anti-religious phase when he wrote this. During this period he was fairly contemptuous of all major religions. Additionally, Churchill reserved his most damning comments specifically for the Islamic Dervish population in Africa who lived under the Mahdiyya, a fundamentalist interpretation of Islam. In Churchill's *A History of the English-Speaking Peoples*, Vol. 6 (1958), he regularly referred to the Dervish Mahdiyya as 'restless fanatics' and 'fanatical hordes', which was actually in step with orthodox Islamic authorities, or the Ulema, at the time.[8] This was because the term 'Mahdi' (or guided one) is the prophesized redeemer of Islam and is roughly equivalent to 'Messiah' (or anointed one).[9] By declaring himself Mahdi, Mohammed Ahmed, the leader of the Dervish Empire, was actually committing something of a heresy against orthodox Islam by suggesting that it was he who was guided by the Prophet and the not the Sultan of the Ottoman Empire who was also the Caliph and, thus, the successor of the Prophet.

Second, this quote exists in this form only in the first edition of *The River War*, which ran for only one year until it was condensed into one volume in 1901, leaving out large swathes of text at Churchill's request, including the section cited here. Moreover, creative editing by journalists and others leave out key portions of the passage (which has been marked in italics) such as the praise for Muslims who 'have become brave and loyal soldiers of the queen'. Additionally, the fact that the figure of Muslims Churchill refers to is 'thousands', indicates this passage is often taken out of context. The Indian census which had already reported as early as 1880 that 'Nearly 41 millions are Mohammedans; so that England is by far the greatest Mohammedan power in the world, so that the Queen reigns over about double as many Moslems as the Khalif himself.'[10] This creative editing also leaves out Churchill's point that the only thing that differentiates Christianity and Islam is Christianity's relationship with science, which reinforces Churchill's broadly humanitarian views. Since this perception of Churchill's view of the Islamic world is clearly faulty, what then were his reflections on Islam as a religion?

Churchill's earliest reflections on Islam were written in a letter to his old schoolmaster, Rev. J.E.C. Welldon, on 16 December 1896 while Churchill was undergoing his self-education in India. Welldon had a major influence in the creation of Churchill's world view, and the two men debated the importance of Christian missionary work in India. Welldon argued for the spread of Christianity in India and elsewhere and argued that 'it is not stranger that a religion issuing its self from London should naturalize itself in Calcutta than a religion issuing itself from Jerusalem should naturalize itself in London'. But Churchill was quick to retort that such an analogy was 'not quite just'. Churchill argued that his main reason for depreciating missionary work was that he thought, 'Providence has given each man the form of worship best suited to his environment.' Though Churchill had not reached the apex of his aggressive atheistic phase, his increasing move away from dogmatic Christianity was evident as he continued his rebuttal: 'I imagine that this religion was originally evolved in a process of time by the influence of material forces – climate and physical – acting on the "innate upward" striving by which all human beings are impelled.' Churchill then turned to the geographic limitations of Christian influence by writing,

> in nearly nineteen centuries [Christianity] has not spread South or East. In all that time no nation of Black or Yellow has accepted it. Centuries of missionary work in China have been barren! [. . .] Nor have the religions of Buddha – Mahomet [the Prophet Mohammed] – and Confucius gained a single white convert.

Recognizing his position as out of step with Welldon, and most British Christians, Churchill then reflected that had he lived in the days 'when the influence of Buddha – of Christ – or of Mahomet began to disturb [. . .] the more primitive forms of worship' he would have 'probably opposed [. . .] the great movements they initiated'. Churchill concluded that 'while religion is natural to man, some races are capable of a higher and purer form than others. I believe the Asiatic derives more real benefit from the perfect knowledge of his religion than of partial comprehension of Christianity.'[11]

This letter is significant because it illustrates Churchill's early ideas on religion, including Christianity and Islam. While his rebuttal was intellectually based on Darwinist concepts and was heavily informed by *The Martyrdom of Man*, it is somewhat remarkable that Churchill seems to hold Islam and Christianity as equals, each playing a part in the progress of civilization in the geographic region that best suits the religion. This was ultimately why Churchill thought missionary work was little more than a fruitless errand. This was clearly echoed in the portion of Churchill's account of Islam in *The River War* that had been regularly left out when the work was cited over the years. That is, when he insinuates that the only thing that separates Islam and Christianity is the latter's relationship with science.

Once Churchill was posted in Sudan he reflected again on Islam in his book *The River War*; however his thoughts were not limited to the often quoted negative reflections of Islam as discussed above. He recognized that the Islamic nature of the Dervish revolt was merely the religious character of a nationalist movement. Yet he believed that this would be lost on many in England who might think the Dervish revolt was one based entirely in religious affairs. He almost maintained a tone of disdain for those who entertained such a concept, and bunked the idea that Islam caused the Dervish revolt:

> Fanaticism is not the cause of the war. It is a means which helps savage people to fight. It is the spirit which enables them to combine the great common object before which all personal or tribal disputes become insignificant. What the horn is to the Rhinoceros, what the sting is to the wasp, the Mohammedan faith was to the Arabs of the Sudan – a faculty of offence or defense. It was all this and no more. It was not the reason of the revolt. It strengthened, it characterized, but it did not cause.[12]

Additional evidence of Churchill's evolving opinion of Islam can be seen in his respect for the Mahdi. He argued that the Mahdi's accomplishments exceeded those of the founder of the Mohammedan faith. His respect for the Mahdi's military accomplishments equals his treatment of Saladin in *A History of the English-Speaking Peoples*.[13] Churchill concludes that he did not know 'how a genuine maybe distinguished from a spurious Prophet, except by the measure of success' and that should an Islamic historian ever write the history of Sudan, he 'will not forget, foremost among the heroes of his race, to write the name of Mohammed Ahmed.'[14]

As Churchill entered the Liberal Party and the most progressive phase of his career, his fascination with the Orient (and to some degree, with Islam) grew. He often spent time with Wilfrid S. Blunt, the political radical, Arabist, and poet, who by 1905 had become 'the avatar for anti-imperial causes' and an active force for the 'regeneration of Islam'.[15] Churchill and Blunt even dressed up in Arab clothes, a tradition they carried on into the twilight of their friendship.[16] In a letter to Lady Lytton during this period, Churchill declared: 'You will think me a pasha. I wish I were.'[17] Churchill's curious fascination with Islamic culture even became obvious to others around him. He received a letter from his long-time friend and soon-to-be sister-in-law, Lady Gwendoline Bertie, who implored him not to convert to Islam:

> Please don't become converted to Islam; I have noticed in your disposition a tendency to orientalism, pasha-like tendencies, I really have; you are not cross my writing this, so if you come in contact with Islam, your conversion might be effected with greater ease than you might have supposed, call of the blood, don't you know what I mean, do... fight against it.[18]

However, Churchill's fascination with Islam proved only to be aesthetic and passing. His knowledge of Islam was largely predicated on Victorian notions, which heavily romanticized the nomadic lifestyle and honour culture of the Bedouin desert tribes. As a result, Churchill never really acquired a deeper understanding of Islam. During the early 1920s when he was Colonial Secretary and was leading the effort to restructure the Middle East, Churchill had to ask about the difference between Shia and Sunni Islam, revealing his ignorance of the Islamic religion. It was perhaps, remarkable that he had the presence of mind to ask the question in the first place. While the aesthetic nature of Churchill's understanding of Islam is unsurprising, his destiny nevertheless became intertwined with that of the Islamic world.

CHAPTER 1

EARLY ENCOUNTERS

An analysis of Winston Churchill's relationship with the Islamic world must begin by examining his preconceived perceptions of the Orient and his earliest encounters with it, first as a soldier along the Indian north-west frontier (present-day Afghanistan and Pakistan), then in the Sudan, and in his travels as Colonial Under-Secretary. This chapter considers those phases of Churchill's life (and what prejudices he might have had from his Victorian, imperial education) and his early encounters with various Muslim sects and tribes to assess how these experiences affected his perception on political matters such as the possibility of a pan-Islamic uprising and Russia's role in the 'great game' in central Asia. In addition, this chapter engages with the influence that abstract issues such as orientalism, frontier ethics, and cultural hierarchies had on Churchill's thinking. While it is true that Churchill shared many Victorian prejudices (such as the belief that British culture was inherently superior to Eastern cultures), this chapter explores how his experiences informed his opinions of the Islamic world and differentiated him from many British politicians of his day.

The Malakand Expedition

It was in 1897 on the frontier of imperial India, along the Chitral road that twists through the Malakand pass, that the British 'Forward

Policy' met resistance from Muslim tribes. 'These clansmen – Pathans, Swatis, Waziris, Mahsuds, Afridis, Bunerwalis, Chitrals and Gilgitis – had lived in remote independence since the dawn of time',[1] and the British Forward Policy, which dictated that imperial forces had a right to secure frontier regions in order to ensure economic stability, brought opposing civilizations into a recurring and bloody conflict. 'Forward Policy' was enacted by the viceregal government of India and made public by dispatch No. 49, 28 February 1897.[2] The tribal uprising against it was led by Mullah Sadullah, nicknamed the 'Mad Fakir', who Churchill described as a 'wild enthusiast, convinced of his Divine mission and miraculous powers, [who] preached a crusade, or Jihad, against the infidel.'[3] Both the British forts at Chakdara and Malakand were attacked. The British losses were severe, with over 153 casualties.[4] A rapid retribution was thought to be required because the Islamic uprising coincided with the recent Turkish victory over the Greek army, which many feared (perhaps due to the lingering memories of the 1857 mutiny) might encourage a Muslim revival.[5] General Bindon Blood was authorized to perform a punitive expedition, which was characterized as the 'Butcher and Bolt Policy' because they often resulted in 'the destruction of tribal villages and crops and then a hasty withdrawal.'[6]

This is also where a 23-year-old Winston Churchill, only a junior officer (subaltern), embarked on his first major assignment as a war correspondent and came face to face with an Islamic adversary. Moreover, it was the first time he was confronted with the threat of a pan-Islamic movement, the fear of which would trouble his entire career in relation to the Middle East. However, it was not Churchill's first taste of war. This came from his brief stint in Cuba as a war correspondent for the *Daily Graphic* during a leave of absence from his regiment, the 4th Queen's Own Hussars.

Churchill arrived in Bangalore in October 1896 and quickly felt isolated from his family, friends, and (more importantly) from politics in Britain. By November, however, he had become somewhat fascinated with the nearby city of Hyderabad, which he explained to his mother contained 'all the scoundrels of Asia' and was an independent city because the Nizam of Hyderabad had remained loyal during the Indian mutiny of 1857. As a result, Churchill continued, 'British officers were not allowed in the city without permission and escort and native customs everywhere prevail. All natives walk about armed and by their arrogance proclaim their appreciation of liberty.'[7] Despite this blatantly imperialist and Anglo-centric perception, Churchill still wanted the adventure of going through the city, though he insisted he would do it on an elephant so that 'natives' could not spit at him.

Churchill's Victorian disdain for day-to-day life in India is evident in several of his early letters from India. Shortly after his elephant ride through Hyderabad, he displayed his indifference to native Hindu culture when he wrote to his mother explaining that he 'shall not learn Hindustani. It is quite unnecessary. All the natives speak perfect English.'[8] When news reached Churchill that he would be able to return home for a short period of leave in April 1897, he wrote to his mother:

> I am looking forward immensely to seeing civilisation again after the barbarous squalor of this country [...] The eight months I have been in this country have as regards Indian information and knowledge been utterly barren. I have met no one who cared to tell my anything about the problems of the hour and if I stay her twenty years as a soldier I see no prospect of my acquiring any knowledge worth knowing of Indian affairs.[9]

These letters demonstrate the first of two cultural paradigms that were intrinsically linked and help to illustrate Churchill's attitudes regarding his early encounters with Islamic civilization, paradigmatic forces that fed on one another and, in a way, required one another for their existence. The first cultural paradigm that greatly influenced Churchill and the British Empire was nineteenth-century British orientalism, as seen in his early letters home from India and in his early field reports from the Swat valley. (The orientalist character of these reports is also evident in Churchill's *The Story of the Malakand Field Force.*) According to Edward Said, orientalism is:

> A way of coming to terms with the Orient that is based on the Orient's special place in European Western experience [...] The Orient is the place of Europe's greatest and richest colonies, the source of its civilizations and languages, its cultural contestant, and one of the deepest and most recurring images of the Other. In addition, the Orient has helped to define Europe (or the West) as its contrasting image, idea, personality, and experience.[10]

Churchill's view of the Islamic world, and indeed the entire East, was shaped by the paradigm of orientalism due to his social background and education in late nineteenth-century England. British academia at the turn of the nineteenth century was firm in its contention that eugenics combined with social Darwinism rationalized the subordination of non-European people because of their inability to use logic. These popular academic and social perceptions of Muslims are best described by Humayun Ansari:

> Interactions between Muslims and British society was largely shaped by contemporary popular views regarding their position in the human hierarchy relative to degrees of civilization. These views were complicated by the juxtaposition of race with religion. As non-European races became subordinate to the British, those from Muslim lands were evaluated disparagingly.[11]

In fact, some have argued that Churchill's perceptions were merely a product of the Victorian England in which he spent his childhood. Historian David Jablonsky has made this argument by referring to letters that an 11-year-old Winston wrote to his mother and father regarding the death of Victorian hero Colonel Fredrick G. Burnaby who was killed in action, 'sword in hand while resisting the desperate charge of the Arabs at the battle of Abu Klea.'[12] Jablonsky also draws on the prolific works of George Alfred Henty who wrote several books about imperial history and was very popular among young, privately educated Victorian boys like Churchill. Richard Toye reinforces this notion in *Churchill's Empire* (2010) by examining the Victorian notions of empire that Churchill inherited from his education at Harrow and from his father, Lord Randolph Churchill, who was briefly the secretary of state for the India Office, and was a Conservative who typically shied away from the Gladstone government's more imperialist undertakings, such as the occupation of Egypt in 1882. Lord Randolph, like most of the Tories of his day, was typically pro-Turk, which had interesting effects on Churchill's understanding of the Ottoman (and thus the Islamic) world.[13] It was from such influences that Jablonsky concludes: 'Churchill created an inner historical world in which there was only the grand and grandiose. Progress was measured through politics and war, rarely in terms of economic, intellectual, and social issues.'[14]

Kirk Emmert further developed this notion in *Winston S. Churchill on Empire* (1986). However, Emmert focuses more on Churchill's personal experiences as a subaltern and explores Churchill's notion of civilization and how it was intrinsically linked to his belief that the British Empire was a 'civilizing empire', which 'is the political relationship [...] which exists when civilized men rule over the uncivilized, without their consent for the sake of the mutual improvement of the rulers and ruled. The civilized are elevated by ruling, the uncivilized by being ruled.'[15]

This school of cultural and racial superiority was evident in almost all aspects of British imperial policy, and was epitomized in the 'Forward Policy'. The wars fought in the Orient were frontier wars, where civilization was confronted with 'militant Mohammedanism' and where (according to Churchill): 'The forces of progress clash with those of reaction. The religion of blood and war is face to face with that of peace.'[16] Churchill later characterized frontier wars as 'little wars' and 'a splendid game' in which 'nobody expected to be killed [...] This kind of war was full of thrills. It was not like the great war.'[17] His racist views are especially obvious after he noted the impossibility of arguing with an Afghan. Churchill repeatedly asserts the impossibility of a 'civilized' European understanding the Muslim thought process:

> A civilized European is as little able to accomplish this, as to appreciate the feelings of those strange creatures, which when a drop of water is examined under a microscope, are revealed amiably gobbling each other up, and themselves being complacently devoured.[18]

However, there is evidence that even at this early stage of Churchill's career, he was not completely dependent on the orientalist paradigm for his perception of the East, especially as it relates to the Ottoman Empire. Before departing for India after his leave, Churchill and his mother had an interesting clash. In a series of letters written during the early spring of 1897, he and his mother argued over the situation in the Balkans and the impending Greco-Turkish War.[19] The Conservative government of the Marquis of Salisbury had adopted a policy of non-intervention, taking the position that Crete should remain with the Ottoman Empire. This was highly controversial and unpopular because the Ottomans had massacred nearly 10,000 Christians on Crete and it appeared as if the Salisbury government was backing 'the cause of Moslem barbarism'.[20] Lady Randolph implored Winston to try to understand that the Salisbury government was acting in the interest of the British Empire in relation to the concert of Europe. However, displaying his orientalist ideas, Churchill saw this political inaction and courting of the Ottoman Empire as an illogical and unethical foreign policy.[21] On 6 April 1897, he wrote what seemed to be his final observation on the subject:

> I am sorry you do not agree with my views on Crete [. . .] We are doing a very wicked thing [. . .] Lord Salisbury is a strong man & a clever man. He does not want Russia to get to Constantinople and with this object he is willing to crush the Greeks or anyone else whose interests do not coincide with his. The Turkish Empire he is determined to maintain. He does not give a row of buttons for the suffering of those oppressed by that Empire. This is not only wrong it is foolish. It is wrong because it is unjustifiable to kill people who are not attacking you [. . .] and because it is an abominable action which prolongs

> the servitude under the Turks of the Christians races. It is foolish because as surely as night follows day – the Russians are bound to get to Constantinople. We could never stop them even if we wished. Nor ought we wish for anything that could impede the expulsion from Europe of the filthy oriental.[22]

Fourteen days later, his mother's response came assuring Churchill that his ideas on the subject were 'premature and wrong' and that while 'no one has any sympathy for the Turks' that 'Greece has taken too much upon herself and she will have to knock under'.[23] However, the next day Churchill completely reversed his position, declaring in a letter to his mother that 'the declaration of war by Turkey on Greece [had] changed all [his] plans.' He then expressed a desire to join the battle between the two Balkan powers. One of his major considerations was which side to join! Churchill goes on to say:

> This [. . .] must depend on you. Of course my sympathies are entirely with the Greeks, but on the other hand the Turks are bound to win, they are in enormous strength and will be on the offensive the whole time. If I go on this side it will be less glorious but much more safe and as I have no wish to be involved in the confusion of a defeated army, my idea is that would be more suitable. You must decide. If you can get me good letters to the Turks, to the Turks I will go. If to the Greeks – to the Greeks.[24]

Despite all of Churchill's musings on the ethics of foreign policy and the morality of war, it appears that he was so motivated by glory and a lust for military experience (to enhance prospects for his political career) that he was willing to fight anyone's battles and, in doing so, would happily skirt off any negative notions regarding the Ottomans. Even at this early stage, Churchill was differentiating himself from his British Victorian contemporaries.

By 28 April he made up his mind to fight on the side of the Ottomans and asked his mother to send money to the Ottoman bank. However, Churchill feared the Balkan War would be over too soon for him to get involved. According to Churchill biographer Bechhofer Roberts, Churchill met Ian Hamilton (later Sir General Ian Hamilton) on the transfer boat, and while Hamilton had promised his service to Greece, Churchill had promised his to Turkey. While Churchill's peculiar allegiance to Turkey largely owes to his lust for glory, an additional explanation might be that he inherited a 'Turkophile' attitude from his father. However, Roberts dismissed such connections, arguing that 'subalterns are often Turkophile' and he noted that the two men shared little love for one another on the boat ride due to their conflicting alliances.[25] Interestingly, Churchill himself recalled the incident years later, saying that Hamilton was a 'romantic' and was thus 'for the Greeks', while Churchill 'having been brought up a Tory... was for the Turks.'[26] However, their formal confrontation was not to be, for by the time they reached their port of call at Port Said in Egypt, the war was over. Churchill lamented his lost adventure in a letter to his mother in late May 1897: 'I have reluctantly had to give up all hopes of Turkey as the war has fizzled out – like a damp firework.'[27]

Once he had arrived back home in England, with the Greco-Turkish War resolved Churchill needed a new adventure. Upon learning of the situation on the north-west frontier he requested to go to the Swat valley to serve under General Blood and retaliate against those 'who have dared violate the Pax Britannica'.[28] Though he could not secure a formal appointment with Blood, Churchill was appointed to Blood's staff as a war correspondent in early 1897. It is from Churchill's field reports and his earliest book, *The Story of the Malakand Field Force*, that a larger foundation of understanding for Churchill's attitude towards the Islamic world can be built.

Moreover, Churchill's active military service on the north-west frontier illustrates the second paradigmatic force that helped construct the context in which his ideas on the Islamic world were formed. The second cultural paradigm was the perception of a geopolitical movement that had haunted the British Foreign Office and military since the mid 1800s: the movement of pan-Islamism.

The pan-Islamic objective was to create a political state which encompassed and united all *Dar al-Islam,* under one leader or imām.

In this perfect and unified Islamic state, the basis for all thought and action would be derived from 'religious rather than racial or national'motivations.[29] The political realization of a unified House of Islam would severely harm British imperial interests in India by effectively forcing British rule out of Asia and parts of Africa.

There are two major schools of thought regarding pan-Islamism. The first and most widely accepted school, which is espoused by Dwight E. Lee and other early twentieth-century writers such as E.G. Bowne and Syed Ameer Ali,[30] depicts pan-Islamism as a spectre created and used by the Western powers (especially the British) to aid in their imperial conquests in the Middle East and Central Asia.[31] The other school of thought is more recent and has been voiced by Nikki R. Keddie. While he agreed that 'pan-Islam [...] was a reaction to Western imperialism', he believed it existed as a political entity independent of imperial propaganda and was therefore only empowered by Western encroachment not created by it.[32] Moreover, Keddie down played the religious dimension and presented pan-Islamism as a proto-nationalist movement. He then criticized Lee's argument because it 'greatly underrated the indigenous roots and strength of pan-Islam.'[33]

Whether pan-Islamism was a phantasm or an actual geopolitical movement, it did have a profound effect on Churchill, his fellow soldiers, contemporary military correspondents, and the military hierarchy. Churchill noted in *The Story of the Malakand Field Force* his theory that the Malakand Field Force was dispatched because of recent victories by the Ottoman army over the Greeks (which Churchill wished to fight in with the Ottomans) and because the Amir of Afghanistan had written several books, including *Advice to Afghans* (*c*.1893), *Rectification of Faith* (*c*.1886), and *Inducement for a Holy War* (*c*.1889), which urged Muslims to engage in jihad. These factors, combined with articles in the Anglo-Indian papers such as 'The Recrudescence of Mohammedanism', created what Churchill called 'a boom in Mohammedanism.'[34] This thought was echoed by one of Churchill's contemporaries, Viscount Fincastle, in his book, *A Frontier Campaign: A Narrative of Operations of the Malakand and Buner Field Forces 1897–1898* (1898). Fincastle served with Churchill in the Malakand Field Force and was a war correspondent for *The Times*. He tended to focus more on the involvement of the Amir and saw him not as a contributing ingredient (like Churchill), but as an *essential* base for the recipe of revolution on the north-west frontier: 'Another belief the tribesmen were imbued with was that the Amir would support them and there were many factorshat lent color to this supposition in the eyes of the people.'[35]

In fact, General Bindon Blood believed that not only was the Amir of Afghanistan inciting jihad but also providing weapons to the tribes in the Dir and Swat valleys to wage a jihad.[36] There is some evidence that he was right. As British influence waned in Central Asia, the frontier Muslim tribes united and attacked the forts along the Chitral road and this caught the British 'totally unawares and so many tribes were involved at once the suggestion was that the whole affair had been planned and was being coordinated [...] and in each of these cases a mullah [...] was heavily involved.'[37] Furthermore, some of the evidence implicated the Amir directly. The political agent responsible for the Malakand, Major H.A. Deane's diary entry for 29 July 1897 indicates he heard that the Amir paid 40,000 rupees 'to an influential Mullah in India to work up this business', and in a letter dated 31 August to Salisbury, who also held the post of Foreign Secretary, Major Deane reported:

> Since the commencement of the Greco-Turkish war the Amir of Afghanistan has sent Maulvis and Talibs to excite frontier Muhammdan [sic] tribes by distributing among them books on jehad [sic]. The Amir has opened shops to sell rifles and cartridges cheap to the different tribesmen. If there were no movement from his [the Amir's] side, Muhammadan [sic] tribes would never dare disturb the British Raj.[38]

Additionally, it is significant that pan-Islamic movements did tend to be more prevalent among 'Central Asiatic and Indian Muslims who, at the mercy of both British and Russian expansionists, frequently discussed the idea of a Muslim league and occasionally appealed to the Turkish sultan for aid.'[39]

Working inside the context of orientalism with an imperial wariness of pan-Islam, Churchill's dispatches focused on the bizarre environment and the strange people who inhabited it. His tone was one of parental concern and dismay for those left on the 'fringe of humanity'.[40] He was quick to cite the social Darwinist concept of 'influence of climate on character'.[41] In his book *My Early Life*, Churchill recalled that 'amid the scenes of savage brilliancy there dwells a race whose qualities harmonize with their environment'.[42] However, Churchill did not accept this argument for the cruelty of the tribes of Afghanistan, noting that their valleys and fields were fertile. He went on to paint a dark picture of the culture and faith of the tribes in Afghanistan: 'Their religion is the most miserable fanaticism, in which cruelty, credulity and immorality are all equally represented.'[43] These aspects of Churchill's writing reinforce the notion that Churchill ultimately supported the Forward Policy.[44]

Moreover, Churchill argued that the clerics of Islam, especially the 'miracle working' Mad Mullah, did little more than oppress and exploit their followers, especially the women, who he asserted 'have no position but that of animals.'[45] Churchill wrote, 'all were held in the grip of miserable superstition'[46] and that 'the Mohammedan religion increases, instead of lessening, the fury of intolerance', and as a result: 'All rational considerations are forgotten. Seizing their weapons, they become Ghazis [Muslims vowed to combat non-believers] – as dangerous and as sensible as mad dogs: fit only to be treated as such.'[47]

Churchill was careful to note that the clerics, such as Mullah Sadullah, were intelligent enough to be aware of what was happening to their situation along the Chitral road: 'Contact with civilization assails the ignorance, and credulity, on which the wealth and influence of the Mullah depend.'[48] Significantly, such insights are not in Fincastle's observations in *A Frontier Campaign*. Fincastle was content to lump the tribe's leaders and members together and simply label them all as 'fanatical'.[49] However, the tribal priesthood clearly recognized the advancement of the British as a threat to their power and drove the people to rise up. Thus, Churchill credited the tribal priesthood with more intelligence, but also revealed them as manipulative and sinister. He thought that despite their zealous religious beliefs and the control of their tribal leaders, the tribes 'would have been willing [...] to remain in passive submission, soothed by the increase of material prosperity.'[50] His disdain for the Islamic clerics and the higher tribesmen reached its apex in a dispatch written on 9 November 1897:

> Their intelligence only enables them to be more cruel, more dangerous, more destructive than the wild beasts. Their religion–fanactic though they are – is only respected when it incites to bloodshed and murder. Their habits are filthy; their moral cannot be alluded to [...] I find it impossible to come to any other conclusion than that, in proportion as these valleys are purged from the pernicious vermin that infest them, so will the happiness of humanity be increased, and the progress of mankind accelerated.[51]

In the midst of Churchill's fighting on the front, he developed a sincere appreciation and respect for the courage and skills of his fellow native soldiers, especially in the 11th Bengal Lancers and the 31st Punjabi Infantry, the two units he spent the most time with while he was in the Malakand.[52] Churchill later recorded his thoughts in his book, *My Early Life: A Roving Commission* (1930) regarding his attachment to the 31st Punjabi Infantry. Though he thought it was an odd experience because of the language barrier, Churchill recalled:

> Although I could not enter fully into their thoughts and feelings, I developed a regard for the Punjabis. There was no doubt they liked to have a white officer among them when fighting, and they watched him carefully to see how things were going. If you grinned, they grinned. So I grinned industrially.[53]

It is remarkable that Churchill's 'letters and writings never refer to those on the same side of the British forces with disrespect and are almost completely devoid of racial epitaphs and common slang.'[54] In fact, in *The Malakand Field Force* when Churchill was discussing the bravery of a *sepoy* named Prem Singh, he argued that natives should be eligible for the Victoria Cross because: 'In sport, in courage, and in the sight of heaven, all men meet on equal terms.'[55]

Churchill's inclusion of 'sport' in this quote is an important one, because his admiration of the skill and tenacity of native Indian polo players (who were almost exclusively Muslim and Sikh) became obvious in Churchill's letters home.[56] In a letter to his mother on 12 November 1896, Churchill was happy to announce that the 4th Queen's Own Hussars (for whom he played) won a polo tournament for the Golconda Cup in Hyderabad and that this victory was a record because 'no English Regiment ever... won a first class tournament within a month of their arrival in India.' Churchill told his mother he would send pictures of the event and that she would be able to see him 'fiercely struggling with turbaned warrior.'[57] The 'turbaned warriors' Churchill, later recalled, were the 'famous Golconda Brigade, the bodyguards of the Nizam himself.'[58] Churchill greatly enjoyed polo matches with the native Indian army officers and even returned to play in the Inter-Regimental Tournament in February 1899, when he stayed with Sir Pertab Singh (the Maharaja of Idar, a British Indian army officer, and a polo enthusiast) for a week prior to the tournament.

It is no surprise that Churchill began to feel the bonds of comradery with the native Indians with whom he played polo. According to ethnologist Magnus Marsden, 'The British [...] cultivated [...] skills like hunting and polo to create commonalities and establish hierarchies with local people.'[59] Undoubtedly, this effect worked both ways, creating a 'cultural consensus' based on 'shared values and practices' in which Churchill would begin to find commonality and establish bonds with his fellow polo players, regardless of their ethnic backgrounds.[60]

Paradoxically, Churchill's respect and admiration also spilled over to the tribes that he had been fighting. 'Churchill had great respect for courage for soldiers regardless for their race or which side of the battle line they were on.'[61] Churchill even drew attention to the fact that the tribes' warlike culture was not so different to that of the British Empire: 'They [Muslims] are a brave and warlike race [...] Nor should it be forgotten that the English are essentially a warlike people.'[62] Though Churchill furiously fought those who stood against the British, he sincerely admired their exceptional courage: 'It would be unjust to deny the people of the Mohmand Valley the reputation for courage, tactical skill, and marksmanship which they have so well deserved.'[63] Churchill made it clear in *The Story of the Malakand Field Force* that he had developed a 'battlefield respect' for the frontier tribes. This dimension of adversarial reverence was also largely absent in Fincastle's book on the Malakand Field Force. While this battlefield respect was, in some ways, typical of Churchill's Victorian contemporaries who were stationed in the East,[64] the extent of Churchill's 'battlefield respect' (for instance, the direct comparison with the English) differentiated him from many of his British Victorian contemporaries.

As his time on the north-west frontier continued, Churchill began to question the punitive expeditions licensed by the imperial 'Forward' and 'Butcher and Bolt' policies that had brought him there in the first place. In his book *The Story of the Malakand Field Force*, Churchill referred to these policies as 'undignified'[65] and criticized them, claiming that 'the words to "extend and consolidate our influence" can [...] have no other meaning than ultimate annexation.'[66] Moreover, he argued that while 'Forward Policy' had yielded territory, it also brought with it war, precluding 'the possibility of peace' because it pushes 'the government of India beyond [its] natural frontier line.'[67] The genesis of this line of thinking might be seen in a letter to his grandmother, the Duchess of Marlborough, where Churchill pondered the value of the Forward Policy by wondering if 'people in England had any idea of the warfare that is being carried out' there. He continued his reflection on the Forward Policy stating:

> I wish I could come to the conclusion that all this barbarity – all these losses – all this expenditure – had resulted in a permanent settlement being obtained. I do not think however that anything has been done – that will not have to be done again. It seems that many years of war and disturbance await the Indian Frontier.[68]

However, Toye has argued that Churchill's relationship with the Forward Policy was actually much more complicated than his musings home suggest. He argues that while Churchill found the tactics of the Forward Policy such as 'Butcher and Bolt' punitive expeditions questionable, Churchill ultimately supported the annexation of the whole of the north-west frontier, even including Afghanistan.[69] Using examples of Churchill's rhetoric of the 'inevitable advance of civilization', Toye indicates that while Churchill finds 'territorial aggrandizement' lamentable, he justifies its aims as inevitable and thus as a 'course that has already been embarked upon' making it 'hard for opponents to contest a policy to which there is, supposedly, no alternative.'[70]

While Churchill's relationship with the immorality of the 'Forward Policy' was clearly paradoxical, he picked up his father's mantle by noting that it was economically unsound: 'Regarded from an economic stand point, the trade of the frontier valleys will never pay a shilling in the pound on the military expenditure necessary to preserve order.'[71] Churchill echoes this point when he recounts the Mamund tribe surrendering their rifles to the Indian army, stating that 'these tribes have nothing to surrender but their arms. To extort these few, had taken a month, had cost many lives, and thousands of pounds. It had been as bad a bargain as was ever made.'[72] However, despite these economic trepidations, Churchill (again revealing himself to hold paradoxical views) believed that to reverse the policy would be far more expensive and morally dishonourable. As Toye put it, 'the forward policy might be costly in terms of men and money, but Britain could not honourably turn its back on its mission to spread civilization.'[73] Churchill's position on imperial economics was summed up when he argued that: 'It was unsound economics, but Imperialism and economics clash as often as honesty and self-interest.'[74]

However, while Churchill was clearly oscillating between condemnation of the Forward Policy's tactics and arguing for it as a strategic necessity, he was clearly becoming more cynical about the policy. In his final dispatch from Nowshera, his disillusionment about the entire operation is evident:

> It is with regret that I do not see any sign of permanency in the settlements that have been made with the tribesmen [. . .] They have been punished, not subdued; rendered hostile, but not harmless. Their fanaticism remains unshaken. Their barbarism unrelieved [. . .] The riddle of the frontier is still unresolved.[75]

Churchill's writing on the north-west frontier was considered so informed by the press that United Service Magazines asked him to write an article for *Military Review* regarding the frontier policies. 'The Ethics of Frontier Policy' was published in 1899. In his article, Churchill recognized the encroaching Russian threat, noting that 'war between England and Russia is possible' and therefore the positions in the north-west frontier must be protected.[76] But he never faltered from his idea that civilization would make the difference in holding the north-west positions. He argued for a proto-variation of winning hearts and minds:

> The wise policy would, therefore, seem to be confined to securing lines of approach, by training the local tribesmen, constructing strong posts, and building roads and railways [. . .] to gradually expose the Frontier tribes, by development of trade and a system of subsidies to the softening, enervating influences of civilization.[77]

However, he also warned that 'interference ends in annexation' and noted that fighting the local mountain tribes is folly, 'to enter the mountain to attack an Afridi is to jump into water to catch a fish.'[78] Therefore, Churchill condemned the 'Butcher and Bolt Policy' while advancing the notion that civilization will help the people throw off their oppressive clerics. Significantly, Churchill's formal article seems to be less harsh towards the tribes than his field reports for the *Pioneer*, where, nevertheless, a degree of magnanimity was evident. This probably owes to Churchill's desire to gain a readership in the *Pioneer*, which can be contrasted with his desire to be taken seriously in the journal article.

Churchill's multi-faceted tone and often paradoxical stance regarding the Forward Policy and the frontier tribes are difficult to reconcile because they represent a blend of paternalistic orientalism, fear of pan-Islamism, and reluctant respect. Toye's argument that Churchill ultimately hoped the Forward Policy to continue and that his 'rhetoric of inevitability' was Churchill's attempt to justify British presence in the north-west frontier overlooks Churchill's increasingly unique view of the situation.[79] While he was reconciled to some of the Forward Policy's intentions, such as exposing the Islamic tribesmen to the 'enervating influences of civilization', and he justified its expansionist ideals by arguing, '[w]e can't pull up now. Annexation is the word which the B[ritish] P[ublic] will have ultimately to swallow', Churchill simultaneously thought it was 'morally wicked' and a political 'blunder'.[80] So while Toye is correct in asserting Churchill's defence of the Forward Policy, this defence was often limited to the public sphere (in Churchill's dispatches, articles, and book) while privately (in letters to his mother and grandmother) Churchill's tone was more cynical. This indicates that Churchill was aware of his audience. Additionally, this is representative of Churchill's romanticized understanding of the British Empire as a civilizing force; he defended its Forward Policy as an inevitable force of progress while saving his harshest criticisms for the abusive tactics of the punitive expeditions on which the Forward Policy depended.

It is notable that the majority of Churchill's writing on the characteristics of the Muslims in the frontier tribes was written upon his arrival from England, but it is clear that an evolution of Churchill's thinking occurred thereafter. His initial observations were still ripe with racist and imperialist views commonly held by his English contemporaries whose perception of the Orient 'is not the Orient as it is, but the Orient as it has been Orientalized'.[81] However, as he lived and fought there, his experiences began to reshape his thinking, not dramatically, but altering it and adding to it. His traditional orientalist tone in letters to his mother prior to his involvement on the frontier, compared with his later dispatches and article, clearly demonstrates a change of mind on the Orient. This explains the 'battlefield respect' that emerged in his writing and how he grew to disdain elements of the 'Forward Policy'. Additionally, Churchill's portraits of the 'fanatical' Islamic warriors were undoubtedly to keep his readers interested and to build a name for himself. Churchill's awareness of his audience allowed him 'to play on deep-seated fears of his audience by presenting a picture of savage tribesmen possessed by an extraordinary fervor.'[82] This idea is reinforced by Churchill's recollection of his experiences on the north-west frontier in *My Early Life*. He argued that the Malakand revolt was 'attributed by the Government to the religion' but was, in fact, 'easily explainable on quire ordinary grounds'.[83] Whatever the case, it is clear that Churchill's view of Muslim society had changed. His foundation of orientalist views became augmented by his experiences with an Islamic society. This new perception helped shape his policies on Middle Eastern affairs later in life and aided his perception in Sudan, his next assignment.

The River War

Churchill's next assignment was in Sudan, where he took part in the final chapter of an unfolding epic.[84] This period of his military career must be understood as part of a larger story. It began in the days of Churchill's father. In early 1884, Gladstone's Liberal government saw the British position in Sudan as too expensive and politically precarious, and thus sought to withdraw their troops to Egypt, which would result in the evacuation of British troops at Khartoum. In order to carry this out, the legendary Victorian hero General Charles Gordon, whom Churchill described as 'extraordinary'[85] and whom historian Robert Rhodes James characterized as the 'T.E. Lawrence of his day',[86] was employed by Gladstone to oversee the evacuation. However, the British forces eventually lost control of the city in January 1885 and, as a result, were totally destroyed, including Charles Gordon.

Six months after the Dervishes captured Khartoum, the Mahdi (the leader of the Dervish Empire) died of typhus and was succeeded by Abdullah Ibn-Mohammed, or the Khalifa. Increasingly, the Khalifa 'gave the Sudan structure and order at the expense of participation and vitality.'[87] However, he also became gradually more erratic and vicious, eventually destroying Khartoum.[88] In April 1889, he sent letters to various heads of state, including one to Queen Victoria, urging her to convert to Islam and assuring her that if she failed to, she should not 'doubt that [her] sins, and the sins of your people, will be on [her] head, and that you will fall into our hands.'[89]

It was not until 1895 that the Second British Brigade was dispatched to reclaim the Sudan from the Khalifa. It was led by General Herbert Kitchener, a major and reoccurring figure in Winston Churchill's life. In 1898 Churchill desperately wanted to join Kitchener's operation; however, his reputation as a glory-hound and his tendency to openly criticize his superiors caused Kitchener to take an especially unfavourable view of Churchill. Yet despite Kitchener's view, Churchill was able to use his mother's influence to obtain a position with the 21st Lancers. Consequently, Kitchener and Churchill shared little love for one another. In fact, Churchill's friend Violet Bonham Carter – daughter of the future Liberal Prime Minister H.H. Asquith – would later describe Churchill as 'a thorn in the flesh [. . .] In the case of Lord Kitchener that thorn pricked on under the skin for many years to come.'[90]

Churchill's second book, *The River War*, is slightly different from the *Malakand Field Force,* because while it chronicles Churchill's time in Sudan and Egypt towards the end, it is more of an authoritative history on the subject. This book is important because it is the work most often cited for Churchill's attitude towards Muslims, as discussed in the introduction. The following passage is especially damning of Islam and has been used by journalists, amateur historians, and politicians to blacken Churchill's reputation.

> How dreadful are the curses which Mohammedanism lays on its votaries! Besides the fanatical frenzy, which is as dangerous in a man as hydrophobia in a dog, there is this fearful fatalistic apathy. The effects are apparent in many countries.

> Improvident habits, slovenly systems of agriculture, sluggish methods of commerce, and insecurity of property exist wherever the followers of the Prophet rule or live [...] Moslems may show splendid qualities [...] but the influence of the religion paralyses the social development of those who follow it.[91]

As discussed in the introduction, Churchill was specifically speaking of the Islamic Dervish population of the Sudan involved in the Mahdiyya, not the entire Islamic culture.[92] Moreover, these lines are confined to the two-volume first edition, which was superseded in 1901. The difference between the two editions is enormous. Historian James Muller points out that, '[the second edition] drops more than half a dozen chapters in whole or in part, leaving barely two-thirds of the original book.'[93] It is unclear whether it was Churchill who opted for a new single-volume edition in order to obfuscate his observations of Lord Kitchener, or if the publishers (Longmans) merely wanted to decrease the size of the text. Because Churchill's official biography only notes a small comparison in a footnote,[94] a thorough comparison of the two editions must begin with James Muller's article 'War on the Nile: Winston Churchill and the Reconquest of the Sudan'.[95]

Muller argues that Churchill wanted to tone down his explicit criticism of his officers, especially Kitchener, because by 1900 'the author was a member of Parliament.'[96] Britain was still at war and Kitchener was still commanding troops, which made him especially difficult to criticize. There were other important omissions as well but the most glaring were those concerning Kitchener'.[97] According to historian Paul A. Rahe: 'There are limits to what a young politician, newly embarked on his career and intent upon ingratiating himself with his colleagues and a wide range of associates, can prudently say.'[98] Whatever the case, most Churchill historians tend to agree that the first edition of *The River War* was reduced in order to preserve Churchill's political ambitions.

Despite the major differences in the first and second editions, both versions of the book employ a great deal of Churchill's traditional orientalist perspective. Like his depiction of Islamic forces in *The Story of the Malakand Field Force*, Churchill was quick to dismiss the Dervish revolt and those who rebelled with it: 'All the warlike operations of the Mohammedan peoples are characterized by fanaticism.'[99] He concluded that the Dervish Empire is the 'worst' in history as: 'All others have compensating virtues [...] but the Dervish Empire developed no virtue but courage, a quality more admirable than rare.'[100] Churchill even described the extreme Dervish Islam as an 'anachronism' and 'paralysing' to the people of Sudan who otherwise displayed 'splendid qualities'.[101]

Churchill also applied the standard Victorian social Darwinist theories, but in *The River War,* he applies them to race as well as the natural environment. An example of this might be seen in Churchill's willingness to employ dumdum bullets against Islamic warriors in both the north-west frontier and in the Sudan, yet he would not consider its use against the Boers in the Boer War, dismissing it as too cruel.[102] Churchill went on to argue that Arabs and Negroes had interbred to create 'a debased and cruel breed, more shocking because they are more intelligent than the primitive savages.'[103] Thus, he created a hierarchy of cultures, which he would return to later in life, and one in which 'the Arab was like an African reproduction of an Englishman; the Englishmen a superior and civilized development of the Arab.'[104] Such notions were present in the nineteenth-century orientalists' thinking. In fact, Churchill succumbs to blatant orientalism when he dismisses the entire affair as a 'complete history [...] which will not interest a later generation [...] One savage army slaughters another.'[105]

However, Churchill's ever-evolving and at times conflicting perceptions towards the Islamic world were slowly changing and becoming prevalent in his writing. His criticisms were balanced by compliments, albeit based in an orientalist paradigm. Though his attitudes and ideas had not yet solidified into a coherent *weltanschauung* regarding the Islamic world, his increasing magnanimous respect and fascination with Islamic culture became more evident over time. Although most probably influenced by Lord Cromer's understanding of the situation, the perfect example of this was Churchill's equation of Charles Gordon's 'Christian mysticism and unstable personality' with 'the Mahdi's fanaticism.'[106]

The development of what Violet Bonham Carter called Churchill's 'unfailing magnanimity towards the defeated' was also coming to light in *The River War*.[107] Churchill biographers Virginia Cowles and Bechhofer Roberts both recall a story about Churchill saving a Dervish baby. In Cowles's version, she interviewed a soldier who she named as Mr Norris, who claimed to have found a Dervish child after the battle of Omdurman and to have given it to Churchill, who promptly 'took it to the Sudanese lines (as they had their wives with them) and that was the last I saw of him.'[108] However, Roberts contends that Churchill found the child and when a Dervish 'happened by to whom Churchill had shown mercy on the battle field after fighting' Churchill gave him the child.[109] Although neither version of this story, if true, is corroborated by Churchill's official biography, both stories display Churchill's magnanimity. As discussed in the introduction, Churchill's veneration and praise of the Mahdi was another illustration of this and can be seen in his declaration 'that the Mahdi's accomplishments exceeded those of the founder of the Mohammedan faith.'[110] Muller further explores Churchill's praise, arguing:

> Though the Sudanese revolutionary [the Mahdi] is often denounced in the West as a false prophet [... Churchill] argues that the Mahdi who 'put his life and soul into the hearts of his countrymen, and freed his native land of foreigners,' deserves not simply opprobrium for having spilt the blood of thousands... but also a measure of respect for his achievements.[111]

However, Churchill's praise for the Dervishes was not totally confined to their leader. In seeing the Dervish warriors stand against the charging Second Brigade (a sight that Churchill would later tell Lord Riddell was the most impressive thing he had ever seen)[112] he wrote:

> 'Mad fanaticism' is the depreciating comment of their conquerors. I hold this to be a cruel injustice [...] Why should we regard as madness in the savage what would be sublime in civilized men? For I hope that if evil days should come upon our own country [...] that there would be some who would not care to accustom themselves to a new order of things and tamely survive the disaster.[113]

The two major competing views – orientalist and magnanimous – in Churchill's perceptions of the Islamic world began to work in tandem. Reflecting his later dismissal of Islam's role in the Malakand revolt, Churchill debunked the idea that Islam caused the Dervish revolt, when he wrote: 'Fanaticism is not the cause of the war. It is a means which helps savage people to fight. It is the spirit which enables them to combine the great common object before which all personal or tribal disputes become insignificant.'[114]

This may help explain why Churchill did not dwell on the threat of pan-Islamism in *The River War*. He most likely saw the Mahdi's movement and Khalifa's empire as specific only to Egypt and Sudan and not a geopolitical religious movement, thus mirroring the caliphate's own interpretation of events. For this reason, Churchill did not see any connection with external Islamic forces such as the Ottoman Empire or the Amir of Afghanistan. In fact, Churchill did not actually categorize the Mahdiyya movement as strictly an Islamic revolution at all. As Muller points out: 'Our author is quick to explain that religion was not the cause of the revolution but rather a pretext. The Sudanese had ample reason for revolt [...] but religious zeal helped the Sudanese people to concert.'[115]

Perhaps the most telling aspect of Churchill's magnanimity towards the Dervishes in Sudan is his condemnation of how Kitchener waged the war. Commenting on the fallen Dervish, he said: 'Yet these were as brave men as ever walked the earth [...] destroyed, not conquered, by machinery.'[116] In a letter to his mother,

Churchill asserted that 'the victory at Omdurman was disgraced by the inhuman slaughter of the wounded and... Kitchener is responsible for this.'[117] Churchill blamed the loss of morality towards the Dervish population squarely on Kitchener, who he described to Violet Bonham Carter as 'the general who never spared himself, cared little for others, {and} treated the men like machines.'[118] Though Churchill altered his book, he did not totally withdraw his criticisms of Kitchener from the public sphere: a daring manoeuvre for a man who wanted to become a minister of the Crown. Kitchener had become incredibly popular, and so speaking against him publicly would have required a great deal of bravery. As Lady Bonham Carter put it: 'Few would have dared to pass such a judgment, however deserved, at a moment when Lord Kitchener, the idol of the nation was enjoying a Roman triumph.'[119] Despite Kitchener's political standing Churchill let his position be known in Parliament. After he was elected in 1900, Churchill voted with John Morley against giving money to Kitchener for his victory in Sudan. In addition, prior to being elected he gave a speech in Birmingham entitled 'A Brutal Act', which concerned Kitchener's actions in the war against the Dervishes:

> It is a matter of dispute whether the desecration of the Mahdi's tomb and the removal of his body were actually necessary to the pacification of the Sudan, but it is beyond all contention that the matter in which the disinterment and removal were carried out was such as to constitute the whole proceeding as a brutal act. I am sorry for those who were concerned with it.[120]

However, there were some who supported Churchill's criticisms of the way Kitchener conducted himself during the Sudan campaign. In London high society, some people found Kitchener's actions completely beneath that of an English gentleman. Among them was Lord Randolph Churchill's old friend (and soon to be Winston's new friend) Wilfrid S. Blunt, the famed orientalist and poet.[121] Blunt became interested in Churchill after hearing of his speech on

Kitchener and of his upcoming book *The River War*, which Blunt thought would '[blurt] out all kinds of inconvenient truths about the Sudan campaign.'[122] Blunt also expressed to John Morley and George Wyndham his admiration of Churchill's bravery for publishing such a work. Blunt's relationship with Randolph, combined with Churchill and Blunt's mutual disdain for Kitchener, would help the two forge a friendship that would last a very long time and would inform Churchill's ideas about the Islamic world. Years later, in September 1909, Blunt recorded in his diary a meeting when he and Churchill discussed Kitchener. Churchill declared that Kitchener behaved like a 'blackguard' and Blunt informed Churchill that he believed Kitchener still had the head of the Mahdi as a trophy, despite being ordered to return it to Sudan.[123]

Churchill's accusations were also cited in *Concord* (a pacifist magazine) on 19 October 1898 in which the editor of *Concord* wrote to the *Westminster Gazette* about the slaughter of the Dervish army at Omdurman. The fact that these attacks were public confirmed that Churchill was not merely trying to gain some form of revenge on Kitchener for having dismissed him as a glory-hound. Churchill, whose ambition was characterized by his son Randolph Churchill as '[s]eeking the bubble of reputation, even in the cannon's mouth',[124] would not have made such a politically unpopular statement out of mere spite. It would have required an issue that truly troubled him. His compassion towards the Dervishes was obvious in the tone of his most embittered disapproval of Kitchener's desecration of the Mahdi's tomb:

> This place had been for more than ten years the most sacred and holy thing that the people of Sudan knew [. . .] It gratified that instinctive desire for the mystic which all human creatures possess [. . .] By Sir Herbert Kitchener's orders the Tomb had been profaned and razed to the ground. The corpse of the Mahdi was dug up. The head was separated from the body [. . .] The limbs and trunk were flung into the Nile. Such was the chivalry of conquerors![125]

Churchill's openness in attacking Kitchener's method of aggressive war against the Dervish population, even though it was politically unpopular,[126] illustrated his genuine concern for the population of Sudan. Churchill's insistence that it was not Islam that caused the Dervish revolution, and his testament to the bravery of the Dervish warriors, can also confirm this. Though there are still tones of traditional racist, imperialist and orientalist views present in his writing, by 1899 Churchill had clearly begun to adopt his magnanimous perception of Islam as his more prevalent opinion. His opinion would not sit well with many of his contemporaries, especially Kitchener, with whom Churchill would have to work in close proximity during World War I. Prior to this, Churchill's political positions would afford him other opportunities to observe and comment on the Islamic world.

Churchill's Early Political Life and Travels

Churchill's display of bravery and renown as a war correspondent in the Second Boer War from 1899 to 1900, and his book *London to Ladysmith via Pretoria* (1900), aided his election to Parliament as a Conservative in 1900. Churchill crossed the floor to the Liberals in 1904 owing to his disagreement with the protectionist ethos of the Conservative Party and he was appointed as Colonial Under-Secretary by incoming Prime Minister Sir Henry Campbell-Bannerman in December 1905, where he would encounter more situations that would require his knowledge of Islamic culture. This appointment did not please everyone, however, especially hardened Conservative imperialists such as F.G. Lugard (the High Commissioner of the Protectorate of Northern Nigeria). Like many Conservatives, Lugard was upset that Churchill had 'ratted out' the Conservative Party of his father and joined the Liberals. Upon hearing of Churchill's appointment, 'Lugard just shook his head and called the appointment bad news'.[127]

Churchill and Lugard had a very antagonistic relationship during this period. In early 1906 Lugard wrote to the Colonial Office for permission to go on a punitive expedition against the Munshi tribe in

Nigeria because they had destroyed the Royal Niger Company's depot. Churchill advised Lord Elgin, the Colonial Secretary, not to give permission as he had witnessed the inhumane and politically self-destructive nature of such expeditions on the north-west frontier of India. Churchill explained to Elgin that 'The chronic bloodshed which stains the West African seasons is odious and disquieting.'[128]

Here, again, Churchill's unfailing magnanimity for his enemies can be seen. Churchill openly reproached Lugard's harsh tactics and his views have been discribed as 'vigorous and by implication very critical of Lugard and the whole forward policy for which he stood and upon which he had now been acting steadily for five years'.[129] Churchill even rebuffed Lugards' wife Flora, when she came to his office to lobby for her husband and complain about Churchill's policies. Churchill even managed to convince Lord Elgin. Despite this, Lugard unilaterally moved against the Munshi tribe anyway, and the tribe was 'defeated and annihilated'.[130] As a result of Lugard's decision to attack, the situation reached crisis level because news of the Munshi defeat reached the Amir of Sokoto (a small Islamic caliphate in Nigeria) and Lugard was afraid that the Amir might rise in jihad. As Perham put it, 'This meant that the danger had now entered the sphere of Muslim passion, of the fierce unifying call of the faith which is the incalculable danger that always haunts the men who carried British power or influence into the world of Islam.'[131] Upon learning of the Sokoto Crisis, Churchill in the House of Commons on 27 February 1906 still urged against the employment of punitive expeditions in this circumstance.[132]

It was during this early political stage of Churchill's life that he began to meet and socially interact with major players in the world of Islam. In 1902, he formally met Sultan Mahommed Shah, Aga Khan III. It was at this meeting that Churchill dazzled Aga Khan with his knowledge of Edward FitzGerald's translation of *Rubaiyat of Omar Khayyam*.[133] According to Aga Khan:

> Churchill [...] quoted freely from FitzGerald's translation of Omar Khayyam. He assured me that he knew virtually the whole poem by heart. I remember being genuinely surprised by

> the enthusiasm which he displayed for those of us whose mother tongue is Persian.[134]

Though Churchill's actions and policies were always primarily governed by his commitment to the British Empire and its interests, they were especially so during this period. However, his knowledge of frontier life, combined with an acute intellect and a compassionate nature, aided his attempts to reconcile the difference between British interests and Islamic sensitivities. For instance, by the end of 1906 he was pushing for a reform of the Aliens Act, on the basis that it charged too heavy a fee for incoming aliens, especially Eastern European Jews but also Muslims. Churchill contested the wording of the Act because it, 'accords the truest enfranchisement to a well-to-do person however undesirable he may be and shuts the door in the face of a poor man however honestly and high-mindedly he may have lived.'[135] Though dictated by British interests, or in some cases his own, Churchill's thinking rarely strayed from the notion of justice for all people, no matter what their religion or ethnicity may be.

One of Churchill's major actions as Under-Secretary for the Colonies was to embark on an unofficial journey to the British colonies in 1907. His interest in the wellbeing of British colonies was obvious, as his tour was not required and ministers such as Lord Elgin rarely travelled to them. However, it was encouraged by Lord Elgin because 'it would put Churchill out of the way'.[136] The first leg of his journey took him to Cyprus, which had been under the control of the British Empire since 1878 and had become a strategic naval outpost for the protection of the Suez Canal and the maintenance of British dominance in the Mediterranean. The next leg of his journey returned Churchill to Africa and the imperial frontier that had fascinated him. During this trip, the appeal of Africa and especially Islamic culture might have been heightened for Churchill by spending more and more time with his friend, Wilfrid S. Blunt.

In October 1907, Churchill arrived in Cyprus and was met with a 'turbulent demonstration in favor of *Enosis,* or union with Greece'.[137] Unimpressed by the 'flag waving', Churchill addressed the crowd and assured them that Great Britain would 'respect the national sentiments of both races [referring to Greeks and Turks]'.[138] While this might be understood as Churchill's commitment to divide-and-rule imperialism, it also demonstrates his magnanimity and at least something of a concern for Islamic Cypriots. Regrettably, many years later, members of the *Enosis* movement would employ his speeches in Cyprus to support the cause of unification with Greece. Churchill's son, Randolph Churchill pointed out: 'A study of the *full* reports in the Colonial Office archives does not lend confirmation to this view.'[139] In one report made to the Colonial Office, Churchill remarked on the ridiculous situation created by Lord Salisbury's promise to the Greek Cypriots that they would never again be under Turkish rule, despite knowing that England was obligated by treaty to respect the Turkish position.[140] Moreover, Churchill argues for the protection of the Islamic, Turkish population in Cyprus by opposing the return of Cyprus to Greece:

> If that were done, the lives of the Muslims in the island, who constitute more than a fifth of the population, and who have always behaved to us with the utmost loyalty and good conduct, would be rendered utterly intolerable, and they would all be oppressed or frozen out [...] Union with Greece means their ruin.[141]

In order to avoid such consequences, Churchill recommended that a large amount of investment and active participation by the British would help both parties come to an agreement. He also noted the imperative need for success in Cyprus because: 'British methods were on trial before the tribunal of Europe. Success in Cyprus, as in Egypt, credits Britain in European eyes.'[142] Though Churchill's protection of the political rights of Islamic Cypriots might have encouraged Lady Bertie to worry about his religious ambiguity and cultural curiosity, it did help validate the British government among the Islamic population in Cyprus.

Churchill had been able to reconcile this multi-faceted international issue by balancing his view of Islamic interests with those of the Greek Cypriots and the interests of the British Empire.

He called for the protection of Islamic Cypriots against overzealous Greeks and unsympathetic English. He also made the case that by helping the Turkish and Greek citizens come to a compromise, they were actually enforcing the wisdom of British methods. Moreover, Churchill did not engage in blatant orientalism in the construction of his colonial policies, as he did in his earlier writings. He understood that by politically securing Cyprus, he had secured the Mediterranean, and by satisfying Islamic concerns, he had avoided the political outrage of the Islamic citizens of the British Empire and elsewhere.

From Cyprus, Churchill continued his unofficial colonial tour of Africa. He recorded his experiences in *Strand* magazine and then compiled them into a book called *My African Journey* (1908). This book mostly recounted his travels in South and East Africa but it also recollected his encounters with Muslims in Africa. While his perception was informed by orientalism, much like in *The River War*, it was also relatively favourable to the Islamic culture. His writing in *My African Journey* captured his distinctive amalgamation of orientalism and magnanimous respect, such as when he proclaimed:

> These Mohammedans have penetrated deeply and established themselves widely in the Eastern parts of Africa. Armed with superior religion and strengthened with Arab blood, they maintain themselves at a far higher level than the pagan aboriginals among whom they live [...] I reflected upon the interval that separates these two races from each other and on the centuries of struggle that the advance had cost, and I wondered whether the interval was wider and deeper than that which divides modern European from both.[143]

This also demonstrated Churchill's hierarchy of civilization. He placed Britain at the top of Europe, and Europe over Asiatic civilizations. While noting their perceived worth, measured with their perceived faults, he placed African civilization under the Asiatic civilizations. This peculiar hierarchy of cultural worth that Churchill ascribes was a clear remnant of his Anglo-centric education. Political scientist Robert Kaplan says that it is important to note that 'Churchill is not a racist: he is concerned with cultural not biological differences.'[144] Moreover, Ronald Hyam supports this concept, noting that historians who try to paint Churchill as 'a malignant racist practising virulent Anglo-Saxon triumphalism' tend to focus too much on 'what Churchill *said* mostly relaxing with cronies, rather than what he *did* or decided'. While he certainly 'believed in British superiority over non-Europeans (and most Europeans), and thought empire was a good thing [...] he loathed racial exploitation'.[145]

However, it is important to note that Churchill was certainly a man of his times and would almost certainly be considered a racist in the parlance of *our* times. Hyam's and Kaplan's hypothesis tends to break down in that they construct racism as a binary differential; either Churchill was a racist or he was not. In reality, there is surely a relative spectrum of racism. For instance, compared with Hitler's deranged and disgusting genocidal machinations, or even with Fredrick Lugard's punitive Forward imperialism, Churchill's 'Anglo-Saxon triumphalism', while technically racist, seems innocuous.[146]

Whatever the case, evidence supporting Hyam's and Kaplan's assertion of Churchill's cultural concerns were evident in Churchill's book, with its obvious concern for the wellbeing of Africa and its future: 'What is to be their part in the shaping of their country? It is, after all, their Africa.'[147] As biographer William Manchester put it: 'The fighter of the Boers had become the champion of the Boers.'[148] In fact, the majority of Churchill's speeches as Under-Secretary of the Colonies urged money for Africa, and South Africa in particular. Churchill's journey clearly inspired his reflection on civilization and savagery. Though this reflection exists in *The River War* and *Malakand Field Force*, it is articulated in *My African Journey*. It appears that disillusionment had once again entered Churchill's thinking because he seems to lose faith in civilization's capacity for justice. He emphasizes that:

> Civilization is ashamed of her arrangements in the presence of a savage, embarrassed lest he should see what lie behind the gold and purple robe of state, and begin to suspect that the all-powerful white man is a fraud.[149]

Churchill's African journey is important because it allowed him to reflect on his perceptions of English imperialism as well as his views of Africans and Arabs. Though Churchill abstractly believed in a combination of his romanticized concept of empire and his altruistic aspiration for justice and the quality of human life, he had to lay the foundation of a more tangible policy for colonial populations, including Muslims. In fact, this paradoxical approach and, at times, sentimental outlook had not gone unnoticed. His official dispatches prompted Lord Elgin to coin the phrase, 'Winston's latest *volte face*'.[150]

Another major result of Churchill's African journey was the reassessment of British policy in Somaliland. Churchill was able to draw heavily from his experiences on the north-west frontier of India and in Sudan to help construct a solution for British interests in Somaliland. Like Sudan and the north-west frontier, Somaliland was plagued by a fundamentalist Mullah, Sheikh Muhammad Abdulla Hassan, who waged a jihad and was another Islamic foe who was given the title of 'mad Mullah'.[151]

However, Sheikh Muhammad, unlike Churchill's antagonist Mullah Sadullah on the north-west frontier, was more of a Somalian nationalist using jihad as a tool to secure his political aims. According to historian Ronald Hyam: 'He was turbulent and tyrannical, but a hero and forerunner for modern Somali nationalism.'[152] Additionally it is noteworthy, that this perception of Sheikh Muhammad would fit into Nikki R. Keddie's version of pan-Islamism or Islamic extremism as a form of proto-nationalism.

Essentially, Britain could not invest the expenditure in order to hold the interior of Somaliland with the sufficient troops required to repel the Mullah's advances, because the return on the investment could never be repaid. As a result, 'Churchill would not seriously entertain the policy of effectively occupying Somaliland and crushing the Mullah.'[153] The alternative course of action, which Churchill thought would be more economically effective, was to move the British forces to the coast where their position would contain the Mullah and control the coast, thus securing the custom duties that raised the majority income.[154] This new position also allowed the return home of the majority of the Indian troops commissioned to hold Somaliland, and would thus cut the military expenditure in half.[155] However, Churchill did not arrive at his solution to the Somali question in a void; he was heavily influenced by Wilfrid Blunt. This notion of withdrawal and coastal control was first suggested by Blunt in 1904 in a letter to his old friend George Wyndham, the Chief Secretary for Ireland, which Blunt recorded in his diary:

> I have written to George Wyndham to get him to stop the Somali campaign, and to provide for the safety of the 'friendly tribes' on the Arab principle of paying blood money so as to end the feud between them and the Mullah. The British forces should then retire to the seaports and leave the interior strictly alone [. . .] The rest of the tribes will very soon come to terms with the others, *only don't leave British garrisons anywhere in the interior* and forbid all travelling and sporting expeditions by our officers for some years to come.[156]

Lord Elgin met Churchill's recommendation with keen interest and approval. However, Lord Elgin wanted to include Grey and the Foreign Office, as the decision would have to include Italy. Grey also liked Churchill's suggestion. In a letter dated 3 February 1908 to Lord Elgin, he wrote: 'This is not a heroic policy, but it finds much justification and many examples in the Indian frontier experience.'[157] Elgin left office before a decision could be reached.

Eventually, a version of Churchill's policy was adopted as a result of the increasing disturbances led by the Mullah. After Churchill and Elgin left the Colonial Office, the Earl of Crewe, Elgin's successor, even entertained the possibility of 'adopting a policy towards the Mullah which was used on the North West frontier of India – persuading him to refrain from raids on British territory in return for an annual subsidy'.[158] However, General Ronald Wingate was commissioned to make a report on Somaliland due to his expertise in the region and he believed that a withdrawal to the coast was a mistake. He also believed that a complete military expedition against the Mullah was the only logical option. Lord Crewe was not receptive to Wingate's proposal. He wished to utilize the friendly tribes to fight the Mullah because 'the Mullah had been discredited [. . .] and the tribes had shown on more than one occasion that they could hold their own against his raiding parties'.[159] Another factor was Churchill's position. Lord Crewe's opinion was most likely informed by Churchill. In a letter dated 19 September 1908 Churchill wrote to Lord Crewe:

> Sometime ago you suggested that we might pay you a visit at Crewe; & you know how anxious I am to have an opportunity of pouring out my soul to you on Uganda extension, on Cyprus tribute, on Malta Constitution & on Somaliland. My views may not command your agreement. But they were honestly & laboriously formed & I should greatly like to put them before you.[160]

It was not until March 1910 that the orders came to withdraw from the interior of the country and hold the coast, as Churchill had pushed for. However, Churchill's plan proved to be a total failure and has been characterized as 'melancholy and even catastrophic'. The interior of Somaliland collapsed into confusion and starvation for many of the tribes dwelling there. However, the Mullah continued to plague the coastal British forces until 1920, when Churchill would employ air power to destroy him. But responsibility of the failed 1910 policy must reside with Churchill because he did not recognize the Mullah's 'unique position as a national figure appealing to the patriotic sentiments of Somali as Muslims irrespective of clan or lineage allegiance'.[161]

Despite the failure of and misunderstandings within Churchill's plan for Somaliland, it is an illustration of how his decisions were informed by his previous exposures to the Islamic culture in Sudan and especially on the north-west frontier. His knowledge of the Mullah's jihad movements was based on Mullah Sadullah and his knowledge of the Dervish warrior was based on the Dervish warriors who fought with the Mahdi in Sudan. Consequently, his misunderstanding regarding the nationalist character of Sheikh Muhammad was an understandable mistake for Churchill to make.

As Churchill was returning from his colonial visit to Africa, James Currie, the principal of Gordon College and director of education in Sudan, had written a report for the Colonial Office. He urged an increase in expenditure for the Sudanese education system, arguing that none of the schools' curriculums were uniform and many of the kuttabs (Muslim teachers in religion and law) were only educated in the Qur'an. In addition, Currie asserted that 'the ignorance of the teachers is incredible, and only equaled by their fanaticism'.[162] Gordon College required more capital in order to correct this and expand the standard itinerary to include 'a primary course and after that a complete course consisting of a compromise between the ordinary literary curriculum and the Law Training College [...] like Borkee College in India'.[163] In addition to these requests, Currie also asked for money to restructure the primary school system to include more English language courses and build more primary schools.

Though Churchill did not reply to this request personally, he did approve the amount of money that the Colonial Office was allowed to expend on Sudanese education. Currie's assessment at the end of 1907 illustrated the difference of the budget for Sudan's education system before and after Churchill's appointment to the Colonial Office. In 1906 the total amount of expenditure on all aspects of the Sudanese education system was £25,048. After Churchill's appointment and James Currie's letter, the expenditure was £33,970. That is an increase of 36 per cent in education spending.[164] This additional spending helped make the Sudanese education system one of the major jewels in the crown of colonial education. In fact, it caught the attention of many of those who had served in the Middle East, including Lugard who, like many in the Colonial Office, felt that 'Muslims had to aquire a modern outlook and come to terms with the modern world.'[165] After reading Currie's reports, Lugard wanted to send several Muslims from Nigeria to Sudan to study and help them become socialized in British culture. Lugard asserted:

> There are many powerful and fairly wealthy Mohammedan Emirs in this country [Nigeria] and [...] a few of the sons of these men might become useful rulers – as in India [...] They should acquire as much English as possible, and it would be useful for them to be able to read and write an English letter [...] This education is of a character, I think, inculcated in our English Public School training [...] I have no doubt that the same estimate [...] applies to the Gordon College.[166]

The Colonial Office's increased expenditure on Sudanese education created a superior reputation and a high standard of colonial education that rivaled India's. Despite Lugard's Anglo-supremisist tone and perception, this passage still illuminates his respect for Gordon College and his desire to implement the new funding to its fullest. The Colonial Office recognized that by educating the Muslim population using British methods, the Muslims would become more socialized and willing to work with British rule. Though Lugard tended to be more rascist and perhaps Anglo-centric in his tone, Churchill also wanted to moderate Islamic fanaticism in Sudanese classrooms. The Colonial Office and Churchill were able to marry the imperialist outlook held by those such as Lugard with a general concern for the wellbeing of the Sudanese population.

When Churchill left the Colonial Office in 1908, he moved through some fairly high positions. In 1909 it was even rumoured that Churchill might succeed Lord Minto as Viceroy of India, despite the condemnation of several Anglo-Indian newspapers.[167] However, this was simply a rumour. Churchill became president of the Board of Trade and in 1910 he sat in the office of Home Secretary, a position he held only for a year. He was now more aware of Eastern matters but still kept the British Empire as his top priority. After a weekend holiday with Blunt, on 2 October 1909 Blunt wrote in his diary, 'Winston sympathizes much with my ideas about the native question in India and in general about the enslavement of the colored by the white race. But his chief interest is the poor in England.' The next day, however, Blunt noted that, 'Churchill is silent, allowing me to attack him without defending himself and I think in his heart he is agreeing with me [. . .] I think Churchill will come round to my views about India, for in all essentials he is at one with me.' Moreover, Blunt was pleased with Churchill's handling of Cyprus and Somaliland. Churchill sent copies of the secret minutes to Blunt outlining the plans that he had created for troop withdrawal in Somaliland and financial aid in Cyprus. Blunt concluded that 'all this is excellent and may lead to real imperial reforms.'[168] In matters pertaining to the Islamic world it was obvious that Churchill respected Blunt's opinions, though sometimes he disagreed with them.

In July 1910 Churchill took a cruise on Baron de Forest's yacht, *Honour*, with his friend F.E. Smith, later the Earl of Birkenhead. They made a stopover at Constantinople, where Churchill met the Sultan, the German ambassador, Marschall von Bieberstein, several leading members of the Young Turk movement and its *de facto* leader Enver Pasha,[169] whom Churchill described as 'a would-be Turkish Napoleon'[170] and whom he had met a year prior in Germany as a guest of the Kaiser to watch German military manoeuvres. Churchill later recalled his first meeting with Enver in his *Thoughts and Adventures* (1932):

> I was attracted by this fine looking young officer, whose audacious gesture had at the peril of his life swept away the decayed regime of Abdul Hamid, and who had become in one leopard-spring the hero of the Turkish nation and the probable master of its destinies [. . .]
>
> Had it been possible for the main lines of British policy to have been more in accord with legitimate Turkish aspirations I am sure we would have worked agreeably with Enver Bey. But all the puppets in the world tragedy were held too tightly in the grip of destiny.[171]

While in such powerful company in Constantinople, Churchill suggested to the Pashas that the Ottomans should remain neutral in any European struggle that might arise, urging them to 'remain the courted party rather than one which is engaged.'[172] Churchill even spoke to Bieberstein about the possibility of Germany and Britain splitting the Baghdad railway as allies.[173] After returning to Britain Churchill promptly saw Blunt in October 1910, who recorded Churchill's thoughts and reflections on his trip:

> At Constantinople he [Churchill] stayed four days and had been taken to see the new sultan, but found him uninteresting indeed senile. Djavid Pasha had shown him about and talked with several Young Turks, also with Bieberstein, the German ambassador, of whose ability he formed a high opinion. The Germans have got the better of our diplomacy there. He had brought away a great sympathy with the Young Turks and was all for them being encouraged and supported.[174]

Churchill was constructing his view of the Islamic world and the role of the British and Ottoman Empire in that world. His magnanimous and compassionate instincts, coupled with a romantic understanding of the advancement of civilization, led to his desire to nurture the new Young Turk movement and disregard the hopelessly weakened and anachronistic Sultan. However, the pragmatic, strategic dimension was not lost on Churchill either, as he understood linking Ottoman and the British interests would help reduce the German diplomatic advantage in the Ottoman court. This proved to become something of an internal balancing act for Churchill, which was not always easy. He found a great deal of antagonism from Blunt regarding the political situation with Turkey and informal British rule in Egypt. Blunt increasingly wanted British rule ended in Egypt, a view with which Churchill was not comfortable, especially in the geopolitical climate of imminent war. On the same evening as Churchill saw Blunt in October, after a discussion concerning Egypt, Churchill finished the conversation by saying:

'You must not quarrel with me if I annex Egypt.'[175] Though Churchill was most likely speaking in jest, Blunt's next journal entry on 19 October 1910, having heard that Grey wanted to annex Southern Persia, concluded that the Ottomans should join the Germans: 'It is the only thing left for any Moslem state to do.'[176] Unwittingly, Blunt had predicted the alignment of the Ottomans with Germany in the coming war, an alliance that would haunt Churchill.

CHAPTER 2

OF OIL AND OTTOMANS

This chapter explores Churchill at the Admiralty (1911–15) during the lead-up to and the first months of World War I. It scrutinizes his correspondence with leaders of the Ottoman Empire, both prior to the war and in the crucial days just before hostilities began. This illustrates Churchill's desire to ally the British Empire with the Ottomans, partly for strategic reasons and partly because he saw the two as natural allies owing to their positions as major powers in the Muslim world. Moreover, the chapter demonstrates the importance of the Middle East and eastern Mediterranean in Churchill's handling of the naval crisis of 1912 and the Royal Navy's switch to oil as its primary fuel. Finally, the chapter considers Churchill's strategy during the Dardanelles campaign and repudiates the notion that Churchill's blunders were caused by orientalist thinking.

Oil and the Ottoman Enigma

In 1911 Churchill became the First Lord of the Admiralty, a position he held into World War I. The first major task that Churchill undertook when he assumed his new office as First Lord was to address the naval crisis of 1912. This crisis arose because Britain had to mask the fact its navy had grown weaker in comparison with the well-funded and ever-growing German navy. In order to keep the illusion of the great maritime power, the British navy was forced to decide whether to limit its scope by reducing its presence in the

North Sea, abandoning the Mediterranean, building more ships for the Mediterranean, or creating a strategic alliance with France, thus sharing the responsibility of guarding the Mediterranean. Churchill was greatly opposed to limiting the navy's presence in the North Sea because 'it would be foolish to lose England in safeguarding Egypt'.[1] However, he was not in favour of abandoning the Mediterranean either, due to its political and strategic significance, especially as the Ottoman Empire might take it as a sign of weakness, thus moving them further into the German orbit. Churchill feared that, 'the shockwaves of any withdrawal would carry through the Middle East to India and the whole empire might be endangered.'[2]

Churchill eventually settled on reorganizing the fleets in conjunction with France, resulting in the Anglo-French naval agreement of 1912. This meant that Britain would move the Atlantic fleet into British waters and station two new, oil-powered dreadnaughts, the *Indomitable* and the *Invincible*, at Malta, to monitor the Mediterranean, rather than keeping the existing outdated fleet there. This would, according to Churchill, accomplish the goal of securing the Mediterranean but at a fraction of the cost; this could be done 'far more effectively than a larger number of equally expensive to keep up, but less powerful or less well advertised ships.'[3] Combined with a submarine and torpedo station at Alexandria this would, in Churchill's opinion, secure the Mediterranean, protect the Suez Canal, make it difficult to invade Egypt, and 'coerce the Turk in minor matters.'[4]

Churchill's solution to the crisis was an example of his ability to marry different interests together to create a situation beneficial for the British navy, while still protecting British colonial interests, thereby protecting the economic and social interests on the British Empire, including its Muslim population. However, there were some who believed Churchill's measures in the Eastern Mediterranean did not go far enough to ensure colonial confidence. Lord Roberts, the previous Commander and Chief of the Forces and veteran of the Indian Mutiny of 1857, wrote a letter to Churchill in July shortly before he announced the Admiralty's plan to the House of Commons, warning him about being too lax in the eastern Mediterranean:

> It is no exaggeration to say that the security of the Empire lies to a great extent in our being able to maintain our position in the Mediterranean and Egypt, and our present weakness at those points is a direct menace to the security [. . .]
>
> Should trouble arise in Egypt, or an attack made on that country by Turkey (which owing to the unfortunate change in our relations with Turkey, is, I believe not an impossibility) we should be forced to send the greater part of [. . .] our small expeditionary Force to that country; for a hostile power dominating Egypt would mean destruction to our communications with India, and a serious blow to our prestige in that country [. . .]
>
> Quite apart from strategical considerations, the importance of showing that we are determined to maintain unimpaired our position in the Mediterranean and Egypt is an incalculable advantage from the point of view of India, for were we once to become seriously embroiled with Turkey, a feeling of unrest would certainly spread to the Mahomedans in India, and this would complicate our defensive arrangements to a dangerous extent.[5]

Lord Roberts's letter was important for two reasons. First, it reinforced the significance of imperial British prestige in the eastern Mediterranean, which was undoubtedly one of the major factors that shaped British policy in the East.[6] However, in 1912 Churchill was weary of the power of prestige. In the Admiralty memorandum of 15 June 1912, one of Churchill's points about removing the existing Mediterranean fleet was that: 'It would be wrong and futile to leave the present battle squadron at Malta to *keep up appearances*. It would be a bluff which would deceive no body.'[7] Though in 1912 Churchill seemed to disregard the issue of British prestige, it would be an issue that weighed more and more heavily on his mind as the Ottomans entered the war on the side of the Central Powers. Lord Roberts's second point referenced Churchill's and Britain's resurgent fear of pan-Islamism being utilized against the Empire; a theme that was already being experimented with and exploited by Germany. Churchill responded two days later, assuring Lord Roberts that the present government had no intention of 'abandoning the Mediterranean', and while he conceded that 'to maintain a naval war singlehanded with a Triple Alliance [Germany, Austria, and Turkey] and a great land war for protection of Egypt against Turkey is beyond our powers', he did not think that such a utilization against the Empire was likely.[8] Perhaps this was because Churchill planned to work at strengthening relations with the Ottoman Empire, as he had tried in 1911.

However, for Churchill's solution to the 1912 naval crisis to work he would have to oversee another major reform: the transformation of coal-burning ships to oil-burning ships. In order to provide the oil, Churchill had to barter a deal with the Anglo-Persian Oil Company (APOC). Churchill's brokerage of an oil deal in Persia illustrates his distinctive ability to merge British strategic interests with what he perceived to be the advance of civilization in terms of helping the Bedouin tribesmen. Churchill's objectives and attitudes can best be observed, as 'concentric circles'. The innermost being strategic 'Admiralty interests' such as oil, and the outermost circle might be described as 'imperial interests' such as infrastructural and political development for Persia and India. The middle circle could be understood as a mixture of 'imperial and strategic' interests.[9] In order to barter the deal successfully with APOC, Churchill had to make all the circles work in tandem. Success would mean the stabilization of British interests in the Middle East; his failure might send Middle Eastern countries and their oilfields into German hands. British oil investments had to be secured while setting up an agreement that 'would serve important Indian [and Middle Eastern] interests as well.'[10] Churchill's pact with APOC was intended to protect and secure British fuel reserves, and keep German interests away from the Middle East, especially Persia and India, while advancing the economic interests of Muslim tribes in India and Persia by way of infrastructure and investment, a notion Churchill had supported as a subaltern on the north-west frontier.

Churchill moved quickly to solidify the pact with APOC, fearing they might sell out to Shell, which would lead to 'upsetting to the detriment of the Indian consumer.'[11] Churchill quickly commissioned Edmund Slade to take experts to Persian oilfields and subsequently used the Slade Commission's findings to convince the wary House of Commons to accept his deal with APOC in the face of ever-expanding naval estimates for 1914–15. Moreover, a dimension of cost-effectiveness of the scheme revolved around the British working with local Bedouin tribesmen. The areas of question in Persia were 'settled and quiet because security was maintained by local authorities in return for annual subsidies.'[12] This was a typical strategy which Britain employed in the Middle East and would work perfectly for the protection of the pipelines. This system was cost-effective and beneficial to the Persians. Echoing aspects of Churchill's article on frontier ethics in 1899, which called for 'winning hearts and minds', Churchill told the House of Commons:

> We are told that the tribesmen are wild and that the Persian government is weak [...] The investment of capital, the development of roads, railways and industries in which the tribesmen and Persian government are both interested, and from which both profit, ought to tend to make the Persian government strong and the tribesmen tame.[13]

This argument won the vote and Churchill's plan was put into action, allowing him to pragmatically unite the British, Persian, and tribal interests while ensuring that Persia would remain in the British orbit. The plan encompassed investment in the Persian infrastructure, while providing oil to the British fleet and keeping German interests at bay. However, there were problems. The reliance on local tribesmen rather than the Persian government for protection of the oilfields and pipelines, led the Persian government to believe that APOC was undermining its authority. While this was certainly the case, it aided the British cause in Persia. This kept capital and political investments in the hands of local tribesmen and away from the relatively centralized Persian government, which could be easily courted by the Ottomans and a pan-Islamic movement.

With British fuel interests protected Churchill was able to focus on preparing the navy for an impending war with the Central Powers. However, Churchill's increasing imperial patriotism saw a change in his outlook in Middle Eastern affairs. In fact, his position at the Admiralty was heavily straining his relationship with Wilfrid S. Blunt, who was increasingly opposed to British imperial aspirations and even wrote a letter to press offices in both Cairo and Constantinople, shortly after reaching the conclusion that Muslim states should join the Central Powers.[14] Early in the year, prior to being appointed to the Admiralty, Blunt noted that Churchill was becoming more imperialistic, recalling a conversation they had in passing:

> As I was going away Churchill called to me – 'What will you say to our making a large increase in the Cairo garrison and putting the expense of it on Egypt as a result of your inflammatory pronouncement?' You may keep 100,000 men there if you like, I said. It will make no difference in the result.[15]

After several months of silence between the two men, Churchill wrote to Blunt, suggesting that they sit down and talk. He also said that he was 'glad to find that [his] belonging to a government wicked enough to send Lord Kitchener to Egypt has not altered [their] relations'.[16] Blunt recorded shortly thereafter that he was happy to see Churchill at the Admiralty but feared that Churchill was too closely aligned with Foreign Secretary Sir Edward Grey's position of British annexation regarding the Middle East, and especially Egypt.

However, Blunt was not completely correct in his estimation of Churchill regarding his views on the Islamic world. While Churchill did insist on keeping a British presence in Egypt, one of his first endeavours at the Admiralty was to try to forge a political and strategic relationship with the Ottoman Empire. Prior to World War I, their allegiance hung in a delicate balance. Both Britain and Germany attempted to sway Turkey to their side. In fact, 'Churchill tried to encourage an actively pro-Turkish policy before 1914.'[17]

This notion of a pro-Turkish alliance came to the fore in Churchill's mind after he received a letter from a war correspondent named H.C. Seppings Wright in late 1911. Seppings Wright had been covering the Libyan War, which arose when Italy annexed the Ottoman prefecture of Libya. He reported to Churchill that the Italians committed 'a wholesale massacre of helpless women, children and old people' and that 'if a nation of cannibals had been let loose they could not have committed more abhorrent outrages.'[18] This caused great concern for Churchill because just a couple of months earlier he had received a letter from Djavid Bey, the Turkish Finance Minister and Churchill's friend from his trip to Constantinople, who wrote (too late) to gauge Churchill's position on a formal alliance with Turkey:

> Knowing and believing you occupy an important and influential position among our friends in England, I will beg you to join our effort using your influence in bringing out this friendship. Has the time arrived for a permanent alliance between our two countries?[. . .] Will you please write me your personal views on these matters? They will be considered entirely personal and unofficial. But I will consider myself happy if we can prepare a possible ground for official purposes.[19]

Before responding to Djavid Bey, Churchill wrote to Grey at the Foreign Office on 4 November 1911 to give his opinions regarding the letter:

> I could not help feeling that our colleagues were rather inclined to treat a little too lightly the crude overture which the Turkish government has made. Italy has behaved atrociously; and I cannot myself measure what the feelings of our countrymen will be as the news of those abominable massacres, resulting as they do from an act of wanton and cynical aggression is amplified and confirmed. I am sure judging by what I hear from every quarter that all the strongest Liberal opinion must be

> stirred against the Italians. On the other hand there is, as you know so well, a strong historical Turkish party among the Conservatives throughout the country [...] Turkey has much to offer us [...] we must not forget that we are the greatest Mohammedan power in the world. We are the only power who can really help and guide her [...] Have we not more to apprehend from the consequence of throwing Turkey [...] into the arms of Germany. Turkey is the greatest land weapon which the Germans could use against us. Italy is not likely to be worth much for or against anyone for some time to come [...]
>
> All this is not intended to advocate a Turkish alliance at the present time but to emphasize the importance of two steps – first a sympathetic and respectful consent of the Turkish appeal, and secondly a clear protest against the vile massacres of woman and little children which have dishonored the Italian arms... But a turn, or even a gesture might produce a lasting impression on the Mahometan world [...] And what I am wondering now is whether we are not at the present time strong enough to confront Germany and at the same time develop a purely British policy in the Orient.[20]

Churchill's letter was remarkable for several reasons. It demonstrated that the concentric circles of Churchill's thinking were in motion; British imperial interests at the centre and humanitarian and logistical circles further out. This was evident in his strategic imperial positioning of British power in the Muslim world and the spirit in which Churchill calculated the value of an alliance with Turkey versus an alliance with Italy. While British geopolitical interests were at the centre of his thinking it would be a mistake to only consider this letter in a geopolitical context. The humanitarian side of Churchill was obviously outraged at the punitive and cruel tactics employed by the Italian military against the Turkish citizens. Having seen such horrors himself in the Sudan, Churchill was quick to point out to Grey that any political action should act as a 'protest' against the 'vile massacres of women and little children.'

Another significant point in Churchill's letter is his appreciation that the British Empire was 'the greatest Mohammedan power in the world'[21] and that Britain was the 'only power who can really help and guide [Turkey].' In fact, it is remarkable that Churchill used this concept in official policy documents. While the notion that the British Empire was 'the greatest Mohammedan power in the world' has been in British academic circles since the early 1880s,[22] and was occasionally referenced by statesmen concerned with the East (especially after the census in 1901), Churchill may have actually come to this notion while he was in Constantinople meeting several members of the Young Turks. One of the Young Turks, named Sabah-ed Din (who was a relative of the Sultan), wrote editorials that appeared in imperial British papers such as *The Advertiser* (Adelaide), *The Singapore Free Press*, and *The Sydney Morning Herald* from 1908 to 1912, arguing for an Anglo-Turkish alliance on the grounds that the large number of Muslim subjects made the two powers natural allies.[23] Having been in contact with such currents of thought, it seems plausible that Churchill heard this notion while he was in Constantinople and adopted it when he returned to London. The fact that Churchill had previously never referenced the number of Islamic subjects in the British and Ottoman Empires despite having an admitted preference for the Ottomans (as opposed to the Greeks) adds weight to the idea that he picked up the notion of an alliance based on religious similarity of imperial subjects. This is further strengthened by the fact that Djavid Bey chose specifically to write to Churchill to propose such an alliance, which suggests he believed that the Young Turks formed a positive relationship with Churchill.

Likewise, Churchill understood the importance of working with the Islamic community, especially in this period. Despite the fact that there were elements of strategic positioning against Germany and a fear of a pan-Islamic disruption in Churchill's motivations here, there was also simply an interest in oriental culture. It must be remembered that this letter was written by a man who had spent a considerable amount of time in Islamic countries as a young subaltern, was a friend of Wilfrid S. Blunt, and was critical of his superiors in the military and in politics for their harsh methods of war and punitive expeditions against their Muslim rivals. So while Churchill's main concern was British interests, his understanding of the Islamic world and his concern for Muslim populations (both inside and outside the British Empire) undoubtedly played a role in his thinking.

Churchill received Grey's response on 9 November,[24] and saw that the Foreign Office wanted to send something 'mellifluous' but 'would not agree to anything substantial' despite Churchill's wish to send an 'encouraging' reply.[25] Churchill wrote back to Djavid Bey on 19 November:

> It is a great pleasure to me to receive your letter, the importance of which I fully recognize. So far as the present lamentable struggle is concerned, we have definitely declared our neutrality, and it is not to be expected that we shall alter policy so gravely decided. My answer therefore to your question must be that at the present time we cannot enter upon new political relations. In the future the enormous interests which unite the two great Mussulman powers, should keep us in touch. That is our wish; the feeling of the British public opinion, as you will have seen from recent manifestations of it, opposes no barrier to the wish, if only the Turkish Government will not alienate it by reverting to the oppressive methods of the old regime or seeking to disturb the British status quo as it now exists and you and your friend, whom I remember to have met with so much pleasure, should bear in mind that England, almost alone among European states, seeks no territorial expansion, and that alone among them she retains the supremacy of the sea. We earnestly desire to revive and maintain our old friendship with Turkey which while we retain the supremacy of the sea should be a friendship of value.[26]

Despite the diplomatic tone that Churchill was forced to adopt by Grey and the Foreign Office, his genuine interest in maintaining an alliance with Turkey is visible. He was disheartened at the Cabinet's decision to remain neutral, but Turkey and the Middle East remained a major factor in Churchill's thinking at the Admiralty, as evidence by his position on the 1912 naval crisis.

Churchill continued to work towards solidifying relations with the Ottoman Empire. He sent Rear-Admiral Arthur Limpus to Constantinople as head of the British Naval Mission, to train the Turkish navy. According to Gilbert, Limpus was 'a popular figure at Constantinople; he represented Britain's desire to help Turkey recover her strength after the crushing defeat of 1912 at the hands of the Balkan States.'[27] Churchill urged Limpus to work closely with the Turks and, as a result, many in the Turkish navy became increasingly pro-British. Limpus even began to lay foundations for a restructuring of the Turkish navy by persuading contractors Armstrong Whitworth and Vickers to make 'an offer to the Turkish government to build necessary installations for new battleships.'[28]

However, Britain was not the only power courting the Ottoman Empire. Germany had been working on relations with Turkey long before the turn of the century, before the Young Turks took control of the government. Sultan Abdul-Hamid II had pursued a pan-Islamic stance for some time, as he believed it would 'give some unity to his ramshackle empire' and that it 'deterred those powers, principally France, Russia, and Britain, who already ruled large numbers of Moslems from further despoiling his empire.'[29] This approach was successful, especially with Britain. In fact, 'fear of a Moslem uprising placed a subtle but nonetheless real constraint on British strategic planning before 1914.'[30] This was not an unfounded fear; the Sultan's agents easily established ties with Muslims in the various European empires, much to European apprehension.

The only European power that saw this as an advantage was Germany. Kaiser Wilhelm II was very friendly to the Ottomans. He sent Sultan Abdul-Hamid II a birthday card in 1896, when other European leaders were denouncing the Sultan as 'Abdul the Damned'.[31] The Kaiser even visited Constantinople in 1898 and proclaimed at a state banquet: His majesty the Sultan and the

300 million Muslims scattered across the globe who revere him as their Caliph can rest assured that the German Emperor is and will at all time remain their friend.[32]

Echoing the British fear of the power of pan-Islamic movements, the Germans also believed in the power of pan-Islamic movements and were aware of British paranoia regarding them. German spies and foreign officers discovered that many of the younger Muslims in the British sphere of influence 'favored an anti-British pan-Islamic struggle to achieve freedom of the Muslim world from Western dominance.'[33] There were several men and groups at work in Britain and the Empire, men such as Nasir-ud-din and Rafiuddin Ahmed from India and Bedr-ud-din from Egypt, all working towards the political mobilization of Islam. As a result, several societies emerged in Britain such as the Pan-Islamic Society, founded in 1903 (later renamed the Central Islamic Society in 1910). Once politically recognized, Rafiuddin Ahmed began arguing that 'Islamic sentiment towards the British was changing for the worse and this would prove harmful to British interests.'[34] German Intelligence tapped into this escalating tension. In fact Max von Oppenheim, architect and leader of the German Intelligence Bureau of the East, had been flirting with the idea of utilizing pan-Islamism against the British for some time. According to historian, Peter Hopkirk:

> Some years before the war, while working in Cairo he had prepared for his chiefs in the Foreign Ministry a secret memorandum showing how in the event of war, militant Islam might be harnessed to the German war machine with what he described as incalculable effects.[35]

Despite the efforts of the Germans and their gifted ambassador, Marschall von Bieberstein, the Ottomans continued to maximize their position in international relations, playing the British and German empires off against one another. This caused each to compete harder and harder for the alliance they both craved. Churchill, however, as early as July 1910 on his cruise to Constantinople when he met Bieberstein and several members of the Young Turks, had seen that the Germans appeared to be ahead in the quest for Ottoman affection.[36]

In an attempt to court the Ottoman Empire in December 1911, Churchill insisted that Turkey 'received what seemed to the British eyes, the most favorable offer ever made to any government in history.'[37] The offer included two battleships, the *Reshadieh* and the *Sultan Osman I*, at reduced prices and an offer to build a dock in which to keep them. The Turkish navy happily accepted the terms and a deal was struck. The construction of a new dock would ensure a British presence in Constantinople and increase trade, commerce, and the living standard for the Muslims residing there: 'Through battle ships and finance, Britain and Turkey were being brought together.' This pleased Churchill because he 'believed in the friendship between the British and Ottoman empires' despite the typical Liberal policy of invoking Gladstone's indignation towards the Turkey of the 1870s.[38] Undoubtedly, one of the primary reasons for Churchill's wish of an alliance, as he told Djavid Bey, was to unite the two largest Muslims powers.

By July 1914 both vessels were almost ready to leave British waters and make their way to Constantinople. But Churchill was wary of letting such powerful warships leave Britain, due to the looming threat of war with Germany. His consideration for British interests overrode his interest in helping Turkey. Dan van der Vat, a naval historian, has used this to argue that Churchill did not appreciate the strategic importance of Turkey. Van der Vat argued: 'Apparently, the addition of two capital ships to the Royal Navy was regarded as outweighing the drastically underestimated importance of Turkish goodwill or neutrality.'[39]

But this does not acknowledge Churchill's notion that German diplomacy had already won Turkish affections.[40] After all, Turkish neutrality was still heavily doubted. It was this diplomatic situation that weighed on Churchill's mind, not a dismissal of the importance of Turkish neutrality. As a result, Churchill was compelled to commandeer the ships and immediately consulted the Foreign Office. Grey's response was, 'we must let the Admiralty deal with this question as they consider necessary and afterwards make such a defense of our action to Turkey as we can.'[41] At first, Churchill was content to let the Armstrong Whitworth workers continue delaying completion. But by the end of July, he convinced members of the Cabinet that both ships would be needed against the German navy and, by 1 August, Churchill had *Sultan Osman I* boarded by British sailors.

The Turkish government was furious. This action alienated several of the pro-British Young Turk ministers such as Talaat Bey and Djavid Bey, and even those who advocated neutrality, which drove Turkey further into the arms of the German Empire. However, according to Hopkirk, the announcement [of British intentions] was made on the very same day that the Germans and the Turks signed their secret alliance. Although, the British had no inkling of this clandestine accord, it would in fact have more than justified Churchill's decision.[42] Churchill's official biographer Martin Glibert, pointed out that the treaty that Enver signed with German ambassador Wangenheim actually was not that official or powerful: 'This treaty was unknown even to the neutralist and pro-British members of the Turkish Cabinet. It did not commit Turkey to enter the war at Germany's side, but gave the Germans the overriding influence in the Turkish capital.'[43] If Gilbert's analysis is correct and the treaty was largely based on control of influence in Constantinople, then Churchill's action actually did push the Turkish opinion against the British and deconstructed Churchill's vision of an alliance of the two largest Muslim powers. Despite this new 'clandestine accord' with Germany, the aborted British deal was perceived as 'an act of piracy'[44] by the Ottoman Empire, which had levelled a tax on their subjects in order to pay the £3,680,650 bill.[45] In fact: 'Thousands of school children who contributed their pocket money to the vessels' purchase marched in protest against the British Government's action.'[46] Churchill even hinted in his *World Crisis* that contributions were not limited to Turkey but spread 'even throughout all Islam.'[47]

The situation in Constantinople was further complicated by the arrival of the German cruisers the *Breslau* and the *Goeben*. On 11 August Admiral Souchon, captain of the *Goeben*, was ordered to 'go to Constantinople as quickly as possible in order thereby to compel Turkey to side with us [Germany] on the basis of the treaty that has been concluded.'[48] Souchon was successful in convincing the Turks to uphold their clandestine treaty. Later that day, Churchill was made aware of the situation and telegraphed Sir Berkeley Milne to keep an eye on the Dardanelles and make sure that the German ships did not re-enter the Mediterranean. On 15 August, Churchill sent Grey a copy of his intended telegram to Enver Pasha, the Turkish Minister of War and an acquaintance of Churchill's. Churchill's brief note to Grey on the cover said: 'Don't Jump; but do you mind my sending this personal message to Enver. I have answered this man and am sure it will do good. But of course your "NO" is final.'[49] Grey approved and Churchill sent a telegram to Admiral Limpus to be personally handed over to Enver, thus making it a personal message from Churchill. The telegram reads:

> I hope you are not going to make a mistake which will undo the services you have rendered Turkey and cast away the successes of the second Balkan War. By a strict and honest neutrality these can be kept secure. But siding with Germany openly or secretly now must mean the greatest disaster to you, your comrades, and your country [...]
>
> On the other hand I know that Sir Edward Grey who has already been approached as to the possible terms of peace if Germany and Austria are beaten, has stated that if Turkey remains loyal to her neutrality, a solemn agreement to respect the integrity of the Turkish Empire must be a condition of any terms of peace that affect the near East.
>
> The personal regard I have for you, Talaat, and Djavid and the admiration with which I have followed your career from our first meeting at Wurzburg alone leads me to speak these words of friendship before it is too late.[50]

This telegram displayed Churchill's personal attachment to his acquaintances in the Young Turks but also Churchill's conviction that a German and Ottoman alliance was a step backwards in terms of advancement of Turkey. From Churchill's perspective an alliance between the Ottoman Empire and the British Empire would be a modernizing force for Turkey. However, Grey and Churchill's desire to keep Turkey neutral by guaranteeing her territorial sovereignty was not without its benefits for Britain, not just in terms of strategic location, but also by aligning the wills of the two great Muslim powers. Logistically, this would have kept 'Russia away from Constantinople and the Straits and the Germans away from head of the Persian Gulf.'[51] Whether Churchill was motivated by opportunism or benevolence for his Turkish friends (or more probably a mixture of the two) he still pushed for Turkish neutrality.

However, as Enver remained silent, Churchill's disappointment turned into anger and by the Cabinet meeting of 17 August, his belligerent tone was audible. After the meeting, Prime Minister H.H. Asquith wrote to Venetia Stanley:

> Turkey has come into the foreground, threatens vaguely enterprises against Egypt and seemed disposed to play a double game about the *Goeben* and the *Breslau.* Winston, in his most bellicose mood, is all for sending a torpedo flotilla through the Dardanelles – to threaten and if necessary to sink the *Goeben* and her consort. Crewe and Kitchener [are] very much against (in the interest of the Moslems in India and Egypt) our doing anything which could be interpreted as meaning that we were taking the initiative against Turkey. She ought to be compelled to strike the first blow. I agreed to this.[52]

Churchill's aggressive posturing and frustration with the situation was on one hand characteristic of his increasing defensive nature regarding British interests in the climate of imminent war, but on the other hand seemed counter-intuitive regarding his hopes for an alliance of the two great Muslim powers. Perhaps ironically, Kitchener (the man Churchill criticized for his harsh treatment of Muslims) was urging the Cabinet not to be aggressive against the Ottoman Empire due to the Muslim population in the British Empire.[53] Grey agreed with Kitchener and thought it best to delay

Turkey's entry into the war as long as possible in order to 'stand well in the eyes of [British] Moslem subjects.'[54] According to Grey's autobiography, he was persuaded to take this position:

> An Indian personage of very high prestige in the Moslem world came to see me. He urged earnestly that Turkey should be kept out of the war: if we were at war with Turkey it might cause great trouble for Moslem British subjects and be a source of embarrassment both to them and to us [...] he then urged that, if it was impossible to avoid war with Turkey, it should come in [a] way as to make it clearly and unmistakably not our fault; that it should be evident that we had done all that was possible to avoid war.[55]

Kitchener and Grey's fear of a pan-Islamic uprising carried the day, despite Churchill's aggressive and almost irrational posturing in the Cabinet meeting. Churchill's behaviour might be explained by the idea that he felt personally betrayed by Enver and his other friends in the Turkish government. In *The World Crisis: The Aftermath* (1929), Churchill included a footnote saying he personally knew the Turkish leaders.[56] After all, Churchill told Grey that he thought he had great sway with Enver and could help the situation, though he had been unable to do so.

However, a turn of events the next day (18 August) raised Churchill's hopes again. Sir Louis Mallet, the British ambassador in Constantinople, telegraphed Grey that Enver was 'delighted with the offer of respect for Turkish territorial integrity' and that 'public feeling would be affected immediately if His Majesty's Government would authorize [...] an announcement at once that the seizure of Turkish ships was not permanent.'[57] Mallet also reported that a 'public promise' for the return of the ships in good order would aide British support in the Turkish population.

Upon hearing this news through Grey, Churchill immediately tried to salvage the British position with the Ottoman Empire. He wrote to Admiral Troubridge, a naval commander in the Mediterranean who was guarding the mouth of the Dardanelles, that he was to 'show no hostile intentions to Turkey' and to 'use no threats' and to 'keep in touch with the Ambassador at Constantinople.'[58] However, later that day Mallet reported to Grey that the Naval Minister in Turkey, Ahmed Djemal, was 'heart broken at the loss of his ships' and that the British 'could not understand what an effect [their] action had had throughout the Mussulman world and to what extent it was being exploited by Germany.'[59]

Churchill telegraphed at once to Enver to try and diffuse the situation:

> I deeply regretted necessity for detaining the Turkish ships because I know the patriotism with which the money had been raised all over Turkey [. . .] I am willing to propose to His Majesty's Government the following agreement:-
>
> (1) Both ships to be delivered to Turkey at the end of the war after being thoroughly repaired at our expense in British Dockyards. (2) If either is sunk we will pay full value to Turkey immediately on the declaration of peace. (3) We will also pay at once the actual extra expense caused to Turkey by sending out crews and other incidents as determined by an arbitrator. (4) As a compensation to Turkey for the delay in getting the ships we will pay £1000 a day in weekly installments for every day we keep them, dating retrospectively from when we took them over.
>
> This arrangement will come into force on the day when the last German officer and man belonging to the *Goeben* and *Breslau* shall have left Turkish territory definitely and finally, and will continue binding so long as Turkey maintains a loyal and impartial neutrality in this war and favours neither one side or the other. Do you agree?[60]

Churchill sent the letter to Admiral Limpus who delivered the letter to the Turkish Naval Minister along with the message, 'that had I had the pleasure of his acquaintance I should have addressed myself directly to him.'[61] This letter illustrated Churchill's desire to keep the Ottoman Empire in the fold of

British friendship. The letter to Enver offered substantial compensation for the two ships and their eventual return, just as Enver had asked. However, already having signed the secret treaty with the Germans, Enver was probably following Churchill's early advice to 'remain the courted party'. Whatever the case, it was a time of great tension and confusion between the great Muslim powers. Churchill later stated:

> I can recall no great sphere of policy about which the British Government was less completely informed than the Turkish. It is strange to read the telegrams we received through all channels from Constantinople during this period in light of our present knowledge. But, all the Allies, now encouraged by the friendly assurances of the Grand Vizier and the respectable-effete section of the Cabinet [...] believed that Turkey had no policy and might still be won or lost.[62]

Churchill's efforts were in vain. Enver decided (without full support of the Turkish parliament) to support Germany and the Central Powers and refused to hear Churchill's proposal. As a result, the next time the British Cabinet met, Asquith reported Churchill's mood as 'violently anti-Turk' and that it was he, rather than Churchill, who was 'against any aggressive action vis a vis [sic] of Turkey which would excite our Mussulmans in India and Egypt.'[63] Gilbert best explained Churchill's anger regarding the situation:

> German officers and German crews remained on board the two warships, making a mockery of the alleged sale of the ships to Turkey [...] While the *Goeben* and *Breslau* remained in neutral Turkish waters and under German command, Churchill felt a personal sense of responsibility for their escape [...] Although Churchill was the foremost British minister to advocate a positive policy of conciliation with Turkey, his ultimate concern and responsibility was German Naval strength.[64]

Despite Churchill's failure to secure Turkish neutrality, it is impossible to dismiss his attempt to make peace with the Ottoman Empire for the wellbeing of Western and Eastern civilzation. Though Churchill's primary aim was to guarantee British interests, he also sought a political relationship with Turkey. However, he was unable to fulfill both goals. At an impasse over pending war with Germany, Churchill had to decide in favour of British security and defence, instead of aiding trade and promoting an alliance between the two largest Muslim powers.

Churchill, the Dardanelles, Gallipoli, and Mesopotamia

As the situation escalated in the Mediterranean, Churchill was anxious to begin the new front. In *The World Crisis: 1911–1918*, he wrote: 'Lest it should be thought that I underrated the gravity of war with Turkey, it must be remembered that I had convinced myself that Turkey would attack us sooner or later.'[65] Despite this, Churchill continued to work towards Turkish neutrality until the very end when Enver committed the Ottoman Empire to the Central Powers in October 1914. As a result of Turkey becoming increasingly coy about their neutrality Churchill resolved: 'If we were not going to secure honest Turkish neutrality, then let us, in the alternative, get the Christian States of the Balkans on our side.'[66]

This shift created a difficult state of affairs for the British Empire, as its Muslim subjects might perceive that a war against the Ottoman Empire was a war against Islam. If this was the case, the situation might spark up the pan-Islamic movements in India, Egypt, and elsewhere in the Empire. This was a precarious situation that Kaiser Wilhelm and the German Intelligence Bureau of the East were eager to exploit. While Enver Pasha was willing to work with the Germans to this end, he was not himself a pan-Islamist. According to Charles Haley: 'It is true that Enver was a Muslim and unquestionably true that he believed in God; yet one cannot derive from his commentaries the idea that he was a devout Muslim.'[67] Moreover, Haley argued that he used pan-Islamism as a political vehicle but only until 1912. After that he saw more opportunity in alliances with European empires, especially Germany. This led Enver to make relations strong with the German Empire, but when it became strategically and politically convenient he was happy to pick up the pan-Islamic banner if it pleased his German allies.

After the outbreak of the war the Kaiser was enraged at the refusal of the British to hear his plea for them to remain neutral. Wilhelm immediately 'issued his celebrated order to all German agents and diplomats in the East to unleash the wrath of the entire Mohammeden world against his British cousins.'[68] Using Max von Oppenheim's previous suggestions as a foundation, several members of the German War Cabinet supported the utilization of militant Islam to enhance the German aims in the East; these included Chief of General Staff, Helmoth von Molkte, and Under-Secretary for Foreign Affairs, Arthur Zimmerman, whose primary belief in the scheme was dictated by economic dimensions. He believed that the holy war would be cheaper on manpower and money.[69] Later, the plan to enfranchise pan-Islamic, anti-British sentiment was dubbed the 'Zimmerman Plan' and was initially successful: 'Three weeks after Turkey joined the Central Powers, Holy War against Britain and her allies was declared by the Sultan.'[70]

This was not confined to the borders of the Ottoman Empire and the Middle East but pushed out into Central Asia with the intentions of threatening the British crown jewel, India.[71] To that end, Constantinople and Berlin sent agents to Libya, Persia, Morocco, India, and Afghanistan where they tried to convince the Amir of Afghanistan to order his troops and the tribesmen under his influence to take up arms against British India.[72] The Turko-German mission linked up with the anti-British and pro-Turkish faction at Kabul, which was headed by the Amir's brother, Nasrullah Khan, and put a great deal of pressure on the Amir to enter the war on the Turkish side. (Despite such pressure, the Amir remained neutral throughout the war.)[73] Additionally, the Germans started helping Sikh and Bengali revolutionaries in Europe and North America.[74]

This all meant that one of the traditional antagonists of the British Empire was making itself visible again. Kitchener, Grey, Asquith, and Churchill all had reason to fear a pan-Islamic revival, as they had all experienced it in various forms. It was a central issue in relations with the 'East'. David French pointed out this reccurring theme in British attitudes since the Indian Mutiny of 1857:

> Although the Indian Mutiny had involved both Moslems and Hindus it had centered around the Moslem King of Delhi, whose dynasty had once ruled most of India. Henceforth, the British saw Islam as perhaps the most potential source of danger to their rule. The lessons of the Mutiny were reinforced by the difficulties and humiliations the British experienced in suppressing the Mahdist movement in Sudan in the 1880s and 1890s.[75]

This took an increasing toll on Churchill's perception and the overall British opinion of the Islamic world. Such writers as John Buchan (who wrote the spy thriller *Greenmantle* (1916)) explored the possibility of the Germans inciting the Muslim world to rise up and wage jihad against the British. This was not just happening in fiction, however, it was actually happening. As early as August 1914, Churchill was receiving intelligence reports of possible pan-Islamic movements. A letter from Lieutenant-Colonel Sir Mark Sykes to Churchill on 24 August 1914 confirmed that Germany was utilizing pan-Islamism to bring the Ottoman Empire into the war against England and the Allied powers:

> From various suggestive scraps I have seen in the Times I infer that the Germans are straining every nerve to involve Turkey and so cause if possible a pan-Islamic diversion against us, and as Caucasian complication for Russia on the Armenian frontier.[76]

Once war was declared between the British Empire and the Ottoman Empire on 4 November 1914, Churchill recognized the relationship with Turkey as a lost cause but he was not particularly concerned with Turkish participation in the war beyond the possibility of a pan-Islamic revival. This fear was reinforced by the Sultan's declaration of jihad on against the British Empire and its allies on 11 November 1914. However, Gilbert contended that: 'For Churchill, the entry of Turkey into the war was of importance entirely because of the effect it would have on the fortunes of the war in Europe.'[77]

This overlooks Churchill's increasing fear for the wellbeing of imperial interests in the Middle East, Central Asia, and India. Churchill saw the Turkish entry as an opportunity to unite the Balkan states against their traditional foe, an idea that delighted Lloyd George and Asquith, who had always pushed for Gladstone's dream of a Europe free from Turkey, a political position Churchill had rejected until the Turkish entry into the war. In October 1914 Asquith wrote, 'few things would give me greater pleasure than to see the Turkish Empire finally disappear from Europe.'[78] Endeavouring to fulfill Gladstone's dream and create a new front that was not bogged down, Churchill, Asquith, Kitchener, and Grey set about to attack what seemed the most vulnerable position of the Ottoman Empire, the Dardanelles. This would have allowed the British navy to demonstrate its power in the East, protect the Suez Canal, and would lead directly to Constantinople, which (if captured) might dissuade any pan-Islamic movements.

It was Churchill's original contention that it would require a large naval and expeditionary force to attack Gallipoli because he knew the tenacity and courage of the Ottoman Muslim warriors. This is reflected in Cabinet Secretary Maurice Hankey's notes from a Cabinet meeting of 25 November:

> Mr. Churchill suggested that the ideal method for defending Egypt was an attack on the Gallipoli Peninsula. This if successful, would give us control of the Dardanelles, and we could dictate terms at Constantinople. This, however was a very difficult operation *requiring a large force*.[79]

This opinion was agreed to by Admiral Oliver, who suggested that 'troop transports should be kept in Egypt sufficient to transport a division of troops to the Dardanelles should it become possible to assemble men in the future.'[80] Churchill sent this to Kitchener, but Kitchener thought that troop transports were not necessary at the present time.

Kitchener's motives might best be explained by the argument that the authors of the Dardanelles campaign were influenced by orientalist motives. For instance, David French argued that: 'In British eyes the Turks were not a western nation but a backward eastern power, whose government was unstable and faction-ridden.'[81] This made Constantinople a 'glittering prize', one that was:

> all the more attractive by the conviction that [it] would fall into the Entente's lap with very little effort because the Turkish Empire would collapse after barely a shot being fired. Nothing else can explain adequately the willingness of Asquith, Grey, Churchill and Kitchener to push ahead with the Dardanelles operation as a purely naval venture.[82]

This, of course, groups Churchill in with the other members of the Cabinet. While French revealed evidence of Grey operating in the orientalist paradigm, there is very little evidence that Churchill did as it relates to his dealings with the Ottoman Empire. However, French made the argument that Churchill was operating in this paradigm based on his testimony at the Dardanelles Commission:

> Churchill claimed that had the fleet reached Constantinople, 'probably a daily shelling of a moderate character at stated intervals, with parleys and bargaining in between would have [been] most efficacious and least costly in ammunition and life as it would have led the enemies of the Young Turks to unite, overthrow them and make peace' [...] Churchill's belief that this would have happened had the fleet got through rested little more on his conviction of the innate inferiority and poor fighting qualities of non-European troops.[83]

This, however, overlooks the idea that Churchill may have considered that those friendly to the British such as Djavid Bey and Talaat Bey could lead a coup against Enver and the pro-German contingent. This was a serious possibility in Churchill's mind. On 19 March 1915, Churchill spoke with Captain William Hall, the director of Naval Intelligence, regarding intelligence from Constantinople. He informed Churchill that he had been in negotiations with Talaat Bey, the Turkish Minister of the Interior. According to Hall, Talaat said: Many of [Constantinople's] most influential citizens would welcome an immediate break with the Germans and prayers were even being offered up at mosques of the city for the arrival of the British fleet.[84]

There were other factors as well which do not indicate an 'orientalist motive' behind the creation of the Dardanelles offensive. The first was that a precedent had already been laid for such an operation. One of the original roots of the operation lay in the previous plans drawn up by the CID (Committee of Imperial Defence) in 1906 in case war had arisen with Turkey over the Sinai boundary dispute.[85] Though the plans included a joint attack and not a strictly naval operation, they did lay the ground work for such an operation.

An Additional factor was the initial military actions taken against Turkey: the Indian government's force landed at Fao and the cutting of Turkish railway lines to Alexandria by the British navy. The latter played a large role in the Cabinet's estimation of the Ottoman Empire's ability to wage war, because Turkish authorities almost immediately surrendered under fire from the British navy and agreed to destroy their own trains. This indicates that the opinion of Turkish military inferiority was derived, at least in part, from their initial military blunders, rather than some preconceived notion of racial inferiority. Gilbert reinforces this point, by noting that this event 'appeared proof that the Turks were not serious opponents and encouraged the hope that no great military effort would be needed to force Turkey out of the war.'[86] Churchill's own testimony in the Dardanelles Commission stated that:

> The incident [was] not without significance, because it had helped to form the opinion in our mind as to the degree of resistance which might in all circumstances be expected from Turkey. What kind of Turk was this we were fighting? [...] I must say that it was always in my mind that we were not dealing with a thoroughly efficient military power, and that it was quite possible that we could get into parley with them.[87]

The final factor affecting the decision to open an attack on the Dardanelles, stemmed from strategic necessity. Though Churchill wanted his attack on the Dardanelles and Gallipoli more and more, there were no troops to help him realize his ambitions. However, the situation in the East was deteriorating, with Russia appealing for a distraction for the Turks to ease its position in the Caucasus. According to Gilbert:

> The Russian appeal supplemented all other considerations. If Russia were forced out of the war, the German Armies then on the Eastern front would be free to reinforce their comrades in the west [...] Once Russia were defeated the Turks could turn their forces against Egypt, where Britain if pressed on the western front, would be most weak.[88]

Upon learning of the Russian appeal, Grey sent a letter to Kitchener and Churchill asking if a 'naval action would be able to prevent the Turks sending more men into the Caucasus and thus denuding Constantinople.'[89] A combination of several expert opinions, including Hankey and Kitchener himself, pushed for an attack at the Dardanelles. It was in this climate that Churchill and Kitchener opted for a purely naval operation due to a coupling of the poor showing of Turkish tactics outside of Alexandria and because of strategic requirement to alleviate the Russians, not because of the 'conviction held by most Englishmen that the Turk was inherently inferior to the white man.'[90] Though this may have played some role in the early thinking of many of the War Cabinet members, it has been overstated in the literature. Moreover, it is impossible to lump Churchill in with the rest of the Cabinet members in this respect.

Churchill sent a telegram to Vice-Admiral Carden asking whether 'forcing the Dardanelles by ships alone was a practical option'.[91] Carden acquiesced to Churchill's wishes, noting that: 'They might be forced by extended operations with a large number of ships.'[92] Seeking glory for himself and the navy that he commanded, Churchill was quick to adopt the plan, with the blessing of Kitchener and Admirals Jackson and Oliver, who later shifted their positions. However, the First Sea Lord, Admiral Jacky Fisher, unfalteringly believed an expeditionary force was required to take the Gallipoli peninsula. Asquith too was opposed to such a scheme. He wrote to Venetia Stanley on 5 December 1914 regarding Churchill's plan, stating that: 'His violent mind is at present set on Turkey and Bulgaria and he wants to organize a heroic adventure against Gallipoli and the Dardanelles; to which I am altogether opposed.'[93]

It is easy to understand why Churchill was apt to adopt Carden's plan. Such a naval victory would redeem Churchill's botched defence of Antwerp earlier in 1914, demonstrate British naval superiority, reduce the number of casualties, and perhaps aid in bringing an end to the war in Europe.[94] Furthermore, such a victory would demonstrate British power in the Middle East and India by essentially stamping out the Sultan's call for jihad, which had acted as 'a direct challenge to British prestige.'[95] Another component that played a role in Churchill's willingness to jump at an all-naval operation on the Dardanelles was his previous interest in such operations. This interest was visible as early as 1900 when Churchill's fiction *Savrola* (1900) was published.[96] The last act of this novel ends with what Churchill would later call in his book *My Early Life*, 'an ironclad fleet forcing a sort of Dardanelles to quell the rebellious capital.'[97]

Though his actions were self-indulgent, motivated primarily by his lust for glory, they were also married with Churchill's desire for Britain to be seen as a benevolent victor to the Turks in *Dar al-Islam*. To that end, Churchill took extra care to protect Muslims sympathies. For instance, he ordered warships in the Red Sea not to attack Turkish vessels containing Turkish Muslim pilgrims on the

Haj to Mecca and ordered them not to fire on Red Sea ports, such as Jidda.[98] When these orders were not obeyed, Churchill sharply rebuked the commanders responsible. Churchill was 'furious' when the *Minto*, a small Indian vessel, 'sank a dhow and put in a Jidda', actions which Churchill felt were 'acts of provocation.'[99]

Churchill believed these considerations would leave the British in good standing with Turkish opinion and Muslim sympathies. He even believed he could still court Turkish favour after the war. In January 1916 in a letter Churchill wrote to his wife Clementine he ended the letter with: 'After the war I shall be friends with Enver and will make a great Turkish policy with him. Perhaps!'[100] According to Gilbert:

> Churchill believed that Enver's followers would abandon the German cause when confronted with so powerful a demonstration of British superiority, and that Enver himself might perhaps take the lead in shaking Turkey from the German grip.[101]

Churchill believed in the success of the Dardanelles. He met Lord Riddell on 29 April 1915 and Riddell recorded Churchill as saying:

> I think the Dardanelles expedition will be successful. This is one of the great campaigns of history. Think what Constantinople is to the East. It is more than London, Paris, and Berlin all rolled into one [. . .] Think how it has dominated the East. Think what its fall will mean.[102]

Assuming victory, Churchill and the Admiralty laid out a principally benevolent policy that concluded with the assertion that 'all religious buildings, especially mosques, and objects venerated by Moslems will be treated with the utmost respect.'[103] Gilbert insinuates that Churchill added this declaration as a warning to Kitchener following his destruction of the Mahdi's tomb in Sudan. However, such statements could have risen from Churchill's fear of angering British Muslim subjects and to prevent a pan-Islamic movement. Certainly, this fear became something of a preoccupation for Churchill. After all, the Sultan had declared a state of jihad against the British Empire when war broke out. Churchill's personal notes from early 1915 reveal the profound nature of his concerns:

> It is in Asia that a natural and appropriate sphere {of} action will be formed for the unorganized armies of Turkey, where the weight of Islam will be drawn into the struggle on the German side. The Mohammedan influence in Asia will carry with it all kindred forces along in Egypt and along the North-African shore. It is in Asia, through Mesopotamia, Persia, Afghanistan, and ultimately India that England will be struck at and her crown of acquisitions cancelled out. India is the target, Islam is the propellant, and the Turk is the projectile.[104]

Churchill was not the only minister who wanted be aligned with Muslim sympathies after the defeat of the Ottoman Empire. At a War Council meeting on 19 March 1915, Sir Edward Grey wanted to set up an 'independent Moslem State in the Arab provinces of the Turkish Empire.'[105] There was, however, still a great deal of disagreement among the various departments as to what should be done in the Middle East once the Ottoman Empire fell. For instance, Lewis Harcourt, the Secretary of State for the Colonies, believed that Mesopotamia should become 'an outlet for Indian immigration and suggested offering the Holy Places as a mandate to the United States.'[106] At the same meeting, Kitchener and Crewe argued to 'transfer Mecca, the center of the Islamic world from Turkish to British control, rather than let the Turkish Empire remain intact and thereby make it possible for the Holy Lands of Islam to fall under Russian domination.'[107] Churchill also sought to determine the fate of the Ottoman Empire and threw himself into the War Council's partitionist campaign. The minutes from the War Council meeting illustrate his position:

> Mr. Churchill, said that the whole question depended on whether we intended to divide Turkey. Surely, he suggested,

> we did not intend to leave this inefficient and out-of-date nation, which had long misruled one of the most fertile countries in the world [i.e. Mesopotamia], still still in its possession! Turkey had long shown herself to be inefficient as a governing Power and it was time for us to make a clean sweep.[108]

This reversed what Churchill had originally thought regarding the Turkish role in the world after the war. This reversal of his opinion has even baffled Gilbert, who wrote: 'These extreme sentiments were in direct and violent contrast to Churchill's earlier sympathies for the Young Turks and their revolution.'[109] These particular minutes have led some historians such as Trumbull Higgins and David French to suggest that Churchill was merely a 'Turko-phobe',[110] and that he 'believed in the innate inferiority of Asiatic troops.'[111] However, these conclusions ignored Churchill's earlier attempts to keep Turkey as a British ally and ignored Churchill's personal relationship with members of the Young Turks. It may be as likely that Churchill simply felt personally affronted by Enver and the other Turks who sided against him.

In order to co-ordinate official British policy in the Middle East, the British government commissioned the De Bunsen Committee in 1915 to make a report of possible policies to pursue in the event of victory.[112] Among the committee's desiderata was the necessity of a guarantee that 'Arabia and the Muslim Holy Places would remain under independent Muslim rule.'[113] Unfortunately, the report never received official approval, but it was very much in step with Churchill's views and designs for the situation.

Despite Churchill's blueprint for victory, and at the behest of Kitchener and Fisher, the War Council decided to send a small battalion of land troops. This decision proved fatal to the execution of the Mediterranean offensive, leaving the expeditionary force outmanned, unsupplied, and unable to assist the naval assaults, which were being repelled by the Turkish forts on the Dardanelles straits. Based on Churchill's first-hand knowledge of the ability of the Muslims to wage war ferociously, he knew that if troops were to be sent it would require a vast number of men. Moreover, the ns in Turkey were armed with German weapons, not old s like the Muslim tribes in Afghanistan – half a world away from Europe. Counter-intuitively, Kitchener, who had originally called for troops, 'would not release his last regular division, the Twenty-ninth',[114] for fear of their requirement in France. Churchill realized that without British regulars the offensive push would fail against their fierce foe. Churchill was furious and tried to intervene at the War Council:

> Mr. Churchill said that the 29th Division would not make the difference between failure and success in France, but might well make the difference in the East. He wished to be placed on record that he dissented altogether from the retention of the 29th Division in this country. If a disaster occurred in Turkey owing to the insufficiency of troops, he must disclaim all responsibility.[115]

As the British forces began to fail in the Mediterranean, Churchill's fears were becoming realized. As Kitchener pointed out, the loss of Gallipoli might incite a pan-Islamic revolt across the British Empire. Since Churchill perceived the British Empire as the largest Muslim power in the world, this was an exceedingly important concern for him. This also troubled Austen Chamberlain, the Conservative recently appointed Secretary for the State of India after the formation of a coalition government in May 1915, who had received reports from provincial leaders such as the Lieutenant-Governor for the United Provinces of Agra and Oudh, Sir James Meston. Meston wrote to Chamberlain in June 1915 concerned about the Muslim population in his provinces and the fallout of the De Bunsen Committee's proposals:

> In the Report of Lord Curzon's committee which was accepted by the Imperial War Cabinet at one of its last meetings, there are references to the future of Mesopotamia 'under British control' and to the desirability of 'an Arab State or congeries of States under the protection of Great Britain'. I do not know

> whether these expressions are intended to define with precision the future method of government in the Baghdad Vilayat, and more especially over the Holy Places of Islam in that area, – Kerbala, Najaf, etc. On the assumption however that the exact degree of British control is not yet fully decided, I suggest that it would be well to ascertain the feeling of our Mahomedan fellow-subjects on the point [. . .] My reason for writing is my belief that any protectorate by a Christian Power or group of Powers over the Moslem shrines in Arabia would actually offend the deepest sentiments of our Mahomedan population. This is true of Mecca and Medina as it is of the shrines near Baghdad.[116]

Chamberlain was growing ever aware of the unrest in the Indian Muslim population, owing partly to the Turko-German missions but also to Muslim political proclivity towards the Ottoman Caliphate. On 27 July 1915, he wrote to the War Council to confirm his and Churchill's fears:

> From our point of view in India, defeat, or the necessity of cutting our losses in the Dardanelles, would be absolutely fatal in this country, since the Mohammedans would then undoubtedly turn their eyes to Turkey, far more than towards us and pan-Islamism would become a very serious danger.[117]

As it became apparent that Churchill's scheme to take the Dardanelles and Gallipoli was failing, Churchill became more depressed. Asked to resign from the Admiralty and appointed Chancellor of the Duchy of Lancaster under the coalition government, on 14 August 1915 he spent some time with his old friend W.S. Blunt. Blunt believed that 'Churchill might go mad' and noted that while Churchill sat painting, he said:

> There is more blood than paint on these hands... All those thousands of men killed. We thought it would be a little job and so it might have been if it had been done the right way...[118]

Churchill's statement of a 'little job' illustrated his frustration with the eastern front and could easily be interpreted as a dismissive imperialist remark. However, it could just as easily be understood as frustration with how the front was waged and the fact there was a front there at all. It must be remembered that Churchill believed until the very end that Turkish neutrality was a possibility and that he personally knew the Turkish leadership; a fact he reminded his readers in *The World Crisis: The Aftermath* (1929).[119] Interestingly, two weeks later, Churchill dined with Blunt at Newbuildings, Blunt's manor house, in full Arab dress (a tradition of his and Blunt's), where he lectured the guests on his opinions of the War Office and its failings.[120]

But Churchill could not take refuge in his friends forever. He took up the post of the Chancellor of the Duchy of Lancaster. The Dardanelles Committee met again and, for the last time, on 6 November 1915. Kitchener had received telegrams from Sir Charles Monroe, which urged immediate evacuation. By November, Churchill had grown frustrated and resigned from the Chancellorship of the Duchy of Lancaster. Rather than hold a post with no power, he resigned in order to fight on the western front, in Flanders. Blunt was impressed and thought Churchill had redeemed his honour. He wrote a letter to Churchill to congratulate him:

> I am commissioned on our joint behalf and on that of the parish of Shipley to congratulate you on your courage in breaking loose from your official bondage to that gang of incapables which has been making a fool of the British Empire.[121]

Churchill left for France and the western front on 18 November to join the Grenadier Guards, expecting to command a brigade.[122] However, Asquith vetoed this and consequently Churchill joined the Royal Scots Fusiliers, only to command a battalion. He would return to the government as Minister of Munitions in 1917, among 'angry protests' and largely owing to the benevolence and political wiles of Lloyd George.[123]

CHAPTER 3

CHURCHILL: MINISTER OF WAR AND AIR

This chapter examines Churchill's tenure of two offices after World War I in relation to his engagement with the Islamic world. The first of these ministerial posts was his position as Minister of War. The first section of the chapter examines what role Churchill's view of the Islamic world played in demobilization after World War I, his condemnation of the Amritsar Massacre, and his increasing disagreement with Lloyd George regarding the postwar strategy for Turkey. The second section considers Churchill's time as the Minister of Air and explores his role in the creation and implantation of the colonial air-policing policy for the Middle East, demonstrating that Churchill's intentions for use of air power were principally benevolent towards the tribesmen.

Churchill: Minster of War

After Churchill rejoined the Cabinet as Minister of Munitions in 1917, he was promoted to Secretary of State of War two years later. This was a significant step up for Churchill as it put him in the War Cabinet, whereas his post at munitions did not. The first crisis Churchill faced in his new post was the demobilization of British forces. After November 1918 there was a great deal of unrest in the British ranks as soldiers clamoured to return to their lives as civilians.

This unrest gave pause to Churchill for two primary reasons: the exorbitant costs of maintaining an army that saw no action, and the fear that 'widespread disobedience would encourage Bolshevism in Britain.'[1] Owing to these factors, Churchill fought to bring the British troops home as soon as possible. However, there was a major consideration that he pointed out to the House of Commons on 3 March 1919: the need to retain at least some portion of the military until the Allies got the terms they asked for at the peace conference. By the summer of 1919 the Prime Minister, Lloyd George, had grown impatient and asked Churchill why the demobilization was not going as quickly as he wanted. Churchill responded in September with 13 reasons why there had been delays to demobilization.

Three of these concerns were to do primarily with areas inhabited by Muslims. The first was a reference to the Anglo-Afghan War and the need to maintain order in India, especially on the north-west frontier. The second was Churchill's wish to raise a new volunteer army to relieve the conscript army in India and the Middle East. This would take time. But Churchill put the most emphasis on the third concern:

> All the above problems have been complicated by the difficulty of arriving at fixed conclusions as to the size and the cost of the post-war army, and by the uncertainty of the political as well as military policy in Palestine, Mesopotamia, and generally toward the Turkish Empire.[2]

Despite these setbacks, the demobilization of the British troops was complete by October 1919 and the cost with which Churchill was so concerned was reduced from £4 million per day to £1,250,000 per day.[3] However, many of the Indian troops were still at their posts in the Middle East. This was a major concern for Churchill because many of the Indian troops in the Middle East were Muslims. Churchill was certainly aware of the 'political consequences of the fact that these predominantly Moslem soldiers were the occupation troops who had been left in place, entrusted with the distasteful task of coercing fellow Moslems.'[4] Meanwhile the situation in India was getting worse.

Concern over using Indian troops was amplified because the House of Commons was debating the actions taken by the British officers during the Amritsar Massacre of July 1919, in which many Muslims and Hindus were killed.[5] The catalyst for the massacre was the passing of a law that extended wartime censors on freedom of expression, which was intended to remove sedition. In protest, Gandhi organized a campaign of non-violence (or *satyagraha*). However, the non-violent intentions were quickly lost and several Europeans were killed. As a result, the acting commander General Reginald Dyer ordered his troops to open fire on an unarmed mob of Indians.

The government of India appointed the Hunter Commission to investigate the masscre and condemned the officer responsible, and 'at Churchill's insistence refused him any further military employment'.[6] Despite this, opinions on Dyer were sharply split. Several in the British government such as Edwin Montagu, the Secretary for the State of India, and Churchill, were horrified at Dyer's actions. However, several Conservative diehards felt that General Dyer should not have been rebuked. They argued that the commission was harsh with him and criticized the government for not supporting him. Montagu was left with the task of convincing Dyer's supporters in the House that they were correct in taking disciplinary action against him (though as disciplinary actions go it was more like a slap on the wrist: Dyer could not hold another post but he enjoyed half-pay and his rank and status were still intact).[7] Montagu's speech was unsuccessful, partly owing to the heated atmosphere of the House and partly owing to Montagu's Jewish ethnicity, which further created a tense atmosphere that now had elements of anti-Semitism injected into the proceedings. Austen Chamberlain noted that the prevailing feeling was that, 'A Jew, a foreigner, rounding on an Englishman, and throwing him to the wolves.'[8]

However, Churchill was quick to save the situation for the government. He 'had no hesitation in condemning the Amritsar shooting'.[9] Churchill addressed the House:

> It is an extraordinary, a monstrous event, an event which stands in singular and sinister isolation [...] Our reign in India or

> anywhere else has never stood on the basis of physical force alone, and it would be fatal to the British Empire if we were to try to base ourselves only upon it. The British way of doing things [. . .] has always meant and implied close and effectual cooperation with the people of the country. In every part of the British Empire that has been our aim, and in no part have we arrived at such success as in India, whose princes spent their own treasure in our cause, whose brave soldiers fought side by side with our own men, whose intelligent and gifted people are co-operating at the present moment with us in every sphere of government and of industry.[10]

Churchill's speech condemned Dyer's actions and revealed his anxiety for the nature of imperial policy. He wanted Britain to extend 'civilization' to the East and India and saw such brutal actions as 'uncivilized'. While this revealed his Victorian prejudices in terms of 'civilization', it also showed a distinct concern for the wellbeing of the Indian subjects. However, Churchill was able to walk a 'middle line' of condemning the massacre (while pointing out its 'unique' nature) and stressing that Dyer was not going to be punished severely.[11] This allowed Churchill to appease the diehards while advancing the government's position. While this clearly demonstrates Churchill's brilliance in rhetoric and political manoeuvring it might also be understood as his oscillation between twentieth-century thinking and Victorian thinking.

Meanwhile, Indian Muslims were ever more fearful that the defeat of the Ottoman Empire would lead to the destruction of the caliphate and removal of the Sultan as spiritual head of the world's Muslims. This alarmed Edwin Montagu at the India Office, especially after 30 October 1919, because the Viceroy 'reported that 10,000 Indians had met at Bombay in support of the Caliph' and things were only getting worse.[12] According to Margaret Macmillan:

> Mosques throughout India prayed for him [the Sultan] as caliph in their weekly prayers. When rumors floated back from Paris to India in 1919 that the powers were planning to divide up the

> Ottoman Empire, depose the Sultan and abolish the caliphate, Muslim newspapers published articles beseeching the British to protect him and local notables formed caliphate committees.[13]

As fear grew among Indian Muslims, one of Churchill's greatest rivals was using the situation to his benefit. Seeing the British position offend Muslim sentiment in India, Mohandas Gandhi used the opportunity to build an alliance between Muslims and Hindus in India against British rule. Churchill's concern for the situation was evident in notes from a Cabinet meeting on 6 January 1920:

> I must bow to overwhelming evidence, supplied by the Secretary of State for India, of the resentment that would be incited in India and throughout the Mohammedan world by the expulsion of the Turks from Constantinople. All our limited means of getting the Middle East to settle down quietly are comprised in the use of Indian troops. We must not do anything that will raise Indian sentiment against the use of these troops or affect their own loyalty.[14]

These notes represent two things. The first is Churchill's concern for the Islamic troops' situation. Churchill naturally feared this might lead to some kind of pan-Islamic unrest, which could be used by the Bolsheviks to further their ambitions in Russia and Central Asia.[15] David Fromkin summed it up neatly: 'Since Britain now had to rely on her Muslim troops, her policies in the Middle East would have to be modified so as not to offend Muslim sentiment [...] and that pointed toward the need for a friendlier policy toward the Turks.'[16]

The second thing these notes demonstrate is the increasing disagreement that would later come to loggerheads between Churchill and Lloyd George on postwar policy in the Middle East, especially with Turkey and the remnants of the Ottoman Empire. Churchill wanted a pro-Turk, pro-Muslim, anti-Bolshevik policy, while Lloyd George was pro-Greek and ambivalent towards the Bolsheviks. Indeed within the government, 'Churchill [...] had been the most severe critic of the Prime Minister's Middle Eastern policy.'[17]

The prospect of controlling the vast Ottoman territory alone was militarily daunting. Moreover, early in 1919 Chancellor of the Exchequer Austen Chamberlain tried to set a cap of £110 million on military expenditure. Churchill did not agree with this restriction of funds and wrote to Lloyd George to protest and explain that the funds were needed to control the Middle East: 'The whole East is unsettled by the disintegration of Turkey, and we shall have large additions of territory in Palestine and Mesopotamia to maintain.'[18]

To help maintain order and to fulfill promises made during the war, Lloyd George allowed Greece to occupy the Turkish port of Smyrna and it did so with great brutality. The Turks were dismayed and their leader, Mustafa Kemal, demanded that all non-Turkish powers leave Turkey. The Greeks dug in and reinforced their positions. They also started annexing large parts of Turkey. Churchill was alarmed at the situation. He wrote to Lloyd George pleading for peace with Turkey and explained again that the military expenditure could not be reduced because the situation required 'exceptional forces in Palestine, Egypt, and Mesopotamia.'[19] According to Gilbert, he 'was convinced that Britain must make peace with Turkey. He saw no merit in either supporting Greek territorial ambitions, or in maintaining control over Constantinople.'[20] Churchill's fears were reinforced by a letter from General Milne, the commander-in-chief of the army on the Black Sea, which concluded that 'it was not the Turkish Government in Constantinople, under allied control, but Mustafa Kemal in Anatolia, to whom the Turks would look for leadership and with whom the Allies must deal.'[21] Even more alarmed, Churchill wrote repeatedly to Foreign Secretary Arthur Balfour and to Lloyd George, who were away in Paris at the Peace Conference, recommending that peace be made with Turkey.

However, Lloyd George supported the Greeks vehemently, as the Hellenic cultural legacy impressed him. Lloyd George was also motivated by a deep distrust of the Ottoman Empire. He believed that the Turks were 'innately despotic and murderous, and the antithesis of civilized Christian Europe.'[22] Moreover, Lloyd George's conception of the Middle East was largely predicated on orientalist and biblical literature that gave credence to the idea that the Ottoman Empire was a cruel and oppressive regime that misruled the Middle East resulting in a decay of its once great civilizations. Lloyd George's hatred for the 'Turkish regime' and his abhorrence for the Ottoman Empire was in part an inheritance from the great Liberal, Gladstone. Channeling Gladstone's positions on Ottoman massacres in Bulgaria in the late 1870s, Lloyd George sought to make common cause with other allied powers against the Ottomans, citing the Armenian genocide. This abusive action of the Ottomans formed the other foundation for Lloyd George's anti-Ottoman outlook. Lloyd George once told Churchill that: 'They [the Greeks] represent Christian civilization against Turkish barbarism.' To which Churchill reminded him:

> The Conservative party is a traditional friend of Turkey. The bias of your majority is pro-Turk, the bias of your cabinet is pro-Turk; the bias of your generals is pro-Turk. We are the greatest Mohammedan power in the world. Very deep oppositions will arise to any prolonged anti-Turkish or pro-Greek policy.[23]

But Lloyd George was unmoved. When his friend Lord Riddell, the newspaper proprietor, challenged him on his zealous backing of the Greeks regarding their acquisition of Smyrna, Lloyd George replied:

> You must decide whom you are going to back. The Turks nearly brought about our defeat in the war [. . .] You cannot trust them and they are a decadent race. The Greeks, on the other hand, are our friends and they are a rising people [. . .] We must secure Constantinople and the Dardanelles. You cannot do that effectively without crushing Turkish power.[24]

Armed with such prejudices, Lloyd George wanted to quit Constantinople, and rather than leave it to the Turks (as Churchill suggested), leave it to the Greeks. Moreover, Lloyd George did not pay any attention to the cries of the British Muslims in India, which caused Churchill and the India Office much worry: 'Lloyd George simply ignored their objections.'[25]

This was the reverse of Churchill's opinion. Since the surrender of Turkish forces, he had supported Turkey. After the war, he believed the Turks were pleased to be conquered by the British, as opposed to the Russians. This notion was perhaps emboldened by Enver Pasha's pleas in his correspondence with Churchill in May 1919. While in central Asia near Afghanistan, Enver wrote, 'Now we [the Turks] are beaten and at the mercy of our enemies. England, as I know all too well, is powerful and generous.' Enver even urged Churchill to appeal directly to Lloyd George on the Turks' behalf, saying: 'Knowing your personal generosity and your chivalrous influence on your colleagues, especially Mr. Lloyd George, I pray you intervene [. . .] I have never forgotten the benefits made to this country when you have intervened in our favour.' Remarkably, Enver warned of the risks in breaking the relationship between the Turks and the Arabs and even warned Churchill of the dangers of 'the deep fire of Islam.'[26]

Echoing Enver's letter in a somewhat disillusioned tone, Churchill characterized what he believed Turkish sentiment was in 1919 after the armistice:

> We have made a great mistake; we have chosen the wrong side; we were forced into it by Enver and Talaat [. . .] We sincerely regret what has occurred; How could we tell that the United States would go to war with Germany; or that Great Britain would become a first-class military power? Such prodigies are beyond human foresight. No one ought to blame us for being so misled. Of course we must be punished, but let us be chastised by our old friend England.[27]

Churchill envisaged an alliance with a restored Turkey, one that maintained its pre-war frontiers and was 'subject to a strict form of international control' rather than dividing up the Empire into separate territorial spheres of exploitation.[28] Churchill wanted to restore an alliance with Enver Pasha as early as 1916. Oddly, even

Lloyd George considered an alliance with Enver, or rather bribing him to leave the war and give terms to Britain, which included the territories of Mesopotamia and Palestine.[29] In Churchill's mind this alliance with a new Turkey would guard against Bolshevik interference in the Middle East and Central Asia. Churchill's hostility towards Bolshevism led him to believe that there might be an Islamic–Bolshevik alliance and he was becoming increasingly fearful of this possibility. It even appeared in one of his air army and navy estimates in the House of Commons:

> [Turkey] looked up at her conquerors and saw with feelings of intense relief that they were British. She asked for our orders and appealed to our guidance [...] A new force of a turbulent warlike character has come into being in the highlands of Asia Minor, who reached out with one hand to the advancing Bolshevik armies from the north and the other offered to the Arabs of the south. A conjunction of forces between Russian Bolshevism and Turkish Mahommedanism would be an event full of danger to many states but to no state in the world would it be more full of danger than to the British Empire, the greatest of all Mahommedan states![30]

In the House of Commons, Churchill often returned to the notion of Great Britain as 'the greatest Mohammedan Power'. Additionally, he echoed this sentiment in his Cabinet notes of 6 January 1920. He disagreed with Lloyd George's push to leave Constantinople in Greek hands, for fear it might push the Turkish Muslims into the embrace of the Bolsheviks:

> If the Turk is in Constantinople, the manhood of the Turkish Empire can be used to prevent the forcible acquisition by Russia of Constantinople and the Straits. If the Turk is gone, there will be nobody to defend Constantinople [...] Once the Turk is out of Constantinople there will be no reason why Turkish Mohammedans and Russian Bolsheviks should not make common cause.[31]

Despite Churchill's objections, Lloyd George supported the Greek Prime Minister Eleutherios Venizelos's bid to make permanent the Greek control of the coast of Asia Minor, Smyrna, and Thrace, thus granting Greece sovereignty as far inland as the Chatalja lines. Churchill appeared to cast a doubt on Lloyd George's policy in the House of Commons: 'We must make peace with Turkey. We must make peace with Turkey soon and must make peace which does not unite against us the feeling of the whole Mahommedan world.'[32] When Churchill saw Venizelos in London on 19 March, he told him that: 'England could not help with troops in either Thrace or in Asia Minor [...] but would be willing to render such assistance as she could in arms and munitions.'[33] Even Lord Curzon, who called himself the last man who would wish to do a good turn to the Turks, was surprised and critical of Lloyd George's decision to stand with the Greeks in this matter.

Lloyd George continued to develop Middle Eastern policy in ways that Churchill thought was disadvantageous. On 24 March 1920 Churchill wrote to Lloyd George to voice his concerns again:

> I am very anxious about your policy towards Turkey. With military resources which the Cabinet have cut to the most weak and slender proportions, we are leading the Allies in an attempt to enforce a peace on Turkey which would require great and powerful armies and long costly operations and occupations. On this world so torn with strife I dread to see you let loose the Greek armies [...] Here again I counsel prudence and appeasement. Try and secure a really representative Turkish governing authority and come to terms with *it.* As at present couched the Turkish Treaty means indefinite anarchy.[34]

Lloyd George did not reply, and a month later the Allied leaders met to draw up a peace treaty with Turkey, which became known as the Treaty of Sèvres. This treaty was put to the Turkish delegates, 'who reacted with dismay and hostility' but were forced to sign it.[35] The treaty called for several harsh anti-Turkish measures. Greece was awarded control of both Smyrna and Thrace. Palestine and Mesopotamia became British protectorates, and Palestine was provisionally set up to become, in rather vague terms, a Jewish homeland. Syria became a French mandate. Arabia and Armenia were given independence. The straits and Constantinople were under Allied occupation. To add insult to this massive territorial loss, the Turkish military was totally disbanded and the Allied powers continued to occupy the Dardanelles.

While the treaty was signed by delegates from the Turkish government in Constantinople, the Turkish nationalists 'denounced it as a betrayal of Turkish national rights and pledged themselves to the total restoration of sovereignty in Asia Minor and Turkey-in-Europe.'[36] Nevertheless, they did accept the loss of Turkish imperial holdings such as Palestine and Mesopotamia.

Everything Churchill was working for in the Middle East was undone by the Treaty of Sèvres. Moreover, Churchill thought that the treaty was a betrayal to the Turks and little more than support for Greek territorial ambitions. He described the harshness of the treaty in *World Crisis: The Aftermath*:

> The whole attitude of the Peace Conference towards Turkey was so harsh that Right had now changed sides. Justice, that eternal fugitive from the councils of conquerors, had gone over to the opposite camp. Defeat must be borne: but the loosing of the Greek Army into Asia Minor, at the very moment when Turkey was being disarmed, boded the destruction and death of the Turkish nation and their suppression and subjugation as a race among men.[37]

Churchill believed that peace could be achieved with Turkey only through the creation of an acceptable and sensible peace treaty. His Cabinet memorandum of 7 June 1920 strongly criticized Sèvres as unjust and noted that it was unenforceable, maintaining that it 'would condemn to anarchy and barbarism for an indefinite period the greater part of the Turkish Empire.'[38] One of Churchill's reasons for seeing the Treaty of Sèvres as unenforceable was because the only army that could enforce it, owing to commitments in Europe and cost, was the Greek army. Churchill argued that this meant, 'it was not Britain and India and Allenby that they had to endure and for a time obey, but Greece the hated and despised of generations.'[39] Despite such warnings, Lloyd George remained unconvinced and decidedly pro-Greek.

Churchill's fears were realized when Mustafa Kemal, the head of the Turkish Revolutionary Congress, and his Turkish nationalists marched towards Ismid in the Dardanelles zone, which was under British control. After avoiding direct conflict by halting his approach, Mustafa Kemal created a separate government in Angora (present-day Ankara) and there he declared that 'the Treaty of Sèvres was a direct act of aggression on Turkey by Britain, France, Italy, and Greece.'[40] He then declared war on the Allies.

Churchill saw his plans for peace with Turkey undone. The Cabinet backed Lloyd George's harsh anti-Turkish policies, which led to the formal declaration of war by the Turkish government in Angora. According to Martin Gilbert:

> This hostility threatened to bring war to Britain's new Arab territory, Mesopotamia and to antagonize Muslim feeling both in Mesopotamia and Palestine. Concerned above all with economy, Churchill feared Muslim antagonism and warned that policing these two territories could become extremely expensive unless Turkey was appeased.[41]

As peace with Turkey became impossible, Churchill focused on his secondary purpose regarding the former Ottoman territories: economy. Since February 1920, Churchill had provided estimates of the cost of conventional warfare and occupation in the Middle East. On 1 May he circulated a Cabinet memorandum that costed the policy at about £20 million per annum: 'To hold these worthless villages sums are being spent varying from £200,000 to £1,000,000.'[42] It was too expensive to maintain a policy of control as long as the Turkish nationalists pursued their cause. This was one of the major reasons why Churchill pursued an air-based policy in the

Middle East. The projected cost was substantially less than conventional military methods. Further, in the memorandum Churchill explained that the Air Ministry would work with the Colonial Office 'for the gradual taking over and development of Mesopotamia without use of large forces; and I believe that economies even more substantial than those I have indicated here may be reached in the future.'[43] As justification for the projected economies created by his new plan, Churchill used the example of the air raid on Somaliland, which had been so effective earlier in the year.

In the summer of 1920 Churchill saw his budgets pressed again as a rebellion broke out along the Euphrates near Mosul. Historians agree that 'events in Mesopotamia shook the British government badly', though they disagree on the causes of the uprising.[44] There were three schools of thought regarding the genesis of the Mesopotamian revolt in 1920. The official British perspective, as expressed by Arnold Wilson, understood the revolt to be mercenary in character as the recalcitrant tribes were being financed and controlled from outside sources.[45] The second interpretation was Fariq al-Fir'aun's account, which, according to Amal Vinogradov, was a regional tribal uprising with little influence from the political parties. Moreover, he saw the uprising as more national in character.[46] The third interpretation is that of historian Elie Kedourie, who gave it a more sectarian character as a battle between Shia and Sunni Muslims. Despite these sectarian differences Vinogradov noted that: 'The ulama preached revolt against the British in the name of Iraqi independence and Arab self-determination.'[47]

Whatever the causes, the British quickly retaliated and Churchill saw the new RAF in action. By the end of the year, the revolt was shattered. Though it proved Churchill's positions on air power, the uprising frustrated his attempts to control the region in an economical way. More and more ground troops were requested and eventually in late July, Churchill dispatched a whole division from India. Moreover, Churchill was beginning to fear the machinations of a pan-Islamic plot to take Mesopotamia, Persia, and central Asia. These fears were bolstered by intelligence from Mesopotamia. A special intelligence officer in Mesopotamia, Major Bray, wrote three influential reports citing a wide conspiracy that sought to fire up pan-Islamism and was backed by the Bolsheviks and Germany.[48] When this news reached Churchill, who had always feared pan-Islamism and had a deep hatred of Bolshevism, he became very anxious. This information, combined with the considerable cost of maintaining control of the Middle East, seemed to be too much for him. In an unsent letter to Lloyd George, he vented his anger and reveled his thoughts on the matter:

> There is something very sinister to my mind in this Mesopotamian entanglement [...] It seems to me so gratuitous [...] we should be compelled to go on pouring armies and treasure into these thankless deserts [...] Meanwhile the military expense of this year alone will probably amount to something like fifty millions, thus by capital expenditure knocking all the bloom off any commercial possibilities which may have existed.
>
> It is an extraordinary thing that the British civil administration should have succeeded in such a short time in alienating the whole country to such an extent that the Arabs have laid aside the blood feuds they have nursed for centuries and that the Suni and Shiah tribes are working together.[49]

As Mesopotamia became quieter, things in Turkey became louder. Venizelos proposed an attack on the Turkish nationalist capital Angora, which the majority of the Cabinet was against. However, on 14 November Venizelos was defeated in an election and forced to step down as priemier. Perceiving a chance to alter Lloyd George's anti-Turk policies, Churchill sent around a Cabinet memorandum, which bluntly explained his opinions regarding Turkey and the policy that ought to be followed there:

> We ought to come to terms with Mustafa Kemal and arrive at a good peace with Turkey which will secure our position and interests at Constantinople and ease the position in Egypt, Mesopotamia, Persia, and India.

> Now is the time to abandon the policy of relying on the weak and fickle Greeks and by doing so estranging the far more powerful, durable and necessary Turkish and Mohammedan forces. We should recreate that Turkish barrier to Russian ambitions which has always been of the utmost importance to us.
>
> In our present state of military weakness and financial stringency we cannot afford to go on estranging the Mohammedan world in order to hand over a greater Greece to King Constantine [. . .]
>
> Finally I must point out that the burden of carrying out the present policy at Constantinople, in Palestine, Egypt, Mesopotamia, and Persia is beyond the strength of the British Army and is producing most formidable reactions upon the Indian Army, upon which we are compelled to rely. I see the very greatest difficulty in maintaining that situation through the new financial year unless our military are aided by a policy of reconciliation and co-operation with the Turks and with the Moslem world.[50]

This memorandum demonstrated several of Churchill's key concerns. Firstly, Churchill's desperation to make peace with Turkey was obvious, as was his contempt for Lloyd George's Middle Eastern policy. But this memo also revealed Churchill's fear that the cost of the continuation of Lloyd George's policy would bankrupt the Empire, and that with British forces spread so finacially thin, the Bolsheviks would take advantage of the British weakness in the East. Most of the people in the War Office agreed with Churchill and thought negotiations should start with Mustafa Kemal. Edwin Montagu, who usually sided with Churchill in this matter, agreed as well. He believed that 'India's Muslims would eventually revolt if Britain set herself up as the enemy of Islam in Turkey.'[51] This was most likely because Muslim leaders, including the Aga Khan, had been sending him letters urging Britain to deviate from Lloyd George's policy. In a letter to Montagu, which Montagu later showed to Churchill, the Aga Khan wrote:

> As long as the terrible Treaty with Turkey remains, as long as Great Britain is the centre of opposition towards the heart of every sincere Muslim, I fear and I beg you to believe me, we will never have real peace and goodwill or moral quiet in the Islamic world or in India.[52]

Additionally, *The Times of India* published an article entitled 'One Final Effort', which called for changes to the Treaty of Sèvres.[53] Despite these warnings from the Muslim world and the defeat of Venizelos, Lloyd George still pursued a strong pro-Greek policy. As tensions in the coalition government between the Liberal and Tory views of the 'East' began revealing themselves, Churchill again tried to sway Lloyd George, in a personal appeal as a friend, in a letter on 4 December:

> I am very sorry to see how far we are drifting apart on foreign policy [. . .] Are you sure that about Turkey the line which you are forcing us to pursue would commend itself to the present H[ouse] of C[ommons]? I feel very deeply that it is most injurious to the interests we have specially to guard in India and the Middle East. I think [. . .] that most ministers who are concerned in this sphere feel serious misgivings [. . .]
>
> It seems to me a most injurious thing that we, the greatest Mohammedan Empire in the world should be the leading Anti-Turk power. The desire you have to retain Mosul – and indeed Mesopotamia – is directly frustrated by this vendetta against the Turks. The terrible waste and expense which the Middle East is involving us in brings the subject forward in a practical and urgent form. I deeply regret and *resent* being forced to ask Parliament for these appalling sums of money for new Provinces – all the more when the pursuance of the Anti-Turk policy complicates and aggravates the situation in every one of them, and renders cheaper solutions impossible [. . .]
>
> We seem to [be] becoming the most Anti-Turk and pro-Bolshevik power in the world: whereas in my judgment we

> ought to be the exact opposite. Our interests in the East require the amenity of the Turks [. . .]
>
> I fear it is going wrong. First, you are up against a shocking bill for Mesopotamia, Palestine, and Persia [. . .] Second, one of the main causes of the trouble throughout the Middle East is *your* quarrel with the remnants of Turkey – not for the sake of the Armenians either [. . .] Third all the soldiers continually say they disapprove of the policy against Turkey and do not care about Mesopotamia or Palestine and that all the extra expense of Army Estimations arises from this evil combination.[54]

This letter not only made clear Churchill's position on Middle Eastern policy, it revealed his slight obsession with Bolshevism. With the Russian Civil War, his open support for the white Russians, and the rise of Bolshevism, Churchill believed there was an international Bolshevik conspiracy that might take advantage of Britain's weakened state, especially in Ireland, India, Egypt, and the Middle East. In Churchill's mind, the only way to obstruct such a force in the Middle East (and the greater Islamic world) was to make strong allies of Muslims who might be persuaded to help fight the fledgling Bolshevik movement. Moreover, in Churchill's Victorian conception of the Islamic world, courting the former seat of the caliphate was the best way to do so.

This notion helps explain why Churchill was so passionate about his position and how wrong he thought Lloyd George's Middle Eastern policy was. But Lloyd George remained unmoved and was now supported by Lord Curzon, who felt that changing the Treaty of Sèvres would result in 'humiliating concession to the Turks.'[55] Despite Curzon's opinion, Churchill continued to prod Lloyd George in another Cabinet memorandum on 16 December 1920 in which he argued that 'certainly it would be very wrong to embroil ourselves with the Mohammedan world for the sake of securing an Empire for King Constantine and his German entourage.' Churchill also stabbed at Lord Curzon by dissenting 'altogether' from his policy on Smyrna and calling it impractical and unwise. Churchill went on:

> There remains the other two great elements in the Middle East, the Turks and the Arabs [. . .] although they have hitherto been divided, they are both Mohammedan influences and our attitude towards them produces reactions throughout the whole Mohammedan world.
>
> We are the greatest Mohammedan Power in the world. It is our duty more than any other Government, to study policies which are in harmony with Mohammedan feeling. It would appear therefore that we should initiate and steadily and consistently pursue a policy of friendship with Turkey and the Arabs.[56]

Despite Curzon and Lloyd George, Churchill did have several supporters for his policy, including the former Cabinet minister and influential Tory figure Lord Derby. In a letter to Churchill on 23 December, Derby pointed out: 'The Treaty with Turkey was, to put it mildly, a rotten one [. . .] and I know it is the fashion to abuse Mustafa Kemal. After all in my mind, he is in his way, a patriot.'[57] Another supporter of Churchill's was his friend Henry Wilson, who noted in his diary on 17 December 1920:

> [Winston] has written a good paper for the Cabinet showing that we are now hated by the Bolsheviks, Turks, Greeks, and Arabs and this *must* be a bad policy and that we ought to make friends with the Turks and Arabs and enemies with the Bolsheviks and ignore the Greeks. This has been my view all along.
>
> He said he made some impression on L[loyd] G[eorge] about the rising feeling of the Conservatives against his pro-Greek pro-Bolshevik foreign policy. I doubt it for LG *is* a Bolshevik.[58]

But such views did not alter Lloyd George's pro-Greek stance, which still held sway over Middle Eastern policy. On 22 December Lloyd George addressed the House of Commons and insisted that it was impossible to alter the British policy towards the Greeks and that the Treaty of Sèvres would stand.

Churchill: Minister of Air

The period after World War I was a pivotal moment for the Royal Air Force (RAF). Its fate was uncertain. It was unclear whether the RAF was to become a new service in its own right or remain as components of the navy and army. However, as the need to police the recently acquired Ottoman territories in the Middle East became evident so did the new role for the RAF. This phase in the development of the RAF has been examined by several historians.[59] While these studies have provided valuable insights into the history of the RAF and the role of its foremost architect, Hugh Trenchard,[60] they have largely marginalized the role played by Winston Churchill. While several aspects of Churchill's contribution to the creation and implementation of the RAF to create economies in the Middle East have been discussed, there are areas such as the adoption of colonial air policing, the influence of T.E. Lawrence, and Churchill's imperial ambitions and ruthlessness, especially concerning the use of poison gas, which require a deeper historical reassessment.

Churchill's influence is generally explained by his desire to create economies while maintaining order in the Middle East. This narrative has been embraced by several historians[61] and is supported by Churchill's numerous letters to his private secretary and other members of the Middle Eastern Department. The best example of this is an often referenced letter that Churchill sent to his private secretary, John Shuckburgh, on 12 November 1921 in which he wrote: 'Do realise that everything else that happens in the Middle East is secondary to reductions in expense.'[62] This narrative tends to cast Churchill in the role of a disinterested Colonial Secretary whose *only* concern was for the reduction of British expense in the Middle East in order to advance his career. While it is certainly true that Churchill's *primary* concern was for saving British taxpayers' money, taken alone it is not enough to fully explain the nuances of his attitudes and policies regarding the strategy of colonial air policing in the Middle East.

When Lloyd George appointed Churchill as Secretary of State for War and Air, in January 1919, the combination of the War Ministry and the Air Ministry was meant to be temporary. Lloyd George and the government thought of dissolving the Air Ministry, making it subservient to the army and navy: 'But Churchill had no intention of weakening the autonomy of the Air Force.'[63]

In February 1919, he appointed Hugh Trenchard as Chief of the Air Staff.[64] Together, the two constructed civilian air routes and military air strategies. Churchill worked quickly to lay out his future plans for the RAF. On 8 February 1919, he wrote to Walter Long, the Secretary of State for the Colonies, and detailed his plans for restructuring the RAF. As a component of his plan, this 'new arm' of the military would be 'in the East and Middle East' to alleviate some of the financial burden of policing the new territories.[65]

Despite minor disagreements regarding civilian air routes and air mail, Churchill and Trenchard found a sphere of common interest: the colonial policing of the Middle East. However, since the end of the war, Churchill looked to drastically cut costs for the British military apparatus, especially in the Middle East and specifically in Mesopotamia. Since Churchill trained as an amateur pilot, he understood the strategic military application of flight, and earlier than many of his contemporaries.

The genesis of the doctrine for colonial air policing might be traced back to a letter that Churchill wrote to the First Sea Lord, Louis Battenburg, just prior to the outbreak of World War I. In the letter, Churchill shared his thoughts regarding air power being employed in Somaliland to restore order and defeat Mullah Muhammad Abdulla Hassan. Churchill complained that 'airships' were not going to be employed in Somaliland because:

> the sweeping opinions expressed by the War Staff do not appear to have been arrived at as the result of a careful study of the facts or with knowledge of local conditions, or after consultation with the officers and administrators serving in the Protectorate.

Churchill went on to mock the Chief of War Staff, Admiral Doveton Sturdee's suggestion that for '£75,000' a traditional military expedition could reclaim Somaliland, by pointing out that Sturdee 'cannot be aware that over £3,000,000 was expended without any good result on the operations of 1904. £75,000 would therefore not go very far towards providing the alternative.' Churchill concluded:

> Generally the question of whether barbarous populations can be controlled by the operations of aircraft in countries whose size and inaccessibility render military expeditions impossible except at inordinate cost, is an issue of novel interest and of very high importance. The authorities of the protectorate are unanimous in thinking that the employment of airships would be most effective from the military point of view and from what they know of the Dervish character and habits.[66]

This letter is significant for several reasons. It demonstrates that Churchill was clearly one of the major architects of colonial air control. This is despite the assertion of T.E. Lawrence to one of his biographers, Liddell Hart, that colonial air-policing in the Middle East had been his idea. In 1933 regarding air control, Lawrence claimed:

> As for the effect of bombing, the war showed me that a combination of armoured cars and air craft could rule the desert: but that must not be under army control, and without infantry support. You rightly trace the origin of the RAF control in Iraq, Aden, and Palestine to this experience. As soon as I was able to have my own way in the Middle East, I approached Trenchard on the point, converted Winston easily, and tricked the Cabinet into approving. (Against the wiles of Henry Wilson) – and it has worked very well.[67]

This was clearly the overactive imagination of the self-advertising Lawrence at work. The editor of Lawrence's letters, David Garnett, even noted that Lawrence admitted in 1920 to Lord Winterton that he supported *Trenchard's* scheme for air control.[68] Despite this, some historians have cited this passage to illustrate Lawrence's influence on Churchill's thinking.[69] While Lawrence undoubtedly influenced Churchill on matters in the Middle East in the 1920s, Churchill had already come to the idea before the war and so would take little or no convincing by Lawrence. The two men probably just happened to agree on the same policy. Though it was unclear who was the foremost architect of colonial air-policing of the Middle East, Churchill's letter of 1914 is evidence that he was a major force in creating the scheme and that Trenchard dealt more with the details that brought Churchill's vision to life; Lawrence's role, while paramount in establishing Churchill's conception of the Middle East, was relatively inconsequential in relation to the air-control scheme.

Moreover, the letter illustrates the significance in Churchill's mind that airpower could be used to police inaccessible frontier areas, especially the Middle East and Northern Africa. Churchill probably arrived at this conclusion from his own experiences in frontier warfare having served in two conflicts in remote frontier environments. It was during these frontier conflicts that Churchill developed considerable expertise in dealing with the geographical and geopolitical landscape.[70] It was in these frontier territories that Churchill learned the importance of geography in determining policy. For instance, he saw the cost in men and materials of traditional military expeditions on the north-west frontier and again in Sudan, where the harsh desert environment meant that any operation or offensive would have to be heavily based on logistics and discourage 'over reach' away from water – and that such infrastructural operations were extremely costly.

Nevertheless, Churchill also made clear in his letter the cost-effectiveness of colonial air control and his desire to test its efficiency. He recognized in 1907, as Under-Secretary for the Colonies, that properly assaulting and controlling Hassan, the Somali Mullah, would require too much in resources and money. As a result, Churchill proposed a disastrous withdrawal to the coast.[71] However, once he realized that air power could achieve control of the interior of Somaliland at a fraction of the cost, he supported the necessary action. Though the outbreak of World War I prevented this happening, it laid the ground work for what became one of the RAF's proving operations in early 1920 under Churchill's and Trenchard's command.

The Mullah Hassan had continually plagued the British administration and trade in Somaliland, especially in the interior of the country, since Churchill's policy of 'coast occupation' had been adopted.[72] The War Cabinet received a report from Major General Reginald Hoskins that 'the Mullah could be defeated in a campaign of two or three months, provided a further four battalions of African and Indian troops were deployed and three squadrons of aircraft were used to scatter the Dervish Soldiers.'[73] However, this was very problematic because the British method for controlling such isolated frontier areas was not systematic; in fact, it was often a hodgepodge of different ideas and tactics that were not always synchronized, were outlandishly expensive, and were very often brutal. These traditional land-based military means of colonial control consisted of two types of operations. The first was the 'punitive expedition' that began by sending large swathes of troops to the objective and was 'followed by the withdrawing of troops to some centralized base.'[74] This was known as 'butcher and bolt' policy. The other was classical full-blown military occupation.

The first method was especially distasteful to Churchill, who had argued against such actions in frontier regions when he was a soldier and had repeatedly urged the Colonial Office not to undertake such efforts when he was Under-Secretary. The second method had been tried and found impossible to achieve in Somaliland because of the cost of maintaining such a force of occupation. These outrageous costs were what prompted Churchill to argue for a retreat to the coast back in 1907 while he was Colonial Under-Secretary. Furthermore, traditional land-based methods, punitive expeditions, and full-scale military occupation were prohibitively costly, inefficient, and rarely created long-term political effects for the area in question. This owed to the fact that the punitive forces 'took an agonizingly long time to reach their targets' and 'the effect of prompt reprisal for a specific act was lost.'[75]

Churchill's experiences clearly shaped his thinking on traditional Forward policy, which he continued to believe was morally indefensible and economically inefficient.[76] However, he loathed the only other option open at that time, which was disengagement.

The British Empire had 'limitless' commitments to 'pacification' or rather control of imperial frontiers, which 'perpetually veered from the "forward" urge to exert complete control [. . .] back to the instinct to disengagement from an untenable situation. The former would be appallingly costly; the latter seemed humiliating and dishonorable, and perhaps strategically dangerous.'[77] So Churchill had to find a way to reconcile the political and defensive benefits of the forward policy with the economic practicality and moral position of disengagement. This would prove impossible with traditional land-based military means of colonial control.

This is where Churchill believed the true promise of air-policing to lie, as it negated many of the economic, strategic, and moral disadvantages of traditional punitive expeditions. After all the objective of air-policing was not to punish – as with traditional methods of colonial control – rather its objective was 'long-term political stability, pacification and administration' of a region with 'with minimum loss of people and material on both sides.' In Churchill's estimation, the people affected by the operations would be the recalcitrant tribesmen and they would be controlled by 'disrupting their normal routines to such an extent that continued hostilities became undesirable.' This policy of violence reduction, Churchill believed, would be 'much more effective (and much cheaper) than the 'burn and scuttle' policy of punitive expeditions by ground forces.[78] In any case, the Mullah in Somaliland presented Churchill with an opportunity to test his theory.

At his wits, end, Lord Milner, the Colonial Secretary, asked Trenchard in May 1919 if he could secure Somaliland primarily using air power. Trenchard approached Churchill and proposed 'a plan by which a singular squadron of bombers would spearhead the campaign, without additional ground troops.'[79] This negated many of the economic, strategic, and political disadvantages of traditional punitive expeditions or the 'army method'.

Understanding such political and fiscal advantages, and eager to depart from traditional punitive expeditions, Churchill approved wholeheartedly. By October, he and Trenchard secured approval from the War Cabinet. Their approval partly owed to the success of the RAF in the third Anglo-Afghan War (May–August 1919). The heavy bombing of Kabul was thought to have produced the desire to find peaceful terms there. Eager to explore the application of air power, the War Cabinet agreed to Churchill and Trenchard's Somaliland campaign. The operation began on 21 January 1920 and only lasted about a month, but it proved extremely economical. Military historian David Omissi recorded that 'the air component of the operations cost £70,000, while the entire cost of the campaign that finally destroyed the Mullah's power was only around £150,000.'[80] Moreover: 'The Colonial Under-Secretary, Amery, pointed out that, at total cost – including army transport and pay, as well as the RAF – of £77,000, what the British called "the Mad Mullah final campaign" was "the cheapest war in history."'[81]

While the outright success of the air operations has been disputed, Churchill certainly interpreted it as a victory for the RAF and air power, as did Trenchard.[82] Having tested his theory in Somaliland and believing it to be dramatically more cost-effective, Churchill sought to fill the gap between political advantage of colonial policing and its prohibitive costs. Revealing aspects of his thoughts on air control, Churchill wrote to Trenchard on 2 March 1920 and asked him to 'submit a scheme and state whether you consider the internal security of the country could be maintained by it. It is not intended that the force holding Mesopotamia should be sufficient to guard it against external invasion.' Moreover, Churchill made it very clear that the scheme would be 'proportioned solely on the duty of maintaining internal security.'[83] This reveals that Churchill believed that air control would be used specifically for policing and not as a defensive military apparatus. Furthermore, it demonstrates that for Churchill any major strategic threat would not come from an external force. Churchill was concerned that the majority of trouble would come from tribal forces within the new and unstable imperial gains in the Middle East.

This was a departure from Churchill's fear of pan-Islam in the traditional sense. Rather than an organized, pan-Islamic threat to British interest coming from the seat of the Ottoman caliphate, as a political weapon, an internal threat (in the form of sectarian violence or anti-British sentiment) might emerge from the newly acquired tribal areas of the recently vanquished Ottoman Empire. As a threat to order would be extremely costly, Churchill was eager to pacify the new Islamic, tribal subjects. Moreover, he was hopeful they would happily work with the British Empire because it was 'the largest Mohammedan power in the world'.[84] In addition, Churchill believed that maintaining order and bringing peace to the new tribal areas formerly controlled by the Ottoman Empire was actually the responsibility of the British Empire as a progressive and civilizing force.[85] This Victorian notion of benevolent imperial imperatives combined with a domestic necessity for fiscally responsible means further ingrained in Churchill the belief of air power as a relatively humane and cost-effective solution to policing the Middle East.

The notion of the British Empire as a civilizing force in Churchill's thinking is also evident elsewhere in Churchill's letter to Trenchard on 2 March. Churchill explained to Trenchard that 'local diplomacy will conform to the conditions of aerial control and that *every effort* would be made to enlist the co-operation of the tribesmen in the establishment and maintenance of peace and order by subsidies and possibly by giving them an interest in the development of oilfields, etc.'[86] Churchill's eagerness to 'enlist the co-operation of the tribesmen' and to barter for co-operation by exchanging subsidies from the oilfields in return for support of the tribes illustrates his hope that the new tribal areas would happily co-operate with British intentions. Moreover, subsidies and infrastructural co-operation were much less expensive than traditional military occupation and, more importantly, this approach helped to create an alliance with Mesopotamian and Middle Eastern tribes. In Churchill's mind, this worked to bring civilization to isolated, peoples throughout the Middle East. Although the use of subsides was a traditional imperial tactic employed by the British, Churchill believed that, in this case, tribesmen well disposed to the British Empire would help maintain control from the air with as little cost as possible. Additionally, these alliances would help act as a buttress against any anti-British, pan-Islamic movements that might occur.

Another aspect of Churchill's thinking revealed in the letter to Trenchard of 2 March opens a discussion regarding the tactics employed by colonial air-policing. Concluding the letter, Churchill considered the means of air control:

> Not only must the air force be able to operate from air by bomb and machine gun fire on any hostile garrison, but it must possess the power to convey swiftly two or three companies of men to any threatened point where ground work is required, and to maintain them [...] The question of chemical bombs which are not destructive of human life but which inflict various degrees of minor annoyance should also be subject of careful consideration.[87]

The letter clearly shows Churchill's sanction of using poison gas and chemical bombs in the Middle East. This theme of Churchill's policy of air control in the Middle East has been attacked by historians such as Niall Ferguson, who argues in *The War of the World* (2007) that 'the idea of flattening cities from the air had captured the public imagination and it remained fashionable throughout the interwar years. As Secretary for War and Air, Winston Churchill used air power without compunction to quell the Iraqi revolt of 1920.'[88] This has been echoed by pacifist historian Nicholson Baker, who contends that Churchill was an 'expert on Mustard gas – he knew that it would blind and kill, especially women and infants.'[89] While Ferguson's point is technically correct, as Churchill did use air power to 'quell' the Iraqi revolt, Ferguson's use of 'without compunction' leads his readers to believe Churchill had no remorse and little organization in his scheme, whereas Churchill's use of air power was thoughtfully designed to reduce casualties. Baker's contention is much weaker. After all, as Churchill pointed out in his letter of 2 March, he wished to employ gas that was 'not destructive of human life but which inflict various degrees of minor annoyance.' Furthermore, Churchill was not an expert on mustard gas or any other kind of weaponized gas. He simply relied on information provided to him by the Air Ministry. In fact, Churchill primarily advocated the use of lachrymatory (or tear) gas, which he conceptualized as a crowd-control weapon that did not inflict lasting harm and had only temporary effects.

However, these criticisms do raise a need to address Churchill's advocacy for the use of gas as one of the tactics of air control. In order to illustrate his thinking on gas it is necessary to examine his memo on its use in Ottoman regions during World War I. In a War Committee memorandum dated 20 October 1915, Churchill argued:

> I trust that the unreasonable prejudice against the use by us of poison gas upon the Turks will now cease. The massacre by the Turks of the Armenians and the fact that practically no British prisoners have been taken on the Peninsula [. . .] should surely remove all false sentiment on this point [. . .] Large installations of gas should be sent out with out delay.[90]

It is reasonable to assume that Churchill is referring to weaponized mustard gas in this memo, because a state of war existed between the Ottoman Empire and Britain and Churchill understood mustard gas to be a conventional weapon of war. It is important to note that this is a stark difference from the 'chemical bombs' that he discussed with Trenchard five years later concerning the air-policing of the Middle East, where Churchill sought to employ lachrymatory gas, not mustard gas. It was also apparent in various War Office memoranda. For instance, in one memo on 12 May 1919 concerning frontier areas, Churchill argued that he did not 'understand this squeamishness about the use of gas. We have definitely adopted the position at the Peace Conference of arguing in favor of the retention of gas as a permanent method of warfare.'[91] Comparing the effects of being shot with the effects of lachrymatory gas Churchill went on to argue that: 'It is a sheer affection to lacerate a man with the poisonous fragment of a bursting shell and to boggle at making his eyes water by means of lachrymatory.' Clearly contrasting the use of lachrymatory gas on the frontier with the use of more heavily weaponized gas (such as mustard gas) during times of war, Churchill concluded:

> I am strongly in favour of using poisoned gas against uncivilised tribes. The moral effect should be so good that the loss of life should be reduced to a minimum. It is *not necessary* to use only the most deadly gases: gasses can be used which cause great inconvenience and would spread a lively terror and yet would leave no serious permanent effects on most of those affected.[92] [Emphasis added]

In another War Office memorandum just ten days later, Churchill's disdain for people questioning the validity of using gas as a weapon and their confusion of deadly mustard gas and the more simple lachrymatory gas was obvious:

> The objections of the India Office to the use of gas against natives are unreasonable. Gas is a more merciful weapon than high explosive shell and compels an enemy to accept a decision with less loss of life than any other agency of war. The moral effect is also very great [. . .] There can be no conceivable reason why it should not be resorted to.
>
> It is fair war for an Afghan to shoot down a British soldier behind a rock and cut him to pieces as he lies wounded on the ground, why is it not fair for a British artilleryman to fire a shell which makes the said native sneeze? It is really too silly.[93]

These memoranda clearly demonstrate that Churchill saw the employment of gas as a tool for controlling 'native tribes' and for creating a crisis of morale among the ranks of the dissidents, a concept Trenchard wholeheartedly endorsed. Poison gas was never meant to exterminate the frontier tribesmen but it did set a precedent in Churchill's thinking on colonial air-policing as he would repeatedly return to the use of gas as a relatively humane and inexpensive way to maintain order. For instance, in August 1920, a revolt had broken out in Mesopotamia that had taken the lives of several officers and laid siege to the town of Shahraban. To control the situation Churchill, then the Secretary of State for the Colonies, wrote to Sir Hugh Trenchard, the Chief of Air Staff: I think you should certainly proceed with the experimental work on gas bombs, especially, mustard gas, which would inflict punishment on recalcitrant natives without inflicting grave injury upon them.[94]

While Churchill's consideration of employing mustard gas is something of a departure from his earlier thinking, it is perhaps understandable. He advocated changing the use of lachrymatory gas to mustard gas because it was a full-scale revolt in Mesopotamia and, even then, he had hoped that it would only 'inflict punishment on recalcitrant natives without inflicting grave injury upon them'. Moreover, this also contradicts Baker's notion about Churchill being an expert on mustard gas. As Churchill noted, the gas bombs were 'experimental' so he could not have been an expert on its effects. So, far from being a blood-thirsty warmonger, Churchill's intention in the employment of poison gas as a weapon was to knock the Iraqi revolutionaries out of action, not kill them. As historian Christopher Catherwood contends, the use of the gas did kill hundreds of Iraqi rebels and did not have the effect Churchill envisaged. Catherwood points out, 'we cannot excuse Churchill from what actually happened as a result of the use of poison gas. But while he did not intend the final results, we can therefore conclude that his suggestion to Trenchard was [. . .] a highly unfortunate one.'[95]

However, it is notable that some historians, including Anthony Clayton, Lawrence James, and most notably R.M. Douglas, do not believe that poison gas was ever actually used in Mesopotamia.[96] Douglas contends that evidence for the use of gas was too vague and no proof exists of it ever being used. While Churchill clearly approved the use of gas shells, the supply chain had broken down and no gas shells were available to be used in the summer of 1920: 'Major operations ceased on October 19 barely a month after Churchill had sanctioned the transshipment of gas shells from Egypt.'[97] The reasons, then, for abstaining from the application of poison gas were not moral but practical, if not political: 'It is equally probable that any actual employment of these weapons would have triggered a public and political storm that might have well had brought an abrupt end to Winston Churchill's career.'[98]

Ironically, Churchill was not the man to blame for the use of poison gas in Mesopotamia, as no gas was ever used. However, had the opportunity been available then Churchill would have undoubtedly authorized the use of poison gas, but not as a lethal weapon. Whatever the case, his desire to use gas as a means of control was an important component of the British doctrine of air-policing in the Middle East.

Despite the role that gas played in the British doctrine of air control, its architects, Churchill and Trenchard, designed the doctrine around using intimidation tactics (such as lachrymatory gas) and the demoralizing effects of the implied omniscience rather than full-blown war and occupation, in an attempt to create order with as few causalities as possible (as reflected in Churchill's memoranda cited above). From the outset, the authors of the British policy for air control based their advocacy on the psychological and demoralizing effects it would have on the recalcitrant tribesmen. As Townshend points out: Air control – defined as 'control without occupation' – was suited only to territories which were (a) administered rather than colonized, (b) markedly underdeveloped, (c) so marginal to the British public opinion that exemplary violence was politically tolerable.[99]

This assumed that the tribes would be 'uncivilized' and thus easily coerced by the psychological effects of air control. As an Air Staff memorandum noted: 'Aircraft depend to a great extent on the moral effect they create: this is at present considerable owing to the ignorance in the native mind.'[100] Therefore, the primary demoralizing psychological effect of the doctrine was the exploitation of fear. Trenchard believed that rebellions must be punished severely, continuously, and over a prolonged period.[101] Trenchard's biographer, Andrew Boyle, refers to this employment of terror as 'frightfulness', and is quick to point out that Trenchard 'insisted that no settlement should be bombed until its inhabitants had received at least twenty-four hours' warning.'[102] Moreover, the same Air Staff memorandum noted that this frightfulness must be 'backed by force but this force is only resorted to when moral persuasion has failed'.[103] However, while actual acts of brutality were heavily discouraged, the implication of a swift and violent rebuke was often considered to be a deterrent to the tribesmen.

The other major demoralizing effect of air-policing was the ever-present implication of the ubiquitous nature of British power. This effect lent itself to the perceived openness of the geographic space in the Middle East. That is to say, the imagined version of Arabia as an open 'desert utopia' that existed in the minds of several British policy makers lent itself to 'a new application of technology', in this case 'aerial control'.[104] This 'new application of technology' combined with the notion of reclaiming and 'restoring' Mesopotamia from the 'state of ruin into which it had fallen under the Turks' would prove that Britain could still act as a civilizing force, even after the horrors of World War I.[105]

This notion of civilizing and restoring the open spaces of the Middle East undoubtedly appealed to Churchill because it fit into his belief that the British Empire was a civilizing force. Moreover, Churchill believed that Mesopotamia's supposed geographic land-scape of deserts and plains (which were inaccessible from land) would not be obstacles from the air. For Churchill, this presented a similar situation as Somaliland, but rather than use outright air power to destroy an enemy, the implication of air power might help control any recalcitrant tribesmen and would certainly save men and materials.

The ever-present airplanes made routine patrols easily visible from the ground and, as Churchill pointed out: 'It must be remembered that from the ground every inhabitant of a village is under the impression that the occupant of an aeroplane is actually looking at him.'[106] This in turn created a 'classic panopticon', which was believed to encourage the tribesmen to reject unrest.[107] Churchill recognized this perceived effect as well. In a letter to Trenchard, he stressed the importance of specially selected landing grounds that 'would enable these air forces to operate in every part of the protectorate and to enforce control, now here, now there'.[108]

Aiding this 'air panopticon' was the fact that the RAF could attack virtually without reprisal and the speed at which it could respond to disturbances. The 'imagined omniscience',[109] combined with swift and harsh retribution, was paramount in Churchill's vision of air control. As he explained to Trenchard on 29 February:

> The staff are convinced that strong and continuous action of this nature must in time inevitably compel the submission of the most recalcitrant tribes without the use of punitive measures by ground troops [...] With certain stubborn races at times it's essential to prove the futility of resistance to aerial attack by a people who possess no aircraft, but it is held that the dislocation of living conditions and the material destruction caused by heavy and persistent action must infallibly achieve the desired result.[110]

However, the notion of 'swift retribution' has led to several historians rejecting the notion of air control as a humane alternative to traditional methods of colonial control. For instance, Charles Townshend does not agree that this policy was merely designed to demoralize the tribesmen, and referred to the 'the gentle vision of air blockade' as a 'self-deception, if not a conscious fraud.'[111] Additionally, Pryia Satia has argued that the '"pacification" of Iraq proved horrifically costly in Iraqi lives – a hundred casualties was not unusual in a single operation.'[112]

It is certainly true that air control was often brutal, indiscriminate, and at time unnecessarily harsh. Moreover, the logic that Churchill and Trenchard relied on in order to justify the demoralizing effects of air power on 'stubborn races' and 'uncivilized tribes' was clearly Victorian, if not blatantly racist. However, in Churchill's mind it remained as a humane alternative. The instruments of fear and demoralization may seem naturally reprehensible today, but Churchill saw these tactics as a way of to bring dissident tribesmen under British control with as few causalities as possible, especially when compared to the brutal traditional military methods previously employed in frontier areas of the Empire. For instance, propaganda was used by dropping leaflets on the tribesmen and intelligence was amassed in order to find specific targets, rather than leveling whole villages.[113] This concept was what Churchill and Townshend referred to as 'minimal force'.[114] While this, of course, implied that air control would require less money and men to maintain, it also focused on saving the lives of the tribes and worked towards arriving at a positive political agreement with them. As military historian David Dean pointed out:

> After a successful air control campaign, it was essential to use the aircraft as a means of positive contact with the former enemy: doctors were flown to remote sites when needed, natives were evacuated to large medical facilities if required, messages were delivered from one local chief to another in the course of normal flying duties, and other acts of good faith were performed.[115]

In fact, because Churchill saw air control as relatively more humane than the previous methods of colonial control, he was 'one of the severest critics of the indiscriminate use of air power.'[116] In June 1921, when Churchill learned that action had been taken against one of the tribes on the Lower Euphrates 'not to suppress a riot but to put pressure on certain villages to pay their taxes',[117] he wrote to Percy Cox, the high commissioner for Iraq, on 7 June: 'Aerial action is a legitimate means of quelling disturbances or enforcing maintenance of order, but it should in no circumstances be employed in support of purely administrative measures such as collection of revenue.'[118]

Cox felt rebuked by Churchill and defended his actions, arguing that the tribal unrest was a 'deliberate defiance to national government' and 'tested whether the local authorities really would call on local support.'[119] This placated Churchill until another report confirmed that a different tribe in the same region had been attacked. In particular, the report stated that 'the tribesmen and their families ran into the lake, making a good target for the machine guns.'[120]

Churchill was enraged. This time he protested directly to Trenchard:

> I am extremely shocked at the reference to the bombing which I have marked in red. If it were to be published it would be regarded as most dishonouring to the Air Force and prejudicial

> to our work and use of them. To fire willfully on women and children taking refuge in a lake is a disgraceful act and I am surprised that you do not order the officers responsible for it to be tried for Court Martial. If such a thing became public it would ruin the air project which you have in view. By doing such things we put ourselves on the lowest level.[121]

This letter illuminates two more aspects of Churchill's thinking on colonial air control. First, it demonstrates that Churchill (as the senior partner in the relationship) understood how to rein in Trenchard. Realizing that Trenchard wanted to solidify the RAF as a separate ministry, Churchill reminded him that the public would never accept such brutal methods and that continued indiscriminate killing of women and children would call into question the moral validity of air-policing, and perhaps the RAF as a whole. Churchill implied this so that Trenchard would take these reports seriously, otherwise Churchill might allow the RAF to return to the army or navy. The second, and most important, aspect of Churchill's thinking revealed by his letter to Trenchard is that Churchill genuinely found the abuse of air power abhorrent, to the point that he called for the court martial of the officers responsible. It is notable, however, that beyond his threat of court martial, Churchill never realized any penalty for the airmen in question. This also fits Churchill's perception of the civilizing role of the British Empire. After all, when discussing Britain's imperial legacy in the House of Commons, Churchill often made a point of quoting Lord Macauley: the most frightful of all spectacles, Churchill would argue, was 'the strength of civilisation without its mercy.'[122]

In reality, the success and benevolent nature of the air-control scheme has rightfully been questioned and criticized by historians. However, for its authors, and especially Churchill, this type of air control represented a fiscally sound and humane way to police the frontier regions of the British Empire, despite the fact that the scheme was rooted in Victorian racism and based around several deplorable concepts such as the implementation of fear and other demoralizing tactics.

In any case, Churchill was very frustrated with his time as the Minister of War and Air. He was unable to persuade his colleagues of the threat of Bolshevism; he was unable to dramatically reduce expenditure in the Middle East; and he could not reverse Lloyd George's policy on Turkey and Mustafa Kemal. His work with the Muslim world had been continually undone by Lloyd George and the various policy disagreements regarding the Middle East. These disagreements were, in Churchill's opinion, due to the gulf between four departments: the India Office, the Colonial Office, the Foreign Office, and his own, the War Office. Churchill sought to remedy this problem in his next office as Colonial Secretary.

CHAPTER 4

CHURCHILL AT THE COLONIAL OFFICE

This chapter considers the features of Churchill's career at the Colonial Office, his creation of the Middle East Department and the Cairo Conference. The first section examines the creation of the Middle East Department and explores his continued policy disagreements with Lloyd George and Lord Curzon concerning Turkey and the Middle East. It also reveals the origin and nature of the 'Sherifian policy' that Churchill and T.E. Lawrence prescribed for the region. The second section looks at the implementation of that policy at the Cairo Conference and reveals Churchill's balancing of three important treaties in the postwar Middle East: the Sykes–Picot Agreement (1916), the Hussein–McMahon pledges (1915–16), and the Balfour Declaration (1917). Moreover, this section illustrates the beginning of Churchill's approach to Jewish and Arab co-operation regarding Palestine, while demonstrating Churchill's willingness to work with Arab sensitivities regarding the creation of Iraq and Transjordan.

The Middle East Department

From his arrival at the War Office, Churchill had urged that a single department be created to co-ordinate British Middle Eastern policy. He believed that a unified policy-making department would provide a logical and coherent policy for the British Empire as well as co-ordinated policy regarding Middle Easterners. Churchill understood that the existing approach was inadequate, expensive, ill-co-ordinated, often contradictory, and unsustainable. The existing system was an 'incoherent' amalgam of policies from the India Office, the Colonial Office, the Foreign Office, and to a lesser degree the War Office, each with its own separate agenda.[1] Since each department was meant to synchronize its work with the others, the geographic lines of responsibility were 'blurred', which resulted in policy confusion.

British policy was further confused by the fact that no one really knew where the Middle East was or which countries were encapsulated by it. The geographical region had a plethora of different monikers. Prior to the last half of the nineteenth century all Asia (including the present-day Middle East) 'had simply been known as "the East".[2] This would eventually be replaced by terms such as the 'Orient', 'Asiatic Turkey', and the 'Near East', which was a French conception and typically referred to the area controlled by the Ottoman Empire.[3] It was not until 1902 that the term 'Middle East' was used for the first time by US naval officer A.T. Mahan in an article in *National Review*, in which he conceptualized 'the Middle East' as the Persian Gulf region. While Mahan was the father of the term, it was slowly popularized by Valentine Ignatius Chirol, special correspondent in Tehran for *The Times*, who wrote a series of articles under the title the 'Middle Eastern Question'.[4] Despite this, the term 'Middle East' remained largely outside official British policy terminology until after World War I.

Additionally, the head of each department was a powerful and intractable personality. At the War Office, Churchill was notoriously stubborn. Edwin Montagu at the India Office was perhaps Churchill's closest political associate of the four departments but the two were still sharply divided over Mesopotamia and the restructuring of the Middle East.[5] Lord Milner at the Colonial Office was a traditional imperialist of the highest order and Lord Curzon at the Foreign Office was perhaps Churchill's principal adversary in Middle Eastern affairs.[6] The synchronization of such strong personalities would have been very difficult, if not impossible. This, combined with larger geopolitical questions of the 'Middle East' would ultimately lead to the creation of a department to consolidate British policy.

Sir Percy Cox, high commissioner for Mesopotamia, supported Churchill's view, stating to the Cabinet on 12 August 1920, 'the need for a separate department to administer all the affairs of the Middle East and to bring an end to the overlapping and at times conflicting polices of the War Office, the Foreign Office, the India Office and the Colonial Office.'[7] Everyone in the Cabinet agreed with this notion though they were unsure whether to place the new department in the Colonial Office or in the Foreign Office: 'Churchill and Montagu favouring the former, Curzon the latter, while Milner was indifferent as long as the responsibility was placed clearly on one or the other.'[8] Both options were explored in the Cabinet meeting of 31 December 1920, and ultimately Churchill and Montagu won out owing to the expressed inability of the Foreign Office to administrate the Middle East. The minutes recorded that 'the temperament of the administrators and diplomats were quite different' and 'that to place Palestine and Mesopotamia under Foreign Office administration would be to court failure and disaster.'[9]

The split between Curzon and Churchill laid the groundwork for many battles regarding the territory of the Middle East. Churchill was usually supported by Montagu and Milner. This further alienated Curzon and the Foreign Office from Lloyd George, who disliked Curzon anyway. Churchill and Montagu did not like Curzon's committee-based approach to administration, with good reason. According to historian Timothy Paris:

> Curzon's committee work was largely ineffectual; he was not determined enough to resolve differences among the departments comprising the committees he chaired. Yet he remained convinced of the value of the policy-making committee. Even in late 1920, long after everyone else had recognized that a coherent Middle East Policy could not be worked out in committee, Curzon was still advocating the approach.[10]

The day after the Cabinet meeting, 1 January 1921, Lloyd George offered Churchill the office of Colonial Secretary, as Milner was 'in failing health and spirits and unwilling to assume such heavy new responsibilities.'[11] Lloyd George's choice for Churchill to replace Milner was a curious one. After all, he and Churchill had clashed a great deal over Middle Eastern policy while Churchill was at the War Office. Lord Derby was Lloyd George's first choice but he declined due to the overwhelming workload it would entail. Lloyd George 'needed a man of imagination and energy' for the Middle East and one who, more importantly, was not Curzon. With that in mind, Lloyd George's appointment of Churchill was logical, for, 'what ever faults [Churchill] possessed, he could not be accused of inertia or want of resolve.'[12] Another explanation might be that Lloyd George was familiar with Churchill's experiences with the 'East' and the Islamic culture in Sudan, on the north-west frontier, and at the Colonial Office 12 years earlier. Despite his experiences, Churchill still hesitated at first. After all, he knew it would be a tremendously difficult office. He would have to tend to policy on the new areas of Middle East, in addition to the nationalist sentiments in Ireland and uprisings against the British in Egypt and India. His worries about the appointment were evident in a letter he wrote on 4 January 1921:

> In view of all the circumstance I feel it is my duty to comply with your wish. I must however ask for the power and means of coping with the very difficult situation in the Middle East [. . .] While I feel some misgivings about the political consequence to myself of taking on my shoulders the burden and the odium of the Mesopotamia entanglement, I am deeply sensible of the greatness of the sphere you are confiding to my charge.[13]

In addition to his misgivings, this letter revealed Churchill's ambitious aim to consolidate Middle Eastern policy under his control. The authority Churchill wrote of in the letter was actually agreed to on New Year's Day 1921. The conditions included 'the widest possible powers to reduce British expenditure' and 'authority to set up the new Middle East department under [Churchill's] supervision.'[14] Despite remaining at the War Office until February, immediate control of the mandates' civil and military administration was turned over to him. This meant that for two months Churchill unofficially was the Secretary of War, Air, and the Colonies. Such blatant consolidation of power alarmed the press. The *Guardian* especially took issue with Churchill's 'wide berth and sweeping powers', but they were not alone. Other newspapers feared that the government 'had lost its bearings and gone wildly native' and that 'Churchill's appointment to Colonial Office in 1921 provoked qualms that he would "rule on an Oriental scale" in the Middle East. His special imaginative gifts made him all the more susceptible to the "seductions of the Orient".[15] These articles illustrated the press's belief that Churchill was somehow familiar and connected with the East – and are not altogether different than the press's treatment of Disraeli in the 1870s as an arch-imperialist. Concerns were not limited to the press either. Lord Curzon was offended because he felt that he 'had suffered a reverse at Churchill's hands [...] His departmental domain had been reduced.'[16]

Upon approval of the new Middle East Department, the Cabinet commissioned the Masterson-Smith Committee to define the department's scope. The committee reported its findings in early January and recommended exactly what Churchill sought: a single department that had wide powers over all aspects of the Middle East. The department's scope included Mesopotamia, Palestine, Aden (Yemen), and the lands collectively known as Arabia. However, the committee also limited Churchill's envisioned scope for the new department, as several Middle Eastern regions such as Egypt, Persia, Hedjaz (Saudi Arabia), and Central Asia were to remain with the Foreign Office. According to Bennett, this was an improvement on the previous policy-making structure, but was nevertheless 'seriously flawed'.[17] Since Churchill did not have complete control of British Middle Eastern policy, he realized he would have to continue to harmonize with Curzon in terms of policy creation, a situation that pleased neither man. But Churchill understood this and on 8 January 1921 wrote to Curzon:

> I am sure I can count on your help in the difficult and embarrassing task I have undertaken [...] But I hope at least to

> have some measure of control. I shall greatly value any advice that you may be willing to give me and also the aid – indispensable at so many points – of the Foreign Office.
>
> In your great sphere you hold controls which alone can make the local solution of the Middle Eastern problem possible. If you can make friends with the Turks and persuade the French not to quarrel with the Syrians, it will not be impossible to arrive at satisfactory results.[18]

This letter illustrates Churchill's appreciation for his new position of power in Middle Eastern affairs. While he politely pursued Curzon's opinions, Churchill also made clear that he expected 'a measure of control' and urged Curzon to reverse his position on Turkey. This further alienated Curzon from Lloyd George who, according to Edwin Montagu, was becoming even more 'violently anti-Turk' and was 'dreaming in Greek'.[19]

Beyond finessing Curzon to his purposes, Churchill also worked to pacify concerned constituents in his then constituency of Dundee (in part, because of negative press regarding Churchill's increased duties). He feared they misunderstood his intentions in the Middle East and why he had set up the Middle East Department. Churchill wrote to his constituent Sir George Ritchie, a wealthy industrialist, and summed up his attitude and intentions in the Middle East:

> The present position is as follows:- We have accepted, by the Treaty of Versailles, mandates for Palestine and Mesopotamia and we have also incurred certain responsibilities in regard to Arabia which are of profound significance to the Mohammedan subjects of the crown. The discharge of our task both in Palestine and Mesopotamia is now threatened by the enormous military expenditure required for the garrisons of these two countries [. . .]
>
> I had hoped that a substantial reduction could be effected in both countries [. . .] Unhappily the reductions so far effected in Mesopotamia are wholly inadequate.

As Churchill continued, it became clear that he was wrestling with his idealized Empire and its cost. Moreover, his concern for the Empire's Muslim subjects came across, if only tangentially:

> On the one hand it is perfectly clear that we cannot go on spending these enormous sums on Mesopotamia and that the forces we maintain there must be promptly and drastically reduced [...] On the other hand, the disadvantages and even disgrace of such a procedure [complete withdrawal] should not be under rated. If [...] we now ignominiously scuttle for the coast, leaving sheer anarchy behind us and ancient historic cities to be plundered by the wild Bedouin of the desert, an event will have occurred not at all in accordance with has usually been the reputation of Great Britain.
>
> It is my hope, therefore, that by means of an Arab Government supported by a moderate military force we may be able to discharge our duties without imposing unjustifiable expense upon the British Exchequer [...] Unless, Arabian affairs can be so handled as to secure tranquility among the tribes at this critical time, the early withdrawal of large numbers of troops from Mesopotamia, and consequentially the reduction of the expense, may be very greatly hampered.[20]

Within the context of this vision for the Middle East, Churchill also received some positive responses to his new role, despite trepidations of the press and the Foreign Office. A letter from Lord Rawlinson, the commander-in-chief of India, congratulated Churchill on his new appointment and reinforced Churchill's positions on Middle Eastern policy:

> For, I know full well from conversations that we have already had together, that the cause of Islam will receive more sympathetic treatment at your hands than ever could have been the case with Curzon.
>
> Whatever you may hear in reference to the effect which matters at Constantinople, and the holy places, maybe said to

> have in India [...] it will be impossible to stabilize the situation, either amongst Mahommedans of India or on the North-West frontier vis-à-vis Afghanistan, until a really drastic modification in the Treaty with Turkey has been effected. It is not too much to say that the eyes of all thinking Mahommedans, both in India, on the Frontier, and in Afghanistan, are turned towards the London conference which is to discuss the Treaty of Sèvres. Their attitude is one of expectancy and so long as their anxieties in reference to the future of Islam remain unsatisfied, it will be impossible for us to either quiet down the Khilafat movement, or to negotiate a satisfactory and lasting peace with our Afghanistan neighbors.
>
> So I sincerely hope that there may be better times ahead of us, and that, by coming to terms with Mustapha Kemal, we may be able to effect a satisfactory agreement with the Moslem world, which will give Turkey a modified suzerainty over the holy places, and permanently cement our friendship with Mahommedans.[21]

The private nature of Lord Rawlinson's letter reveals that his and Churchill's expressions of 'friendship with Mahommedans' were sincere. Moreover, he clearly supported what Churchill had in mind for the Middle East. He saw the necessity of a strong alliance with the Muslim world in order to create a bulwark against Bolshevik encroachment in Central Asia and the Middle East. This completely echoed Churchill's strategy of friendly British relations with the Muslim world, which might in turn create a strong alliance with Muslims outside the British Empire and would garnish favour with those inside the Empire. In this way, Churchill's fear of a pan-Islamism would be neutralized and the Muslim world might act as a shield against Bolshevik expansion. However, Churchill knew that to enforce and empower such strategies he would have to bolster his control over British Middle Eastern policy because this was at odds with Lloyd George's wishes and Curzon's foreign policy.

Churchill, therefore, moved forward quickly in establishing the groundwork of the Middle East Department. He sent Sir Percy Cox a letter explaining the remit of the new department and explained his desire for the establishment of a new Arab government in Mesopotamia, 'through whose agency the peaceful development of the country may be assured without undue demands on great Britain.' Moreover, Churchill wanted a domestic police force for Mesopotamia that was made up of 'Indian military units specially recruited from India.'[22] This policy had a dual purpose for Churchill. It provided great economy in Middle Eastern matters, as was Churchill's primary goal, and it empowered the Arab rulers by providing them with states in the Middle East, thus fulfilling the pledges of the Hussein–McMahon correspondence (1915–16).[23] Additionally, Churchill's desire for an Indian police force demonstrated that he was aware of the Muslim trepidation of being policed by non-Muslims. Churchill's solution was to use the Muslim troops of India to help maintain order. He was trying to marry his need for economies with the sensitivities of the Islamic people of the Middle East. In that way, or at least compared to his contemporaries such as Lloyd George and Curzon (who John Fisher described as the 'high priest of war imperialism'), Churchill was relatively progressive in his approach to the Middle East.[24]

Another demonstration of Churchill's relatively progressive thinking on the Middle East became evident in the staffing of his new department. He appointed John Shuckburgh as secretary and Major Hubert Young as his assistant secretary. Both men were very sympathetic to the Arab cause. On the other hand, his adviser on military affairs in the Middle East, Col. Richard Meinertzhagen, was a fierce Zionist.[25] Churchill's most significant appointment to the department was the famed T.E. Lawrence.[26] Churchill immediately offered the position of adviser on Arabian affairs to Lawrence, despite apprehension from the Masterson–Smith Committee.[27] Lawrence was known to greatly favour Arabian self-determination, a fact that Churchill was exposed to when he first met Lawrence at the Peace Conference in 1919. Bringing Lawrence into the department began an enduring friendship between the two men, which had long-term effects on British policy in the Islamic world. Among the things they discussed in their first official meeting in January 1921 was Lawrence's support of King Hussein's son, Feisal, in his designs for Mesopotamia. As they were discussing possibilities for the region, Lawrence pointed out that if the British supported Feisal (as he had supported them in World War I), it would 'tend towards cheapness and speed of settlement.'[28] This was 'music to Churchill's ears and played [. . .] the key role in Churchill's agreeing to install a Hashemite regime' in the Middle East.[29]

Interestingly, Churchill's relationship with Lawrence was characterized by 'deep mutual admiration and respect' and 'Lawrence's influence on Churchill was considerable', resulting in 'Churchill's adherence to Lawrence's recommendations even on issues which the rest of the Middle East Department dissented.'[30] Although not exactly a reliable source, Col. Meinertzhagen recorded in his diary that he was 'struck by the attitude of Winston towards Lawrence, which almost amounted to hero worship.'[31] Churchill's admiration of Lawrence became a thorn in the side of Meinertzhagen because Lawrence typically steered Churchill towards Arab sympathies. As a result, Lawrence and Meinertzhagen became rivals for Churchill's attention and mouthpieces for the opposing Arab and Zionist causes in the Middle East. Typically, Lawrence won out. Churchill's admiration for Lawrence might be explained by his similarities to Churchill's old friend Wilfrid S. Blunt. After all, in many ways Lawrence was a 'caricature' of Blunt.[32] Churchill even tried to arrange a meeting of his two greatest influences in Islamic and oriental matters in early 1922, before Blunt's death.[33] Whatever the cause for Churchill's admiration for Lawrence, he sometimes trusted to a fault Lawrence's positions on the Middle East.

In furtherance of establishing the Middle East Department, Churchill sent a flurry of letters on 23 January 1921 to Arthur Hirtzel at the India Office.[34] In the first letter, he insisted 'that a uniform system of spelling and pronouncing Arab names should be adopted from the outset' and that 'all deviations would be strictly forbidden.' Moreover, Churchill called for the creation of a committee to 'make proposals to me [Churchill] regulating the methods of spelling and pronouncing to be employed. At present everybody follows his own caprice.' His next letter, in Churchillian fashion, asked for 'a *large* map of Arabia and Mesopotamia' that illustrated where 'all the principal Arabian potentates exercise influence.'[35]

These letters are important because it helps illustrate how Churchill helped shape how we discuss and conceptualize the Middle East. First, it is significant that Churchill chose the title 'Middle East Department': the term 'Middle East' was still not official British terminology and was not often used in Cabinet social circles, with the notable exception of Mark Sykes who tried to 'popularize the term from the summer of 1916'.[36]

Additionally it has been argued that the switch from 'Near East' to the 'Middle East' in British terminology was a form of propaganda that drew from 'the longstanding discourse on Ottoman despotism' as well as 'the Orientalist idea of the ancient East as the cradle of civilization'. That is to say that 'the Orient had been a flourishing and vibrant region that had given Europe the seeds of civilization, but had [been] forced into dramatic decline by Ottoman mis-rule'.[37] From this perspective, the lands of the 'Near East' or 'Asiatic Turkey' were actually the nations of the ancient East such as Mesopotamia, Syria, and Palestine, and were subjugated by Ottoman despotism. Moreover, in this construct, the British Empire's altruistic role in this region was to liberate and revive the region 'to regain the glories of its ancient past.'[38] Therefore, 'reflecting this idea of a new and independent future "Asiatic Turkey" was increasingly referred to as the "Middle East": A revived nationalized landscape between East and West, that was to be free of Ottoman despotism and would achieve redemption under Allied protection.'[39]

Though Churchill's view of the Ottoman Empire was actually rather favourable (especially when compared to Lloyd George's), the Ottoman Empire no longer existed and as such Churchill's idea of uniting the two largest Muslim powers was dead. Despite this, it is notable that as late as 1919 Churchill called for Britain to return Mesopotamia and Palestine to Turkish control.[40] Even so, the notion of the British Empire offering guidance to independence for the Middle Easterns who were recently liberated from the Ottoman

Empire would have undoubtedly appealed to Churchill's belief in the British Empire as a civilizing force. It is unsurprising, then, that he adopted the term 'Middle East' in his new department and that he used the term in an official capacity, firmly planting it in the lexicon of British policy.

Additionally, Churchill's request for the map in order to familiarize himself with the Middle East is also significant in that it demonstrates that his knowledge of the region was not merely aesthetic or mythologized like Lloyd George's, whose knowledge of the Middle East was based more on biblical stories than on factual information.

Churchill's next letter asked Hirtzel to show all fiscal expenditures for 1920–1 and the expected expenditures for 1921–2 in 'all territories in the Arabian group, including Mesopotamia, Palestine, Arabia, and Aden'. Churchill also sent another important letter containing five points:

(1) Will you please let me have a note on whether it would be right or possible to form a Mohammedan Guard of Indian volunteers for the protection of the holy places.

(2) I had not appreciated the weakness inherent in King's Hussein's position [...] What other important chiefs of the Sherifian family are there still alive? It seems to me that all this has a bearing upon our committing ourselves irrevocably to one of King Hussein's sons as the ruler of Mesopotamia. If the father's title is defective, the sons' influence may fall with it. Probably you will be able to re-assure me.

(3) Will Bin Saud be offended if a son of King Hussein is made ruler over Mesopotamia, or will he not care? Will not the selection of Feisal or Abdullah strike him as a hostile act on our part if it is accompanied with a substantial reduction in his subsidy? From the papers you have sent me it would seem Bin Saud is much the stronger figure in the Arabian Peninsular.

(4) I have succeeded in disentangling Saud Bin Rashid from Bin Saud. It will simplify matters if you make up your mind once and for all whether you will call them 'Bin' or 'Ibn'.

(5) The Wahabi sect is at feud with the Sunni. Is it also at feud with the Shia? What are the principal doctrinal and ritualistic differences involved between the Shia, the Sunni, and the Shabi Mohammedans?[41]

The first point made clear Churchill's desire to dispel Islamic unrest in India that the holy places of Islam would not be as well protected under the British Empire as they were under the Ottoman Empire. Who better to protect Muslim holy sites than Islamic British subjects? This would help quell the Islamic British subjects in India who feared that without the Ottoman Empire the Islamic world's holy sites would not be protected. Moreover, adopting this policy reduced situations that tribal Muslims could exploit to create a pan-Islamic uprising.

The second and third points, however, demonstrated something more central to Churchill's aims in the Middle East: his desire to create a new Arab state, which would act in accordance with British wishes but also remain autonomous. This arrangement, as Churchill envisioned it, greatly reduced costs while reinforcing British supremacy in the Middle East. After speaking with Lawrence in December 1920, Churchill was almost certain that Feisal should become the sovereign power of the new Arabian state in Mesopotamia. Curzon also supported Feisal in his telegram to Churchill on 9 January 1921, stating that 'Feisal behaved like a real gentleman and with a fine sense of honour and loyalty. Further his attitude is in my view the best possible one for us in the present circumstance.'[42] Cox also agreed that Feisal should be the sovereign. With all the major players in concurrence, this became the British design for the Middle East.

This design for the Middle East is what Winston Churchill referred to as the 'Sherifian solution' and its implementation and design owed largely to Lawrence and himself. The idea was that power should be vested with the Hashemite family. This was for several reasons. They were loyal to Britain in World War I and helped lead the Arab uprising against the Ottoman Empire, which gave them the premiere status of being the head of the Arab nationalist movement.

This added to their already influential standing in the Islamic world, as King Hussein was the keeper of the holy city of Mecca. Through them, the British could honour their pledge to the Arab nationalists, as laid out in the Hussein–McMahon correspondence, and to the family who negotiated the pledge. Further, they were moderate Sunni Muslims, while other powerful Islamic leaders, such as the Wahhabist Ibn Saud,[43] were considered far too fundamentalist to work with British interests. Another reason that Churchill was a proponent of the 'Sherifian solution' was its cunning political advantages. Churchill believed that 'Britain could bring pressure to bear in one Arab country in which a Sherifian prince reigned [in order] to achieve goals in a different region ruled by another family member.'[44] For example, if Hussein knew his son's rule in Mesopotamia was dependent on his co-operation with British interests in Mecca, he would be more likely to oblige British wishes.

However, there were those who opposed the 'Sherifian solution'. The India Office principally rejected the idea because Muslim sentiment in India was against the Hashemite family. The Indian Muslims feared Hussein was renouncing the authority of the Caliph and endangering the Muslim holy sites.[45] Additionally, Arnold Wilson, the previous commissioner of Mesopotamia and understudy of Cox, opposed the self-determination of Arabs in general and preferred to keep Iraq as a sort of India. He was an old-fashioned imperialist in the spirit of Curzon and felt that an Arab state was too progressive, and that the Arabs were not ready for such an undertaking. There were also strategic flaws in Churchill and Lawrence's plan; namely that 'the plan was predicated on family affinities that in fact did not exist.'[46] Yet whatever the policy's pros and cons, the die was cast in Churchill's mind and the policy moved forward.

The fourth point of Churchill's letter to Hirtzel reinforced his concern regarding the standardization of language and spelling of names: that Churchill reinforced this point helps to illustrate the vague nature of the language of British policy for the Middle East. It further demonstrates a genuine concern for politeness, which would address Muslim sympathies.

The fifth point demonstrates that Churchill felt that he should have a greater understanding of the different sects of Islam. It is somewhat remarkable that he even knew there were multiple sects of Islam and that there were ongoing conflicts between them. Rather than viewing the Middle East as an aesthetic monolith of otherness, Churchill was probably made aware of such differences in the Islamic world by Wilfrid S. Blunt in their many talks on the Middle East – and this point goes some way in further illustrating that Churchill's thinking was not purely orientalist.

The difference between the two major sects of Islam is in fact not a theological difference but a doctrinal one. Essentially, Sunni Muslims believe that the position of Caliph, or religious leader, should be elected from among those capable of the task, whereas Shia Muslims believe that the caliphate should stay within the Prophet's own family, among those appointed by the Prophet, or among imáms appointed by Allah. To further complicate the issue, the Wahabist sect is a fundamentalist branch of the Sunni sect, which was founded in the eighteenth century by Muhammad ibn Abd al-Wahhab in the Nejd (present-day Saudi Arabia). The major schism occurred after the death of the Prophet Mohammad, when the search began for a new Caliph. According to Arun Sinha:

> There were two candidates for the post of caliph; Hazrat Ali, the Prophet's young son-in-law and Abu-Bakr, an uncle of the Prophet. The tribe chose Abu-Bakr. The first caliph, being very old, died very soon. Again, Haz-rat Ali's name was proposed as the successor but the tribe voted for Usman Gani. After the death of Usman, Hazrat Ali's name came up once again; the post however went to Umar Faruq. When this third caliph died, the tribe, considering that Hazrat Ali had been the loser every time, elected him. Ali was to be the last caliph. The controversy between Shias and Sunnis is this: the Sunnis believe in all the four caliphs; but the Shias believe only in the fourth and last caliph Hazrat Ali [. . .] The Sunnis, believing in the order of caliphate, recite 'Madhe-sahiba' in which they venerate and eulogise all the four caliphs, including Hazrat Ali.

> The Shias recite 'Tavarra' in which they curse Ali's three predecessors, Abu-Bakr, Usman and Umar. The Sunnis cannot tolerate the three caliphs being cursed; the Shias resent their being eulogised.[47]

While Churchill was at least aware of these religious differences, he undoubtedly did not have a firm grasp on the significance of the Islamic schism. His failure to appreciate this issue demonstrated another fault with the envisioned Arab state and the 'Sherifian solution'. Churchill and the others wanted Feisal, who was a Sunni Muslim, to become the new regent of Mesopotamia (Iraq), which was a predominantly Shia country. As historian Christopher Catherwood points out:

> So even if Feisal (and his branch of the Sherifian clan) could be said to be the right ruler for Iraq, as his supporters argued, that would still not have given him any degree of legitimacy among the vast majority of his new – and loyally Shia – subjects. It would also mean minority Sunni rule over a predominantly Shia population.[48]

Despite this complication, Churchill's designs for the Middle East and his power to enforce them were continually expanding. Seeking to further his role in the Middle East, he wrote to Lloyd George on 12 February:

> It is absolutely necessary for me to have effective control of the general policy and to be able to communicate directly with the commander-in-chief of Mesopotamia [...] Unless in this way I secure the effective initiation and control of the whole policy, I could not undertake the task with any prospect of success.[49]

Churchill was pleased that Lloyd George agreed with his expansion of powers. The entire general policy of Britain regarding the Middle East was placed in Churchill's hands. This did not please Curzon, however, who at the Cabinet meeting on 14 February expressed his fear of Churchill's eminence in Middle Eastern affairs. Despite Curzon's reservations, the Cabinet agreed with Churchill's increased authority. Exasperated, Curzon wrote to his wife saying that there was a 'rather long and worrying controversy between Winston and myself over the Middle East. He wants to grab everything in his new department and to be some sort of Asiatic Foreign Secretary.'[50]

Curzon was not the only person who represented an obstacle to Churchill's vision. Churchill became ever more frustrated with Lloyd George's anti-Turkish policies. Churchill saw a decent treaty with the new Turkish nationalists as a crucial step towards pacifying the Middle East and the entire Islamic world. After Lloyd George insinuated in mid January 1921 that the Turkish entry into World War I was Churchill's fault, Churchill reached a boiling point. He wrote a letter to Lloyd George defending his acquisition of the two Turkish warships, and reminding him that German and Turkish alliance was signed on 4 August and that he and Churchill were in 'full sympathy' during the war.[51] Upon reflection on his first letter, Churchill wrote a second, more direct one that revealed his frustration with Lloyd George's anti-Turkish policies; however, he did not send it for fear it was too damning. The second letter stated:

> The present misfortunes from which we are suffering throughout the Middle East are in my opinion the direct outcome of the invasion of Smyrna by the Greeks. The fact that we are the greatest Mohammedan power in the world makes us the chief sufferer in all our vital interests in the East from a policy which makes England the bitterest enemy of the Turks and which exalts the Greeks over them. The treaty of Sèvres, as I warned you in writing at the Conference [...] contains clauses which the Turks would never accept and which we have no power to enforce [...] If now Britain is to proceed alone to ratify this Treaty we shall draw upon ourselves the whole hostility of the Mohammedan world and our position in the Middle East will only be maintained by the expenditure of enormous sums of money.[52]

A month later, Churchill received an intercepted telegram from the Greek Foreign Office to the Greek Embassy in London. The telegram contained a conversation in which Lloyd George told President Venizelos that 'he was happy to have succeeded in solving the Smyrna question in favour of Greece' and asked for more information 'so that he might be in a better position to support the Greek point of view'.[53] Churchill was infuriated. He told Lloyd George he needed to stop supporting Greek ambitions in Turkey. He then wrote another harsh letter of protest, which he did not send. In the letter, Churchill noted that several officials and people of importance such as Allenby, Percy Cox, T.E. Lawrence, John Shuckburgh, Montagu, and the Aga Khan all agreed that Lloyd George's unrelentingly pro-Greek policies were disastrous for the Middle East. Churchill continued his tirade:

> I have yet to meet a British official personage who does not think that our Eastern and Middle Eastern affairs would be enormously eased and helped by arriving at a peace with Turkey. The alternative of the renewal of war causes me the deepest misgivings [. . .]
>
> The Turks will be thrown into the arms of the Bolsheviks; Mesopotamia will be disturbed at the critical period of the reduction of the Army there [. . .] the general alienation of Mohammedan sentiment from Great Britain will continue to work evil in every direction; and we will everywhere be represented as the chief enemy of Islam. Further misfortunes will fall upon the Armenians.
>
> In these circumstances it seems to me a fearful responsibility to let loose the Greeks and to reopen the war. I am deeply grieved at the prospect and at finding myself so utterly without power to influence your mind even in regard to the matters with which my duties are specially concerned.[54]

Though unsent, this letter illustrates Churchill's desperate hope to alter the Middle Eastern policy to one that was more amicable with Muslim sentiments. The entire Middle East Department saw its work being undone by Lloyd George's Grecophilia. Moreover, this letter demonstrated Churchill's desperation in trying to influence Lloyd George's opinion on Middle Eastern affairs, as his tone seemed more like the pleading of an old friend, rather than a concerned departmental minister. Whatever problems the two might have had on Middle Eastern policy, Churchill had been given nearly a *carte blanche* for the region to achieve his design and he intended to use it.

One of the first things he set out to do when he moved to the Colonial Office was to see Mesopotamia at first hand as he believed that several issues needed his personal attention. The first was to evaluate the troop situation in Mesopotamia. There was a major uprising going on there and Churchill wanted to control it with the RAF rather than traditional ground troops, but General Haldane did not approve of Churchill's withdrawal of army troops in exchange for RAF squads. In a telegram dated 13 January 1921, Haldane urged Churchill 'that his use of air power as the main instrument of control would not work.'[55] This was followed by a telegram from Percy Cox, which offered his resignation and stated that 'he supported Haldane's fears that any substantial reduction of troops would be a mistake and that the Royal Air Force could be nothing more than a valuable auxiliary.'[56] Churchill responded the next day and reassured Cox that his quest for economies in the Middle East did not translate to complete withdrawal: No province in the British Empire has ever been acquired by marching in and maintaining a large regular army at the cost of the British Exchequer, but always by skilful and careful improvisations adapted to its special needs.[57]

However, the War Office became increasingly obstinate as a reduction of troops in Mesopotamia (and replacing them with RAF squadrons) essentially transferred power from the War Office to the Colonial Office and the Air Ministry. For this reason, General Haldane refused to co-operate with Hirtzel and Churchill. This infuriated Churchill. In an unsent letter to Under-Secretary for War, Sir Laming Worthington-Evans, Churchill complained: 'At present the attitude of your Department is inveterate hostility and obstruction to a policy with which you are a party.'[58] The unreliability of the War Department reminded Churchill of the disastrous Dardanelles campaign 'where his policies had been undermined by his departmental subordinates in London and by his officers in the field.'[59] This was amplified by Haldane's and Cox's unrelenting resistance to Churchill's air control scheme and his reduction of expenditure.

In the midst of the troop discussions, Churchill also personally desired to examine Britain's situation regarding three treaties, each of which proposed seemingly different arrangements for the Middle East. Ultimately, he hoped to somehow make these three pledges work together to balance British and Islamic interests.

The first was the Sykes–Picot Agreement (1916),[60] the secret treaty between Britain and France drawn up by Sir Mark Sykes and François Georges-Picot in 1916, which split the remains of the Ottoman Empire between the two countries. It gave control of Syria, Lebanon, and Damascus to France, while the majority of Mesopotamia, Transjordan, and Palestine went with Britain. Churchill thought that the British policy in the Middle East should not antagonize the French claims there, in order to prevent more conflict. Moreover, French collusion might aid in making the region easily administered and, most importantly, cheap to maintain. Churchill met with the French president, Alexandre Millerand, on 11 January and reported to Lloyd George that the French were now of the same mind as Britain and were 'utterly sick of pouring out money and men on these newly acquired territories'. Consequently, Churchill confided to Lloyd George that he thought the French were 'ready to be conciliatory and accommodating' to British interests.[61]

Despite these agreements, however, Millerand also told Churchill that 'Feisal had been intolerable in his relations with the French.' Churchill heard from Major Hubert Young, the new assistant secretary in the Middle East Department, that both Feisal and his brother Abdullah were participating in anti-French intrigue. According to Young, Abdullah wanted 'to get Feisal back to Damascus', thus consolidating himself for Mesopotamia.[62] If Britain appeared to support this, it would destroy Anglo-French relations. Lord Curzon was increasingly anxious the British alliance with the Arab leaders might scupper the peace negotiations in Europe. Churchill knew that if his designs were to be successful Arab intrigue had to stop. He assured Curzon that Britain was in a position to prevent any attack that might befall French interests through Transjordan.

The second so-called treaty Churchill had in mind was the pledge that was believed to have been struck between King Hussein, the Sharif of Mecca, and Sir Henry McMahon, the high commissioner for Egypt during World War I, in their correspondence (1915–16).[63] McMahon urged Hussein to revolt against the Ottoman Empire in exchange for an Arab state (it was ambiguous if it was to be an independent state or one under the umbrella of the British Empire). The boundaries of this supposed state were also ambiguous, which resulted in much dissention, especially regarding Palestine. Despite the indefinite nature of the pledge, Churchill felt that it was a debt of honour to pay to the Hashemite family for their support during the war. Moreover, Lawrence was determined to see it fulfilled and he had Churchill's ear. David Fromkin has emphasized Lawrence's influence, stating:

> Unaware of the extent to which Lawrence [. . .] had exaggerated the role of Feisal's Arabs in winning the war, Churchill was prepared to accept Lawrence's thesis that Britain owed a great deal to Feisal and his followers.[64]

The final accord that Churchill wanted to settle was the Balfour Declaration (1917).[65] It stated that Britain would work towards the aim of establishing a national home for Jewish people in Palestine, which at that time included Jordan. This pledge was also ambiguous and could be interpreted as a contradiction of the pledges made in the Hussein–McMahon correspondence. On this point, the French were decidedly against the Balfour Declaration. Millerand told Churchill that he believed that Zionism was a cause that was 'disturbing the Arab world.'[66]

Churchill was not opposed to the Balfour Declaration and often fought for it. Gilbert describes Churchill as having 'high hopes for Zionism' and the Jews despite their supposed connection to Bolshevism. In his notorious article in the *Illustrated Sunday Herald* (which was littered with anti-Semitic language), Churchill identified 'praise worthy National Jews' who were loyal to their respective countries, and the 'International Jews' whom he believed had a major hand in the Bolshevik revolution. He asked the Jews of the world to choose between Zionism and Bolshevism and noted that they 'are the most remarkable race which has ever appeared in the world'.[67] He clearly hoped that the advent of Zionism would become a new outlet that might offset any perceived Jewish connection to Bolshevism. Interestingly, Churchill was not a lone voice on the matter. This was not dissimilar to the views of Lloyd George and Balfour', both of whom believed in the power of an 'international Jewry'.[68]

Churchill's relationship with Zionism did not necessarily contradict his view of Islamic Arabs. In fact, he believed that the shared history of the two groups, based on similar religious origins and shared Semitic ethnicity, would unite them in a symbiotic relationship. This helps to illustrate why Churchill believed that all three treaties might work in tandem to create a unified policy that would please all parties. Rather than try to orchestrate such complicated Middle Eastern policy from London, Churchill resolved to go to the Middle East personally and take with him all the experts he could gather, to create a comprehensive Middle Eastern policy for the Empire that was equally amicable for people in the Middle East, Jews and Muslims alike.

The Cairo Conference

On 6 February 1921 Churchill decided to abandon his idea to go to Mesopotamia and instead decided that Cairo in Egypt was the best place to call a comprehensive meeting for the Middle East. He wrote to Cox immediately to inform him about his plans for the conference, revealing his objectives in a telegram:

> The questions at issue cannot be settled by an interchange of telegrams. I cannot [...] find time to visit Mesopotamia [...] Main questions to be settled are following: – First, the new ruler. Second, future size, character and organisation of the future garrison. Third, the time-table of reduction from the

> present strength to that garrison. Fourth, total amount of grant-in-aid. Fifth, arising out of above the extent of territory to be held and administered.
>
> After such a conference I shall be in a position to make definite recommendations to the cabinet for action. I shall also endeavour to use this new conference as an occasion for getting into personal touch with various British authorities in the Middle Eastern triangle who are being placed under the Colonial Office.[69]

Churchill went on to inform Cox of the new Middle East Department and assured him that it had 'effective control of all factors in the Arabian problem.' Churchill also continued his quest to find savings in Middle Eastern expenditure. He wrote to the ever more obstinate Haldane and rebuffed his proposal of paying £100,000 for the cavalry in Mesopotamia along the Upper Euphrates. Churchill fumed:

> We are maintaining this regiment in region named for the purposes of collecting taxes and that the taxes gathered do not exceed one quarter of the cost of their collection. I expect this is typical of a great deal of the waste of force and of money which is going on in Mesopotamia.[70]

Churchill wrote to Hirtzel complaining, 'Why have we got to pay £300,000 a year for wretched shanties in Baghdad?'[71] An equally stubborn Haldane immediately responded, revealing his racist perceptions by arguing that the 'inherent respect of the Arab for the "strong hand" necessitates the troop presence.'[72] The next day, this combined with Haldane's obstructive nature prompted Churchill to declare his intentions to the Cabinet. He informed them he was calling a conference in Cairo, and that after the conference he planned to dismiss 'the present Commander-in-Chief in Mesopotamia' and replace him with 'an officer whose junior rank will be more appropriate to the reduced permanent garrison.'[73]

Interestingly, Churchill was not completely a slave to reducing expenses. Concerning annual subsidies to the rulers of Arabia, he was not willing to reduce expenditures at all. This was another example of

Churchill's ability to combine pragmatic necessity with his ideals for the region, as he sought to make a partner of Islamic Bedouins. In order to promote stability and peace, Cox wrote to the Treasury asking for £100,000 per annum to pacify Ibn Saud. The Treasury refused and Churchill protested in letters to Hirtzel:

> It is clearly folly to haggle about fifty or sixty thousand pounds a year in subsidies to particular Arab chiefs [. . .] My view is that in this critical year, while withdrawal from Mesopotamia is in progress, we should be generous with subsidies to the Arab chiefs. It would seem necessary to act on Sir Percy Cox's suggestion to pay £100,000 to Bin Saud. Similarly King Hussein's should be renewed up to its full previous level.[74]

Churchill planned to leave for Cairo on 1 March. He drafted an outline for the agenda of the conference with regards to Mesopotamia, which echoed his telegram to Cox. He also noted that Palestine needed a similar solution. While preparing to go to Egypt, however, he was confronted by a Palestinian issue. Pinhas Rutenburg put forward plans to build a dam on the Jordan and Auja rivers to electrify Palestine. On advice from Shuckbrugh, Churchill agreed to the project as it 'would provide employment to eight hundred people, both Jews and Arabs.'[75]

This concept of benefitting both Arabs and Jews simultaneously was the framework in which Churchill operated in relation to Palestine. Any position taken by Britain in Palestine or the greater Middle East had to work for both Jews and Arabs and ultimately facilitate the creation of an Arab–Jewish symbiotic relationship. A day before Churchill left for Cairo, Chaim Weizmann, the president of the Zionist Organisation, assured its members that Churchill had 'a low opinion of the Arab generally'.[76] He took the opportunity to write to Churchill urging the inclusion of Transjordan in the Palestine mandate. However, foreseeing that this would work against Arab sentiments in Transjordan, Churchill refused.

Another minor issue that crept up on Churchill before he left for Cairo was a letter he received from Curzon urging him to change the location of the conference, because 'Curzon feared Churchill's public criticism of Egyptian independence might lead to hostile demonstrations.'[77] Churchill believed that Curzon was merely interfering with his Middle Eastern agenda. Churchill wrote to him, obstinately declaring that if the location was to be changed, then Allenby had to make the decision. However, in the letter, Churchill took out a particularly angry paragraph which argued:

> I wish you were going to this work. I greatly repent ever having allowed the consequences of the last two years in the Middle East to be thrust upon me. I shall be delighted to hand them over at any moment if the cabinet agree.[78]

Curzon's wish for Churchill to hold his conference elsewhere owed largely to Lord Allenby, the high commissioner of Egypt, confirming to Curzon that the Egyptians 'bitterly resented being put on par with Palestine and Mesopotamia' and that Churchill's view of Egypt as an informal imperial holding greatly offended them.[79] While this illustrates the increasing rift between Churchill and Allenby regarding Egypt's status, Allenby's fears were sound. It was only logical that the Egyptians would be insulted. After all, why should Mesopotamia receive state status, with its own sovereign, while Egypt remained an imperial possession, still under formal control of a British commissioner? Nevertheless, Churchill was unmoved by these arguments and Egyptian sensitivities and was resolved to go to Cairo. Upon his arrival he and Clementine were met by several protesting Egyptian nationalists flying banners that said '*Iskut* Churchill' (shut up Churchill) and 'Down with Churchill'.[80]

The Cairo Conference opened on 12 March 1921 at the Semiramis Hotel. It was attended by 'some 40 British experts from London and the Middle East', including A.T. Wilson from Persia, the high commissioners Percy Cox (Mesopotamia) and Herbert Samuel (Palestine), T.E. Lawrence, Gertrude Bell (Cox's oriental secretary and the only woman among the delegates), as well as several representatives of Somaliland and Aden.[81] Bell had served in Mesopotamia under Cox since the end of World War I as a political officer. Moreover, she was an avid supporter of the cause of Arab self-determination, but eventually came round to supporting Lawrence and the Hashemite family for the new state's leadership. She and Lawrence worked in tandem to promote Feisal; Lawrence 'smoothed the way with Churchill in London and Gertrude had done the same with Cox in Baghdad.'[82] However, unlike Lawrence, Bell was not impressed with Churchill. She believed that he had repeatedly made errors in regard to Asia and the Middle East, especially at the Dardanelles and Gallipoli during World War I. Upon learning of his initial desire for withdrawal from Mesopotamia on account of its cost, Bell sneered to her father that: 'As far as statecraft, I really think you might search our history from end to end without finding poorer masters of it than Lloyd George and Winston Churchill.'[83] Despite these differences, Bell resolved to work with Churchill and Lawrence because she saw a real opportunity to have an effect on the creation of Iraq.

Churchill's plan for the Middle East might be categorized in two parts, sitting under an umbrella issue, which was, of course, the reduction of expenditure. This had always been Churchill's primary goal, even to the detriment of the others. Churchill and Lawrence thought the Sherifian solution was a mere cog in the machine of Churchill's fiscal designs: 'Churchill's main goal in Cairo [. . .] was financial, not the advancement of one rival dynastic claim against another [. . .] the Hashemites were simply the best means to an end.'[84] The first part under the umbrella dealt with the Arab regions such as Mesopotamia and the Arabian kingdoms. The second part dealt with the Zionist aspiration for Palestine. The first was 'dictated by British strategic requirements' and the second was 'motivated primarily by Britain's commitment to the establishment of a Jewish national home.'[85] As chairman of the Cairo Conference, Churchill set the tone and shattered any illusions that members of the War Office might hold:

> The first consideration is the reduction of British military commitments in Mesopotamia. No local interest can be allowed to stand in the way of an immediate programme for reducing

> the British army of Occupation. Whatever maybe the political status of the country under the Mandate, it is out of the question that forces of anything like the present dimensions should be supported by the British taxpayer.[86]

The structure of the conference was set up so that there were two primary committees: one political, chaired by Churchill, and one military, chaired by General Congreve. There was also a third committee that dealt with finances. While the primary objective of all the committees was the reduction of expenditure, the conference was to create and enforce Churchill's vision for the Middle East using the Sherifian solution. This was a hugely importance conference because 'Churchill not only meant to formulate policy. He also intended to address the fundamental conditions on which it was grounded.'[87] When the conference was over, Churchill's vision had radically altered the traditional British imperial model and ushered in 'a new kind of colonial policy, and formalized the end of direct British rule in Iraq.'[88]

When the political committee opened, Churchill immediately pushed for the sovereignty of Mesopotamia, while the Military Committee supported Churchill and Trenchard's air strategy and began by reducing ground troops in Mesopotamia in exchange for RAF squadrons. This theme was followed in the subsequent meetings. In the Political Committee's first meeting it was decided unanimously that Feisal was the candidate who Britain supported for the kingship. This, of course, had already been decided back in England, but as a gesture of goodwill Cox nominated some other candidates. One was a Turkish prince named Burhan al-Din who had been a member of the Committee of Union and Progress (CUP) in the Ottoman Empire, was a son of the previous Sultan Hamid, and was appointed as Amir of Mecca once Hussein resisted Ottoman rule. This disqualified him. Another candidate was Ibn Saud, who was considered but ultimately ruled out due to the fundamentalist nature of his Wahabist Islamic beliefs, which were thought to be incompatible with the theological tenets of the large Shia majority in Mesopotamia. Churchill reported to Lloyd George that Ibn Saud would 'plunge their whole country into religious pandemonium'.

Another candidate was Sayyid Talib, the Minister of the Interior, but Churchill described him as a 'man of bad character and untrustworthy', perhaps owing to Talib's pre-1914 reputation as 'the boss' of Basra.[89] The Aga Khan was also considered briefly but he was not really interested in the position.

The elimination of these candidates left Feisal and his brother, Abdullah, as the only viable options. Churchill asked Cox which of the two Hashemite brothers might be best suited for the role of Iraqi sovereign. Cox cited Feisal's military experience with the Allies during World War I as a primary reason to choose him; however, this endorsement avoided 'French antipathy towards Feisal {and} it was supported by Colonel Lawrence, who depicted Abdullah as lazy and by no means dominating, while Mesopotamia needed a ruler who would be active and inspiring.'[90] And so Feisal officially received British support as the ruler of Iraq. This ignored the fact that Feisal had been pursuing his kingship of Damascus in French-held Syria and that Abdullah had already been positioning himself as King of Iraq. In fact, he had been declared King in absentia by the Iraqi Congress in March 1920.

Nevertheless, Churchill still had the business of selling this solution to Lloyd George and the Cabinet. In his telegram to Lloyd George on 18 March, he echoed Lawrence's warnings of Abdullah's laziness and weakness. He also noted that putting Abdullah on the throne in Iraq would 'ensure failure of policy in both directions at once' because it would 'put the weak brother on the throne in Irak {sic} while the active and powerful brother was loose and discontented to work off grudges against the French by disturbing Trans-Jordania.'[91]

At a joint meeting of the political and military committees on 14 March, Churchill re-emphasized the need to cut expenditure. He asked for a comparative cost survey to be presented to both committees, which illustrated that the annual cost of the garrisons in Palestine and Mesopotamia was approximately £30 million and that only £3.5 million was needed in Palestine.[92] This led to an exploration for savings, which in its first phase cut cost by approximately £4 million by reducing staff and military personnel. This reduced the expenditure to about £27 million. The second phase, set to start in October, reduced the military personnel down to about 15,000 men. The success of these reductions depended on Churchill and Trenchard's air scheme, backed up by newly levied Arab and Kurdish troops.

After the meeting closed, Churchill wrote to Lloyd George informing him of the major reductions in expenditure, which relied on his and Trenchard's air-control scheme and Feisal's candidature as the ruler of Mesopotamia. On 16 March, Lloyd George replied that he was 'in full sympathy with your desire to cure the waste and reduce troops in Mesopotamia.' However, he remained dubious about Feisal as the potential Iraqi King, due to French sympathies. Lloyd George argued that 'real initiative in any demand for Feisal should come from within Mesopotamia' otherwise '[the British] position with the French will be embarrassing, and we think it will be very difficult to reconcile procedure you propose with the attitude we have adopted with the French Foreign Office in this matter.'[93]

The next Political Committee meeting on 15 March met to discuss the possibility of an independent Kurdistan. Cox and Bell were of the opinion that the areas that would make up Kurdistan – Kirkurk, Sulaimaniya, and other districts north of Mosul – actually 'formed an integral part of Iraq' and should be kept in a united Iraq.[94] This was also Feisal's opinion. He feared that 'if any separate Kurdish state were to be encouraged, the Iraqi Kurds would join with their fellows in Turkey and Iran and thus constitute a permanent menace to Iraq.'[95] Bell furthered the argument by adding that the area north of Mosul was also the 'breadbasket' of Mesopotamia, 'its fertile soil provided grain for the entire country'. Additionally, the Kurds (who are traditionally Sunni Muslims) would help redress the strong Shiite majority in the south.[96]

However, Major H. Young and Major Edward Noel, the British authority on Kurds, quickly objected on the grounds that the Kurds would prefer home rule and Kurdistan might make a 'useful buffer state against both Turkish pressure from without and anti-British pressure from within.'[97] Lawrence also broke ranks with Bell and suggested that the Kurds should not be under Arab rule. To retort, Bell, who felt Lawrence was becoming unruly, famously called

Lawrence a 'little imp', to which 'his ears and face turned red and he retreated in silence.'[98] Churchill agreed with Young, Noel, and unsurprisingly, Lawrence because he was fearful that the future ruler might 'outwardly accept constitutional procedures [but] at the same time despise democratic and constitutional methods.' In this situation it would prove all too easy for the new king to 'ignore Kurdish sentiments and oppress the Kurdish minority.'[99] Ultimately, the committee adopted Young's position but it placated Cox and the others by agreeing to wait until a congress of Kurds could be formed to vote on whether they wanted to remain in Iraq or not.

The next day the Political Committee met to discuss the subsidies in Arabia. In this matter Churchill kept with his earlier remarks to Hirztel and decided to pursue direct subsidies to Arab chieftains, because it was cheaper than maintaining British garrisons and because it fit into his relatively progressive imperial view. For these reasons, Churchill encouraged the Political Committee to increase its subsidies in order to move closer to peace. Fahad Bey, a Bedouin chieftain, was awarded £36,000 annually for use of his territory as air fields. Cox wanted to double Ibn Saud's subsidy from £60,000 to £120,000. Unsure of how to move forward, Churchill asked for a sub-committee to be created to explore the different options regarding the subsidies. Among its members were Lawrence and Cox.

The sub-committee decided that Ibn Saud's subsidy should be £100,000 per annum paid monthly in exchange for his acquiescence and absence of violence against Hussein's and his sons' kingdoms. The sub-committee commented that Ibn Saud was a powerful factor in Arabian politics and, Middle Eastern historian Aharon Klieman, 'a moderating influence on his Wahabi subjects, who were restrained mainly by his useful skill of the British subsidy'. Klieman's interpretation of the sub-committee's findings is somewhat paradoxical, because Ibn Saud was refused the Iraqi throne on the grounds that his Wahabism was too religiously extreme. Gilbert's interpretation reveals the more fiscal nature of the sub-committee's findings. He contends that Ibn Saud's subsidy was 'as large as the total revenues of his government from other sources, and would therefore act as a means of encouraging him to restrain the warlike desire of his desert followers.'[100]

Regardless, Ibn Saud was a powerful force in the Middle East, so powerful that Major Young warned Churchill and the committee not to give him the title of 'king' because he might try to 'claim membership of the League of Nations, and thus remove himself from British control.' This, according to Young, would be 'undesirable in view of British interests in Arabia.'[101]

It was decided that Hussein should be paid in identical terms as Ibn Saud, but he had more obligations. He would not only have to 'maintain an attitude of goodwill towards the British Government' like Ibn Saud, but he also had to 'abstain from and entirely disassociate himself from anti-French propaganda, both by himself and by his son Abdullah in Transjordan.'[102] The final stipulation addressed Churchill's recurring fears; Hussein had to promise 'not to allow the Muslim Holy Places at Mecca to become a focus for anti-British or pan-Islamic intrigue.'[103]

That evening, after the meeting of the Political Committee, Churchill and Clementine went to Lord Allenby's ball. When Herbert Samuel showed up around midnight, he and Churchill retired upstairs to discuss Palestine. The morning after the ball, in a combined Political and Military Committee meeting Churchill announced that Palestine would be discussed in relation to two basic concepts. The first was the development of Palestine in regards to a Jewish homeland; the second was how Palestine would fit inside the Sherifian solution. In order to satisfy the second concept, Churchill announced that Transjordan would be partitioned away from Palestine and that Abdullah would make a good sovereign there. This was odd, since Churchill had just explained to Lloyd George why Abdullah would not work in Mesopotamia.

Churchill's change in tone can be explained by exploring the pragmatic political issues. Samuel feared that Abdullah might continue his anti-French agitation and that he might encourage anti-Zionist activism, which would make him a real destabilizing force in the region. Even Lawrence was cautious of Abdullah as ruler at first, fearing the French might push the throne of Damascus towards

Abdullah, which would put Transjordan in French orbit.[104] Additionally, Herbert Samuel was mortified in that Palestine and the Jewish national home had just been reduced in size, dramatically. However, Churchill overruled Samuel and was not swayed by these arguments. Churchill explained:

> A Sherifian candidate was essential. To support Feisal in Mesopotamia, but to refuse to support his brother in Trans-Jordan would be courting trouble especially if, by subsidizing Abdullah's father in Hedjez and paying Ibn Saud not to attack the Hedjez, we could obtain general peace and prosperity in Arabia [. . .] It seemed inevitable that in these circumstances we should adopt a policy elsewhere which would harmonize with our Mesopotamian policy.[105]

Lawrence quickly reversed his position, in part because he supported an overall Sherifian solution to the Middle East, as Churchill suggested, but mostly because he believed that 'neither Britain nor Amir Abdullah were strong enough at present to hold Trans-Jordan without the assistance from the other.'[106] He helped Churchill in his argument by assuring Samuel that anti-Zionist activity would be kept under control. Lawrence assured the committee and Samuel that:

> He trusted in four or five years, under the influence of a just policy, the opposition to Zionism would have decreased, if it had not entirely disappeared and [. . .] that it would be preferable to use Transjordania as a safety valve, by appointing a ruler on whom he could bring pressure to bear, to check anti-Zionism. The ideal would be a person who was not too powerful, and who was not an inhabitant of Transjordania, but who relied upon His Majesty's Government for the retention of his office.[107]

Samuel was still aghast and his secretary, W.H. Deedes, simply washed his hands of the scheme saying he was 'opposed to the appointment of Sherif Abdullah.' However, Abdullah already held sway in Amman so removing him for someone else would prove very difficult. This was why Deedes recanted his earlier position, saying that 'the only course was to accept his appointment as a *fait accompli*.'[108] Though other options were discussed, such as ejecting Abdullah from Amman by force, or promoting a governor with Abdullah's endorsement, promoting Abdullah as the regent of Transjordan was ultimately decided upon because it kept with Churchill's larger view of a Sherifian Middle East controlled by Great Britain – and because it was the cheapest solution.

Later that day Churchill wrote to Lloyd George informing him that 'occupation of Trans-Jordania on the basis of an arrangement with Abdullah is the right policy for us to adopt, and that it will afford best prospect of discharge of our responsibilities with future reduction of expense.' He also explained that he planned to meet Abdullah in Jerusalem after the conference in Cairo had finished. Churchill wanted Lloyd George's approval to move forward with Abdullah but also to quiet his fears about French resistance to the plan. In the telegram Churchill also included what they might say to French diplomats:

> So far from our acquiescence in a Feisal candidature for Mesopotamia, if desired locally, being an embarrassment to you, it is, in fact through our concomitant arrangements with Abdullah in Trans Jordania the surest means of securing you from disturbance and annoyance from Arabs in [the] south.[109]

Once that had been settled, the Military Committee met separately and decided that the make-up for Palestine was to mirror Mesopotamia, with a small division of ground troops under control of the RAF. Samuel suggested that there should be two battalions, one Jewish for Jewish areas and one composed of Arabs for Arab areas. Samuel argued that this would enable the Jews to 'share in bearing the brunt of defending their National Home' and illustrate to the tax-weary British public that the Jewish homeland was not totally dependent on the Empire for its existence.[110] This same deal would be offered to the Arabs. However, General Congreve (chair of the committee) was opposed to a strictly Jewish army in Palestine on the grounds that 'they had just agreed to an Arab force for Abdullah in Transjordan.'[111] He did, nevertheless, concede that a Jewish gendarmerie might be needed to fend off local Arab disturbances.

This argument continued into 18 March, when the combined committees on Palestine met. Samuel urged Churchill to adopt his solution. Churchill acquiesced and summed up why: 'bearing in mind the world-wide character of the Zionist movement and the desire expressed by the Jews to help in their own defence, it would be better to decide on the troops.'[112] Christopher Catherwood attributes this to Churchill being 'consistently pro-Jewish and pro-Zionist'.[113] However, this was not the case, strictly speaking, because Churchill cut off western Palestine at the Jordan River and placed everything east of the Jordan under Arab control and excluded it from all provisions made in the Balfour Declaration. Furthermore, out of necessity, 'Churchill undoubtedly paid more attention to the Arab than to the Zionist cause.'[114] Nevertheless, a Jewish army was never created because General Congreve and Samuel could not decide on an appropriate uniform.

During the conference's recesses, which were brief, there was not much to do. These recesses were described by Jessie Raven, the wife of the senior War Office official Joseph Crosland, who said that 'when things were boring in the hotel everyone would cheer up when Winston came in'. She also noted that Churchill was not popular with the locals and that he had to endure signs that said 'Down with *Churchill*', but that he did not mind: 'He took his easel out and sat in the road painting.' She also remembered that Churchill 'didn't like the Arab's coming into the Hotel, not even into the Garden.'[115] This seems out of character for an erstwhile associate of Wilfrid S. Blunt and may, in fact, be completely created by Raven. Despite the questionable authenticity of such utterances by Churchill, it has been remarked that these comments were unfortunate because Churchill was about to 'determine the fate of millions of Arabs'.[116]

On 20 March, the first break of the Cairo Conference, Churchill and Clementine went with Gertrude Bell and T.E. Lawrence to visit the pyramids. They chose to ride camels, which Churchill had never done before and he was not very adept at it. According to Gertrude Bell, he fell off his camel like 'a mass of sliding gelatin.'[117] Clementine laughed, 'How the mighty had fallen.'[118] Churchill barked back that he had 'started on a camel and... would finish on a camel.'[119] It was at the pyramids that the famous picture of Churchill in Cairo was taken marking the occasion of the conference as one of the major shaping events of Middle Eastern history. The conference has been best summed up by Gilbert: 'In three days, two new Arab states had been created, their sovereigns chosen, and part of the Zionist case lost by default.'[120]

The modern Middle East was born, but it was not the result of a single conference. It was the culmination of several factors: the creation of the Middle East Department, the development of the 'Sherifian policy' (under T.E. Lawrence's guidance), and the strategic balancing of the three important treaties in the postwar Middle East. In every instance, Winston Churchill left his mark.

CHAPTER 5

THE LEGACY OF THE CAIRO CONFERENCE

While Churchill's views of Zionism weighed heavily on the conference, he was also fair to the Arabs, at least according to T.E. Lawrence who said: 'Mr. Winston Churchill [...] was entrusted [...] with the settlement of the Middle East; and in a few weeks, at his conference in Cairo, he made straight all the tangle, finding solutions fulfilling (I think) our promises in letter and spirit.'[1] The creation of Transjordan, which was originally a part of the Palestinian protectorate, honoured the pledges in the Hussein–McMahon correspondence, despite those who had hoped it would never be honoured. Taken together, these factors help construct a more balanced understanding of Churchill's design for the Middle East; one that took into account all sides, Arabs and Jews alike. This interpretation moves away from the traditional concept of Churchill as a rabid imperialist and purely pro-Zionist policy maker, which certain historians have tried to ascribe to his legacy, and leans more towards the school of historians who have illustrated that Churchill's relationship with Zionism was significantly more complex than is typically realized.

Churchill saw the opportunity for his designs for the Middle East to marry British interests with the Arab world's desire to achieve, at least in part, a unified, self-controlled government. In Churchill's mind, this would create a major pro-British sentiment among the

Middle Eastern Arabs that would reverberate through the Islamic world as a whole, achieving two goals: the old Victorian dream of having consenting subjects who would advance British interests while shouldering part of the cost, and the creation of a strong flank in the Middle East and central Asia to help contain Russian Bolshevism and to counter Turkish nationalism.

Churchill's solution was in some ways very similar to what his old friend Wilfrid Blunt had prescribed for the Islamic world in his *Future of Islam* (1882). Blunt's far-sighted design interpreted the collapse of the Ottoman Empire as inevitable. Once it had collapsed, Blunt reasoned that: 'The Caliphate – no longer an empire, but still an independent sovereignty – must be taken under British protection, and publicly guaranteed its political existence, undisturbed by further aggression from Europe.' According to Blunt's design, the English were singular among Europeans because they had a 'tradition of tolerance towards Islam', which would result in Muslims 'recognizing this', and looking to 'England as their advisor and protector.'[2] While Churchill's solution was clearly informed by Blunt's, it had major differences such as its secular nature. Rather than revolve around Blunt's envisioned Arab caliphate or being split into separate minor *vilayets* as the Ottoman's had done, the Middle East would be composed of strong Arab nation-states in orbit around the British Empire. This was the noble role that Churchill envisioned for the British Empire, an opportunity for the Islamic world to gain its own nations, and dramatic savings for the British taxpayer.

Transjordan

The creation of Transjordan was one portion of the Sherifian solution that can largely be attributed to Winston Churchill and T.E. Lawrence. In fact, Churchill later boasted that he 'created [Trans]-Jordan on a Sunday afternoon with the stroke of a pen.'[3] There are even myths that have grown from Churchill's boast, that lend credence to this notion and at least confirm Churchill's role as a primary architect of Transjordan. The eastern boundary of Jordan, which borders Saudi Arabia, has a large notch, or zigzag in it which is still known as 'Winston's Hiccup'. According to the myth, after lunch with Abdullah, Churchill literally drew the map of Transjordan and as he drew it, he hiccupped causing the large zigzag in the border with Saudi Arabia.[4] While this is clearly fantasy, it does demonstrate the importance of Churchill's role in creating the kingdom of Transjordania.[5]

Churchill met with Abdullah in Jerusalem after taking a midnight train journey from Cairo with Lawrence and Samuel. The primary purpose of his journey was to tie up a loose end of the Sherifian solution, to find a place for Abdullah. Though thought unsuitable to be king of Iraq by Churchill and Lawrence, he had been 'the front runner in the race for the would-be Mesopotamian kingdom.'[6] He was even declared King of Iraq by the Iraqi Congress in March 1920. But since Churchill had awarded Iraq to Feisal, Abdullah had to be pacified, otherwise he might make trouble for the British Mandate of Palestine by working against the Jewish population, or by mounting a revolution against the French in Syria to press his kingship there. In order to avoid Abdullah thwarting their designs, Churchill and Lawrence were eager to change their tune regarding Abdullah's character.

In order to avoid such a catastrophic collapse of Middle Eastern policy, Churchill sought to reconcile Abdullah by making him the Amir of Transjordan. This involved severing everything east of the Jordan River out of the British Mandate for Palestine and making Transjordan a nominally independent state under an Arab master. This was contrary to Herbert Samuel's wishes, who confided to Lord Curzon in 1920 that not including Transjordan in the British Mandate for Palestine was 'a grave error of policy.'[7] If it was contrary to Herbert Samuel's views, it was mortifying to Chaim Weizmann, the leader of the Zionist movement in London. Before the Cairo Conference, he appealed to Churchill for the Jewish national home to be 'as far East as the Hejaz railway' including the 'Western most tip of the Trans Jordan territory.'[8] But Churchill had already made up his mind in favour of the Sherifian policy and he was intent on seeing Transjordan as a home for the wayward Abdullah.

On 28 March at their second meeting Churchill assured Abdullah that he 'wanted to revert back to the British policy of the war years of supporting Arab nationality on constructive lines, using the Sherfian family as a medium.'[9] Some historians have interpreted this as Churchill expressing 'his intention to abide by McMahon's promises regarding Arab independence.'[10] If this was so, Churchill did not make such a promise to the exclusion of the Balfour Declaration, rather he envisioned a system based on Jewish and Arab co-operation. He believed the two pledges complemented one another. While Churchill happily carved Transjordan out of the side of Palestine in order to fulfill one, he did not intend to renege on the British policy of supporting the Jewish national home, thus supporting the other. Abdullah, who had expressed concerns regarding the Jewish national home, was quick to embrace the idea as he fully expected Jewish capital to enhance his kingdom too. Churchill explained this to Abdullah saying that promises had been made to other parties, namely the French regarding Syria and the Jews regarding the land west of the Jordan River. In addition, Abdullah agreed that 'Britain was not free to act in Syria and in Western Palestine.'[11]

Churchill thanked Abdullah for supporting his brother's throne in Iraq and noted that Britain 'recognized Trans-Jordan's Arab character' but feared it economically too weak to stand without British support.[12] Churchill suggested that Transjordan might be linked with Palestine for this support. Remarkably, Churchill had originally envisioned that 'Abdullah might become governor [of Transjordan] under the High Commissioner of Palestine.'[13] Lloyd George's telegram of the 22 March to Churchill expressed 'misgivings' about this policy because Abdullah might refuse the position offered. It went on to say that 'the general desire of His Majesty's Government to fulfill earlier promises to King Hussein about independent Arab territories, undoubtedly favour an Arab solution.' However, the Cabinet was also wary of installing Abdullah without linking him to Palestine because 'the simultaneous installation of two brothers...in regions contiguous to French sphere of influence would be regarded with great suspicion.'[14]

Abdullah's counter-offer mirrored Churchill's. Abdullah suggested that Palestine and Transjordan should unify under an Arab Amir, believing this to be the easiest way 'that difficulties between Arabs and Jews would be most easily overcome'.[15] He also argued that the system that was adopted for his brother's kingdom in Mesopotamia should also be adopted in his kingdom. This proposition was indicative, not only of Abdullah's ambition but also of the sibling rivalry between the two Hashemite Amirs. 'If Feisal were to receive the largest (remaining) imperial prize, Iraq, then Abdullah should have his cake too.'[16] This, demonstrated Abdullah's frustration with Feisal for accepting Britain's offer of Mesopotamia. Though Churchill and Abdullah argued, Abdullah eventually accepted Churchill's plan but 'he showed no enthusiasm for the idea', noting that 'he declined Churchill's request to write Mesopotamia in favor of his brother's candidacy' and 'lost no opportunity to besmirch his brother.'[17] However, in Abdullah's memoirs he insisted that regarding Feisal's placement on the throne, he told Churchill he would be 'pleased to use [his] influence to both Feisal and [his] father to take this course.' However, perhaps revealing his a lack of enthusiasm, Abdullah stated that 'as for the people of Iraq, I cannot write them to them as I have no contacts with them.'[18]

In any case, Churchill rejected Abdullah's offer, arguing that there were fundamental differences in the two kingdoms: Mesopotamia was an independent state while Palestine and Transjordan were part of a mandate entrusted to Britain from the League of Nations. As a counter-offer, Churchill assured Abdullah that if he did not 'interfere with Zionist activity in Western Palestine, the British Government would promise that the Zionist clauses of the Mandate would not apply to Trans-Jordan.'[19] In addition, Abdullah would have to promise to stop all anti-French intrigue. Churchill reminded Abdullah that 'he was taking a great responsibility as the new Minister of the Middle East in advising his colleagues to join hands with the Sherifian family' and then warned Abdullah that 'he had been told by other people that this was a dangerous policy', and he was told that His Majesty's Government would be better advised 'to split up the Arabs into distinct and Local Governments.' After all, 'this had been the policy of Rome and Turkey in the past.'[20] This phase in their negotiation seemed to win Abdullah over to Churchill's thinking (with some reassurances from Herbert Samuel) but it also illustrates an important point in Churchill's thinking towards the Islamic world.[21]

In Churchill's mind there were two ways to administer the Middle East. The first was the conventional *vilayet* system, which the Ottoman and Roman empires had prescribed for the Middle East, and which Churchill described as:

> The policy of keeping [the Arabs] divided, of discouraging their national aspirations, of setting up administration of local notables in each particular town or city and exerting influence though their jealousies of one tribe against another. That was largely the Turkish policy before the war and as cynical as it was it undoubtedly achieved a certain measure of success.[22]

Since Churchill sought to create strong and economically viable Arab nation states that were nominally controlled by the British Empire, he rejected this system. Though it may have made easy administration of imperial outposts, it did not give the Arabs nation states or fulfill the McMahon pledges, which Churchill felt the British were honour-bound to fulfill.[23] Instead, Churchill wanted to pursue the other policy, which he believed was solely 'compatible with the sincere fulfillment of the pledges we gave during the war to the Arab leaders.' He went on to describe the policy as one that builds 'around the ancient capital of Baghdad in a form friendly to Britain and her allies an Arab state which can revive and embody the old culture and glories of the Arab race.'[24] In this way, Churchill's approach to Mesopotamia and Transjordan were inexorably linked with his understanding of the British Empire as a civilizing force in the world. Rather than control the Arabs, they would be allowed to control their own destinies (to a degree). These Islamic nation states would have to work with the British Empire and its aims. In Churchill's mind, they would keep Turkish nationalists in check, help contain Bolshevik expansion and, most importantly, they would be fiscally responsible for themselves. This explains Churchill's preference for nation building, rather than provincial maintenance. Though this system created difficult issues for the future Iraqi state (which are still unfolding), it seemed logical to push the Middle East towards nation states at the time.

Churchill and Abdullah met again on the morning of 30 March and Churchill urged him to 'stay in Transjordan for six months, with a British Political Officer as his chief adviser to set the revenue of the country on a proper basis'. To accomplish this Churchill implied Her Majesty's Government would happily give money and troops to Abdullah but in return for its support, Churchill expected Abdullah to guarantee no 'anti-French or anti-Zionist agitation on the country.'[25] Abdullah accepted these terms and Transjordan had found its ruler, though on an informal and temporary basis. Churchill's memo after their meeting, noted that Abdullah's position was 'an informal arrangement' and left the questions of governorship and sovereignty in the air.[26] Therefore, Churchill left the official policy open. With the worries of the Cabinet on his mind, Churchill believed he had to sweeten the deal so Abdullah would remain in Transjordan. However, it has been argued that this was not actually the case, that Abdullah was 'a spent force' who was 'passed over in the division of the remaining Ottoman territories' before the Cairo Conference, and that Churchill's policy had essentially established him as 'a key Hashemite player with...a territory of his own.'[27]

Neither the Cabinet nor Churchill understood Abdullah's position in those terms, so during negotiations Churchill insinuated that the Damascus throne might eventually go to Abdullah, an idea Churchill had picked up from Lawrence's earlier postulation on Abdullah's fate.[28] Churchill stated that 'the French might come around to the British way of thinking' and that 'every personal effort must be made by the Emir himself to improve his relations with the French.'[29] Churchill went even further to say that once Abdullah had 'succeeded in checking anti-French action for six months he would... greatly improve his own chances of a personal reconciliation with the French, which might even lead to his being instated by them as the Emir of

Syria in Damascus.' This position however, could not be guaranteed.[30] Of course, it was 'just what Abdullah wanted to hear' so he could use Transjordan as a 'spring board for the realization of his imperial dream: a vast kingdom comprising Syria and Palestine under his leadership.'[31]

However, some commentators doubt whether Churchill was completely honest in his implication to Abdullah regarding the throne of Damascus and that it was done merely to force the final piece of the Sherifian solution into place. George Antonius, the author of *The Arab Awakening* (1938), argued that 'What Churchill did in fact do was...trick Abdullah into remaining in Amman as ruler of Transjordan on the promise of a real settlement which was never realized.' This was also echoed in Abdullah's own memoirs. He maintained that:

> It was eventually agreed provisionally that the British Government should use their good offices with the French to secure their eventual restoration of an Arab administration under the Amir Abdullah's leadership; that he should remain in Trans-Jordan, check anti-French movements there and thus prepare for eventual reconciliation with the French.[32]

However, Churchill maintained that it was made clear that he could not guarantee Abdullah's position with the French in Syria; this much is recorded in the minutes of the meeting. Moreover, Churchill even conversed with Monsieur de Caix, the French representative in Syria saying, 'I explained to him the arrangement I was making with Abdullah about Trans-Jordan, and told him that the key stone of it was the prevention of attacks on the French.' Then Churchill went on to note that de Caix had told Samuel that, 'if Abdullah was able to maintain order all would be forgotten and forgiven in six months. There is no doubt that the French have already been trying to get in touch with Abdullah themselves.'[33] This indicates that Churchill made a wholehearted effort to see through his suggestions regarding Syria and Abdullah. After all, it would have been beneficial for the British to see Abdullah on the throne of Syria, as it might have created a large swathe of territory under their nominal control, without the burden of the cost.

Churchill's policy on Transjordan was pragmatic and effective. While his intention of keeping Abdullah in Transjordan on a British leash were motivated by Churchill's aspiration to secure a fiscal and strategic position for his beloved Empire, they also demonstrate the lengths to which he was willing to go to uphold the McMahon pledges in order to preserve British honour in the region. Ironically, the place where Churchill and Lawrence assumed the Hashemite ruler was the weakest is today the only place where a Hashemite remains in power.

Mesopotamia

Churchill's strategy for Mesopotamia (or Iraq, the name adopted for Mesopotamia in August 1921) is often explored solely on the grounds of fiscal economies. Several historians specializing in the Middle East stress this as Churchill's *raison d'etre* in Middle Eastern policy and especially in Mesopotamia. Peter Sluglett, David Fromkin, Robert Fisk, and others explore this notion.[34] While this is true and provides an over-arching context for Churchill's policies in Iraq (and the greater Middle East), it limits others factors in his thinking, which culminated in the policies outlined at the Cairo Conference for Iraq.

The Sherifian solution dictated that a Hashemite be put on the throne of Iraq. This gave Churchill and the Middle East Department two options, Feisal or Abdullah. Churchill's choice of Feisal over his brother was informed by T.E. Lawrence, who made his preference clear in *The Seven Pillars of Wisdom*. Lawrence characterized Abdullah as lazy, self-indulgent, and bland. Lawrence further revealed his repugnance by noting that Abdullah's 'causal fits of arbitrariness now seemed a feeble tyranny disguised as whims; his friendliness became caprice; his good humour, love of pleasure. The leaven of insincerity worked through all the fibres of his being.' Lawrence's depiction of Abdullah was made all the more severe by his heroic and regal depictions of Feisal, who he described as 'tall, graceful, and vigorous, with the most beautiful gait.' He also noted that Feisal was a 'master of diplomacy' and a 'careful judge of men.'[35]

After the conclusion of the Cairo Conference it fell on Cox to install Feisal on the throne of Iraq before a largely ambivalent population. This was not an easy task as there 'was no Iraqi equivalent of the Sharif of Mecca; the nearest parallels being the Naquibs (keepers of the shrine in Baghdad and Basra).'[36] Moreover, the situation was further complicated by Sayyid Talib's continued desire to resist Hashemite rule in Mesopotamia, despite the findings of the Cairo Conference. He was a powerful local figurehead who had a secure power base in Baghdad and had some support from British officials, such as Henry St John Philby, advisor to the Minster of the Interior. Upon returning to Baghdad, Cox got word that Talib had reached an agreement with the elderly Neguib of Baghdad, Saiyid Abdu Rahman, whereby 'the former would support the candidacy of the latter in return for a chance of succession.'[37] Interestingly, Rahaman had previously opted out of candidacy on the grounds of his age and because he had been 'talked around by Cox'.[38] Despite this, Talib toured the country proclaiming his slogan of 'Iraq for Iraqis' and British intelligence reported that Talib had been getting 'a magnificent reception everywhere'.[39] Rather than address the issue and upset the balance Churchill had created in the Middle East, Cox simply invited Talib for tea, and had him promptly arrested and deported to Ceylon. Cox's action upset several British Middle East officials including Philby, who complained but was quickly dismissed.[40] Churchill was simply pleased that his plan was moving forward.

Feisal, however, had not proved as malleable as Churchill had hoped. Feisal immediately sought full independence for Iraq, and argued that relations between the two countries should be defined by a formal treaty, rather than informal British rule. Feisal was in a difficult position because on the one hand he had to seem independent of Britain in order to win the support of his subjects, and on the other hand, he had to remain true to British interests so as not to alienate the very power that put him on the throne. Churchill was unimpressed by Feisal's more independent position and drafted a letter to him on 17 August 1922:

> I have learned with profound regret the course in which Your Majesty is resolved to preserve. It can only lead to the downfall of the hopes of cooperation between the British Government and the Sherfian family in pursuance of which we have with so much labour and expense facilitated Your Majesty's accession of the throne of Iraq. Having laboured so long to serve your interests and create for Your Majesty a stable throne and prosperous country I cannot view without sorrow the return which the exertions and sacrifices of Britain have received.[41]

Churchill decided ultimately against sending the letter as he realized it would only exacerbate the situation. However, Churchill's desire to use his personal influence with Feisal and appeal to his sense of honour was evident in the draft, as was Churchill's frustration. Churchill concluded the draft, threatening to withdraw from Iraq completely and asking whether Feisal and his government were 'prepared to assume sole and unaided responsibility for the Government of the country'. Churchill then wrote to Lloyd George venting his frustration: 'Feisal is playing a very low and treacherous game with us.'[42] Churchill further aired his frustration a few days later in a Cabinet meeting:

> King Feisal had been making great difficulties and confusing the situation in Iraq. He had made objections to the Mandate but had stated his willingness to agree to a treaty. He was not, however, prepared to recognise the mandatory basis as he thought the mandatory system was a slur on Iraq. No argument had been of any effect on him. He had recently taken up the Extremists who now regard him as their patron.[43]

In subsequent letters after the Cabinet meeting, Churchill's position became clear. He told Lloyd George, Feisal should be given an 'ultimatum; if it were not accepted' Britain should 'clear out'.[44] This further reinforced Churchill's commitment to lower expenditure, as he was willing to allow his entire solution for the Middle East to collapse and retreat from the Middle East in order to stop the considerable expense if Feisal refused to play the part Churchill assigned him. However, Cox was able to negotiate Feisal towards a friendly solution and the Anglo-Iraqi treaty was signed in October 1922. The Mandatory system continued in Iraq until 1932 and Feisal's descendants remained on the throne until 1958.[45]

Kurdistan

Another peculiar issue in Churchill's Sherifian solution for the Middle East is the absence of Kurdistan. This was one of the great failures of Churchill's policy as Kurdistan was lost to a combination of departmental rivalries and *realpolitik*. At the Cairo Conference, Churchill, T.E. Lawrence, Hubert Young, and Major Noel all agreed that 'a Kurdish State ought to be set up without delay'.[46] In Churchill's mind, Kurdistan would act as a buffer state for Mesopotamia against Kemalist Turkey and Bolshevik Russia, and this was reflected in the official minutes of the meeting:

> We are strongly of the opinion that purely Kurdish areas should not be included in the Arab state of Mesopotamia, but that principles of Kurdish unity and nationality should be promoted as far as possible by H.M.G. The extent of the area within it will be possible for H.M.G. to carry out this policy must necessarily depend upon the final terms of peace with Turkey.[47]

Beyond Churchill's strategic buffer-state reasoning, there were other reasons why he thought it best to pursue a policy of a separate Kurdistan. The first, suggested by Major Noel, was that besides working as a buffer from 'Turkish pressure from without', Kurdistan would help regulate any 'Iraqi anti-British movements from within'.[48] This would be reinforced by including the proposed Kurdistan under the jurisdiction of the Mesopotamian, British High Commissioner and thus, under similar air-control structures as Iraq. The second was that Churchill was fearful that the future ruler of Mesopotamia would 'ignore Kurdish sentiment and oppress the

Kurdish minority'. Churchill's intention throughout the Kurdistan debate was to create a situation in which the rights of the Kurdish minority were protected. His letter to Cox on 9 June 1921 reflected this notion, saying that 'so long as British officials form the only link between the two countries [the British High Commissioner] shall be in a strong position to deal with any future Arab ruler whose advisers may persuade him to attempt to interfere in Kurdish affairs.'[49]

However, Cox and Gertrude Bell were opposed to the idea of an independent Kurdistan. Cox's position was that the heavily Kurdish, northern districts of Kirkuk, Sulaimaniya, and parts of Mosul were integral to Iraq and should be incorporated into the new Hashemite kingdom. Cox was more inclined to keep a larger Iraq, for two reasons. The first, like Churchill's, was strategic. He believed that Iraq alone could act as the buffer state against Kemalist Turkey and that any deal offered to the Kurdish leaders would have to be 'more attractive than any alternative that the Turks might offer and must be broad enough to satisfy the more ambitious Kurdish nationalists.'[50] Moreover, the northern parts of the proposed Kurdish state were not even under Cox's authority, as the Turks were contesting the region in the mountains between the two Zab Rivers west of Arbil. The second reason was perhaps more political, if not religious. Cox had reported the situation to Feisal and explained that Churchill wanted to remove the northern districts to create Kurdistan. Cox recorded Feisal's response:

> The question of Kurdistan had a further aspect for him as King of Iraq which had probably not been fully considered by us. This was the question of preponderance of Sunnis or Shias with special reference to the question of constitutional (Assembly) shortly to be convoked. As we were aware there was already technical and numerical preponderance of Shiahs and excision of a large slice of Sunni districts of Iraq out of state and exclusion of their representation from National Assembly would place Shiahs in a very strong position and fill [Feisal] with misgiving.[51]

Feisal then offered a solution that he had learned under Ottoman rule: the Ottoman *millet* system that 'allowed for non-groups to live as self regulating communities under Arab law'[52] and was very similar to the approach Abdullah would take with the Jewish settlers in Palestine prior to World War II. Feisal suggested that,

> As long as [the Kurds] were assured of being administered by Kurdish officials [...] rather than resort to the possible alternative of becoming part of a mandated State under the control of some European State Senate they would prefer to be nominally under the rule of a Muhammadan King.[53]

Feisal's interpretation of the matter offered two points of insight into the situation. The first is that Feisal had unwittingly challenged his already faltering relationship with Churchill by reinforcing Cox against Churchill's design for the region. This move reflected Feisal's desire to appear independent. The second point is that Feisal highlighted one of the essential flaws of the Serifian solution for the Middle East: it placed a Sunni king on a Shia throne. Churchill, however, had more difficulty coming to grips with the subtleties of Islamic doctrine. Moreover, Feisal's argument was reinforced by the notion that if Kurdistan remained independent and was understood to be a purely British dependency, this would increase the Turk's 'ability to use Islamic propaganda against the British'.[54] Such a situation was anathema to Churchill who was increasingly desperate to find tenable terms with Turkey and reduce British expenditure. In any case, Feisal's position on the matter, combined with the Turkish challenge of the northern-most regions, forced Churchill to reconsider his position on the Kurdish state.

Meanwhile, as a sort of cunning bluff, Cox proposed to Churchill that if he intended to support an independent Kurdistan, then perhaps British policy should aid the Kurdish rebellion against the Turks in support of the Greeks.[55] Cox postulated that such an action would only offend 'kaliphate fanatics' in India and that while the Iraqis would 'not like the idea of supporting the Greeks against the Turks', after the successful conclusion of the Kurdish rebellion, the more 'farsighted among the Arabs could be induced to accept it.'[56] Churchill understood Cox's point. In his reply, Churchill forbade Feisal from entering into any kind of negotiation with the Turks as 'negotiations were already in train with a view to a general peace with Turkey.' Churchill concluded, 'I deprecate any attempt at the present moment to encourage the Kurds.'[57]

Churchill's change of mind represented the death of an independent Kurdistan. While, the change of policy denoted a departmental and diplomatic victory for Cox, Churchill's reconsideration was understandable. Churchill's desire for economies in the Middle East overrode all other considerations, and the quickest means to this end was to reach terms with nationalist Turkey. Secondly, Cox's telegram of 28 October illustrated to Churchill the larger issues of his Kurdish policy. While Lloyd George would have undoubtedly leapt at Cox's notion of support for the Kurds (and thus the Greeks), Churchill believed the quickest way to create peace was to pacify the Islamic world, which in his mind meant peace with Turkey, the former seat of the caliphate. Churchill's Victorian view of Turkey as a special seat of power in the Islamic world led him to believe that any further notion that Britain supported the Christian Greek against the Islamic Turks would result in the Middle East exploding in unrest. Cox's letter certainly brought this to the fore in Churchill's mind when he mentioned the 'kaliphate fanatics' in India and the reluctance of the Iraqis to fall in line with such a policy. In this way, Churchill chose to pursue the long game of supporting Islamic and Turkish opinion as his desire 'for peace with Turkey [. . .] subordinated Kurdish policy.'[58]

Palestine

Palestine was not really discussed at the Cairo Conference beyond the need for economies, air control, and formal borders. It was in the last instance that a major concession was made for the Arabs. The eastern boundary of Palestine, and the western boundary of Abdullah's future kingdom, was marked along the River Jordan because it was 'a clear and natural demarcation line.'[59] This meant that everything east of the river was in Arab-controlled Transjordan, and was therefore outside the remit of the Balfour Declaration. This also meant that the area of Palestine that was subject to the Balfour Declaration had been almost halved. This change aroused much resentment from Chaim Weizmann, the Zionist representative who unsuccessfully appealed to Churchill not to alter the mandate of Palestine. This appeal was formally made in the Cairo Conference by Herbert Samuel, where Churchill and Lawrence 'out argued and out manoeuvred' Samuel and ultimately overruled him.[60] In fact, it has been pointed out that, 'the Zionists were to be the first ones sacrificed in the cause of Abdullah's desert fiefdom.'[61] In exchange for this, Abdullah promised his support for the Jews.[62] Despite this massive alteration of Palestinian borders, Britain had committed itself to Zionism and to making a national home for the Jews in Palestine, as expressed in the Balfour Declaration. Churchill's challenge then was to balance the pledges of the British Empire with making deep reductions in expenditure.

After the conference had ended in Cairo, Churchill went to Jerusalem, where he met Abdullah, and then an Arab delegation from Haifa, first on 28 March 1921. The Arab delegation asked for a halt to Jewish immigration and requested 'the establishment in our country of a native government similar to those established in other countries.'[63] This implied that to allow the Jews a national home in Palestine was a negation of the British pledges made in the McMahon–Hussein correspondence. This point, in particular, offers insight into the nature of the Arab demands and Churchill's thinking on Palestine, and the position in which the Palestinian Arabs found themselves. It is significant that 'not before 1921 were accusations of betrayal and double dealing hurled against Britain.'[64] Moreover, this line of argument was first introduced officially by Amir Feisal himself in January of 1921 at an interview with the Foreign Office.[65] After being removed from Damascus by the French it was a logical, though unfounded, argument for Feisal to make in order to procure more of the region for himself and to use the Arab frustration to further his ambition. This ideological move away from a Damascus-centred pan-Arabism to a Palestinian Arabism centred in Jerusalem was common among many Arab intellectuals such as Mohammad Amin al-Husayni, the future (and especially problematic for the British) Grand Mufti of Jerusalem.[66]

However, King Hussein and Amir Feisal's own accounts repudiate the notion of 'double dealing'. King Hussein repeatedly gave consent for a Jewish national home in Palestine and even published an article in *al-Qibla,* his official published representation, which argued that Palestine was 'a sacred and beloved homeland [...] of its original sons (*abna'ihil-l-asliyim*) – the Jews'. Furthermore, the article added that it would be difficult for native Palestinians to develop 'the virgin soil' but that Jewish immigrants would develop Palestine as:

> Experience has proved their [the Jews] capacity to succeed in their energies and their labours [...] The return of these exiles (*jaliya*) to their homeland will prove materially and spiritually an experimental school for their [Arab] brethren [...] in the fields, factories, and trades.[67]

Amir Feisal echoed these sentiments at the Versailles Peace Conference in 1919 when he discussed the matter with Weizmann, who recorded that 'Feisal appeared well disposed to a Zionist presence in Palestine.' However, Feisal did warn that he had to be careful of Arab opinion.[68] This proves that at least in principle Feisal was 'prepared to give Zionism a free hand in Palestine.'[69]

Churchill's position was similar to the British official position, which was that Palestine was left outside the McMahon–Hussein pledges. (Curzon was the only senior member of the British government at the time who believed that the Balfour Declaration clashed with the pledges of McMahon.) Churchill's belief was reinforced by two things. The first was a statement from McMahon, which argued that it was always his intention that Palestine should be excluded from the Arab states.[70] Though McMahon's statement was published after the Jerusalem meeting in 1921, it clearly demonstrated the official British position. The second was that, in Churchill's mind, the Palestinian Arabs had fought *with* the Ottoman

Empire *against* the British, unlike their Arab cousins elsewhere in the Middle East. While the reality of the situation was that the Bedouins fought for the Ottomans in the same if not greater numbers than the Palestinian Arabs, this did not fit into the British narrative of 'Middle Eastern' states being oppressed by the despotic Ottomans.[71] As it relates to Palestine, Churchill was happy to pragmatically adopt Lloyd George's anti-Ottoman narrative since it was more convenient to cast the Palestinian Arabs as enemies who found themselves on the losing side. By casting them in with the defeated and deposed Ottomans, this would, in Churchill's mind, bar them from any pledges of the McMahon–Hussein correspondence. Churchill made this abundantly clear during his testimony at the Royal Palestine Commission (Peel Commission) in 1937. When Sir Harold Morris asked, 'What makes you say we conquered the Arabs? I thought they were our allies?' Churchill retorted, 'The actual inhabitants, the Palestinian Arabs, were making their quota in the Turkish Army. The Arabs from the Hedjaz were our allies.' Dismayed, Morris quipped back that they were forced to fight with the Turks and that eventually 'they came in and fought with us'. Churchill dryly replied, 'Not the Palestinian Arabs.'[72] Churchill repeatedly returned to this notion of Palestinian separateness throughout his career.[73]

Another facet of Churchill's belief in Palestinian separateness was his Victorian notion that the Palestinians were somehow culturally less valuable than the other parts of the Islamic world. The Palestinian Arabs were different from the Bedouin Arabs romanticized by Wilfrid Blunt and T.E. Lawrence, the two men who did most to help shape Churchill's thinking on the Islamic world. Both men heavily disliked Palestinian Arabs. Blunt, like Lawrence, believed the Palestinians 'were as monkeys and the Bedouin Arabs were Lions.'[74] Lawrence even characterized the Palestinian Arabs as 'stupid, materialistic, and bankrupt'.[75] This notion of the Palestinian Arabs as degraded Arabs or 'Levantines, of mixed race and questionable character' had been present in British Intelligence since World War I. In 1918, the head of the military administration in Palestine, Gilbert Clayton, wrote to Gertrude Bell saying, 'The so-called Arabs of Palestine are not to be compared with the real Arabs of the desert or even of other civilized districts in Syria or Mesopotamia.'[76] Interestingly, Chaim Weizmann recorded that this notion was even echoed by Feisal who was 'contemptuous of the Palestinian Arabs' and that he 'doesn't even regard them as Arabs'.[77]

Undoubtedly armed by these opinions, Churchill constructed a cultural hierarchy of Islamic culture similar to the one he imagined during his trip to Africa. At the top of his hierarchy were Bedouin Arabs, romanticized as a sort of 'noble savage' or 'warrior king' in the Victorian mindset, who contributed to the advancement of civilization and its ideals. This characterization was largely based on the travel writing of Charles Doughty, Wilfrid S. Blunt, and T.E. Lawrence. Beneath the Bedouins, were Middle Eastern merchants, and under them were Middle Eastern farmers, or *fellaheen,* who would have had the same 'cultural value' as Islamic peasants in India. At the bottom of Churchill's Islamic cultural hierarchy were the mountain tribesmen on the north-west frontier, and the Islamic Dervishes. These groups made up the bottom of the hierarchy partially because Churchill saw them as highly uncivilized, but also because they made themselves enemies of the British Empire, which in Churchill's mind was the pinnacle of progression and civilization. The Palestinian Arabs started as *fellaheen* on Churchill's scale, which put them at a disadvantage as he believed that *fellaheen* cultivation techniques were obsolete and unproductive. This only reinforced the idea that they were somehow weaker or inferior compared with the idealized Bedouin Arabs in Iraq and elsewhere in the Middle East. This perceived inferiority was obvious in Churchill's testimony to the Peel Commission when he argued that the injustice in Palestine was that 'those who lived in the country left it to be a desert for a thousand years' and 'you have seen the terraces which used to be cultivated, which under Arab rule have remained desert.'[78] In Churchill's opinion, their seemingly constant rebellions in addition to their alliance with the Ottomans in World War I also lowered their 'cultural value' in his eyes and would have made them enemies of the Empire.

It is no surprise, then, that Churchill's response to the Arab delegation in Jerusalem was fairly dismissive when he remarked: 'You ask me to repudiate the Balfour Declaration and to stop immigration. It is not in my power and it is not my wish to do this.' Churchill then seemingly acknowledged the argument of a betrayal of the McMahon–Hussein pledges by arguing:

> The British Government passed its word, through Mr. Balfour, that it would view with favour the creation of a national home that involved immigration and it has been ratified by the Allied powers, the victors in the great war [. . .] Our position is one of trust but our conquest makes it a position of right, your statements sound as if you over threw the Turks; this is not so.

The final part of that sentence implied that the Palestinian Arabs were not the victors, as they were allied with the Ottomans and were thus subject to British terms. Churchill then rationalized that Palestinian Arabs and Jews both benefit from the Zionist enterprise. He argued that:

> We think [the Jewish national home] will be good for the world, good for the Jews and good for the British Empire, but also good for the Arabs who dwell in Palestine and we intend it to be so; they shall not be supplanted nor shall they suffer but they shall share in the benefits of Zionism [. . .] If a national home is established in Palestine [. . .] it can only be by a process which [. . .] wins its way on its own merits and carries increasing benefits, prosperity, and happiness to the people of the country as a whole [. . .] [The Zionists'] success will bring general prosperity and wealth to all Palestinians [. . .] Instead of sharing in miseries through quarrelling Palestinians should share blessings through cooperation.[79]

Churchill's genuine belief that the Jews and Arabs would work together to better Palestine seems strange and incredible given the current instability in the Middle East. However, in 1921 Churchill's theory of co-operation was perfectly logical given that the Hashemites gave their consent (and blessing in King Hussein's case) for the Zionists to make a national home in Palestine. Churchill's belief in the co-operation between the two races was also evident in his testimony at the Peel Commission, when he defended his position arguing there would be 'wealth and work for everybody' and that 'we want these races to live together and to minister to their well being', which would 'be greatly enhanced if they did not quarrel'.[80]

However, some historians have disparaged this notion. For instance, Michael Cohen argued that Churchill 'adopted an arrogant and scolding tone' with the Arab delegation, and that Churchill's insistence that the Jews should accept the Arabs because it would benefit them as well, was little more than some kind of paternal imperialism and was akin to Churchill 'explaining the benefits of white civilization at the African natives.'[81] Yet while Churchill's preference was almost certainly for the Jews over the Palestinian Arabs, as he considered the Jews a more 'civilizing' force, he would not have been disdainful. Cohen concluded that 'the general consensus' was that 'Churchill's blunt remarks to the Arabs were insensitive and self defeating.'[82] Cohen's evidence, however, relied on statements from Mohamed Osman, a Palestinian Arab (who was far from unbiased) and British Intelligence officer C.D. Burton, who Col. Meinertzhagen described as 'a notorious anti-Zionist'.[83] Yet despite the biased or unbiased nature of Osman and Burton's statements, their opinions taken together hardly constitute 'a general consensus.'

Cohen's criticism seems anachronistic and, in the case of the 'general consensus', unproven. While Churchill was something of a progressive Victorian, he was still a Victorian and subject to the prejudices of Victorian England. He believed in the benefit of 'white civilization' and it is unfair to hold his positions to the standards of today. Moreover, the second part of Churchill's remarks dealt almost exclusively with the second portion of the Balfour Declaration, which espoused the protection of the rights of the native population of Palestine. While Churchill's next remarks were somewhat patronizing they still seem to contradict the notion he had a 'scolding' tone:

> I draw your attention to the second part of the declaration which emphasises the sacredness of your civil and religious rights [. . .] It is vital to you and you should hold it and claim it firmly, if one promise stands so does the other [. . .] The establishment of a national home does not mean a Jewish Government to dominate the Arabs. The British Government is the greatest Moslem State in the world, it is well disposed to the Arabs and cherishes their friendship.[84]

Protection of Arab rights, coupled with Jewish and Arab co-operation, were further emphasized when Churchill addressed the Zionist delegation on the same day. He told them that the process of creating a Jewish national home 'must be without prejudice or unfairness to the existing Arab and Christian inhabitants' and that he was convinced the Zionist cause would be 'good for the whole world and the Jewish people' and would 'bring welfare and advancement to the Arab population of this country [Palestine]'. Churchill even alluded to the 'alarm felt by the Arabs that they will be dispossessed by their lands' and the Arab (and Churchill's own) fear of the 'Bolshevik character of some of the Jewish immigrants'. Churchill concluded his remarks by saying: 'I hope that in a few years there will be a greater feeling of well-being and unity among Palestinians and that Arab fears will prove to be unfounded.'[85]

Despite Churchill's public position on the Arabs, it must be noted that at the Peel Commission, Churchill gave evidence that did indicate that he was contemptuous of the Islamic world as a whole. In fact, Churchill requested that his evidence not be published as it was so controversial. He said: 'I have a great regard for the Arabs but at the same time, where the Arab goes is often desert.' When questioned on the ability of the Arabs to create civilization, such as in Spain, Churchill simply responded, 'I am glad they were thrown out.' He went on to argue: 'When the Mohammedan upset occurred in world history and the great hordes of Islam swept over these places they broke it all up; smashed it all up.' But perhaps the most damning and most revealing statement was Churchill's comparison of the Native American Indians to Palestinian Arabs (not the Arabs in general). After being asked by the Commission chairman if it was morally wrong 'to keep downing the Arabs [. . .] when all they want is to remain in their own country', Churchill proclaimed:

> I do not admit that the dog in the manger has the final right to the manger, though he may have lain there for a very long time [. . .] I do not admit for instance that a great wrong has been done to the Red Indians of America or the black people of Australia. I do not admit that a wrong has been to those people by the fact that a stronger race, a higher grade race or. . . a more worldly wise race. . . has come in and taken their place. I do not admit it. . . I do not think the Red Indians had any right to say 'the American continent belongs to us'.[86]

Journalists and historians have used these passages to justify the idea that Churchill was contemptuous of the entire Islamic world.[87] There are often comparisons of Churchill's attitude with other 'typical British Arabists' who, 'developed a somewhat paternalistic, if not actually contemptuous opinion of Arabs'.[88] It has been rightly stated that Churchill relied heavily on his Middle Eastern experts and might therefore share the same opinion; however, this fails to take into account Churchill's past experiences with Arabs and other Islamic peoples, such as the Muslims with whom Churchill had served and played polo on the north-west frontier, and that he would, therefore, be predisposed to make unique judgments based on his own experience. While Churchill did criticize Muslim historical movements, his barbs are relatively tame compared to the statements on the Palestinian Arabs. However, these statements were products of the turbulent context of massive Arab unrest surrounding the Peel Commission during the 1930s, which frustrated Churchill. Moreover, Churchill's comparison to Native Americans revealed a position based more on the advancement of civilization than hatred of another race. For Churchill, the progression of civilization was the most important function of a state, and the best example of this progression manifested itself as the British Empire.

After Churchill returned to London, Herbert Samuel was left in Palestine to deal with the increasingly recalcitrant Arab protests. As things deteriorated in Palestine and the Middle East in general, owing to anti-Turkish policies, Churchill suggested to Lloyd George the desirability of 'quitting the two countries [Palestine and Mesopotamia] at the earliest possible moment.'[89] This was due to Churchill's fear that the cost of continuing the British role in the Middle East was unsustainable as long as Lloyd George pursued his resolute pro-Greek agenda. However, Lloyd George dismissed Churchill's worries and the British mission in the Middle East continued. Since Britain was committed to Palestine, Herbert Samuel appointed Mohammad Amin al-Husayni as Grand Mufti of Jerusalem and created a Supreme Muslim Council to help calm the Palestinian Arabs. However, this proved a disastrous decision as al-Husayni continued to pursue anti-British, pan-Arabist ends, including intensifying the protests and riots. In May, Samuel made another concession to the Arabs by suspending Jewish immigration. This also backfired, as the Arabs saw the suspension as a vindication of their behaviour thus reinforcing the notion that increased violence produced their desired political ends. Ismar Elbogen eloquently described the situation: 'The British administration had nurtured an adder in its bosom.'[90]

Once news reached Churchill, he immediately wrote to Samuel and urged him to 'do whatever is necessary to bring to justice persons guilty of murderous violence.'[91] On 14 May Churchill wrote again saying that he 'approved of Samuel's actions', which included pursuing the guilty parties but also included Samuel's concessions such as the creation of a non-representative Muslim Council. Moreover, Churchill did not discard the possibility that such a council could become representative, but he could not answer that definitively 'off hand'. Churchill concluded by saying that the timing of such concessions were important because 'to make such a concession under pressure is to rob it of half its value', and that concessions should be made 'on their merits and not under duress'.[92] Samuel, still eager to win favour with the Arabs, wanted to announce that there would be a representative Christian–Muslim committee, which had the same responsibilities as those of the Jewish committee during his speech to the Palestinian mandate goverment planned on 3 June. However, Middle East Department officials such as Shuckburgh and Major Young thought it was a mistake to do this because it would 'crystallize the communal distinction between Jews and Arabs'.[93] Churchill approved of this position, as he firmly believed in the co-operation of the Jewish and Arab elements in Palestine, and Samuel was forced to leave that part out of his speech.

Two days later, Churchill wrote to Samuel to explain why he did not allow him to publicly make such a policy concession to the Arabs:

> I am certainly in no way opposed to the step by step establishment of elective institutions or *any measures* which you may take to secure constant and effective representation of non-Jewish opinion. I am willing to receive proposals from you on the subject at any time. I did not think, however, that the best moment for making such a concession was on the morrow of the Jaffa riots.[94]

This revealed that Churchill was increasingly open to such representative organizations for Muslims. He made it clearer to John Shuckburgh in a letter on 15 June, stating: 'I am strongly in favour of introduction of representative institutions in Palestine and I consider it impossible to deny them to a country while little backwards places like Trans-Jordan are given them.' Churchill then relayed his position that as long as the 'elective institutions provided for the execution of our pledges to the Zionists' and immigration was '*ultra vires*' then an agreement would be 'reinforced by leading Arabs as to the proportion of Jews to be admitted.'[95] These exchanges further establish Churchill's hope for Palestinian co-operation and his genuine desire to work with the Arabs while fulfilling the Balfour Declaration.

Churchill's position was also evident in a meeting with Chaim Weizmann, Lloyd George, and Balfour in July. Weizmann visited London to protest Samuel's concessions to the Arabs and demonstrate his concern that Britain might quit Palestine and thus the Balfour

Plate 1 This photo is believed to be Winston Churchill playing polo against an Indian team which may have been 'The Turbaned Warriors' which Churchill referred to in his letter home on 12 November 1896. (Source: Churchill Archives Centre, The Broadwater Collection).

Plate 2 Winston Churchill standing between the Ottoman leaders, Mehmed Talaat Pasha (on the left) and Mehmed Djavid Bey (on the right) during his holiday in the Eastern Mediterranean in the summer of 1910. (Source: Churchill Archives Centre, The Broadwater Collection).

Plate 3 Winston Churchill and Ottoman guards on an armed escort 'against brigands' for a British train on the Aydin Railway in Turkey during the summer of 1910. Churchill later wrote to Sir Edward Grey that that his party traveled the whole length of the railway from Smyrna to the interior of the country. (Source: Churchill Archives Centre, The Broadwater Collection).

Plate 4 On 20 March 1920, after the Cairo Conference, Churchill, Clementine, T.E. Lawrence and Gertrude Bell visited the Pyramids and Churchill spent part of the day painting them. (Source: Churchill Archives Centre, The Broadwater Collection).

Plate 5 Winston Churchill with T.E. Lawrence and Emir Abdullah (who was to become King of Jordan) at the Government House in Jerusalem. (Source: Churchill Archives Centre, The Broadwater Collection).

Plate 6 Winston Churchill shares some food and drink from his picnic with a young Moroccan man during a visit to Marrakesh in January 1936. (Source: Churchill Archives Centre, The Broadwater Collection).

Plate 7 Winston Churchill with Punjab Prime Minister, Sir Sikander Hyatt Khan in Cairo, 1942. (Source: Churchill Archives Centre, The Broadwater Collection).

Plate 8 Winston Churchill on the steps of the British embassy in Cairo in December 1943. He is standing next to Lady Killearn and behind him is his daughter Sarah. Nahas Pasha (the Egyptian Prime Minister) and Hussein Pasha (the Chief Chamberlain to the King of Egypt) also appear in this picture. (Source: Churchill Archives Centre, The Broadwater Collection).

Plate 9 Winston Churchill salutes at a passing Sherman tank while visiting his old Regiment, the 4th Hussars in December 1943. With him are his son Randolph Churchill, his daughter Sarah and Lieutenant General Stone. (Source: Churchill Archives Centre, The Broadwater Collection).

Plate 10 In the absence of Winston Churchill, Mrs. Churchill receives a sword presented by the Emir Faisal amd the Emir Khalid on behalf of King Ibn Saud in June 1943. (Source: Churchill Archives Centre, The Broadwater Collection).

Plate 11 Winston Churchill with King Abd al-'Aziz Ibn Saud of Saudi Arabia at Auberge due Lac, Fayoum, in February 1945. (Source: Churchill Archives Centre, The Broadwater Collection).

Plate 12 Winston Churchill's famous 'Let Us Go Forward Together' poster in Arabic. (Source: Australian War memorial, Canberra, Australia).

Plate 13 A Persian man gives the 'V' sign. This photo was sent to Winston Churchill by Major-General Robert Cotton Money, G.O.C. Balochistan. (Source: Churchill Archives Centre, The Broadwater Collection).

Plate 14 Winston Churchill inspecting the Guard of Honour in Tinerhir, Morocco, January 1951. (Source: Churchill Archives Centre, The Clementine Churchill Papers).

Declaration. At a meeting at Balfour's house, Weizmann made the case that 'the Balfour Declaration meant that a Jewish majority should develop in Palestine, leading to an eventual Jewish state' and that Samuel's concessions to the Arabs would never allow for that eventuality. Churchill demurred as his interpretation of the Balfour Declaration called for a Jewish national home in Palestine, not a Jewish state. Both Lloyd George and Balfour agreed with Weizmann's reading of the Balfour Declaration. Churchill found himself alone, on the defensive, and 'astonished' at his colleagues' interpretation.[96] Recalling his telegram to Shuckburgh, Churchill argued that the Colonial Office was contemplating self-government for Palestine in the same spirit that had been adopted in Mesopotamia and Transjordan. Weizmann responded that, 'you will not convince me self government has been given to these two lands because you think it right, it has only been done because you must. The representative character of the governments of Mesopotamia and Trans Jordan are a mere farce.' Weizmann then challenged Churchill by asking: 'Why don't you then give representative government to Egypt? [. . .] Is it because you don't want to abandon Egypt, and you don't really care what happens to Palestine?' By forcing Churchill to examine the hypocrisy of his position by challenging his devotion to the British Empire, Weizmann won out. Churchill left, but not before Lloyd George told him, 'You mustn't give representative government to Palestine.'[97] Though Churchill was defeated, his aspiration for a representative government for Arabs and Jews was clear in his dissension from his colleagues.

On 12 August the Palestinian Arab delegation met with Churchill in London and continued to take a defiant position. They again argued in favour of repealing the Balfour Declaration and asked for an elective government composed of the 'natives of Palestine who lived in the country before the war.'[98] Churchill still refused to alter the Balfour Declaration and, in the light of his discussion with Weizmann, added in a conciliatory tone: 'The matter is binding on me as well as you.'[99] After a lengthy and futile discussion in which Churchill reminded the Arabs that the British policy had 'safeguards for Moslems and clauses for Jews' and that the Arabs should 'give the

Jews their chance', he advised the Arab delegation to see Weizmann and to come to an arrangement with him.[100] The delegation refused on the grounds that they did not recognize the Zionist cause and consequently did not recognize Weizmann as its spokesman.

As the situation in Palestine deteriorated, Churchill clung 'to the chimera that the Arabs and Jews should sort out matters by themselves.'[101] In fact, Churchill began to retreat from the matter entirely. Col. Meinertzhagen noted in his diary that Churchill 'does not care two pins and does not want to be bothered about it [...] He is too wrapped up in home politics.'[102] Churchill's attitude in this has been characterized as one of 'outer optimism and inner pessimism' that created an atmosphere of indecisiveness that left the Colonial Office 'unable to present a coherent and well worked out position.'[103] This was true, as Churchill realized that any position that favoured the Zionists would enrage the Arabs, which in turn would complicate matters in Middle Eastern affairs by stirring up hostilities with the Turks and costing huge quantities of money. Churchill revealed his ambivalence twice in November by failing to make an appearance at joint Jewish and Arab delegation meetings in which he was meant to give firm policy statements. Each time he cited health problems. As the policy regarding Palestine was adrift, the Colonial Office continued to steer it back on course and eventually settled on Major Young's plan, which had four basic principles: 1) British policy in Palestine would continue to be based on the Balfour Declaration; 2) the rights of the present inhabitants would be protected; 3) Jewish immigration would be permitted up to the absorptive capacity of the country; 4) a legislative council would be established.[104] These principles came to be the backbone of Churchill's 1922 'White Paper on Palestine'.

However, before it became official Churchill tried to find a middle ground between the Zionists and Palestinian Arabs. In March 1922 he made further concessions to the Palestinian Arab delegation, accepting Samuel's decision to limit Jewish immigration into Palestine. He then explained his constraints to the House of Commons in July stating that 'he had decided to go to the utmost possible lengths to give the Arabs representative institutions, without getting into a position where he could not fulfill the pledges the government was committed to.' He also reminded the House that while there was a pledge to the Zionists, 'an equally important promise was made to the Arab inhabitants of Palestine – that their civil and religious rights would be effectively safeguarded and that they should not be turned out to make room for new comers.'[105] This demonstrated Churchill's interpretation of the Balfour Declaration as creating a Jewish national home in Palestine and not a Jewish state, at least initially. However, despite these concessions, the Arab delegation rejected Churchill's white paper.

While Churchill had been at the Colonial Office, Palestine had been a thorn in his side. He tried to solve the situation in the 'Churchillian' fashion of finding a solid middle route that pleased both the Palestinian Arabs and the Zionists, but he found the Arabs too extreme in wanting a repudiation of British pledges, and the Zionists too eager to transform their position into a Jewish state. Churchill could not turn his back on the pledges of Balfour, as that would be tantamount to shirking one's duty and would, therefore, damage British prestige. In the same vein, despite political and ideological differences, the continued antagonism of Palestinian Arabs was likely to upset the precarious balance upon which Churchill's Middle Eastern solution rested. Complete concessions to either party were impossible and neither party, especially the Arabs, wanted to compromise. Frustrated and bewildered, Churchill walked away after his white paper was published. While this temporary solution sustained the status quo until the 1936 Arab riots, the inability to solve the problem in 1922 became a recurring problem for Churchill for years to come.

CHAPTER 6

THE TWENTIES AND THIRTIES

This chapter traces Churchill's career through the 1920s and 1930s and explores three episodes of his life. The first section examines how and why the Chanak Crisis altered Churchill's policies regarding the Middle East and the role of the British Empire in the region. The second section examines Churchill's interventionist Middle Eastern policies and attitudes as Chancellor of the Exchequer. The final section of the chapter is devoted to Churchill's often overlooked political alliance with Indian Muslims in the 1930s during his campaign to keep India firmly in the Empire. This section differentiates Churchill's views on Muslim Indians and Hindu Indians and reveals the origins of his prejudice concerning Hindus, and how this prejudice led him to an alliance with Indian Muslims.

The Chanak Crisis

While Churchill was busy at the Cairo Conference dealing with the former Ottoman territories, Mustapha Kemal (Atatürk) and the Turkish nationalists were continuing the war against Greece over Turkey's European lands, which the Treaty of Sèvres reserved for Greece. To enforce the treaty, the Greek army marched towards Angora (Ankara) and attempted to remove Atatürk's forces. Churchill still opposed the Treaty of Sèvres and protested Lloyd George's pro-Greek policy,[1] while Lloyd George 'began to become wary and suspicious of [Churchill's] ambition' and was more motivated against Churchill's cause in the Middle East.[2] In a draft letter to the Prime Minster on 22 February 1921, Churchill submitted a list of experts, including T.E. Lawrence, Percy Cox, and the Aga Khan, who all agreed that 'our Eastern and Middle Eastern affairs would be enormously eased and helped by arriving at a peace with Turkey.' Churchill went on to argue that the Greek forces could not end the war with a favourable conclusion. Then he reminded Lloyd George of the political consequences of his policy:

> The Turks will be thrown into the arms of the Bolsheviks; Mesopotamia will be disturbed at the critical period of the reduction of the army there [...] the general alienation of the Mohammedan sentiment from Great Britain will continue to work evil consequences in every direction [...] and we shall be everywhere represented as the chief enemy of Islam.[3]

Churchill had several allies against Lloyd George's pro-Greek policy. The Conservative Party was typically friendly Muslim aspirations and their interests in the Islamic world were 'dictated [by] susceptibility to Moslem sensibilities and the friendship with Turkey.'[4] Even Liberal members of the Coalition Cabinet supported Churchill's position. Edwin Montagu, who, according to Churchill, 'was for peace with Turkey on almost any terms', believed like Churchill that 'England should be the friend and head of the Moslem world; and above all Constantinople should be restored to the Turks.'[5] However, Lord Curzon and the Foreign Office typically sided with Lloyd George. As a result of the infighting, a coherent Cabinet policy towards Turkey was not created.

Meanwhile, the Greek offensive fizzled out in September 1921 when the Greek army was defeated at the Sakaria River. Much to Lloyd George's dismay, Greece agreed to the terms of the Turkish national government in Ankara, which included a Greek evacuation from Asia Minor. However, the Turkish government refused to acknowledge the Armistice until the terms were met by the reluctant

Greeks. According to Churchill, it was at this point that public opinion in Britain switched to violent opposition of the Turkish aspirations. He claimed that news of Turkish atrocities committed on Christians 'appeared daily'.[6] While this was probably hyperbole on Churchill's part, there were several reports of Turkish violence. The *Manchester Guardian* headline for 1 July 1922 was 'Atrocities in the Near East: Turks Worse than Greeks' and the headline for *The Times* on 27 September 1922 was 'Near East Crisis: Reported Massacre at Bigha, Christians beheaded or shot.'[7] The atrocities against the Armenians in the Caucasus and the continuing crimes against the Greeks in Anatolia became common knowledge and the shock of these massacres reverberated through the public, or so Churchill thought.

It was in this political climate in August 1922 that Atatürk reclaimed Smyrna and moved onward towards the Dardanelles. As his forces approached the Dardanelles in early September, they came across a British contingent of troops in occupation of Chanak, on the Gallipoli peninsula, under the command of General Harington. He was ordered by the Cabinet to deliver a harsh ultimatum to Atatürk, with the threat to open fire. He chose instead not to deliver the ultimatum and to keep a 'diplomatic stance and keep communications with Atatürk and the Turkish commanders in order to avoid military confrontation'.[8] Churchill wrote to Harington on 27 September and encouraged that Chanak be held as a defensive position but 'entirely approve[d] of all you are doing to avoid a conflict.'[9]

However, Lloyd George was resolved that 'a firm stand' was needed to illustrate the British position and 'would have a good effect on all Mohammedans'.[10] Despite wishing to avoid conflict, Churchill echoed that sentiment, fearing that: 'If the Turks take the Gallipoli peninsula and Constantinople, we shall have lost the whole fruits of our victory and another Balkan war would be inevitable.'[11] Churchill feared a loss of the strategic gains of World War I, including a fairly open path to the Middle East. He was also concerned with the effects it might have on the British Empire. He argued that losing their position in Turkey would be 'the greatest loss of prestige which could possibly be inflicted on the

British Empire'.[12] But Churchill was still careful to tread a middle line. While he was supporting Lloyd George's policy with Turkey, he did not want to divorce himself from the Muslim world. In a Cabinet meeting on 15 September, Churchill warned that 'there would be a grave danger if the British Government were isolated and depicted as the sole enemy of Islam.'[13] So he and Lloyd George decided to notify the dominions of the crisis, and released a provocative press communiqué the next day in order to keep the public informed. However, the press communiqué would ultimately have disastrous results for the Lloyd George government.

The communiqué stated that 'the allies being driven from Constantinople by the forces of Mustapha Kemal would be an event of the most disastrous character, producing no doubt far-reaching reactions throughout all Moslem countries, and not only through all Moslem countries, but throughout all the States defeated in the late war.'[14] Though the communiqué implied that France, the dominions, and the Balkan states were all as resolute as Lloyd George and Churchill to halt Atatürk's march, it was released to the public before the dominions actually received word of it. While it called for a peace conference with Turkey, its aggressive if not war-mongering tone alienated the British public who were still recovering from World War I. For instance, the *Daily Mail* headline was 'STOP THIS NEW WAR!'[15] Moreover, the communiqué completely misread the nature of Turkish national government, illustrating the larger flaws in Lloyd George's and Churchill's thinking. They assumed that Atatürk's government and aspirations were of an Islamic character, when in fact they were almost completely nationalist and divorced from political pan-Islamism.

This communiqué revealed that Churchill's previously pro-Turkish stance had completely evaporated and that he 'came to the rescue of Lloyd George's policy.'[16] This was the second time that Churchill had pursued a peaceful, pro-Turkish, pro-Muslim policy for the sake of the Empire only to change his mind at the last minute (the other being prior to World War I). The traditionally pro-Turkish Conservatives were alarmed by Churchill's switch. Lord Beaverbrook was 'astonished to find Churchill [...] in complete agreement with the Prime Minister's Near East Policy.'[17] Sir Maurice Hankey, Lloyd George's Cabinet Secretary, recorded in his diary on 27 September 1922 Churchill's transformation at a dinner with Lloyd George: We talked late into the night. Winston hitherto a strong Turko-phile had swung round at the threat of his beloved Dardanelles and become violently Turko-phobe and even phil-Hellenic. All the talk was of war.[18] After years of squabbling with Lloyd George, Churchill had agreed to take up his banner. He explained his relocation of loyalty in *World Crisis* (1929) saying:

> The reader is perhaps convinced that I tried my best to prevent this hateful and fearful situation from coming into being. But here it was. The resuscitated Turk was marching upon the Dardanelles and Constantinople and beyond them, Europe. I thought he ought to be stopped. If indeed, unhappily he reentered Europe it should be by Treaty, and not by violence [...] So having done my utmost for three years to procure a friendly peace with Mustapha Kemal and the withdrawal of the Greeks from Asia Minor, and having consistently opposed my friend the Prime Minister upon this issue, I now found myself whole-heartedly upon his side in resisting the consequences of the policy I had condemned.[19]

Churchill echoed these sentiments to Sir Archibald Sinclair, a future Liberal Party leader, in a letter after the crisis:

> Thank God that the awful pro-Greek policy against which we have so long inveighed has come to an end. We have paid an enormously heavy price for nothing. However, at the very end I had to throw my lot in with LG [Lloyd George] in order to try and make some sort of front against what would have otherwise been a Turkish walkover and the total loss of all the fruits of the Great War in this quarter.[20]

Churchill's *volte-face* was rather abrupt and oddly out of character for someone that Hankey and others described as a 'Turko-phile'. It is notable that a similar situation with Turkey at the outset of World War I caused Churchill to change his position. Hankey seemed to believe that Churchill changed his position partly for the fear of the strategic loss of position in Asia Minor against the Bolsheviks and the undoing of the 'fruits of the Great War', but primarily because Churchill was simply spoiling for a fight. He recounted in his diary that Churchill confessed to him after the crisis that 'he quite frankly regretted that the Turks had not attacked us at Chanak.'[21] This notion has been supported by Curzon and Charles Hardinge, a former viceroy and ambassador to France in 1922, who told Curzon that Churchill 'always advocates expeditions and military operations which end in failure.'[22] This was public sentiment as well. Writers such as A.A. Milne and E.M. Forster echoed the notion to the *Daily News* in October 1922 that Churchill and Lloyd George simply wanted a war in letters.[23] However, some historians have suggested that the communiqué was harsh and threatening in an attempt to reveal 'that the diplomacy [. . .] had force behind it' or, as Birkenhead put it, war 'could not be averted by peace.'[24] This, according to Inbal Rose, was 'viewed as a step toward peace, not war', which would allow Britain to 'negotiate from a position of strength.'[25]

The traditional school of thought tends to reject that idea and leans more toward the notion that 'the possibility of violent action exercised as irresistible fascination' for the former Lord of the Admiralty. It would then follow that perhaps Churchill saw a second chance to correct his failures at the Dardanelles and Gallipoli during World War I.[26] Perhaps it was personal. After all, Churchill felt personally betrayed by the former leader of Turkey, Enver Pasha, and suffered his greatest personal and military defeats at the hands of the Turkish army. For instance, David Walder concluded that Churchill's decision to join Lloyd George's cause was a personal one:

> Friendship? Loyalty? Duty? Something of all three, plus a zest, of which Lloyd George once complained, for military conflict [. . .] The possibility of a fight had roused again the Calvary subaltern never far below the surface of the statesman

> [. . .] The truculence and perniciousness that a later generation was to know were at once displayed. Lloyd George had found an ally.[27]

Another explanation is an orientalist one which argued that: 'There was a generally consistent and negative view of the Turks in British officialdom.'[28] This argument focuses on the almost racially motivated desire of some members of the British government, such as Lloyd George, to keep the Turks out of Europe. For instance, Gladstone's campaign in the late 1800s to drive the Turks from Europe and the tendency of British officials to see the situation in a medieval fashion of Christian crusaders fighting barbarous Muslims. This approach, however, cannot be strictly applied to Churchill who had previously been virtually uninterested in religious differences, very pro-Turk and whose father fought political battles against Gladstone. Therefore, to cast Churchill in such a generalization would be an historical misrepresentation.

However, there was another, more abstract reason for Churchill to change his mind: his fear of pan-Islamism. Churchill was clearly aware of implications for 'the largest Mohammaden power in the world' in the event of a pan-Islamic movement in the Middle East and India, and the communiqué that he and Lloyd George authored demonstrated their concern. After all, the Cabinet had been receiving reports from the violently anti-Turk High Commissioner of Constantinople, Sir Horace Rumbold, which stated that Atatürk's victory 'will have stimulated Moslems all over the world and have even raised the question of Islam versus Christianity'.[29] His warnings of pan-Islam did not stop there. He also painted a picture of the spectre that Churchill, Montagu, and Curzon had fought for years by arguing that Atatürk and the Turkish nationalists sought to: '[put] Turkey in a position of hegemony in a great Islamic combine. For these Great Britain not only is, but will remain the enemy. They desire nothing less than the collapse of our position, first in Mesopotamia, then in the East generally.'[30] Other intelligence reports reflected this concept but added a new and even more frightening aspect: Bolshevism. In fact, it had been reported that 'Bolshevik agents in Turkey [...] had been instructed to work solely on nationalist and pan-Islamic lines.'[31]

However, this British perception of impending pan-Islamic chaos caused by Turkish nationalists was a complete misunderstanding of Atatürk's intentions. While it was true that Atatürk developed diplomatic ties with Soviet Russia and that Turkish Unionist elements 'were promoting a pan-Islamic-Bolshevik alliance', Atatürk's 'policy could not be dignified by the term pan-Islamist, except in a degraded sense of the expression.'[32] This misconception led to Churchill and the rest of the Cabinet completely misunderstanding the nature of the Turkish national movement; Atatürk was far from being a pan-Islamist. Atatürk maintained a serious 'contempt for religion' and absolutely 'loathed primitive fanaticism.' For him 'Islam – and its leaders and holy men – were a 'poisonous dagger' pointed at Turkey.[33]

Atatürk's position on Islam was similar to Churchill's own. For Atatürk, the fanatical aspects were a 'poisonous dagger'; for Churchill they were the 'horn of a Rhinoceros or sting of a wasp.'[34] The fundamental and reccurring theme of Churchill's comments on the Islamic world were that any kind of political movement would use Islam as its weapon. This conception was informed by his experiences on the north-west frontier and Sudan. For Churchill, a purely nationalist movement could not happen in an Islamic region and so any political movement therein must take on some form of pan-Islamism or fanatical Islamic identity. Perhaps because Islam was regarded by many English policy makers as 'retro-grade and incapable of change, and that pan-Islamic or Mahdist uprisings were imminent'. Churchill had not yet moved beyond this type of 'pre-war thinking' and so like many European observers he was 'extremely slow to comprehend the challenge posed by nationalism.'[35] In cases where an Islamic identity was not present, such as the Turkish nationalist movement, Churchill, like several other members of the Cabinet, would try to find (or in the case of Rumbold, even create) pan-Islamic elements. So, in this way, it is correct to attach Churchill to the rest of the Cabinet. Moreover, it is reasonable to assume that this weighed heavily in Churchill's understanding of the Chanak Crisis and thus offers additional ground for Churchill's change of mind.

Whatever the reason, Churchill did change his mind and stand with Lloyd George and it paid off, at first. Atatürk, fearing 'what Lloyd George and Churchill in their recklessness might do' agreed to postpone 'Turkey's occupation of some of the territories she was eventually to occupy.'[36] Atatürk and the Allies agreed to negotiations, eventually resulting in the Treaty of Lausanne (1923), which undid the harsh and unfavourable terms of the Treaty of Sèvres and 're-established the Turk at Constantinople', giving Turkey control over the Straits and most of Eastern Thrace.[37] Atatürk, much to Churchill's surprise, worked to reform Turkey into a more secular Westernized nation. Years later, Churchill even regarded Atatürk as a 'Warrior Prince' and spoke of his quality as a military tactician.[38] These and other praises induced T.E. Lawrence to comment to Churchill upon reading *World Crisis* that he 'was glad to see [Churchill] say a decent word about Mustapha Kemal.'[39]

While Churchill respected Atatürk, and despised the Treaty of Sèvres, he felt that the new Treaty of Lausanne went too far in addressing the terms of the Turkish national government. In *World Crisis* he lamented: 'The capitulations which for so many hundred years had protected the traders and subjects of western nations in Turkey against Oriental misgovernment or injustice were abolished.'[40] In an election speech at the Reform Club in Manchester in 1923, Churchill aired his harshest criticism of the Treaty of Lausanne:

> A Treaty which at a stroke abandoned almost every tortured population with whom our sympathy was of a historic character, which condemned large portions of the East to a cruel reversion to barbarism and which robbed European nations of right which they had enjoyed in the Turkish Empire ever since the year 1534.[41]

Churchill's position on the Treaty of Lausanne was clear. His anti-oriental tone in the speech and his blatant mistrust of Eastern government in *World Crisis* illustrated that he believed the Treaty of Lausanne went too far. However, this cannot remove the fact that he believed the Treaty of Sèvres was too harsh and needed to be abolished. Moreover, this cannot be seen as a rejection of Churchill's relationship with the Islamic world. Indeed some of the 'tortured populations' that he referenced were the Arabs in the Middle East. But, rather, it should be understood as a personal and perceived geopolitical loss for Churchill.

Churchill believed that the halting of Atatürk's army would win him some political popularity back home. He was wrong. At first, the resolution of the Chanak Crisis seemed to be a major victory for Lloyd George and Churchill, appearing to be 'a brilliant triumph [...] given the weakness of their position.'[42] However, the Cabinet's unwavering stance against the Turks was beginning to be viewed as irresponsible by the press and public, and political colleagues alike, and 'gave the impression of being anxious to provoke another war.'[43] *The Times* accused the Cabinet of being: 'Rash and vacillating and incapable.'[44] This opinion was echoed in the *Daily Mail* and several other national papers. Lloyd George made a political miscalculation because he failed 'to understand the war weary mood of his countrymen and [was] oblivious to the fact his personal views ran counter to a growing isolationist trend in postwar Britain.'[45]

Meanwhile, political machinations in the Conservative Party began to brew against Lloyd George's Coalition as Conservative politicians saw their chance to usher in a defeat of Lloyd George. Stanley Baldwin told his wife that Lloyd George had 'schemed to make this country go to war with Turkey so that they should have a "Christian" war [...] versus the Mahomedans and turn the Turks out of Europe' – and this was enough, Baldwin believed, to call for a general election that 'would return them [the Conservatives] to office for another period of years.'[46] The previous leader of the Conservatives, Andrew Bonar Law, went a step further, publishing a letter to *The Times* and *Daily Mail* that argued: 'It was wrong for Britain, as the leading Muslim power [...] to show any hostility toward the Turk.' His letter concluded that, 'we cannot act alone as the policeman of the world.'[47] Churchill was having his own policies thrown back at him.

Churchill must have realized that altering his principles on the Turkish question might create massive political reverberations. At the Carlton Club on 19 October, Baldwin gave a speech warning the Conservatives that Lloyd George was a 'great dynamic force' but a 'dynamic force was a terrible thing' and that he had already broken up the Liberal party and [...] would break up the Conservative party too.'[48] Though Bonar Law's additional speech undoubtedly played a role, several historians have pointed to Baldwin's as the one that 'effectively brought down the Lloyd George Government.'[49] The general election was in November. The Conservatives formed a new government and then won the elction. Lloyd George was more or less sentenced to political exile, while Churchill, due perhaps to his bout of appendicitis, which limited his campaigning, failed to place the pro-Greek policy on the shoulders of Lord Curzon.[50] Churchill was not re-elected in Dundee, finishing fourth behind a Prohibitionist, and was left 'without an office, without a seat, without a party and without an appendix.'[51]

Egypt, Eastern Economies, and the Meddling Exchequer

After Churchill's defeat in the general election of 1922, he ran unsuccessfully again for the Liberals in 1923. Like Lloyd George, Churchill seemed to remain on the outside of the political sphere. However, in 1924 Churchill stood for Epping as a Constitutionalist (though he was adopted by the Epping Conservative Association) and won. Immediately after the election, he donned his father's robes and 're-ratted' to the Conservative Party.[52] Stanley Baldwin named him Chancellor of the Exchequer later that year despite a great deal of criticism from some of his Conservative colleagues and *The Times*, which believed it was a mistake to appoint to the second most powerful position in the Conservative government a man who had recently been a Liberal.[53] It has been hypothesized that Baldwin did this to help keep Churchill out of trouble, because while the Exchequer was 'prominent, it was less politically sensitive than other departments.'[54] However, Churchill saw his appointment as a way to 'vindicate his father's brief tenure of the Exchequer' and to 'act as a moderating and reforming influence on the Conservative Party.'[55]

Though the Chancellorship was a promotion for Churchill, his new office kept him mostly outside the sphere of the newly restructured Middle East. Yet despite his distance from the Orient, he still managed to involve himself in some of the political and economic issues related to the Islamic world. He continued to support Jewish immigration into Palestine and reduced economies in Iraq and the Middle East. After being notified by the Duke of Devonshire of the new reductions of commitment in Iraq, Churchill replied that he felt that the arrangements (he designed in Cairo) were 'an honourable fulfillment of our obligations'. However, Churchill also noted that he was concerned that 'we are rather letting ourselves in for all the work and costs, and excluding ourselves from any chance of returns.'[56]

Churchill's focus on fiscal austerity in Middle Eastern affairs was evident in a note to George Barstow, a civil servant, when he declared that he 'had been struck by the length of and number of telegrams coming from Persia'. Churchill continued: 'Every day pages and pages are sent about obscure matters which only rarely eventuate in action of any kind [. . .] What is the rate per word with Persia? What is the total expenditure of the Foreign Office on telegrams? What proportion of this expenditure arises from Persia and the Persian Gulf?'[57] Barstow wrote back defending the necessity for the telegrams, to which Churchill retorted: 'I still think the Foreign Office representatives in Persia are unnecessarily verbose in their telegrams.'[58]

Churchill's meddling with Middle Eastern affairs had a long history that rarely stopped with economic issues. For instance, a situation arose in Egypt in the early 1920s as a result of the British government releasing Egypt from its status as a protectorate. A new Egyptian Sultan, Ahmed Faud, was placed on the throne in 1922, much in the way that Churchill placed Feisal on the throne in Iraq. However, the Egyptian nationalists (the *Wafd)* led by Saad Zaghloul Pasha were in fierce opposition with the British policy and had been since 1918, to the extent that Zaghloul was exiled in 1921. Churchill opposed his exile, stating later that the treatment of Zaghloul was 'a perfect cameo of how not to do it' and that his being exiled 'made a martyr of him, while admitting the justice of the cause of Egyptian Independence.'[59] Churchill's position was informed at least in part by his old friend Wilfrid Blunt, who sent a letter from his deathbed on 5 December 1922 urging Churchill to convince the Cabinet that it should 'send the exiled Zaghloul back to Cairo: You will be fools in Downing Street if you do not.'[60] Despite the fact that this foreign controversy was entirely the prerogative of the Foreign Office, Churchill offered his opinion frequently and interfered with Foreign Office policy. Lord Curzon noted in his Cabinet memorandum of 21 April 1921 that Churchill stepped boldly on 'ground ordinarily reserved for the Foreign Office' when he met unilaterally with the then Sultan of Egypt and discussed the difficulties of installing sovereign governing institutions.[61]

Naturally, Churchill's meddling in Foreign Office affairs continued when he entered the Treasury. Once Zaghloul returned from exile in 1923 and led a movement calling for British withdrawal, he became the first Prime Minster of Egypt and established a Wafdist government. In the Cabinet minutes for 30 December 1924, Churchill revealed his frustration with the situation and the Foreign Office, despite not being directly involved with Egypt. He was quick to offer his position saying, 'if Ziwar Pasha's administration fails we must choose between annexation and evacuation.' Churchill explained his position with a history lesson as well, noting the missteps of the British policy in Egypt such as putting Ahmed Faud on the throne 'against public opinion' and then abandoning him to Zaghloul and the Wafd party. Churchill continued, recalling the government's treatment of the Sultan in a particularly insightful passage that goes some way in demonstrating that Churchill's opinions transcended (at least to some extent) the conventional orientalist paradigm of his youth:

> When this unfortunate puppet, whom we had hoisted into precarious eminence, was repeatedly assured that we were about to desert him, he naturally began to look about for a local

> foundation and seek for friends among those forces hostile to British influence [. . .] When we saw him taking these reasonable precautions, we made naïve comments upon Oriental 'duplicity' and 'love of intrigue'. Duplicity is the natural resource of the weak when the strong fail in their duty. Intrigue may be the only recourse when policy is non-existent.[62]

However, Churchill's faith in paternalistic imperialism revealed itself when he argued that Britain should 'shoulder the burden' and remain in place to see Egypt through to a condition that would create the 'internal good government of Egypt.'

Churchill's memorandum made it clear he enjoyed meddling in the affairs of the Foreign Office, especially matters concerning the Islamic world. He spent a great deal of his time and energy creating a system of checks and balances for the Middle East which might have, at least in his own mind, rivaled Metternich's Concert of Europe. For Churchill to see his work undone by the Foreign Office was too much for him to bear. In this way his meddlesome attitude is very understandable.

The memorandum also revealed Churchill's critique of the Foreign Office's treatment of Ahmed Faud and criticized those who might dismiss Faud's actions simply because he is a Middle Easterner. Churchill defended Faud's actions as sound for any leader in a weak political state when they have been abandoned by their guarantor. This represented a rejection of an orientalist viewpoint on Churchill's part. He mocked the idea that Faud was behaving duplicitously because he was oriental or 'naïve' and implied that there was no room in practical politics for such nonsense. However, while Churchill's disdain for such blatant orientalist views was evident, his desire to bring Egypt back under control of the Empire via total annexation tells something of a different story. His fear that Egypt might fall into 'oriental misgovernment' (a phrase Churchill used to describe Atatürk's national movement in Turkey) as a result of leaving Egypt with Zaghloul and the Wafd's in control, demonstrated that orientalism was present in Churchill's thinking too.

Since neither the Foreign Office nor the Cabinet was willing to alter the course created by their policies, Churchill withdrew back to the Treasury and focused on economic matters. However, this did not totally remove him from the Islamic world. He sought to control the budget in Middle Eastern areas of the Empire. He argued that Sudan and Egypt ought to remain together and that Egyptian revenues ought to pay for British troops in Sudan.[63] He also sought to apply his model for the rest of the Middle East on Sudan by suggesting to Foreign Secretary Austen Chamberlain that traditional military means in Sudan were far too expensive and that the 'cheapest way of keeping the Sudan was to let Trenchard run it as he does Iraq.'[64]

Churchill continued to pursue the reduction of Middle Eastern cost throughout his entire tenure at the Exchequer. He argued that British money should not go to Iraq beyond what was paid in to maintain the air squadrons and that Palestine should pay its own way and not be a 'burden on the exchequer.'[65] However, as the 1929 general election drew closer Baldwin, expecting to win, mulled over the idea that Churchill might be better suited to the India Office, which was the same position Churchill's father had held in the 1890s. Thomas Jones, the Deputy Secretary of the Cabinet, noted in his diary that Baldwin asked him 'What do you think of Winston at the India Office', to which Jones replied that he thought it was 'a splendid idea' but that Churchill would need officials around him 'who were not afraid to stand up to him at critical moments when he was going off the deep end.'[66] Baldwin then tried out his idea on Lord Irwin, the Viceroy of India, arguing that Churchill was 'good all through the Irish trouble: he has imagination and courage; he is an imperialist; he is a liberal.' However, Baldwin revealed his cautious side by noting that appointing Churchill was a 'risk' but wondered if it was one worth taking.[67] Lord Irwin was almost completely against the idea. He said in his reply that his 'doubts tend to outweigh [his] confidence that it would be a good appointment.' He arrived at this idea by arguing:

> [India] needs the guidance of somebody with courage and vision of a real desire to help India and making themselves felt through sympathy with all their difficulties [...] How would

> [Churchill] fit with these necessities? FE [Smith, Lord Birkenhead] did an incredible amount of harm here – not by policy [. . .] but by the impression he produced upon sensitive self important Indians visiting England [. . .] Frankly I should fear that Winston at the bottom would have rather the same point of view & would never be able [. . .] to conceal it. And he has become – or perhaps it is more true to say – has always been, a much more vigorous Imperialist in the 1890–1900 sense of the word than you and me.[68]

Churchill later recalled this possible office change in a draft version of his war memoir:

> Mr. Baldwin seemed to feel that as I had carried the Transvaal Constitution through the house in 1906, and the Irish Free State Constitution in 1920, it would be in general harmony with my sentiments and my record to preside over a third great measure of self government for another part of the Empire. I was not attracted to the plan.[69]

These conflicting comments from Churchill's contemporaries are important because they demonstrate that 'Churchill's reputation on imperial issues was by no means set in stone.'[70] Churchill's Conservative colleagues were unsure of his position on imperialism. Baldwin thought him perhaps too liberal for a position in India; Lord Irwin thought he was too imperialist; others such as Leo Amery thought he was 'definitely hostile to Empire.'[71] These conflicting understandings of Churchill's position on imperialism represented a conflict within Churchill himself. On the one hand, he was an imperial reformer and did (as he suggests Baldwin said) carry the Transvaal Constitution and the Irish Free State Constitution through the House of Commons, as well as create new sovereignties in the Middle East. On the other hand, Churchill loved the British Empire and sought to preserve its power at all costs.

Either way, Churchill's position at the India Office was not to be. In 1929 the Conservatives lost the general election and he became increasingly estranged from the party leadership over imperial issues such as the resignation of Lord Lloyd from Egypt. Churchill's vacating of the Exchequer led him into his 'political wilderness' where his comments on another aspect of the Islamic world (Indian home rule) would help illustrate his position on British imperialism.

Churchill: Champion of the Indian Muslims

It was from the political wilderness that Churchill engaged with another issue wrapped up with the Islamic world, India. Though there has recently been some notable exceptions, typically historians have approached this topic by depicting a fiercely imperialist Churchill whose policy 'rested on the simple concept that British power in India must be preserved without qualifications' against meek and well-intentioned Mahatma Gandhi, whose policy of *ahimsa* (non-violence) helped make Churchill seem all the more fanatical about imperialism.[72] That Churchill's primary motivation for his position on Indian independence and the India Act of 1935 was related to his wish for the Empire will not be disputed.[73] Even into the twilight of his career, Churchill was still clearly tied to his Victorian conception of the Empire as a means to spread and defend civilization. While Churchill's view of the Empire was that it was well intentioned, his view was nevertheless limited. Robert Rhodes James argued that Churchill had 'a lifelong lack of serious interest in Empire [. . .] He made speeches and wrote fine passages in his books about the Empire, but he never visited any part of it except Canada after 1908.' While this is not technically true, since Churchill visited Egypt and Palestine in 1921, the point was that Churchill's understanding of the Empire remained Victorian because he viewed the Empire 'essentially through English eyes – as an asset of incalculable value in world power terms.'[74] Churchill's Victorian conception of the Empire relative to India was laid out in his biography, *My Early Life: A Roving Commission* (1930) when Churchill recalled the 'good old days':

> If you liked to be waited on and relieved of home worries, India thirty years ago was perfection. All you had to do was hand over all your uniform and clothes to the dressing boy, your ponies to the syne, and your money to the butler and you need never trouble any more.[75]

Despite Churchill's quasi-racist views and limited grasp of empire, his 'diehard' imperialist position allowed him to pick up the banner of Indian minorities, such as the lower castes, the sheiks and, of course, the Muslims. His hatred of Gandhi and the Hindu-controlled Indian Congress ultimately created an alliance with Islamic political movements in India. After all, in Churchill's hierarchy of civilization Islam, with its shared Judeo-Christian traditions and monotheistic structure, was understood to be infinitely more civilizing than polytheistic Hinduism.

In this way, Winston filled a role that Wilfrid Blunt envisioned for Lord Randolph, which was 'to make himself, in Parliament, the champion of Islam.'[76] After a trip to India in 1883 Blunt decided to take up a cause he 'specially made [his] own, that of the Indian Mohammedans.' Upon returning, Blunt told Lord Randolph of his new cause and found him 'more than half disposed to go with me in my plans for them.'[77] Though Lord Randolph's tenure at the India Office was short, and ultimately failed to live up to Blunt's expectations, this position of Blunt's might illustrate the origin of Churchill's alliance with Indian Muslims. The influence of Lord Randolph Churchill on Winston Churchill has been explored by a large number of historians and Churchill himself even said that he had taken his politics 'almost unquestionably from his father.'[78] It is reasonable to assume that his politics did not stray too far from his father on Indian matters as well. After all, he often quoted his father's passage that British rule in India was 'a sheet of oil spread over and keeping free from storms, a vast and profound ocean of humanity.'[79]

Beyond Churchill's English conception of empire and his father's influence, several other factors helped to make his political alliance with the Indian Muslims logical, in Churchill's view. His ever-present fear of pan-Islamism was a powerful force in his thinking. For instance, 'the increased importance Churchill attached to India [...] came most of all from an international context. It was the conjunction of events in India with those in the Middle East that persuaded Churchill of the seriousness of the problem.'[80] From the political sidelines, Churchill saw the new Labour government's policies as increasingly lax on imperial matters. The 1929 Arab riots and acts of violence in Palestine, Lord Lloyd's dismissal from Egypt, and rumblings from the Middle East seemed to reinforce to Churchill that for 'the discontented factions among the Arabs, the hour to strike had come.'[81] Such 'rumblings' combined with Churchill's perceived lack of imperial will on the part of the Labour government and the British people would plague Churchill's thinking through the 1930s.[82] This fear was reinforced in 1932 by a letter from Waris Ameer Ali, a prominent Islamic judge and a close friend of Churchill's; it relayed that trouble from the Persian government regarding the Anglo-Persian Oil Company was linked with events in India because the Persian government 'like our other neighbors in Asia have observed events in India and obviously consider that a people who can be talked out of the sub continent can be assailed with impunity.'[83] Churchill agreed in his response, noting: 'Now anyone thinks they can give us a kicking.'[84] Further evidence of Churchill's fear of a pan-Islamic movement and disdain for the Labour government's policies was evident in his article for *Answers* on 26 October 1929; the concept that India was inexorably linked with Egypt and the Middle East was obvious:

> From the moment that the British Parliament divests itself of responsibility for the welfare and forward progress of the Egyptian and Indian masses – from that moment our position in those countries is fatally weakened. Unless the British race has high confidence in its mission to guide forward these Eastern peoples along the path of material, social and moral advancement, there remains no justification for our continued presence in their midst, except that of material self-interest. Such a foundation could never endure.[85]

The MacDonald government's imperial polices continued to frustrate Churchill. He was also angered by Baldwin and the Conservative's lack of help on the India question. Just prior to the first Round Table Conference in September 1930, Churchill gave a speech at the Conservative meeting in Minster Hall, dismissing the idea of dominion status for India and lambasting the government's policy there. According to Churchill, the government was turning a blind eye to the increasing attacks of the frontier tribesmen on Peshawar. Revealing his longing for the height of the Victorian Empire, Churchill lamented:

> Such a [. . .] spectacle would have been impossible in former times [. . .] Thirty years ago when I knew something of the Indian frontier, those marauding invaders would have been destroyed [. . .] It marks the lowest ebb in British authority in India.

He also drew the conclusion that the only reason the tribesmen attacked in the first place was because they believed that 'Lord Irwin's government was clearing out of India and that rich spoils lay open to their raids.' Despite his wish for the British to maintain control in India, at least for a generation, Churchill still qualified himself by arguing:

> Let me however also reaffirm the inflexible resolve of Great Britain to aid the Indian people to fit themselves increasingly to the duties of self government. Upon that course we have embarked for many years and we assign no limits to its ultimate fruition.[86]

If there was one thing that Churchill disliked more than the government's policies (which provided another reason for his alliance with Islamic Indians) and the timidity of the Conservatives, it was Hinduism and Gandhi.[87] Churchill's loathing of Hinduism was obvious in his speech at the Albert Hall in London on 18 March 1931:

> To abandon India to the rule of the Brahmins would be an act of cruel and wicked negligence. It would shame forever those who bore its guilt. These Brahmins who mouth and patter the

> principles of Western Liberalism and pose as philosophic and democratic politicians are the same Brahmins who deny the primary rights of existence to nearly sixty millions of their own fellow countrymen whom they call 'untouchable'.[88]

The leader of the Indian Hindus, Mahatma Gandhi, offended Churchill the most. At a speech in Winchester House in Epping, Churchill famously called Gandhi 'a seditious Middle Temple Lawyer, now posing as a fakir of a type well known in the East, striding half naked up the steps of the Vice-regal Palace.' If there were any doubts about Churchill's hatred, he clarified in his conclusion that he believed Gandhi to be a 'subversive malignant fanatic.'[89] This speech had adverse effects for Churchill, as parts of the Conservative Party were prepared to part with such notions. Lord Irwin, the Viceroy, agreed to negotiations with Gandhi and the Indian press reported that Churchill's views were 'not necessarily popular even with white opinion.'[90] Churchill's speech resonated against the public because it demonstrated that 'for Churchill, Gandhi's decision to abandon Western Dress was repellant, marking a retreat from civilization itself.'[91] This seemed to be an out-of-touch position, especially as seen by the press.[92]

But from where did Churchill's hatred of Hinduism come? Certainly his opinion tended to flow against Indian self-rule, which was overwhelmingly promoted by the Hindus. Moreover, his friend F.E. Smith, the Secretary of State for India, 'reinforced a hardening of Churchill's views.'[93] This was evident in Churchill's memoirs when he stated: 'My friendship with Lord Birkenhead had kept me in close personal touch with the movement of Indian affairs, and I shared his deep misgivings about that vast-sub-continent.'[94] But other factors were at work as well in Churchill's thinking.

Some historians point to the influence of a book called *Mother India* (1927) by Katherine Mayo, an American who wrote in the muck-raking tradition with assistance from several high-ranking British officials. Though Mayo's book was a 'startling exposé of the exploitation of Indian women by Hindu and Muslim society',[95] it contained a 'profound anti-Hindu bias.'[96] While Mayo attacked both

Muslims and Hindus, she reserved her harshest criticisms for Hindus, especially regarding the treatment of 'untouchables' and the tradition of child marriage. She included a particularly gruesome appendix called 'Medical Evidence' that contained a collection of 14 horror stories regarding the medical results of sexual activity in child marriages.[97] In every instance the husband was Hindu. She also maintained that Muslim women had a better diet, which was closer to Western standards and differentiated the 'utterly democratic' nature of Islam (which she linked to Christianity) with the untouchability of the lower castes in Hindu society.[98] More evidence of Mayo's preference for Muslims over Hindus was evident in her treatment of Islam as 'the religion of the conqueror' and her descriptions of a grand Islamic past in which 'Perisan was the language of the court, the language of literature and verse, [and] the language of the law.'[99] This contrasts sharply with her depiction of the ascendancy of Hindu culture, which she alleged came about partly because of the persistent contented nature of the Islamic rulers and partly because the Hindus took advantage of opportunities that arose from British colonization.[100]

While this pro-Islamic tone undoubtedly appealed to Churchill, so did Mayo's conclusions. She argued that mounting divisions and aggravations between the two fundamentally opposed cultures would end in a cataclysmic civil war, and that the British presence in India was all that prevented such a catastrophe and insured that the Indian civilization did not slide into anarchy. Churchill echoed this point in his speech at the Albert Hall on 18 March 1931: 'Were we to wash our hands of all responsibility and divest ourselves of all our power, as our sentimentalists desire, ferocious civil wars would speedily break out between Moslems and Hindus. No one would dispute this.'[101] To give weight to this fear, Mayo noted the 'Solemn verdict of the Ulema of Madras', which stated: 'Verily, Polytheists are unclean. In the case the British Government were to hand over administration as desired by the Hindus it would be contrary to the sacred laws of Muslims to live under them.'[102] To further argue her point she included the notes of several meetings between the Viceroy, the Secretary of State for India, and an impressive list of Islamic political organizations, which included the All-Muslim India League, the United Provinces Muslim Defence Defiance Association, the Indian Muslim Association of Bengal, the Indian Muslim Association, the Association to Safeguard the Muslim Interests in the Province of Bihar and Orissa, the South India Islamia League, Muttialpet Muslim Anjuman, and the Muhammadans of the Bombay Presidency. Each group echoed Mayo's case for a sustained British presence in India. The South India Islamia League argued that:

> we realise the value of the British government in holding the scales even between different classes in this country [...] and are opposed to any scheme of political reconstruction which tends to undermine the authority of the British Government in India but are strongly in favour of gradual progressive political development.[103]

Virtually every group agreed with this sentiment.

Mayo's *Mother India* engaged with Churchill's sense of imperial duty to spread and ensure civilization's progress in the world, a Victorian notion that he never let go. He loved the book and its subsequent volumes.[104] Churchill was 'delighted' and 'sent copies to his friends, including Birkenhead and Roger Keyes. Sir George Lloyd remarked to Lord Irwin that he had recently stayed for a weekend with Churchill, who was 'immensely struck' with *Mother India*.[105] Victor Cazalet recorded in his diary after spending the day with Churchill that: 'He admires the book *Mother India* and would have no mercy with the Hindus who marry little girls aged ten.'[106] In fact, Churchill so admired Mayo's work that he wrote to her on 5 March 1935 regarding helping her with *The Face of Mother India*, a photographic book that supported her earlier work. Churchill said he was 'thankful' she was 'moblilising her powerful pen and vast knowledge upon these burning and all-important topics.'[107] To what extent the book affected Churchill's thinking is debatable but while 'Churchill had been no enthusiast for self government before reading Mayo [...] it seems plausible to suggest that she provided the basis for much of the anti-Hindu tinge of his later arguments.'[108]

It is notable that Mayo was not the only author who may have influenced Churchill's stance on India. Sir Harcourt Butler's *India Insistent* (1931) rejected the idea that India was ready to move away from British rule, which won praise from Churchill in a letter to Harcourt's publisher saying 'I have read [the book] with entire agreement'; he also wrote a glowing review for the *Daily Mail*.[109] Additionally, Churchill was fascinated by a book called *Warrior* (1933).[110]

Despite the possible influence of these other books on Churchill's position towards India, his speeches suggested that he was most heavily influenced by Mayo. His speech in the Albert Hall on 18 March 1931 (quoted above) fits with Richard Toye's argument and demonstrated Churchill's utter preference for Muslims over Hindus, due to their 'martial' nature and because the Hindus 'do not possess among their many virtues that of being a fighting race', and, Churchill added, 'incapable of self defense.' Churchill also quipped that 'while the Hindu elaborates his argument, the Moslem sharpens his sword.'[111] His respect for the Muslims as warriors was ingrained in him while as a subaltern on the north-west frontier, where the majority of Indian officers he played polo with and the soldiers he served with were predominately Muslims, especially in the 31st Punjabi Infantry.[112]

Moreover, Churchill held on to this idea of courageous and loyal Muslims soldiers through World War I and after. In his note on 'the importance on fair dealings with Moslems of India', he recalled that: 'During the Great War the Moslems of India confounded the hopes of their disloyalty entertained by the Germans and their Turkish ally and readily went to the colours, the Punjab alone furnished 180,000 Moslem recruits.'[113] Clearly, he was impressed with Muslim Indians' martial nature, but more importantly by their loyalty. In this way, Churchill's experience of fighting with the loyal Muslim *sepoys* as a young man offers an additional explanation of his alliance with Indian Muslims against (what Churchill concerned to be) disloyal and non-confrontational Hindus.

Since a political alliance with Islam was a logical (if not personal) move for Churchill, the inevitable question that arises is 'why did the

Muslims of India seek an alliance with Churchill?' The most obvious reason seems to be 'Churchill's fear that they and other Indian minorities would be subject to Hindu tyranny led some Muslims to consider Churchill as a sympathetic figure.'[114] His speeches, like the one regarding the Cawnpore Massacre in June 1931, resonated with the Islamic population because Churchill effectively vilified the Hindus (and Gandhi) and placed the blame for the violence at their feet, while portraying the Muslims as good imperial subjects who were brutally victimized:

> Look at what happened at Cawnpore [. . .] A hideous primordial massacre has been perpetrated by the Hindus on the Moslems because the Moslems refused to join in the glorification of the murder of a British policeman. The most horrible event which has occurred since the Mutiny has been the direct outcome of the Irwin–Gandhi pact with its smooth ambiguous equivocal formulas.[115]

Churchill's alliance with Islam was also solidified by his relationship with prominent Muslims who were well known in British society such as the Aga Khan, Baron Headley (president of the British Muslim Society), and Waris Ali, who was on the executive council of the Indian Empire Society. The Aga Khan had known Churchill since he was in India as a subaltern and they became friends in 1902 when Churchill impressed him with his ability to quote from FitzGerald's translation of *Omar Khayyam*. The Aga Khan in his memoirs, *World Enough in Time* (1954), lamented that Churchill was never appointed as Viceroy of India.[116]

Baron Headley heard Churchill address the Albert Hall audience and wrote to Churchill that he agreed with him and that, in his opinion, the Qur'an expressly forbids all sedition 'which leads to breaking the Law.'[117] Baron Headley wrote again a couple days later, thanking Churchill for his speech:

> I trust you won't think I am taking too great a liberty in writing to express my gratitude for all you have recently done

> for us – particularly with respect to India & the danger of the Muslims opposed to Sedition and the cruelty of deserting the poor wretched 'untouchables.'[118]

Baron Headley connected Churchill to important pro-Islamic groups such as the British Muslim Society, whose members were mainly 'from the middle classes and the aristocracy, with experience of the Muslim World.'[119] Headley played a major role (along with Mark Hunter, a civil servant and one of the founding members of the University of Yangon in Burma) in coupling Churchill with the Indian Empire Society, which Churchill often spoke for (his first speech for them was on 11 December 1930 against the impending Round Table Conference), and later linked him to the Indian Defence League. The Indian Empire Society often wrote for British newspapers, and wanted Britain to adopt a policy along the lines of those suggested in the Simon Commission in 1930, which among other things called for separate electoral commissions for Muslims and Hindus, at least on a temporary basis.[120] Later, Churchill even published a collection of his speeches on India for the society, in a volume called *India: Speeches and Introduction* (1933). In the introduction, Churchill rebuked his critics (such as Baldwin) who argued that his views on India were inconsistent by citing his speech regarding the Amritsar Massacre. Churchill noted that:

> An interval of nine years separates [the Amritsar speech] from the earliest of the others. It was delivered in circumstances very different from those in which we now find ourselves. It has been quoted against me, if to show an inconstance of view. I [. . .] feel that my statement upon India would be incomplete without it. I abhor Terrorism. Nothing is to me more repulsive than the wholesale shooting of unarmed people and nothing is less necessary for the re-establishment of British authority in India.[121]

Additionally, Churchill's support of Edwin Montagu's Government of India Act in 1919, which pushed for 'the progressive realisation of responsible government in British India', has often been cited to illustrate Churchill's inconsistency on India.[122] This is an unfair criticism because Churchill maintained that once he believed India was ready for home rule, he would support it. He just had not arrived at that belief yet, most likely owing to Mayo's book and Birkenhead's influence; although it is doubtful that Churchill would have reached such a belief. The Indian Empire Society, of which Churchill was an influential member, also reflected this notion in a letter that the society wrote to *The Times* saying: 'The society is not in the least opposed to the political advancement of India and we shall all welcome any *sound* scheme that would promote this.'[123]

Of all Churchill's prominent Muslim friends in Britain, Waris Ali probably held Churchill's attention the most regarding the Muslim population of India. In this way, he was probably as influential on Churchill's thinking as Mayo. Waris Ali and Churchill became good friends; their correspondence lasted into the postwar years and they worked closely together on the Indian Empire Society, which later became a part of the Indian Defence League. Waris Ali used his connections in India to keep Churchill informed on Muslim opinion on the ground in India. When Lord Irwin released Gandhi in January 1931 and proceeded to recognize him as a legitimate Indian leader (eventually culminating in the Gandhi–Irwin Pact), Waris Ali sent Churchill the first issue of *Crescent,* a new Muslim publication that was created to address the need for 'an independent organ truly reflective of Muslim opinion.' It condemned the Cawnpore riots and linked their outbreak to a 'well thought out [...] programme for [...] the terrorization of the Muslim minority into submission and surrender of their demand for effective safeguards in the future constitution of India.'[124]

Just prior to the second Round Table Conference in 1931, where Gandhi claimed that the Indian National Congress spoke on behalf of all India (despite the protests of the Indian Muslim League), Waris Ali sent Churchill a letter at the behest of several 'prominent Muslims in Northern India' that included an article entitled 'The Muslim National Conference', which proclaimed – in an attempt to show a split among the Muslims – that Muslims who joined the

National Congress and nationalist organizations were propped up by rich Hindus.[125] Churchill thanked Waris Ali for his letters, articles, and help. Churchill also implied that Waris Ali had influenced his position, saying that he had 'availed himself fully of [the letters and articles]' and he would recur to Waris Ali if he needed more help.[126]

Waris Ali also helped inform Churchill of the Cawnpore Massacre and continually sent him information that he might use in the House of Commons to defend his position on the opposition to home rule for India. One such letter in July 1931 included the graphic deposition of a Muslim couple at the Cawnpore Enquiry, after the massacre that prompted Churchill to write: 'I have read with great distress the terrible evidence of the Cawnpore massacre and of the treachery and brutality with which it was accompanied.'[127]

Waris Ali also connected Churchill with several prominent Indian Muslims such as Shujaud din Khan, Moului Mahood ul Hasan Kermon, Nawab Zeda Muhammad Azim, and even Muhammad Ali Jinnah, who stayed in touch with Churchill well after World War II. These figures kept Churchill informed about what was happening with the Muslims in India, which illustrates that Churchill was not just observing from a distance but took an active interest in Islamic affairs. Moului Mahood ul Hasan Kermon and Shujaud din Khan wrote to Churchill pledging their support for his cause in Parliament.[128] Shujaud din Khan also thanked him for his support of the Indian Muslims saying: 'It is high time that the masses and especially the depressed classes were protected and saved from the killing axe of those ministers unscrupulous, corrupt, and with no sense of propriety.'[129] Nawab Zeda Muhammad Azim also wrote offering his services to Churchill by 'voicing Moslem opinion hostile to the White paper' and said that he hoped the two could meet.[130] Churchill replied to Nawab Zeda that he was so busy that he would not be able to meet until May 1935. Illustrating his notion of a kindred warrior spirit Churchill mused that they were both 'combatants in the same army fighting for our King Emperor and for our Empire and we must help each other to the very best of our ability.'[131] It was not until 1935, just before the Government of India

Act, that Churchill heard from M.A. Jinnah via Waris Ali and the Indian Empire Society. Jinnah, discontented with *The Times*'s coverage of his statement on the impending bill, sent his own account to the Indian Empire Society and it was forwarded to Churchill. Jinnah spoke for the Muslim League saying:

> With respect to the scheme for central government called the All Indian Federation, this house is clearly of the opinion that it is fundamentally bad and totally unacceptable to the people of British India and therefore recommends the government of India to advice His Majesty's Government not to proceed with any legislation based on the scheme.[132]

Churchill was so connected with the Islamic cause in India that it attracted the attention of his former private secretary (and future Secretary of State for War), P.J. Grigg. Grigg wrote to Churchill joking about visiting 'his old haunts' on the north-west frontier but also warned him saying, 'you should not readily assume that the Muslims were Britain's eternal friends: There is a damned sight too much of that pan-Islamic nonsense flying about out there and the Muslims are only being our friends for what they can get.'[133]

Despite support from Indian and British Muslims and the Indian Empire Society, Churchill was still out of favour with the majority of British subjects at home and in India. In 1933 the government released its white papers on India and Churchill declined membership of the Joint Select Committee on India.[134] His speech on 29 March 1933 in the House of Commons further revealed his true desire to keep India in the bosom of the British Empire. Thinly veiling paternalistic orientalism with a moral duty to advance civilization Churchill said:

> During the last 50 years the population of India has increased by one hundred million. The prevention of wars, famines and the control of infanticide and pestilence by British rule has brought that accession to mankind [...] You cannot desert

> them, you cannot abandon them. *They are as much our children as any children could be.* They are actually in this world as the result of what this nation and this Parliament have done.[135]

That October, Churchill presented evidence to the Joint Select Committee on India and, according to Rhodes James, revealed his knowledge of the Indian situation to be minimal:

> Had the violence of his language been compensated for by informed judgment, his reputation with those who were struggling with the issues would have been higher. That he felt passionately about India could not be gainsaid, but his policy really rested on the simple concept that British power in India must be preserved without qualifications.[136]

This sentiment was certainly evident in several Indian newspapers such as the *Times of India*, *The Times*, and the *Bombay Chronicle* to illustrate a united feeling that Churchill was out of his depth. Churchill's memorandum, which called for home rule in India along the lines of the Simon Commission, had several safeguards for minorities (including Muslims) but did not allow for any kind of federation and maintained a centralized government under the control of the Viceroy, who still was to 'restrain strong powers.'[137] While this concept protected his Muslim allies with safeguards, it also undermined any form of autonomy, which the Indian Muslims had hoped for. It was generally rejected by all parties and denounced in the *Free Press Journal* as 'intelligent stupidity and hypocritical sympathy for the India cause.'[138] Even Churchill's old friend the Aga Khan told him, 'you have what I may call a cursory knowledge of Indian affairs.'[139]

While Churchill's meddling into affairs of the Islamic world was perhaps politically precarious and displayed a lack of current knowledge on the ground, it also illustrates his desire to influence issues that he felt strongly about such as the wellbeing of Muslim subjects in India. However, his imperial appetite overshadowed his connections with the Islamic world and his genuine concerns for the

Muslim population of India. In 1934 the Joint Select Committee agreed with the government's white paper, which ultimately led to the Government of India Act in 1935. As Churchill's attention pulled away from India to the closer, more ominous threat of Nazi Germany, he decided to lay down his banner for the Indian Muslims. His speech in the House of Commons on 5 June 1935 'marked the end of Churchill's long battle over India.'[140]

CHAPTER 7

CHURCHILL, THE MIDDLE EAST, AND INDIA DURING WORLD WAR II

This chapter explores and argues the importance of Churchill's policies and thinking regarding the Middle East and India during the war years. The first section engages with Churchill's continuing struggle to create order in Palestine, by examining his positions on the situation and how it was linked to other Arab situations such as the Iraqi revolt of 1941. The second section considers the larger Middle East such as Turkey, Syria, and Saudi Arabia, and how Churchill married his military strategy with the larger diplomatic strategy to ally Britain with the Islamic world. The final section considers Churchill's attitudes and policies regarding India, demonstrating his desire to see the creation of Pakistan and refuting the notion that Churchill was contemptuous of all Indians, by illustrating his continued support of the Indian Muslims.

As the 1930s progressed, Churchill's interest in India and the Islamic world waned as his attention moved to the European problem of Nazi Germany. After the failure of Prime Minister Neville Chamberlain's diplomacy, war with the expansionist and militarist Third Reich became inevitable. As militant Japan and fascist Italy solidified their positions in the Axis alliance, the scale of the impending struggle became obvious: it would be a world war.

This meant Churchill would once again be confronted with the issues of the Middle East and India. However, Churchill's focus would be different. Unlike his previous altrusic concerns regarding the role of the British Empire in the Levant or India, his focus was almost totally strategic. First at the Admiralty and then as Prime Minister, Churchill's energies were laser-focused to defeat Germany. All other considerations, even his hatred of communism, became secondary. It is in this context that Churchill's opinions and policies regarding the Islamic world were implemented during World War II.

Churchill's strategic aims for the Middle East set out to accomplish two things. The first, and most obvious, was that he sought to consolidate British tactical control in the Middle East. Such control would protect the Suez Canal, ensure communication and shipping to India, and protect the Empire's oil reserves in Persia and Iraq. This was undoubtedly the most important aspect of strategy in Churchill's mind as it protected the basic infrastructure of the British Empire, to which all other considerations in the Middle East were secondary. The second prong of his approach to the Middle East, and to which this chapter will pay closest attention, was more abstract and based on strategic influence in the region. The primary object of the second aim was to ensure that the Islamic world remained allied with the British Empire. Each part of this strategy informed and influenced the other. Issues such as Palestinian concerns (though it is arguable that these were more ideologically driven), the Iraqi revolt in 1941, and the protection of the Suez Canal are best explored in terms of tactical and physical control of the region. The larger strategic goal of maintaining an alliance with the various Muslim powers in the Middle East and Central Asia concerns issues such as Turkey's neutrality, Syria's freedom, and potential postwar structures in the Middle East, such as an Arab Confederation headed by Ibn Saud.

Palestine and Iraq

Palestine was central to Churchill's Middle East strategy. However, in Churchill's ministerial absence from 1929 until he returned to the

Admiralty in 1939, the political climate in Palestine had deteriorated. Tensions between Jews and Arabs had increased dramatically. The radical Palestinian nationalist, Mohammad Amin al-Husayni was given the title of Grand Mufti of Jerusalem by the High Commissioner, Herbert Samuel (while Churchill was still Colonial Secretary) and al-Husayni used his title to amass a political power base among the Arabs of Palestine, which he used to antagonize British policy and Zionist aspirations. In 1929, some thought he masterminded the first major Arab attack on Palestinian Jews,[1] and in 1936, after a brief power struggle, al-Husayni led an Arab revolt that lasted until 1939 when it was crushed by British troops. However, the rebellion did force the British government to make large concessions to the Palestinian Arabs, culminating in the removal of the Peel Commission's suggested Palestinian policy (which argued for a partition) and the adoption of the Chamberlain government's 1939 white paper. This argued that the large number of Jewish settlers in Palestine had fulfilled the Balfour Declaration's pledges to the Jewish people for a national home in Palestine, that an independent Palestine governed by both Jews and Arabs should be established within ten years, and that Jewish immigration would be limited to 75,000 over the next five years, after which all Jewish immigration would be subject to Arab consent.[2]

Chamberlain's white paper was almost universally reviled in Palestine. It was condemned by both Arabs and Jews, which was ironic because it was calculated to help increase support from the Arab world in terms of the imminent war with Germany. Additionally, it was based around Chamberlain's concept that 'the Jews in any case had no choice but to side with the allies, whereas the Arabs, as they frequently reminded the British, did [have a choice]'.[3] The white paper received little support in England, owing to the policies of the Nazis, which led to the mass evacuation of Jews from Central and Eastern Europe. Churchill roundly rejected the white paper and the concept of Arab consent for Jewish immigration and saw the government's new policy as a breach of the Balfour Declaration and especially heinous during the 'cruel and forced exodus of the Jews from Nazidom.'[4] While several historians, have used Churchill's speeches on this matter to illustrate his ideological support of Zionism,[5] there was more to Churchill's position than just exclusive Zionism.[6] As Churchill said, he was strongly 'wedded to the Zionist policy'[7] but he was not a Zionist in the truest sense at least until 1950.[8] Therefore, his approach to Zionism, as much else in his life, offered many contradictions and might be categorized as uniquely Churchillian.

So while Churchill was something of a Zionist, at least in a Churchillian manner, his drive to see Palestine as a bi-national state might alternately be explained in two ways. The first and most obvious way was in fiscal terms and was almost purely strategic. The fact that in the 1920s, Zionist capital provided the majority of fiscal investment to relieve the British Empire's burdens of keeping Palestine garrisoned and the Arab world harmonious is evidence of this notion. For instance, Jordan was unable to pay for its frontier forces and relied on Palestine for nearly 'one half of Trans Jordan's administrative costs', which in 1927 was almost increased to two-thirds of the cost.[9] This created a situation that Churchill wholeheartedly endorsed while he was at the Exchequer, where 'Britain financed the services it provided to the Arabs of Palestine (not to mention a part of Trans-Jordan), from taxes derived primarily from the Jews and very little, if any, of the said income was channelled back to the Jewish community.'[10] In Churchill's mind, a unified Palestine would allow for more space for Zionist immigration and thus more Zionist capital, which would help secure the Sherifian policy he put forth in 1921 for the Middle East.

While the first phase of this thinking was along financial lines, the other was tactical. Palestine was a key strategic position in the Middle East as it provided a space to defend the Suez Canal and check German and Italian expansionism in the Middle East and Mediterranean. In light of the coming war with Germany this was most likely Churchill's primary lens for seeing the Palestinian situation. Supporting Zionist aspirations in Palestine, Churchill reasoned, would help convince the 'American Jewry' to place pressure on the Roosevelt administration to enter the war in a timely fashion.[11] However, keeping a large garrison there after the war officially began caused Churchill concern because he believed the garrison should be withdrawn and returned to Britain in case of an invasion. In order to make up the shortfall, he relied on his 'old idea that the Jews be armed in order to relieve the British troops there'.[12] However, while still at the Admiralty in 1939, Churchill checked Zionist aspirations by suggesting that mixed Palestinian units be created. Churchill believed:

> It would be desirable to make use of the man power in Palestine by balancing the Arabs against the Jews in the units which might be formed. Not only would an outlet be provided for the more adventurous spirits in those peoples, but each community would be enabled to keep watch upon the other.[13]

But Churchill's idea was rejected by officials in the Colonial Office and the War Office on the grounds that it would be unacceptable to the Palestinian Arabs, because it would appear that Britain was arming the Jews against the Arabs, not to mention that Churchill's view, which rested on his Victorian ideas, was largely out of touch. The First Secretary of the Middle East Department, Harold Downie, argued that any such force could not be used domestically in Palestine because 'the use of Jewish force to put down an Arab disorder in Palestine would set Palestine and surrounding Arab countries ablaze.'[14] Echoing such concerns Lord Halifax thought Churchill's proposal 'raised a fundamental issue: were they to allow Jews and Arabs to arm, and then leave them to fight it out alone?' He also, along with Chamberlain and Malcolm MacDonald, rightly accused Churchill of viewing the plan 'as if the issue was confined to Palestine alone', whereas they believed 'the problem was far wider, with repercussions extending throughout the Moslem world.'[15] Churchill's mixed unit was ultimately put on the scrapheap. When Churchill tried later in 1940 to arm the Jews again, Lord Lloyd, Secretary of State for the Colonies, refused his idea on the same grounds. Churchill replied: 'If the Jews were properly armed, our forces would become available, and there would be no danger of the Jews attacking the Arabs, because they are entirely dependent upon us.'[16] In this reasoning we can glimpse that Churchill continued to see the world through Victorian lenses. His concept of Jewish dependence on the British Empire in a bi-national situation echoed the British Victorian rule in India.

Another reason Churchill pursued a united Palestine might best be explained by his fundamental (and Victorian) belief in the advancement of civilization via British imperialism. Churchill believed that under British authority, the Arabs and Jews working together would aid in the advancement of civilization in the Middle East. Discussing the situation in Palestine in 1938, Churchill compared it to the situation in 1922 (as he often did), when his white paper set the policy for Palestine. His desire for their co-operation was evident:

> The Zionist policy, to which we had pledged ourselves in the stresses of the Great War was being continued with remarkable success. The Jews were coming in a steady stream, bringing with them [...] wealth, development and civilisation. The Arabs – and here again it is common ground – were prospering and greatly increasing in numbers [...] I know of no case where the population had so increased in numbers and prosperity [...] You could not have had more satisfactory development.[17]

Churchill's primary concern in 1938 was that order be restored in Palestine. Once that happened, a ten-year plan would aid in finding a compromise between the two parties. In describing his plan Churchill noted that 'we have obligations to the Palestinian Arab, as well as too the Jews', and he saw it as British duty to 'make a fair offer to the Palestinian Arabs.' However, Churchill also warned that if they refused to come to terms Britain 'must still endeavour to do justice; but justice unhampered by any special understanding with [the Palestinian Arabs]'. In this ten-year plan Churchill argued that Jewish immigration should be set at a 'figure which after the ten year period will not have decisively altered the balance of the population as between Arab and Jew.' He also believed that since the Jewish quota would be determined by the population numbers of the Arabs, this would give 'the Zionists an interest in stimulating an increase in Arab population', which would result in the Jews helping the Arabs 'in their employment and bring the two into a common interest in the matter.'[18]

Churchill believed in this concept so much that he refused outright to consider a two-state system proposal by H.T. Montague-Bell, a travel writer and opinionated commentator on Middle Eastern affairs. His proposal called for Palestinian Arabs to be 'absorbed' by Iraq 'so as to counter the critical shortage of population in Iraq for the requirement of agriculture and public works.' Montague-Bell sought to gain travel rights so he might 'put the idea to the Iraq mind without allowing it to appear as a suggestion from the outside.'[19] His requests for a passage had already been denied by the Foreign Office and the Colonial Office, so Montague-Bell believed that Churchill, being interested in Middle Eastern affairs and as Prime Minster, might give him right to passage. However, Churchill believed in a bi-nationalist approach leaving Palestine as a single state with a mixed population. In his notes, it was apparent that he thought Montague-Bell's scheme was destined to fail because 'there is no evidence that the Iraqi government would make such a request' and 'the Palestinian Arabs would reject any such proposal outright.' Furthermore, Churchill reasoned that any transfer of population between the projected Arab and Jewish states would cause 'great indignation among the Arabs of Palestine.' Another interesting reason for rejecting the scheme that Churchill included in his notes was that 'the scheme takes no account of the climatic differences between Palestine and Iraq. It is rash to assume the Palestinian *fellaheen* could adapt themselves to the summer heat of the Tigris and Euphrates valleys.'[20]

This final note stressed the difference of the Palestinian Arabs and the nomadic Bedouin Arabs in Churchill's thinking. His notes imply that the rural and largely agricultural Palestinian Arabs were somehow weaker or inferior than the idealized Bedouin Arabs in Iraq and elsewhere in the Middle East. This notion partially derived from his belief that the Arab's *fellaheen* farming cultivation techniques were obsolete and unproductive, but mostly was informed by his

Victorian understanding of the world and echoed the thinking of both Wilfrid Blunt and T.E. Lawrence.

Churchill had other policies that illustrated his genuine belief that the two ethnic groups would work together for a better Palestine. Besides his Palestinian mixed-unit idea, as discussed above, the majority of his agricultural schemes reflected this belief. In December 1939, Churchill supported the idea that Jewish immigration aided Arab development. He noted that the government's new white paper policy would 'stop agricultural progress in Palestine' and that: 'It was a sticking fact that the Arab population had shown the largest increase in those areas where land had been purchased by the Jews.' Churchill arrived at this conclusion because he believed the Arabs were inferior farmers and could not cultivate the land due to their 'primitive methods.'[21] This echoed some of Churchill's utterances in his Peel Commission testimony. However, it does not represent the 'utter contempt' that Cohen has argued,[22] rather it illustrated Churchill's own version of an Islamic cultural hierarchy.

In fact, Churchill regularly defended his policies regarding Arabs. After the British victory over the Italians at Bardia, the governor of Aden reported that there was 'jubilation' in the streets, and photographs of Churchill as the 'Victorious Vizier' were in demand.[23] Lord Lloyd also sent a letter that stated that he believed Churchill would like 'to see that *some* Arabs have virtue in them'; Churchill replied that he was 'one of the best friends the Arabs ever had, [he] had set up Arab rulers in Transjordania and Iraq which still exist.'[24] Churchill defended his policies in the House of Commons again, after being heckled for treating the Arabs unfairly by James Maxton:

> I cannot feel that we have accorded to the Arab race unfair treatment after the support which they gave us in the late war. The Palestinian Arabs, of course, were for the most part fighting against us, but elsewhere over vast regions inhabited by the Arabs, Arab independent kingdoms and principalities have come into being such as had never been known in Arab history before. Some have been established by Great Britain, some by France. When I wrote this despatch in 1922 I was

> advised by, among others, Colonel Lawrence, the truest champion of Arab rights whom modern times have ever known. He has recorded his opinion that the settlement was fair and just – his definite, settled opinion.[25]

Churchill went on to lecture about Abdulla still ruling Transjordan, and the descendants of King Feisal ruling Iraq, clearly fulfilling the Empire's pledge to the Arabs.[26] However, Churchill also acknowledged that he believed that the promise of the Balfour Declaration must be kept as well, as a matter of honour, despite what the nationalist Palestinian Arabs had to say and whose status, in Churchill's opinion, was outside the pledges of the British Empire anyway. After all, from his perspective their credibility was wasting away with each act of rebellion and insurgence. This made the concessions in the white papers of 1939 to the Palestinian Arabs tantamount to appeasement, which Churchill had continually condemned in regard to Chamberlain's policy with Germany. In fact, the two matters 'became inexorably linked' in Churchill's mind and Churchill had no other option but to oppose the policy, though he did not alter it through the war, save for occasional refugees from Central and Eastern Europe.[27] When Churchill allowed the refugees to enter Palestine, he was criticized by Lord Lloyd. Churchill defended himself by saying:

> I wonder whether the effect on the Arab world will be as bad as you suggest. If their attachment to our course is so slender as to be determined by a mere act of charity of this kind, it is clear that our policy of conciliating them has not bore much fruit so far.[28]

While Churchill hoped the Arab world at large was convinced of the British course, he learned that not every Arab was. The Iraqi Revolt of 1941 (or the Rashid Ali Coup) quickly demonstrated to Churchill how alienating British policy in Palestine had been for some of his would-be Arab allies. In essence, Iraqi nationalist leaders, Colonel Salah al-Din al-Sabbagh, Colonel Kamal Shabib, Colonel Fahmi Said, and Colonel Mahmud Salman led a coup against the Iraqi Crown Prince Abd al-Ilah and installed the pro-German Rashid Ali Al-Gaylani as Prime Minster, seeking to kick the British out of Iraq and increase trade relations with Germany.[29] Because Iraq contributed greatly to the Allied war effort's oil supplies, Churchill sent an Indian infantry brigade and units from the Arab Legion in Jordan to quash the rebellion. By the end of May, Iraq was returned to the Allied fold.

While securing Iraq from the Nazis was primarily a tactical operation to protect oil interests, it also had roots based on the British strategic desire to keep an alliance with the Arabs. As Churchill noted in his history of World War II, another figure in the Iraqi revolt was the Grand Mufti of Jerusalem, Mohammad Amin al-Husayni. After he was exiled from Palestine he took refuge in Baghdad, where he became a mouthpiece for the Axis powers.[30] The Mufti regularly facilitated Nazi propaganda, usually via the German Arabic radio service that was used to recount 'British wickedness in Palestine' and to lavish listeners with 'expressions of German sympathy for the Arab cause.'[31] He also regularly harassed the Arab rulers that Britain supported in the Middle East such as Amir Abdullah. In fact, the Mufti had been courted by the Nazi diplomatic service in the Levant since 1938 and Germany helped bankroll the Palestinian revolt that he led.[32]

The Mufti and other Arabs who supported the Germans in the Middle East believed Germany might help remove Britain from the Levant and support pan-Arab nationalism, because Germany 'lacked any imperialist ambition in the region' and this 'lack of colonial experience [...] bolstered Germany's reputation with Arab nationalists.'[33] As matters were intensifying in Iraq, Hitler extended German friendship to the Arab nationalists on 23 May 1931, with his Directive No. 30, which stated:

> The Arab Freedom movement is, in the Middle East, our natural ally against England. In this connection, the raising of the rebellion is of special importance. Such a rebellion will extend across the Iraqi frontiers to strengthen the forces which are hostile to England in the Middle East, interrupt British

> lines of communication, and tie down both English troops and English shipping [. . .] For these reasons I have decided to push the development of operations in the Middle East through the medium of going to the support of Iraq.[34]

Luckily for Churchill and the British, this proposed alliance lacked the expertise and conviction that the Kaiser had shown during his attempt to court the Muslims as allies. The alliance between Nazi Germany and the Muslim world was superficial for two primary reasons. The first was that Nazi policy supported the Zionist movement for Jewish people to migrate to the Middle East throughout the 1930s.[35] This was of course diametrically opposed to the wishes of Arab nationalists. The second reason, which was that Arab intellectuals tended not to engage with 'the deeper meaning of Nazi ideology and especially its racist elements.'[36] If they has they had, the Arabs intellectuals would have realized that the Nazi's considered the Arabs Semitic as well. Therefore, there was no deep bond between the 'Aryan' Nazis and the Arab nationalists who were willing to court anyone who would back their cause. After all, 'Great Britain was always Baghdad's most important trading partner', despite increased economic relations with Germany.[37] In fact, Rashid Ali only moved Iraq from neutrality to the Axis side once Italy entered the war in the Mediterranean because it appeared as though Britain would be defeated. The German effort to approach potential allies in Jordan met with even less success as there were very few who did not support Abdullah, who wholeheartedly supported Britain. He came out in full favour of Britain and 'defined Germany as an enemy State.'[38] Consequently, Germany supported opposition to Abdullah outside Jordan. For instance, the Mufti became Amir Abdullah's' self-appointed 'arch enemy' once Baghdad was under Allied control. From Berlin, the Mufti continued his Arabic propaganda campaign against Britain and its Hashemite dynasties in the Middle East. However, Churchill was quick to secure Iraq against such Axis propaganda by sanctioning an urgent and complete overhaul of the Iraqi education system after the Allies reclaimed Iraq, which took the curriculum away from pan-Arabism and an emphasis on the Qur'an, to a more conventional, albeit Westernized, model.[39] This aided in keeping a strong British presence in the Middle East for strategic purposes, such as protecting the Suez Canal and the oilfields, as well as keeping the Islamic world in the Allied camp.

Turkey, Syria, and the House of Saud

The second prong of Churchill's overall strategy was to ally the Islamic world with the Allies and the British Empire. While this prong played a part in undoing German–Arab nationalist propaganda in the Iraqi Revolt, it also played a major role in relations with Turkey, in the future of Syria, and with Saudi Arabia's prospects as a regional leader. While each of these areas took on the purely geographically strategic dimension of protecting oil and the Suez Canal, the larger geopolitical aim of ensuring an Islamic alliance with Britain cannot be ignored, especially in Churchill's approach to the Middle East.

However, it is worth exploring where and what exactly the 'Middle East' was in Churchill's mind as his views on the subject had undergone few adjustments since he had been Colonial Secretary in the early 1920s. Facing difficulties in the North African theatre of war, Churchill proposed to restructure the Middle East Command and his suggestion illuminates how he came to conceptualize the Middle East of the 1940s. Churchill proclaimed, 'I had always felt that the name "Middle East" for Egypt, the Levant, and Turkey was ill chosen. This was the Near East. Persia and Iraq were the Middle East; India, Burma and Malaya the East; and China and Japan the Far East.'[40] This clearly represents another Churchillian *volte-face* from his earlier view of an expanded modern 'Middle East'.

Churchill's change of mind may have been prompted by a desire to nail down a fairly mercurial term that was often referenced in official documents but never given a true geographic designation. Even Churchill used the term loosely, often with conflicting geographic designations. This could get confusing because Churchill would, at times, include Turkey in the 'Middle East' and was thus 'prepared to see the Middle East jump into Europe.'[41] This was obvious in

Churchill's letter of 26 November 1940 to General Wavell, who was head of Middle East Command at the time. Churchill believed there was a possibility that the 'centre of gravity in the Middle East' might shift from 'Egypt to the Balkans and from Cairo to Constantinople.'[42]

This letter also reveals that Churchill's failure to form a static version of the 'Middle East' was, at least in some way, connected to Turkey's role as the former caliphate and its position in the war. This is further evidenced by Churchill's tendency to revert back to the use of 'Near East' in official letters such as his letter to Lord Lloyd on 28 April 1940, in which he argued that the British position in Palestine would not prejudice 'Arab feeling in the Near East and India [...] Now that we have the Turks in a such a friendly relationship, the position is much more secure.'[43]

This goes some way in revealing that British diplomacy with Turkey during World War II was one of Churchill's major concerns. Almost alone he sought Turkish neutrality and the possibility of an alliance. 'By 1940 [Churchill] had convinced himself that he alone could bring Turkey into the war as an ally. Few people [...] agreed with him.'[44] Despite the fact that the Foreign Office 'had been hard at work improving Anglo-Turkish relations since the 1930s', the relationship began to deteriorate going into the 1940s because of a reduction in the Anglo-Turkish chrome trade.[45] After that time, the Foreign Office seemed to be unable, or unwilling, to develop a policy that took into account in any coherent way 'the realities of the Turkish economy and the daunting facts of German expansionism [...] This had to wait until Churchill took over Turkey personally.'[46]

In courting Turkey, Churchill had little help from his colleagues in the government or the alliance: 'Anthony Eden, Secretary of State for Foreign Affairs, did not like the Turks and was not liked by them.'[47] Harold Macmillan, who as resident minister at Allied headquarters in North Africa was responsible for relations with many Mediterranean countries, was basically forced out of Turkish relations and forbidden to return.[48] The British ambassador to Ankara, Sir Hughe Knatchbull-Hugessen, was not particularly concerned about an alliance and believed it would never materialize. Additionally, America tended to see Turkey in terms of a possible second front, with little geopolitical significance, while Stalin was keen to control the Dardanelles Straits and had expressed interest in 'the absorption of Dobruja as a Soviet province.'[49]

The War Cabinet's reluctance was understandable, as was Ismet Inonu's (the Turkish president), reluctance to commit Turkey to the Allied cause. Turkey had been devastated by revolutions and war from 1908 to 1922. Inonu was determined to try to keep Turkey from suffering the fate of another catastrophic war with either Germany or the Soviet Union. To this end, Inonu maintained a large army in case an invasion occurred, even to the detriment of the Turkish economy.[50] This helps explain why, after the Molotov–Ribbentrop pact of 1939, Turkey moved away from the Allied powers because their traditional security policy relied on the Soviet Union as a counterweight to Germany. Furthermore, Turkey's geostrategic realignment made several in the War Cabinet and Foreign Office give up hope for Turkish neutrality, especially Knatchbull-Hugessen. While Churchill remained confident of inducing an alliance with Turkey, or at the very least continued neutrality, Knatchbull-Hugessen was regularly 'less hopeful' because he was convinced that all Britain could gain from Turkey was, at best, 'benevolent neutrality' and he resisted putting additional pressure on the Turks for an alliance – for fear of 'making them suspicious'.[51]

Despite this, Churchill continued his fight to sway the War Cabinet and met with some success in altering British foreign policy with Ankara. In late Novemeber 1940, once it became obvious that the Germans were moving towards the Balkans, the War Cabinet decided to 'try to bring the Turks into the war at once', in part because they were now 'under the influence of the Prime Minister's opinion that we should put pressure on Turkey.'[52]

The tension between Churchill and the War Cabinet regarding Turkish neutrality and the value of pursuing Turkey as an ally became increasingly evident as the war went on. By early 1943 Churchill wanted personally to meet Ismet Inonu when he left the Casablanca Conference before going to Cairo, but the War Cabinet was very hesitant and advised him not to. Churchill replied that he was 'not at all convinced by their arguments' and planned to meet with Inonu.

He then wrote back saying, 'I am most grateful to you for allowing me to try my plan. We may get a snub, in which case it will be my fault, but I do not think it will do to wait [. . .] I think there is a shade of odds in favour of their coming.'[53] Churchill had a successful meeting with Ismet Inonu at the end of January 1943 and wrote to him after the war saying that the Allies had 'staunch friends and allies and not least among them is Turkey.' Churchill continued his praise for Inonu and Turkey, saying that he was 'impressed by the firm and sagacious policy which your Excellency, your government and your warrior nation are pursuing [. . .] I see in Turkey a barrier defended by stout hearts ready to withstand and hurl back the Nazi aggressor.'[54] Churchill's positive relationship with Inonu can further be seen in a telegram to the War Office after their secret meeting, in which Churchill reported that he 'pursued a method of perfect trust and confidence, asking for no engagement but giving to the utmost in our power.'[55] Churchill's high regard for Turkey was also evident in his speeches when he often referred to Turkey as an 'ally' and 'friend'.[56]

Since Churchill almost unilaterally sought to court Turkey as an ally, Britain's policy on Turkey was 'a personally directed policy' of Winston Churchill's.[57] He sought this for several reasons. Primarily, Turkey was perfectly placed geographically in the Mediterranean and occupied a space that might provide an eastern front in Europe, or a staging ground to launch attacks on Nazi-occupied Europe, while simultaneously shoring up the Balkans and protecting oil installations in the Middle East. There were, however, more personal reasons as well for Churchill. The first was that he remembered how deadly a foe Turkey was in World War I and the great disasters at the Dardanelles and Gallipoli. Churchill referred to his earlier experiences in Cairo in February 1943: 'Certainly it is clear that the old friendship between Great Britain and Turkey, which was so grievously slashed across by the tragedies of the last war is now in fullest strength and sincerity.'[58] With Turkey onside, Churchill would not have to worry about being undone in the same fashion and reliving his defeat at the hands of the Turkish powers. He was not the only one who saw Turkey in light of World War I: 'The parallel [. . .] as far as Germany was concerned was clear and von Falkenhyn in

1914, as Jodl would do in 1943, promoted the view that a threat to the Suez would weaken British forces in the West.'[59]

Another of Churchill's reasons for courting Turkish favour was to ally Britain with the Islamic world. This notion was a holdover from Churchill's earlier, more Victorian understanding of the world; after all, he had sought just such an alliance off and on since 1911. This might also help explain why Churchill reverted back to the Victorian geographic designation of the 'Near East'. He continued to fear that Germany might seek to inflame the Muslims in India and the Middle East, as they had done in World War I. The Mufti's propaganda almost certainly confirmed this fear in Churchill's mind. Churchill thought that the perfect way to offset anti-British, Arab sympathies was to have the seat of the former caliphate as an ally. This was evident in a BBC broadcast on 12 November 1939 when Churchill stated: 'Turkey and the whole of Islam have ranged themselves instinctively but decisively on the side of progress.'[60] Churchill referenced this concept in dealing with the Palestinian issue when he wrote to Lord Lloyd regarding arming Jewish units. He concluded by saying, 'I do not admit that Arab feeling in the near East and India would be prejudiced in the manner you suggest. Now that we have the Turks in such a friendly relationship the position is much more secure.'[61]

Churchill's response indicated that his understanding of the Islamic world never really evolved past the views he held in the early 1920s. Back then his approach would have certainly been logical, but it seems strangely anachronistic in the 1940s. First, Turkey was an increasingly secular and relatively 'Westernized' country after Atatürk's reforms. The Turkish connection to Islam as a religion was nowhere near as prominent as it had been in the 1920s and all pan-Islamic aspirations had died out with the Caliphate Movement in India and central Asia. Second, the Arabs who did take issue with Britain, such as the Palestinians, were not recalcitrant for specifically religious reasons. They were, in fact, Arab nationalists and were politically motivated, not religiously motivated. While prominent anti-British Arabs such as the Mufti and Rashid Ali used arguments of an Islamic identity to enforce their positions, they were primarily fighting against British imperial rule in Iraq and Palestine for political reasons. Churchill's understanding of Arab nationalism and its relationship with Islam seemed hopelessly outdated and even uninformed by his own earlier writing regarding the use of Islam as a tool for personal or political gains.[62]

Despite this, Churchill was very serious about garnering Islamic support to the Allied cause. In October 1940, during the darkest days of the Second World War, Churchill approved plans to build a new mosque in central London and even set aside £100,000 for the project.[63] Lord Lloyd and Lord Halifax believed that building a mosque would 'have a good effect on Arab countries of the Middle East' and Lord Lloyd privately told Jock Colville that 'this was the best piece of propaganda that {Britain} could undertake with regard to the Moslem world.'[64] Though the Central London Mosque project was primarily championed by Lord Lloyd, it met with Churchill's happy approval.[65] It is significant that Churchill embraced this course of action despite negative feedback from the public. J.A. Kensit of the Protestant Truth Society wrote to Churchill on 3 December 1940 to rebuke him for supporting 'the erection in London of a Mosque' because while appreciative of the 'loyal support of our righteous cause in the present conflict by Mohammedans' the "Truth Society" believes Islam 'stands in active rivalry to the Christian faith.'[66] In the House of Commons, Ian Hannah sarcastically quipped that Churchill should 'take steps to make better known the gift by the Government of a prominent London site for a mosque.' Churchill retorted that Hannah 'will be glad to know that our many friends in Moslem countries all over the East have already expressed great appreciation of this gift.'[67] This reveals that Churchill did not just have Arab appreciation in mind, but Muslims everywhere, including Turkey.

He pursued Muslim alliances and Turkish neutrality along these inclusive lines and eventually met with some success. In April 1944, Turkey broke economic ties with Germany. Four months later they broke all diplomatic ties and, on 23 Febuary 1945, just before the end of the war, Turkey joined the Allies, largely as a gesture of goodwill as no Turkish troops saw combat.

Churchill also hoped to keep the Islamic world as an ally by promoting Arab independence (at least titularly), another of his principles from the 1920s. Prior to Operation Exporter, the campaign to liberate Syria from Vichy France in July 1941, Churchill wrote to General Charles de Gaulle, the leader of the Free French, to confirm that they were operating along the same lines:

> You will [...] agree that this action, and indeed the whole future policy in the Middle East, must be conceived in terms of mutual trust and collaboration. Our policies toward the Arabs must run on parallel lines [...] I welcome, therefore, your decision to promise independence to Syria and Lebanon and, as you know, I think it is essential that we should lend to this promise the full weight of our guarantee. I agree that we must not in any settlement of the Syrian question endanger the stability of the Middle East. But subject to this we must both do everything possible to meet Arab aspirations and susceptibilities.[68]

De Gaulle acquiesced; however, he feared this was a ploy to supplant the Free French in Syria with a permanent British force. De Gaulle stated in his memoirs that he believed 'British policy [was] to replace France at Damascus and at Beirut.'[69] Some historians have validated de Gaulle's fears and typically cite Churchill's Cabinet minutes of 19 May 1941, which, in the event of a French obstruction to the British Arab policy, called for 'an independent Sovereign Arab state in Syria in permanent alliance with Turkey [...] and Great Britain.' However, there is another school of thought which notes that Churchill's minutes were 'remarkably crass and made hastily' and were most likely Churchill thinking out loud, as he often did. As the conclusion of the minutes illustrated, Churchill reflected that such a proclamation 'might well gratify the Arab race and rally them to a strong nationalist movement to expel all European masters, or would-be masters from their country.'[70] This demonstrates that Churchill was simply mulling over ideas because most of the 'European masters' in Arab regions were British.[71] In any case, Churchill promoted Syrian independence in order to stabilize the region and to keep the largely Islamic, Arab world in the Allied camp. In the Cabinet meeting of 19 May 1941, Churchill overtly argued, 'we must get the Syrian Arabs on our side. For this purpose, we should proclaim that the French mandate has collapsed.'[72]

Once the Axis powers were defeated and had abandoned Syria to the Allies in July 1941, de Gaulle sought to keep a Free French presence in Syria. Churchill received a telegram from de Gaulle that stated his intention of naming General Georges Catroux as 'Commander-in-Chief of the Levant with all powers exercised hitherto by the French High Commissioner', and another telegram from General Wavell, the British commander in the area, stating that 'de Gaulle did not recognize British military authority in the Levant.'[73] Churchill felt betrayed. In a Cabinet meeting the next day he expressed his displeasure about de Gaulle reneging on his promise for Syrian independence and revealed his hope that pushing for Syrian independence would help keep the Arabs allied with Britain. Churchill argued that: 'It was never our intention that [...] de Gaullist should virtually replace the Dentz administration [...] It is therefore for de Gaulle [...] to make the same kind of arrangements with Syria as we made [in] Iraq.'[74] Churchill sent this off to Oliver Lyttelton, the Cabinet's representative in Cairo, who thought it too harsh. This further upset Churchill. Revealing his desire to court the Arab world, Churchill responded by saying:

> the Arabs bulk far more largely in our minds [and we must] satisfy them and convince them that they have not merely exchanged one set of Frenchmen for another [...] You must not over look the main point which is to gain the Arab world by establishing a proclamation, at the earliest, of Syrian independence in whatever form is most acceptable.[75]

Eventually, in November 1941 Syria claimed its independence, but it was not until 1944 that the Free French and de Gaulle recognized it. This delay continued to frustrate Arab leaders such as Ibn Saud, who wrote to Churchill to complain on behalf of the Arab community about the Free French administration in Syria. During the Lebanese Crisis of 1943 Saud pleaded to Churchill to use his 'practised influence [. . .] with the French authorities [. . .] who administer the country regardless of their promises' and warned that the situation has 'created the worst impression on the Arab peoples in general and on us in particular.'[76] After pressure from the British and Syrian nationalists France eventually removed all its troops in 1946.

The final and perhaps most significant portion of Churchill's strategy to cultivate the Islamic Middle East as an ally was the scheme to create a postwar Arab Confederation with Ibn Saud as the overlord or 'boss of bosses', as Churchill put it. This was known as the Philby Plan,[77] because Harry St John Philby, a Middle East expert with an eccentric personality and a dubious record in Arabian affairs, reportedly tried to gain momentum for it in 1939 by explaining it to Lewis Namier, an academic, Zionist and political acitvist, and Zionist leader Chaim Weizmann. His initial idea was to allow the Jews to have Palestine and, in return, Palestine would exist as a Jewish subdivision of a larger Arab Confederation in which Ibn Saud was the leader of the Arab region. The Palestinian Arabs would be relocated in Transjordan or perhaps Syria. Namier and Weizmann both became advocates of the plan because Namier, like Churchill, believed that Ibn Saud was 'the only really independent Arab' and that 'he fitted the romantic image of the proud [. . .] desert Arab.'[78] Weizmann, on the other hand, jumped at the idea because, like Churchill he saw the situation in terms of the First World War: 'Dr. Weizmann who believed that history was repeating itself for the Jews, saw in the Philby Plan the reincarnation of his own aborted agreement with Emir Faysal, in January 1919.'[79] Philby went at once to Saudi Arabia and found Ibn Saud reticent regarding the plan. Meanwhile, Namier and Weizmann pushed for the plan in areas where they held influence. Weizmann took the idea to America and Napier planted it within London social circles where, according to Philby, it had reached Lord Lloyd and Lord Moyne, who in turn discussed it with Lord Halifax, who introduced it to Churchill in passing.[80]

Churchill then mentioned the concept to Weizmann in their meeting of 12 March 1941. Weizmann recorded the meeting:

> At the end of our conversation the PM said that he was thinking of a settlement between us and the Arabs after the war. The man who we should come to an agreement with is Ibn Saud. He, the PM would see to it and would use his good offices. IS [Ibn Saud] would be made the Lord of the Arab countries, the boss of bosses, as he put it. But he would have to come to an agreement with Weizmann [. . .] with regard to Palestine.[81]

Weizmann maintained that Churchill arrived at the idea on his own and created it *ad hoc.* This might have been the case because Churchill offered up the plan as a concession for the delay in the creation of a Jewish division in Palestine.[82] However, it seems more likely that Weizmann was already aware of the plan before this meeting with Churchill as the two had actually discussed elements of the plan as early as 17 December 1939.[83] Moreover, its even possible that Weizmann purposefully made it look like the plan's author was Churchill in order to distance himself from Philby after the plan collapsed. However, Weizmann's own account stated that 'Churchill himself had taken the initiative, independently, without any prior knowledge of Philby's plan.'[84] While at first this seems highly unlikely, the fact of the similarity to Churchill's plan for the Middle East at the Cairo Conference – and that Churchill and Philby were both admirers (and in Philby's case, a formal protégé) of Wilfrid S. Blunt – does seem to make the coincidence of similar plans more plausible.

Whether the author of the scheme was Philby or Churchill or some coincidental amalgam of the two, Churchill wholeheartedly pursued the scheme, at least until late 1941. Churchill's minutes of the War Cabinet meeting of 19 May 1941 reveal how seriously he considered it. While the first part of the meeting regarding Syria was rather crass, anti-French and flippant, the second part seemed more serious and even included an independent Syria:

> I have for sometime past thought we should try to raise Ibn Saud to a general overlord ship of Iraq and Transjordania. I do not know whether this is possible but Islamic authorities should report. He is certainly the greatest living Arab and has given

> long and solid proofs of fidelity. As the custodian of Mecca, his authority might well be acceptable. There would therefore, be perhaps an Arab King in Syria and an Arab Caliph or other suitable title over Saudi Arabia, Iraq and Transjordania.

Churchill also included the Palestinian lynchpin of the scheme in the minutes:

> At the time of giving these very great advancements to the Arab world, we should, of course, negotiate with Ibn Saud a satisfactory settlement of the Jewish problem; and if such a basis were reached, it is possible that Jewish State of Western Palestine might form an independent Federal unit in the Arab Caliphate.[85]

The scheme appealed to Churchill for a number of reasons. The first was that it avoided the proposed partition of Palestine outlined in the 1939 white papers. Moreover, by positioning a complete Palestine in an Arab Confederation, Britain would be relieved of the economic burden of continuing responsibility for Palestine. This echoed Churchill's attempts to offload the Palestine mandate on the United States or the League of Nations after World War I. Additionally, a grateful, Arab confederation in the Middle East would provide support against the Germans and, after the war, ensure British prestige and dominance in the oil-rich region for a very long time.

Churchill was also a proponent of the scheme because it allowed for a restructure of the Middle East, which took its roots from Blunt's proposal in the 1880s and was along the lines that Churchill and Lawrence had proposed in the 1920s. This scheme, called for an interconnected Middle Eastern Arab bloc, heavily influenced by British hegemony. In fact, US diplomatic cables commented on the similarity of Churchill's scheme in the 1920s and the one he proposed during the war. Under-Secretary of State, Sumner Welles, who was one of Roosevelt's most trusted advisers, commented that making Ibn Saud 'the boss of bosses was out of the question' because Churchill's use of the term 'Arab World' would have to include 'Iraq, Syria, the Lebanon, Palestine, Egypt, Libya, Tunisia, Algeria, and

Morocco in addition to the Arabian peninsula.' Welles concluded that this would be impossible and noted, 'as you will recall British experts on Arabia during the last World War picked out Hussein, Sherif of Mecca, as the coming man and leader of the Arab world [. . .] This was a bad miscalculation.'[86]

However, this plan differed from the previous one in that the Arab bloc would be ruled by a man Churchill considered to be 'the greatest living Arab' Ibn Saud, who had come to personify, the Victorian image of the noble Arab Bedouin. Churchill's admiration for Ibn Saud was most prominent in his history of World War II when he recalled meeting him at Lake Fayyum, outside Cairo, near the close of the war. His account reads like a Victorian travel writer's in the Levant:

> I had arranged a meeting with Ibn Saud. He had been transported to the conference aboard the American destroyer, *Murphy*, and travelled with all the splendour of an Eastern potentate, with an entourage of some fifty persons including [. . .] his astrologer and flocks of sheep to be killed according to Moslem rites [. . .]
>
> King Ibn Saud made a striking impression. My admiration for him was deep, because of his unfailing loyalty to us. He was always at his best in the darkest hours. He was now over seventy, but had lost none of his warrior vigour. He still lived the existence of a patriarchal king of the Arabian desert, with forty living sons and seventy ladies of his harem, and three of the four official wives, as proscribed by the Prophet, one vacancy being kept.[87]

This is a stark contrast to Ibn Saud's account of meeting Churchill. Churchill immediately wanted to discuss the Palestine situation and Ibn Saud noted that Churchill 'opened the subject confidently, wielding the big stick', but after Ibn Saud declared that he could not come to a compromise he said 'Churchill had laid down the big stick.'[88] In fact, the meeting was something of a diplomatic failure, allowing the United States to form a strong bond with Saudi Arabia. For instance, Roosevelt refrained from drinking and smoking in Ibn

Saud's presence, but Churchill, after learning that Ibn Saud would not tolerate smoking or drinking in his presence, commented:

> If it was the religion of His Majesty [to deprive himself of smoking and alcohol] I must point out that my religion prescribed as an absolutely sacred rite smoking cigars and also drinking alcohol before, after, and if need be during all meals and in the intervals between them.[89]

This offended the King, despite the British agreeing to be served their whisky and sodas in coloured glasses and their distributions of the whisky as medicine.[90] Moreover, Ibn Saud did not like the British food or his quarters aboard the HMS *Aurora* on his return to Jidda.[91] In fact, Ibn Saud even confided to William Eddy that he did not like Churchill's gift of a Rolls Royce because 'it would require the king to ride on the driver's left, a side of dishonor' and that he thought, 'Mr. Churchill speaks deviously, evades understanding [and] changes the subject to avoid commitment, forcing me repeatedly to bring him back to the point.'[92] Despite such diplomatic failures, Churchill seemed unaware of his impression on Ibn Saud or, alternatively, Ibn Saud was simply playing the United States off against the British in order to maximize the Saudi position in the Middle East.

Another reason Churchill was attracted to the plan was that it established an Arabic federation, an idea that had pleased Churchill since World War I. While this illustrated his fossilized, post-World War One mindset and his anachronistic, Victorian understanding of the Islamic world, it also demonstrated his genuine belief that the Arab world could be bettered by absorbing the Jewish community in Palestine as a part of a larger Arab federation.

That Churchill still saw the Islamic world through Victorian eyes as a religiously and thus politically interconnected monolith is further reinforced by Churchill's (and Leo Amery's) enlistment of Sir Firoz Khan Noon in the Philby Plan. Churchill merely asked Noon to speak with Weizmann to determine which outcome was most acceptable to both the Islamic and Zionist communities. This was undertaken to see what the Muslim feeling would be in India towards any such scheme. Interestingly, Noon suggested that 'the kingships of Iraq and Transjordan be abolished' if the new scheme were to proceed.[93] This might indicate that Noon saw the problem of minor Hashemite kings under a Wahabist Arab overlord.

Despite heavy support for the scheme among such influential figures as General Smuts and the Secretary of State for India, Leo Amery, it was destined to fail for several reasons. First, the 'virulently anti-Jewish' Ibn Saud never actually gave his consent for the scheme because 'no Arab leader could have retained yet alone, improve his position by handing over Palestine to the Zionists.'[94] Second, the scheme failed to take into account the dynastic rivalries of the Middle East; in the same way Blunt had warned that the Wahabists would never consent to a Hashemite Caliph in 1921,[95] it was unreasonable to think that the installed Hashemite rulers, like Abdullah, would accept a Wahabist overlord, and especially one who overthrew his father. In those terms, Churchill's Middle Eastern solution made the same mistake twice. The harsh realities of 'the Middle East after World War II were substantially different' from those after World War I and those realities would make Churchill's attempts to fix relatively Victorian solutions to modern issues little more than 'day dreams of doing now for the Wahabists what in 1921 he had done for the Hashemites.'[96]

As the problems of the scheme became evident and the realities of war set in, Churchill laid the idea to rest in November 1941 to 'get on with the war.'[97] In the absence of any viable alternative, Churchill's support of the scheme demonstrates that he was no less committed to working with Muslims to find a solution that was acceptable to them. While his perusal of such an anachronistic plan reveals his outdated approached, it also illustrates his respect for what he imagined the Muslim aspirations to be, and his long-term view of their place in the British Empire.

Churchill and India during World War II

The coming war did not alter Churchill's views on India. Though it consumed most of his thinking, he continued to promote British imperialism in India under the guise of equal rights for Muslims and other minorities. The Chamberlain government sought to unify the different sects of India in order to have a ready and unified ally in the Pacific theatre. In fact, 'British attitudes were now heavily conditioned by the war effort. To secure India's military support and its political acquiescence, initiatives and incentives came fast and thick.'[98] However, remaining largely informed by his Muslim contacts in India and at home, such as Waris Ali, Churchill continued to oppose Indian independence. In a War Cabinet meeting in February 1940 he argued: 'Such a unity was in fact almost outside the realm of practical politics and if it were to be brought about the immediate result would be the united communities showing us the door.' The War Cabinet minutes conclude saying that the First Lord 'regarded the Hindu–Moslem feud as the bulwark of British rule in India.'[99] Churchill even wrote to Chamberlain warning that Gandhi was not to be trusted and that he supported the Simon Commission's recommendation of waiting for the development of a centralized political system that was representative of all classes. In his letter, Churchill essentially condemned the Indian Congress Party and noted that continued support of them would result in 'serious results in all directions, to ourselves, to the Moslems, to the Princes, to the depressed classes and indeed a very large body of Hindus.'[100] It was in this climate that Jinnah, Sikandar Hayat Khan, Abul Kasem Fazlul Huq, and Muhammad Zafarullah Khan first articulated the so-called Pakistan Resolution in Lahore in early 1940, calling for Muslim separation, though the Lahore text did not mention Pakistan specifically.

Once news of this reached Churchill, he was pleased. On 12 April 1940, he noted in the War Cabinet, 'the awakening of a new spirit of self reliance and self-assertiveness on the part of the different communities, of which the Moslem League's resolution was a sign of hopeful development.'[101] Churchill even went along with the idea that an Indian sovereign state might be given dominion status; in theory this would have applied to a Muslim state as well.[102] Jock Colville, Churchill's favourite private secretary, recorded in his diary: 'Winston rejoiced in the quarrel which had broken out a fresh between

Hindus and Moslems [and] was glad that we made the suggestion of dominion status which was acting as a cat among the pigeons.'[103]

Since 1939, when the British Empire officially declared war, India had provided Britain with troops that fought in the Middle East, the Mediterranean, and eventually Italy. Jinnah and the Muslim League supported the war from the beginning. Churchill's old alliance with the Indian Muslims was paying off. Not only did The Muslim League support the war, Jinnah echoed Churchill's belief that without British help, India would 'break into a hundred pieces in three months and lie open [. . .] to external invasion.'[104] Churchill's allegiance with India's Muslims produced other demonstrations of kindness from Muslim leaders such as Sahibzada Mirza Bashird-ud-Din Mahmood Ahmed, the leader of the Ahmadiyya movement in Simla. His secretary wrote to Churchill and described a vision that:

> certain verses in the Holy Quran which appear indubitably to refer to the present conflict indicate that in case of invasion of Great Britain by Germany the only defences that would ultimately operate as a check against the invading forces are steel fortifications which have been [. . .] reinforced with molten bronze.

He went on to describe these fortifications as 'pill boxes' and continued to stress that 'the Quran distinctly specifies molten bronze being poured over the iron or steel fortifications.' In the letter's conclusion the significance of the connection with Churchill was clear, 'I am afraid these suggestions might appear ridiculous to your advisors, but both the head of the Movement and myself feel that at this stage no sense of false modesty should prevent my conveying these suggestions to you.'[105] Though mostly likely written by a private secretary, Churchill's response was that he found the letter to be 'an earnest of the determination of India to fight this war to the end' and thanked the Ahmadiyya movement for its support.[106]

It was not until the fall of Singapore in February 1942 that the hitherto unsupportive positions of both the Indian Congress Party and Gandhi became a major issue to Churchill. As he put it: 'The atmosphere in India deteriorated in a disturbing manner with the westward advance of Japan into Asia. The news of Pearl harbour was a staggering blow. Our prestige suffered with the loss of Hong Kong.'[107] As Japan's victories loomed in the minds of the Indian subjects, some extremists such as Subbas Bose (who formed the Indian National Army) actively sought an Axis invasion in order to rid India of Britain once and for all. Despite this, the majority of Indians under the leadership of Gandhi and the Congress Party continued to support a passive and neutral position. However, there were other factors that led to many Indians wanting the British to quit India. After the loss of Burma to Japan later in 1942, India (and especially Bengal) was struck by a major famine and bad weather. Burma had provided 15 per cent of all India's rice, and fearing a Japanese invasion of India via Bengal, a policy of scorched earth was adopted by the British government.[108] This policy, compounded by a difficult monsoon season, created a dire situation for India in which approximately three million people died due to malnourishment.

Some historians, have blamed Churchill's anti-Indian (if not racist) attitudes and policies as Prime Minister for the severity of the famine. Others, have maintained that the famine's severity was due mostly to infrastructural inabilities to deliver grain and wheat.[109] While Churchill's anti-Hindu rants were shamefully racist, his intention, for right or wrong, was to protect Britain and its Empire. The unfortunate Indians, both Hindus and Muslims, who suffered through the famine were seen by Churchill as little more than collateral damage in the war against the Axis powers.

With the threat of Japanese encroachment, Churchill swiftly decided to support the idea of dominion status for India and authorized Leader of the House Stafford Cripps to go to India and put the idea to the Party Congress and the Muslim League.[110] However, he probably did so due to his 'political weakness.'[111] Neither Churchill, Jinnah, or Viceroy Lord Linlithgow really wanted the offer to be accepted. For Churchill and the Viceroy this meant that Britain would have to concede to self-government in India; for Jinnah, if the offer was successful, 'he would have to join a national government and play second fiddle to Nehru and the Congress.'[112]

Churchill was fearful that American sympathies were with the Hindu opinion, so he sought to 'let them see the Moslem side of the picture.'[113] He wrote to Roosevelt on 4 March 1942 saying that the British Cabinet was considering dominion status for India but was wary that such a step towards self-governance would alienate the princes, the untouchables, and the Muslims of whom Churchill said he was not willing to break with, for two reasons. The first was that the Muslims 'represent 100 million people', the implication being that Churchill did not want to deny them a government that would represent their community. The second reason, which was purely strategic, was that Muslims make up 'the main army elements on which we must rely for immediate fighting.'[114]

To convince Roosevelt of the Muslim plight and to vindicate his wariness of dominion status, Churchill included letters from Jinnah, Sir Firoz Khan Noon, one of Churchill's Islamic contacts in India who was a member of the Viceroy's council, and a military adviser from the India Office. While the last two echoed Churchill's strategic concerns, Jinnah's letter addressed both reasons for Churchill's wariness. Jinnah wrote: 'If the British Government is stampeded into the trap laid for them, Moslem India would be sacrificed, with most disastrous consequences, especially with regard to the war effort.' He also made the case for Britain to stay in India, arguing that if self-government were taken up at present, all power would go to a:

> Hindu all-Indian Government, thus practically deciding at once far reaching constitutional issues in breach of the pledges given to the Moslems and other minorities in the British Government's declaration of 8 August 1940, which promised no constitutional change [...] without Moslem agreement and that the Moslems would not be coerced to submit to an unacceptable system of government.

Also fearing for the future of the speculative Pakistan, Jinnah argued that giving the all-Indian government over to the Hindu majority would 'torpedo the Moslem claim for Pakistan, which is their article of faith.'[115] In his history of World War II, Churchill noted: 'Pakistan meant a separate domain and government for the Moslems, and the consequent partition of India.' However, he did not enter into any discussion on whether he favoured the partition. Churchill's discussions with Jinnah after the war revealed that he did, in fact, favour a separate Pakistan and that it might be offered dominion status.[116]

At any rate, Roosevelt was not interested in Churchill's caveats and wrote back referencing the American system for government when they threw off the British in 1787, which further illustrated the American point of view that Britain needed to give up its empire in India. The largest concession Churchill could bring himself to offer was dominion status, which was made by the Cripps mission in late March 1942 and was basically rejected by Gandhi and large portions of the Hindu population because they felt that 'it was impossible for Congress to consider any schemes or proposals which retain even a partial measure of British control in India [. . .] Britain must abandon her hold on India.'[117] The Indian Congress had passed the 'Quit India Resolution' but before Gandhi could put the campaign in full swing, Lord Linlithgow had the Congress leaders arrested. This only radicalized the younger Indian nationalists such as Subbas Bose, whom Gandhi had subdued. The instability in India infuriated Churchill. He proclaimed privately that he hated Indians and that they 'are a beastly people with a beastly religion.'[118] Churchill was clearly in a rage and was referring to the polytheist Hindus and not the monotheist Muslims. Despite the Cripps report that Nehru 'came out with a fine statement of total war against the Japanese', the majority of Hindus continued with a neutral attitude and India remained under nominal British control.[119]

Interestingly, the major reason the Cripps proposal was rejected is because it 'betrayed a British willingness to appease Muslim nationalism and princely autonomy by endorsing the possibility that some provinces and states might eventually secede. This was an anathema to all shades of Congress opinion.'[120] However, it illustrated a willingness by Churchill to allow Jinnah to pursue the possibility of Pakistan. This was not because Churchill personally sought an idealized Islamic state in the region, but because he believed that any such state would remain allies and friends to the British Empire, thus advancing British interests in the larger Islamic world. This line of thought was evident in Churchill's statement in the House of Commons on 10 September 1942, when he spoke against the Indian Congress Party saying it 'does not represent India. It does not represent the majority of people in India. It does not even represent the Hindu masses. Outside that Party and fundamentally opposed to it are 90 million Moslems in British India who have their rights to self expression.' Churchill went on to note that 'it was fortunate that the Congress Party has no influence whatever on the martial races, on whom the defence of India [. . .] really depends.'[121]

His preference for the loyal Muslims was evident. From Churchill's perspective, Muslim India had largely been loyal throughout World War I, with the exception of the Caliphate Movement in the early 1920s. In that case, it only made sense to ensure British authority in the Islamic world (including Central Asia) by supporting Jinnah's nationalist aspirations. Through Churchill's secret support for Jinnah and India's Muslims, he still hoped he could deny Gandhi his ultimate victory.'[122]

Churchill's support of Jinnah and the Muslims' national aspirations was evident in several remarks in his private life. After reading *Verdict on India* by Beverley Nichols, another book that heavily influenced Churchill's thinking and that has been described as 'a sequel to *Mother India*' by Katherine Mayo,[123] Churchill wrote to Clementine:

> It certainly shows the Hindu in his true character and the sorry plight to which we have reduced ourselves by losing confidence in our mission. Reading about India has depressed me for I see such ugly storms looming up there which, even in my short flight, may over take us.

However, in the letter's conclusion, Churchill's thinking on the solution for the Indian situation is evident, 'I agree with the book and also I agree with its conclusion – Pakistan.'[124]

Another example that Churchill's thinking was turning towards a Muslim state was his remarks at dinner with the President of the Board of Education, R.A. Butler, in March 1943 when Churchill was lecturing his dinner guests on India. He 'launched into a most terrible attack on the "baboos" saying they were gross dirty and corrupt.'[125] Churchill then feared that the only reason Britain remained in India was to prevent 'one section of the population mauling and murdering the other'. He concluded that 'the answer was Pakhistan [sic]'. However, R.A. Butler refused to acknowledge this, because Indian unity was 'the thing which the British Raj has always stood.' Churchill snapped back: 'Well if our poor troops have to be kept in a sweltering, syphilitic climate and lice infested barracks for the sake of your precious unity, I'd rather see them have a good civil war.' At that point, Clementine scolded Churchill for his tone: 'Winston! You don't mean what you are saying.' Churchill admitted he did not want a civil war but assured Butler that he supported the reality of Pakistan by adding that what he really felt about the Indian government was that 'we might sit on top of a tripos – Pakhistan [sic], Princely India, and the Hindus.'[126] Churchill continued to support the Muslims of India, even if it meant breaking up the country. The fact that he gave such weight to Muslim opinion was displayed by his political alliances with Muslims in different areas of the British Empire.

This period of Churchill's career saw him continuing to grapple with issues involving Muslim populations of the British Empire in the midst of World War II. While these problems were complex, for Churchill they understandably remained secondary to the war effort. Despite this, there is clear evidence of Churchill's continued consideration of Muslim and Arab aspirations, which would continue into the postwar world.

CHAPTER 8

THE POSTWAR WORLD

This chapter examines Churchill's attitudes and policies concerning the Islamic world after World War II and during his final premiership. The chapter is divided into three sections. The first explores Churchill's views on Indian independence and the creation of Pakistan, taking into account his relationship with M.A. Jinnah and other prominent Muslims. The second considers the advent of the new state of Israel and how it affected Churchill's views of the Zionist position in the Middle East. The third analyzes Churchill's attitudes and policies concerning the greater Middle East, especially Egypt, and demonstrates how he was forced to surrender some of his more antiquated views of the Islamic world in order to keep a united front with the United States and preserve British prestige.

The United States emerged from World War II as the premier world power, followed closely by the Soviet Union. The 'once magnificent' but 'still considerable' British Empire had suffered greatly, but survived the onslaught of the Nazi war machine, with Churchill at its helm.[1] However, near the close of the war on 26 July 1945, Churchill lost the 1945 general election and became the leader of the opposition in Parliament. Yet the significant changes of this period were not limited to strategic and political changes; Churchill's views were also changing but not in the progressive manner as they had during the Edwardian period – if anything Churchill's views were becoming more conservative, if not more Victorian. Churchill was certainly a 'victim of illness and age' (this would become increasingly obvious after his series of strokes) and his policies and beliefs were also increasingly effected by 'Arteriosclerosis [...] dementia, as well as habit, nostalgia, and self centeredness.'[2] This might help explain Churchill's reversion to a romantic, Victorian world view because, according to medical historians, 'a feature of Arteriosclerosis is an increased rigidity of view.'[3]

Despite such influences on Churchill's policies and views he still had a relatively solid grasp on geopolitical issues. Because of the divisions caused by the Cold War, Churchill's engagement with the Islamic world during the postwar period remained largely strategic, much as it had been during the war. His strategic aims had three primary goals. The first was to stay as diplomatically close as possible to the United States; the second was to contain communism and keep Stalin and the Soviets in check; and the third was to maintain the prestige of the British Empire as far as possible. All of Churchill's interactions with the Islamic world from the end of World War II to the Suez Crisis must be examined in this context.

India

After the war, as leader of the opposition, Churchill continued his support of the Muslims in India, partly out of genuine concern for their situation but mostly because he thought this alliance might keep India (and perhaps Pakistan) as a dominion of the British Empire. In Churchill's mind this would keep parts of India loyal to Britain and serve as a strategic location against the Soviet Union, much in the same way as it had been in the 'Great Game' against the Russian Empire. In a letter to Prime Minister Clement Attlee on 1 May 1946, Churchill claimed that he remained 'committed to the Cripps Mission in 1942', which sought to eventually grant independence to India, but that he was not happy about it. He noted that the 'imminence of Japanese invasion' and the hope of rallying as many forces as possible 'compelled [Churchill] to take the line he did.'[4] In the run-up to the Indian Independence Act of 1947, Churchill continued his parliamentary tactics of the 1930s by repeatedly reminding his colleagues that 'the large Muslim and Untouchable minorities were under serious threat in Hindu-majority India' and that: 'The British, in their role as paternalistic rulers, had a moral duty to protect them. If the British left, it would be a dereliction of that duty; therefore the British could not leave India.'[5]

Churchill was frustrated by the rejection of the Indian interim government in May by the Hindu-controlled Indian National Congress and reminded his colleagues in Parliament that:

> attention should be particularly directed at the Muslim Community of nearly 80 million who are the most warlike and formidable of all the races and creeds in the Indian sub-continent and whose interests and culture are a matter of great consequence to India as a whole and to peace in India.[6]

Equally frustrated by the situation in India, though for different reasons, Indians (both Hindus and Muslims) began to mutiny in the armed services due to the increasingly complicated and slow repatriation from Britain.[7] This was largely due to Viceroy Wavell's inability to keep the debate under control and move towards British withdrawal. In this climate, M.A. Jinnah resumed his correspondence with Churchill on 6 July 1946 and solidified their political alliance. However, 'just how far the alliance went between Churchill and Jinnah was hard to tell from the remaining few records.' However, Churchill's letters do reveal a 'keen interest in the Muslim League.' Additionally, historians have implied that Jinnah and Churchill had 'made a secret pact' during the war, in which Jinnah would have Pakistan in return for the Muslim's League's support fighting the Japanese' – though no real evidence exists of any such pact.[8] Regardless, Jinnah sought help from Churchill and appealed to him for his continued support of the Indian Muslims. Believing Viceroy Wavell to be too soft towards the aspirations of the Indian National Congress in the interim government, Jinnah argued that the British government had 'shaken the confidence of Muslim India and shattered their hopes for an honourable and peaceful settlement.' He also enclosed several press clippings and statements from himself to the press to illustrate the situation to Churchill, who was fascinated by Jinnah's statement and even underlined portions of it that stated:

> As regards the resolution of the Congress, I most emphatically repudiate their bogus claim that they represent India and their claim to 'national' character. The Congress are a Hindu organisation and they do not represent any other community except Caste Hindus [...] The Congress [...] have no right to represent or speak on behalf of the Muslims and their refusal to accept the proposals for the formation of an interim government is based on sinister motives.
>
> As regards the safeguard that no decision on any major communal issue could be taken if the majority of the main parties were opposed to it, of which assurance was given by the Viceroy, this is absolutely necessary to protect the Muslim interests as [...] there is parity between the Caste Hindus and the Muslims, the Muslims will be a minority of little over one-third in the whole executive.[9]

Jinnah's letter made such an impact on Churchill that in his speech to the House of Commons on 18 July 1946 he echoed many of Jinnah's points, which he had underlined, and made a bold case for the Muslims of India. He began pointing out to his colleagues that during the war 'The Congress party gave us no assistance; on the contrary, they did us the greatest injury in their power.' When asked, 'What did the Muslim League do?' Churchill retorted that while 'the Muslim League did not give active co-operation as a League' there were 'upwards of 800,000 volunteers from the Punjab State alone.' Churchill then moved to speak about the Muslims as a minority and how the gulf between the Hindus and Muslims 'was never more acute [...] than at the present moment.' This was due, Churchill argued, to what the Muslim community saw as a 'departure' from the Viceroy's declaration of 16 June, which stated that if one community failed to enter a coalition interim government, then the mission would move forward as best it could in the most representative way possible with only one of the major parties present. According to Churchill, 'The Muslim League entered this, when the Hindu Congress members refused [. . .] I understand that the Muslim League made a violent complaint.' Churchill then asserted that it would be difficult to make a coalition government with only one party and that 'there is a feeling among the Muslims of India that faith has been broken with them.' Churchill then noted that 'the General Secretary of the Muslim League has gone as far to say that unless the situation is clarified, it would be suicidal for the League to enter into a Constituent Assembly'. He then warned the House:

> The agreement of the Muslims to the new system affects the whole foundation of the problem. One cannot contemplate that British troops should be used to crush the Muslims in the interests of the caste Hindus. Whatever, our responsibilities may be [. . .] we must not make ourselves agents of a caste government, or a particular sectional Government in order to crush by armed force and modern weapons, another community.[10]

Churchill wrote back and assured Jinnah in his reply that he was 'very much opposed to the handing over of India to Hindu Caste rule', and that he has 'always strongly espoused the rights of Moslems and the Depressed Classes.' Churchill also noted that he felt 'it is most important that British arms should not be used to dominate the Moslems, even though the caste Hindus might claim numerical majority in a constituent assembly.' However, it is important to remember that though 'he was a supporter of India's Muslims, Churchill was not uncritical of Muslim attitude.'[11] Churchill became gradually more upset about the violence and anti-British rhetoric issued by some members of the Muslim League. This, of course, hardened his opinion of the Indian Muslims, just as such riots had hardened him towards the Palestinians before the war. In a letter to Jinnah Churchill expressed his concerns:

> I was [. . .] surprised to read all the insulting things that were said about Britain at the Moslem Congress in Bombay, and how the

> Moslems of India were described as 'under-going British slavery'. All this is quite untrue and ungrateful. It also seems to be an act of great unwisdom on the part of the Moslems. The tendencies here to support the congress are very strong in the Government party and you are driving away your friends. I am sorry to see you taking up an attitude towards Great Britain which cannot be reconciled with your letter to me asking for help.[12]

Jinnah received Churchill's letter as negotiations were breaking down between the Muslim League and the government. Fearing no support from England, Jinnah moved to start a protest on 16 August 1946, which came to be known as 'Direct Action Day'. The original intention of Direct Action was a planned strike for Muslims to protest the interim government and to support the creation of a Muslim homeland. However, the protests turned into riots. In Calcutta alone nearly 5,000 people died, and these riots led to country-wide sectarian violence between Hindus and Moslems for nearly a year.[13]

Jinnah retorted to Churchill after Direct Action Day that he was 'surprised' to read such a paragraph and that it illustrated that 'even you have not got a full grasp of the situation in India and that it seems that your press is not very helpful in that direction while the Congress propaganda of misrepresentation is so widely spread.' Jinnah then emphatically pleaded 'What do you expect the Mussalmans to do?' He noted the tendency in England for support for the Congress and that the Muslim league was 'steam rolled' by the Viceroy and Cabinet delegation. He concluded by arguing that this could have created 'only one result and that [was] a general revolt against the British.' However, in an attempt to keep up their relationship Jinnah included more press statements in order to keep Churchill informed.[14]

Jinnah's assessment seems unfair (though probably accurate) because Churchill did remain relatively informed by other people such as Waris Ali, Walter Monckton, and members of the Muslim League and the Royal Empire Society, though he probably lacked a 'full grasp' of the situation. For instance, Walter Monckton wrote to

Churchill earlier thanking him for his speech on 16 May and, in his letter, Monckton explained that the 'princes and the Muslim League and Jinnah will all be pleased.'[15] He also forwarded a letter to Churchill from Ahmed Said, the Nawab of Chhatari, on 5 August 1946 explaining the Muslim dilemma in the Indian situation to Monckton:

> This controversy between the Muslim League and the Cabinet Mission has driven the Muslims also into the wilderness of direct action and unconstitutional agitation [. . . The] British Government has failed in making friends of their enemies but has succeeded in creating a feeling of hopelessness and helplessness in the minds of their friends.

In the letter's conclusion, Said reminded Monckton that he wished to remain out of the press and out of the House of Commons but that he saw 'no reason why the Leader of the Opposition should not know the difficulties of those in India who are willing to remain with the British provided they are willing to stay in India.'[16] Churchill enjoyed the conclusion of the letter immensely, as he was just as frustrated with government policy in India as his friends were. Likewise, Waris Ali continually informed Churchill about the Indian situation, much as he had in the 1930s, and often included newspaper clippings and articles that further reinforced Churchill's position.[17] In December 1946, Waris Ali wrote to Churchill to vent his frustration and urge him to continue his quest of keeping India as a dominion of the Empire.[18]

Additionally, Churchill received many letters from other members of the Muslim League and its allies, keeping him informed. For instance, also in December, Liaquat Ali Khan wrote to Churchill regarding the massacres of Muslim villages by Hindus in Meerut.[19] Upon receipt of this letter, Churchill spoke in the Commons of the 'frightful slaughters over wide regions and in obscure uncounted villages that have, in the main, fallen upon Muslim minorities.'[20] Moreover, the Muslim league wrote two letters to Churchill in the spring of 1947. The first asked to keep Bengal in Pakistan and pleaded with Churchill to 'kindly see that injustice is not done to those who have been peaceful and loyal during the war.'[21] The second letter argued that partition and a Muslim state was the only real logical solution to the Indian issue.[22] Both these concepts were used by Churchill in speeches to Parliament.

In December 1946 Churchill and Jinnah met for lunch at Chartwell while Jinnah was visiting Britain. They discussed 'the fate of India's Muslims under a Hindu majority government.'[23] Both men supported the concept of Pakistan. For Churchill, 'the creation of Pakistan with ties to the empire seemed the one way to "save a bit of India" for Britain and to snatch victory from Gandhi, the Congress and Attlee.'[24] Churchill wrote to Jinnah afterwards and confirmed how 'greatly [he] valued their talk the other day' and attached an address where Jinnah could reach him. Churchill said he would always sign himself 'Gilliant' (the name of his secretary) so not to 'attract too much attention in India.'[25] In this correspondence, Churchill repeatedly 'assured Jinnah that Pakistan would have a strong protector in the British and would never be expelled from the British Commonwealth.'[26] However, after this letter very little evidence of an exchange between the two exists, save for the stray press statement and thank you card, which seems odd, as this letter instructed more to follow. It has been argued that there were probably 'letters of substance' but they had most likely been 'destroyed'. Historian Alex Von Tunzelmann has theorized that the two men 'were up to something' due to the 'cloak and dagger' nature of the correspondence. Whether they were or not, Churchill certainly played a prominent role in the creation of Pakistan. As Tunzelmann put it:

> There can be no doubt that [Churchill's] public championing of the Muslim League's cause in the House of Commons throughout 1946 and 1947, and of Pakistan's thereafter, was crucial both to the creation of Pakistan and to the British government's support for its interests over the years to come. If Jinnah is regarded as the father of Pakistan, Churchill must qualify as its uncle; and, therefore, as a pivotal figure in the resurgence of political Islam.[27]

After Churchill met Jinnah, he spoke to the House of Commons on 12 December 1946 to illustrate his concern that the situation in India was headed towards a 'ferocious civil war [...] between the Muslims and the Hindus.' In this speech, Churchill's paternalistic imperialism came to the forefront. Quoting his father on India more than 50 years previously (and thus illustrating his fossilized perception of India) Churchill quipped:

> There are now 400 millions who are affected by those powerful forces, to bind them and to weld by the influence of our knowledge, our law and our higher civilization in process of time into one great united people to offer to all the nations of the West the advantages of tranquillity and progress in the East.[28]

In 1947, Clement Attlee lost confidence in Viceroy Wavell's ability to negotiate a peaceful settlement for India and installed Lord Mountbatten, a former naval officer, as Viceroy. Unlike Wavell, Mountbatten believed that an independent, united India was an impossibility and was content moving forward with a two-state solution, much to the happiness of Jinnah and Churchill. Even Hindu leaders such as Nehru began to warm to the idea. However, Gandhi remained convinced that a united India must be the only outcome.

In May, Mountbatten received orders from the Cabinet to move forward with a plan to transfer power to two separate states, whereby India and Pakistan would be split along a line determined by the Government Commission. Upon revealing it to the Indian leaders, Nehru objected for fear of a 'Balkanization' of the Indian subcontinent.[29] However, Nehru eventually decided that he could accept dominion status if nominal independence was granted before the end of the year. Interestingly, Mountbatten met with the leaders of the opposition including Churchill and 'reassured them, off the record, that it might be worth their while to take up Nehru's concession. If they were prepared to offer India a very early transfer of power, they could expect it to accept dominion status rather than full independence.'[30]

Churchill jumped at this opportunity to keep India as a part of the Commonwealth, partly because this would gain favour with the United States, which took a stern view of the British Empire in India, but mostly because it ensured India (and Pakistan) were still connected with the British Empire. In Churchill's mind, the scheme also helped contain communism's spread in Central Asia. He wrote to Attlee on 21 May 1947, that he:

> had an opportunity of consulting my colleagues terms of the possible settlement in India [. . .] As a result, I am in a position to assure you that if those terms are made good, so there is an effective acceptance of Dominion Status for several parts of a divided India, the Conservative party will agree to facilitate the passage, this session, of the legislation.[31]

However, Churchill was never actually satisfied with how the legislation played out. He objected to the name of the bill,[32] and later recalled to Julian Amery (Leo Amery's son) in July 1952 that had he sent a small force to suppress the Congress uprising in 1942 and believed that:

> we could have maintained law and order in India after the war. We could then have held a Constituent Assembly with British troops holding the ring, in which the Princes, the Untouchables, the Moslems and others would have made their influence felt much more effectively than they did in the chaos that followed our withdrawal.[33]

There still remained one minor issue: getting Jinnah to accept the terms of separation. At the meeting, Mountbatten told Churchill that convincing Jinnah would be 'the real problem'. To which Churchill barked, 'By God he is the one man who cannot do without British help!' He then told Mountbatten to give Jinnah a message from him, 'Tell him this is a matter of life and death for Pakistan if he does not accept this offer with both hands!'[34]

Mountbatten delivered the message and 'the immovable Jinnah' had been swayed by Churchill; the plan to partition India finally moved forward.[35] Jinnah might have realized he could not push the scales further in his favour after having negotiated for the position of Governor-General of Pakistan, while Lord Mountbatten remained the Governor-General of India.[36] Alternatively, Jinnah may have simply respected Churchill's opinion on the matter. After all, 'Jinnah admired Churchill more than any man alive.'[37] One cannot dismiss the effect of Churchill on M.A. Jinnah – and the effect of Jinnah, the Muslim league, and their allies on Churchill's view of India.

After partition and independence in August 1947, rioting and bloodshed washed over India as the confusion of the partition became a reality. Churchill still supported Pakistan and the Indian Muslims by echoing their concerns in his speeches. In a speech in the House of Commons, Churchill argued that 'Hyderabad should remain independent' rather than go to India as portions as Kashmir had done.[38] Another case of Churchill helping the Muslims in this period was his exchange on behalf of his old friend Sir Feroz Khan Noon. A certain Mr Keeling forwarded a letter to Churchill of Noon's (upon his request) that said: 'We in Pakistan shall be most grateful if you can persuade your government to sell us sufficient arms to save our freedom. We are being attacked by the Hindus [...] Can Mr. Churchill please use his influence with the USA to persuade them to sell us arms.'[39] Mr Keeling was fearful that such a letter would give cause for the arrest of Sir Noon, to which Churchill assured him that he had 'obtained the fullest possible personal assurances that no action had been taken against Sir F Khan Noon.' Noon next wrote to Churchill directly to ask for help and explain what the situation was in Pakistan.

Interestingly, Noon played on several of Churchill's strategic fears in his letter. Knowing Churchill to find communism abhorrent, Noon argued:

> The Musalmans in Pakistan are against communism like the Musalmans of Turkey. However, the Musalmans by religion are against communism and on the whole Pakistan will fight against it just as Turkey is doing [...] In Pakistan communism

> does not exist at all. However, Hindus have got an ambassador in Moscow.

Noon continued that, 'if fighting continues in India communism will have quick rise there on account of the Hindus.' Noon then touched on one of Churchill's principal strategies for the region: 'It seems very desirable that Pakistan should be made a strong bastion in the East against communism, as Turkey has in the west.' He also warned Churchill that: 'Should India invade Pakistan, Pakistan will side with anyone against the Hindu and may even look to Moscow.'[40] Undoubtedly, Churchill agreed with several aspects of Noon's letter, especially in regard to using Pakistan as a bulwark against the Soviet Union. Noon successfully combined Churchill's hatred for communism and Hinduism in order to gain his support. Churchill sent both of Noon's letters to Lord Mountbatten to illustrate how grave the situation in Pakistan was.[41] In Churchill's letter to Mountbatten he said: 'No doubt it is one sided, but none less poignant [...] I have your promise that the writer will suffer no ill on this account.' Churchill then revealed that Noon's second letter had sparked his fears. He concluded his letter by saying: 'I am too grieved with what is happening in India to write more.'[42]

In many ways, Churchill's long-term political alliance with the Muslims resulted in something of a victory for Churchill. Like Burma (in 1948), India and Pakistan were no longer held by the British Empire. However, unlike Burma, they both remained as dominions, India until 1950 and Pakistan until 1956, just after the end of Churchill's final period as Prime Minister. This arrangement owed largely to Churchill's alliance with Jinnah and the Indian Muslims during the rush to get Britain to quit India. From Churchill's point of view, it could have been worse. After all, Pakistan did help contain the Soviets in Central Asia as signatories to the Baghdad Pact in 1955 and as members of the Central Treaty Organization (CENTO). This, of course, was not a long term solution. But when Churchill left office in 1955 CENTO appeared as strong as ever. As a bonus, the new gift of relative freedom in the dominions pleased the United States, fulfilling Churchill's other postwar objective.

Palestine/Israel

While in opposition after the war, Churchill continued to struggle with the situation in Palestine. His stance towards the Zionist leadership had cooled. After the assassination of Churchill's friend Lord Moyne by the Stern Gang, extremist Zionists, Churchill stayed away from the cause and, in fact, never again personally met with Chaim Weizmann, the leader of the Zionists. As Cohen pointed out: 'Churchill's reputed sympathy for the Jews [... was] not translated into the coinage of action.'[43] A.J.P. Taylor even commented:

> Only Churchill continued to show sympathy with the Jews until the murder of Lord Moyne, and there is nothing more striking in the story than the total failure of the supposedly all powerful Prime Minister to enforce his will on numerous occasions.[44]

Remarkably, the feeling was fairly mutual. 'The Zionists were in agreement that Churchill's government had betrayed the Zionist cause and even worse, tricked them into silence, by making promises it had never had any intention of keeping.'[45] Weizmann even feared that Attlee's government would renege on the promises to the Zionists in the Anglo-American Committee on Palestine and recommend an 'abolition of Jewish Agency and the establishment of an Arab state in Palestine.'[46] Churchill's distance from the Zionists was obvious in his speech to the House of Commons on 1 August 1946 when he reiterated his preference for a bi-national solution, stating that 'Palestine was not to be a Jewish National Home, but there was to be a Jewish National Home in Palestine' and that: 'It was quite true that the claims and desires of the Zionists went beyond anything which were agreed to by the Mandatory Power.' Churchill also defended his bi-nationalist approach by speaking on Arab and Jewish solidarity. He argued that each community had helped the other, resulting in: 'The Jews multiplying six fold and the Arabs 500,000, thus showing that both races gained a marked advantage from the Zionist policy which we pursued.'[47]

However, just because Churchill had cooled towards the Zionists did not mean he warmed towards the Arabs of Palestine. He also noted in his speech that the Jews had been 'vehemently and undividedly on our side in the struggle' while the Zionist policy of Great Britain caused a 'divergence in Arab sentiment'. Similarly during World War I, the Palestinian Arabs allied with the Ottomans, an alliance for which Churchill never forgave them. Despite this damnation, he went on to comment on how the Middle Eastern Arabs had been treated by Great Britain:

> We have treated them very well. The House of Hussein reigns in Iraq. Feisal was placed on the throne, his grandson is there today. The Emir Abdullah, whom I remember appointing at Jerusalem, in 1921, to be in charge of Transjordiana, is there today [. . .] He has never broken his faith and loyalty to this country. Syria and Lebanon owe their independence to the great exertions made by the British Government [. . .] We have insisted on those pledges being made good. I cannot touch on the Arabs without paying my tribute to the splendid king, Ibn Saud, of Saudi Arabia, who in the darkest hours never failed to send messages and encouragement of his unshakeable faith that we should win and gain through. I cannot admit that we have not done our utmost to treat Arabs in a way which so great a race deserves and requires.

Churchill's monologue on the Arabs revealed that his thinking on the Islamic world remained much as it had in the 1920s. He praised the House of Hussein, whom he put in power, and their arch-rival, the House of Saud, despite their rivalry. While Churchill's newly found confidence in the Saudis represented the largest change in this thinking since the 1920s, it also illustrated a very limited grasp of the world as it was in 1946. However, Churchill went even further in demonstrating his romantic, if not Victorian, understanding of the Middle East by evoking the memory of T.E. Lawrence:

> There was no greater champion of Arab rights that the late Colonel Lawrence [. . .] When Lawrence gave me his book

> *The Seven Pillars of Wisdom*, he wrote in it that I had made a happy end to the show. I will not have it that the way we treated this matter was inconsiderate to the Arabs. On the contrary, I think that they have had a very fair deal from Great Britain. With all those countries which are given to their power and control, in every way they have had a fair deal. It was little enough [. . .] that we had asked for the Jews – a natural home in their historic Holy Land, on which they have the power and virtue to confer many blessings for employment, both of Jew and Arab.[48]

While Churchill's understanding of the Middle East was clearly a romanticized construction in which all Arab and Islamic sects allied themselves along nationalist aspirations, he had a point. He had helped create and empower 'Transjordania' and Iraq, embraced Ibn Saud's powerful position in Saudi Arabia, and created a situation in which an independent Syria became a reality. It was only in Palestine that Churchill had not empowered the Arabs along the same lines. This was not only due to the Jewish national home but also to Churchill's belief that the Palestinian Arabs were outside the pledges to the other Arab countries. Despite these issues, Churchill genuinely believed, like Abdullah and other members of the Hashemite clan, that pursuing Zionism also advanced the Palestinian Arabs, as the Zionists provided skills and capital for the region.

Another theme in Churchill's speech was his return to an insistence that Palestine should remain unpartitioned, as the presence of Jews and Arabs was beneficial to its future development. However, Churchill did imply 'that had he been re-elected as Prime Minister in 1945, he would have implemented the partition scheme for Palestine.'[49] However, this was after the Arab–Israeli War in 1948, which created the State of Israel and solidified Jewish dominance in a partitioned Palestine. Churchill merely returned to the two state solution for Palestine 'once the Israelis themselves had made it into a *fait accompli*.'[50] What is particularly curious is that this can be inferred from Churchill's statement in the House of Commons on 26 January 1949 (after the defeat of the Arab armies by the Zionists) in which Churchill sought not to create a partition for the sake of the Jews, but for the sake of the Arabs. Churchill criticized the government, arguing that 'the Foreign Secretary's [Ernest Bevin's] policy has been the worst possible for the Arabs. I am sure we could have agreed immediately after the war upon a partition scheme which would have been more favourable to the Arabs.'[51]

Churchill, like most politicians of the time, was surprised that Zionists had won the Israeli–Arab War. In fact, 'prior to the spring of 1948, there was a general consensus in the West that the Jews in Palestine would be defeated by the Arabs'. The war changed two things in Churchill's thinking on the Middle Eastern area of the Islamic world. The first was that he found a new respect for Israel. After the war Churchill's 'sentiments were governed [...] by admiration and respect for the military prowess of the Jews, an asset which might yet be turned into an imperial asset in the region.'[52] This was clear in 1950 when Churchill was interviewed by Israel's first ambassador to Britain, Eliahu Elath. Demonstrating some Churchillian inconsistencies, he told Elath that the creation of Israel was a 'great event in history' and that he was 'proud of his own contribution towards it.' He concluded by saying that he had 'been a Zionist all his life'.[53] This statement was made despite Churchill's earlier claims of just being wedded to Zionism.

This alteration in Churchill's stance was an advantageous political move. The political *zeitgeist* in England (and the United States) was to 'count oneself among the friends and admirers of the heroic young state.'[54] Appearing closer to the Zionist cause offered Churchill another relatively powerful partner in the Cold War, and a political opportunity to rebuke the Labour government. Churchill's change of opinion was made clear in his speech to the Commons on 10 December 1948 when he chastized the Labour government for not recognizing the new Israeli state. Revealing his functionary view of the situation Churchill argued:

> But whatever part we belong to, and whatever view we take, we must surely face the facts. The Jews have driven the Arabs out

> of a larger area than was contemplated in our partition schemes. They have established a Government which functions effectively. They have a victorious army at their disposal and they have both the support of Soviet Russia and the United States [. . .] It seems to me that the Government of Israel which has been set up at Tel Aviv cannot be ignored and treated as if it did not exist.[55]

However, it would be unfair to say that Churchill's move towards accepting Israel meant he turned his back on the Arabs. On the contrary, he had received intelligence from Marcus Seiff that 'recognition of Israel by Gt. Britain will be the method by which a settlement between the Jews and the Arabs will be most likely reached' and would prove 'a face-saving device for the Arabs.' Another such memorandum came a few days later and argued that: 'Recognition now of the State of Israel would strengthen the moderate elements amongst the Arabs and the Jews who desire to reach agreement' and that it was believed that, 'King Abdullah, Ibn Saud, and the Lebanese are desirous of reaching a settlement but, until Gt. Britain recognizes Israel they must [. . .] align themselves with their extremists whose declared plans are the elimination of the Jewish State.'[56] While this intelligence was no doubt skewed in favour of the Israelis, Churchill would have leapt at such a notion. It returned to the idea that the Jews and Arabs aided one another, which was something Churchill believed and mentioned repeatedly in his speeches and it provided an economic solution that was tenable for Britain. Moreover, there were larger geopolitical reasons that motivated Churchill to support Israel. The memorandum hinted that without British recognition of Israel there would be a 'vacuum in the Middle East', which Churchill feared would be filled by the Soviet Union.

The second way that the Arab–Israeli War affected Churchill's perception of the Middle East was that it reinforced a sort of sympathetic approach to the Islamic Arabs. In fact, in the same speech where he urged the government to recognize Israel, Churchill mentioned his previous desire for a partition scheme that 'would have taken into account the legitimate rights of the Arabs, who [. . .] had not been ill used in the settlements made in Iraq and Transjordania and in regard to Syria.' Churchill then laid out his old wartime vision for the structure of the Middle East complete with 'an Arab Confederation, comprising three or four Arab States – Saudi Arabia, Iraq, Transjordania, Syria, and Lebanon – however grouped, possibly united amongst themselves, and one Jewish state.' In Churchill's mind this would have 'given peace and unity throughout the whole vast scene of the Middle East'.[57] Churchill once again showed himself to be out of touch and unable to grasp the reality of the Middle Eastern situation. The rival houses of Hussein and Saud would never join in a federation with one another, let alone with a Jewish state.

Another example of Churchill's reinforced sympathy with the Arabs and the Islamic world was his fear that Israel might invade Transjordan. He remarked that Britain 'had a duty to Abdullah', and that it had been 27 years since Churchill 'proposed and supported his appointment as the Emir of Transjordania'. Churchill then pointed out that he was not willing to discount a loyal ally:

> During all that time [. . .] he has acted with wisdom to his own people and with fidelity to the Allies, irrespective of the fortunes of war. We cannot remain indifferent to his fate and treat him as we have treated the Nizam of Hyderabad.'[58]

The last part of Churchill's speech was a dig at the government for abandoning certain areas of India to their fate and illustrated Churchill's perception that the Islamic world was somewhat interlinked.

He virtually repeated these arguments in the House of Commons a month later when he spoke during an emergency debate.[59] In this speech he condemned Foreign Secretary Ernest Bevin's handling of Palestine and the Middle East, arguing that: 'During all this period the Foreign Secretary has not been able to inform Abdullah, our faithful adherent, where he stood or what he would be wise to do. He has had to wait and guess.' Churchill then remarked that he was sure Abdullah would have 'done everything in his power to work for a peaceful solution with the Jews.'[60] While this seemed like a false sentiment, it was fairly accurate.

Abdullah had generally worked with the Zionists in Palestine and actively encouraged Jewish immigration because, like Churchill, Abdullah thought that 'Zionists could bring skills and capital which the Arab world seriously lacked.'[61] It has even been argued that the Hashemites and the Zionists held secret negotiations to have a partition whereby a Jewish canton would exist in the Abdullah's Jordan.[62] This solution might have resembled the Ottoman *millet* system, 'which allowed for non-Islamic groups to live as self-regulating communities under Arab rule.'[63]

Churchill also dwelt on the historical significance of a new Jewish state, arguing that, 'the coming into being of a Jewish State in Palestine is an event in world history to be viewed in the perspective, not of a generation or a century, but in the perspective of a thousand, two thousand or even three thousand years.'[64] This utterance revealed in Churchill a Whiggish approach to the creation of a Jewish state and echoed a bit of Lloyd George's biblical understanding of the Middle East. It also seemed somewhat at odds with the paternalistically kind approach to the Arabs in other portions of the speech. This might be because Churchill ultimately returned to the theme of a united Palestine where 'both of these races have lived [. . .] for thousands of years side by side' and that 'the Jews need the Arabs'. In this way Churchill, even after the Arab–Israeli War, continued to hold the genuine belief that Arabs and Jews would work together. In his mind, he was simultaneously pro-Zionist while maintaining a fair acknowledgment to the Arabs as well, since he believed the races needed one another.

Of course, this symbiotic relationship seems very odd in a modern context, but for Churchill it was completely logical (if not hopeful) and advanced his Cold War strategy on all fronts. First, Israel demonstrated that it was a powerful state by defeating the Arab armies and, thus, was a powerful potential ally against the Soviet Union in the Middle East. Churchill believed that Israel would reward Britain for supporting it since the Balfour Declaration and, by recognizing Israel's existence as a state, trans-Atlantic relations between Britain and the United States would harmonize in the region, creating a united front against the Soviets. Additionally, Churchill hoped his conciliatory stance towards the Arabs would convince the Islamic world to stand firm against communism, while allowing the British Empire to keep nominal control in Pakistan and the Middle East, which, for Churchill, kept his dream of the British Empire alive.

As the general election in 1951 approached, Churchill was hurriedly working on his history of World War II when he got the news of Amir Abdullah's assassination by an extremist Palestinian Arab, a member of the Husayni clan and the clan of Abdullah's arch-rival, the ex-mufti of Jerusalem. Churchill, who had once remarked that 'Abdullah [. . .] had proved the only reliable and stable ruler in the region', was upset by the news,[65] not least because he believed that 'King Abdullah was the only leader in the Arab world who sought consistently to maintain close ties with Great Britain.'[66] In the House of Commons he praised Abdullah as a 'worker for peace and prosperity' and 'champion of Arab rights' and a man who sought 'reconciliation between the Arabs and Jews.' Churchill concluded by simply saying that 'the Arabs have lost a great champion and the Jews have lost a great friend.'[67] Though Abdullah's dynasty continued, Churchill saw the last of his Sherfian kings vanish into history. The question, then, for Churchill was: could Britain maintain the foundation of his Middle Eastern solution even without the men he placed in power? Since both Hashemite house were still in power in Iraq and Jordan, and the United States and Britain were on friendly terms with Saudi Arabia, Churchill remained hopeful. The only wild card was Israel.

That October the Conservatives won the general election and Churchill once again became Prime Minster. One of the first letters Churchill received was from Chaim Weizmann congratulating him on his return to power. Churchill responded to thank Weizmann and express how happy he was about 'the wonderful exertions which Israel is making in this time of difficulty.' Churchill also noted that he hoped that Weizmann would 'work with Jordan and the rest of the Moslem World. With true comradeship, there will be enough for all.'[68] In a speech in Washington on 17 January 1952 Churchill continued with this cautionary blend of admiration for Israel but concern for the Arabs. He praised the fledgling Jewish state saying he 'desired the Jews to have a national home and I have worked for that end' and that he 'rejoiced' at paying 'tribute [to] those who have founded the Israelite State.' However, Churchill also displayed his concern for the Arabs, arguing that 'if [the Israelis] are to enjoy peace and prosperity they must strive to renew and preserve their friendly relations with the Arab world without which widespread misery might follow for all.'[69]

Churchill's cautionary tone was a unique blend of strategic necessity and a personal *weltanschauung.* His admiration and praise for Israel reinforced British diplomatic synchronicity with the United States and encouraged Israel to remain in the anti-Soviet camp, while his concern for the Arab world reflected his desire to create a peaceful region in which British prestige still held sway. This would help contain the Soviets and continue to uphold British honour in the Middle East. It was an example of Churchill's dynamic and pragmatic realism that sought to keep the British united with the United States, combined with his rigid Victorian and romantic view of the world that sought to maintain a part of the Empire in the Middle East. As the Aga Khan once noted regarding these 'interlinked facets' of Churchill's character:

> Part of his being responds with instantaneous romanticism to a highly coloured conception of empire, to the Union Jack unfurled to the breeze in some distant out post [...] to all the trumpet calls of more than a century of British Imperial History. But in the other part of his being he is capable of resolute practicality and common sense, solid and realistic, yet magnanimous.[70]

As the Middle East became increasingly important to the foreign policy of Churchill's government, Israel's role became more solidified as an antagonist of the Arabs. Despite this, the British policy in the Middle East to safeguard against Soviet expansionism began to stand on two columns: its alliance with Israel and its alliance with Turkey, which joined NATO in 1952, and was the largest politically secular, and yet Islamic nation in the region. Since Pakistan was the bulwark against communism in Central Asia, and Turkey was the buttress in the West, the 'northern tier' of the Islamic world worked with the British geopolitical aspirations in the East. However, the alliance with Israel continued to destabilize the Middle Eastern portion of Churchill's strategy. While Israel proved a staunch ally against Soviet expansion, it continually antagonized the Arab world, especially in Jordan where the descendants of Abdullah were not as patient or as loyal as Churchill's old ally.

In October 1953, in retaliation for an Israeli family being killed by 'Palestinian Arab infiltrators', the Israeli government sanctioned a military raid into Jordan against the village of Qibya, which resulted in the destruction of 'forty-five houses, a school, and a mosque', and resulted in the deaths of nearly 70 Arabs, most of whom were 'women and children'.[71] This raid was condemned by virtually every Western nation, including the United States. The British government told its embassy to send 'an expression of horror' to the Israeli government.[72] Remarkably, Churchill 'did not respond' after being shown the telegram and, a few days later, sent an armoured division to Jordan, and said that 'it should be made clear' that the British forces in the region do not represent a threat to Israeli interests.

Gilbert understates the effect of the massacre on Churchill, simply stating that he did not 'send a personal message to [Israeli Prime Minister] Ben-Gurion deploring the Kibya attack.'[73] However, in the Israeli Foreign Minister Moshe Sharett's diary, Eliahu Elath reported that '[t]he old man [Churchill] was furious over Qibya' and that 'since the murder of Lord Moyne [...] Israel had not aroused such outrage in him.' Churchill even proclaimed 'that as a Zionist he had been hurt to the depths of his soul', and that if 'Weizmann had been alive, such a thing would have never happened.'[74] This suggests that Churchill was angry enough to send a message, and a complete review of the Cabinet minutes reveals that he wanted to provide a 'stabilising influence in the area' that would reassure 'the Jordan Government of our fidelity to our obligations to them'.[75] However, in a Cabinet meeting in September, Churchill expressed his fear regarding a war with Israel and even considered going to the UN in the event of a war, and wanted to see what the US position was 'in relation to the pacification of [the] Israel/Arab situation.'[76]

In 1954, border clashes between Jordan and Israel came to the forefront when another border incident took place on the Scorpion Ascent to the Negev. Tensions were so high that the Cabinet tried to arrange for secret talks between the countries.[77] At the next Cabinet meeting, plans were drawn up for an Anglo-Jordan alliance in the event of hostilities with Israel. In these plans, Britain would invade Israel from the south. The Minister of Defence, Earl Alexander of Tunis, wondered if the plan should be communicated to the Jordanians. The Chief of Imperial Staff, General Harding, noted that the other Chiefs of Staff did not want to disclose the plan, to which Churchill said 'he was much relieved to hear that the Chiefs of Staff were not in favour of disclosing to the Jordanians a plan involving British invasion of Israel'. Churchill feared that: 'Leakage of such a plan would have very grave consequences.' In the meeting, Foreign Secretary Anthony Eden suggested that Churchill might send Ben-Gurion a letter reminding him of the British 'obligations under the Treaty with Jordan' and urge him 'to avoid any provocative action.'[78] In Churchill's letter to Ben-Gurion, he promised to do what he could to 'influence the Arab States', but warned that all Britain 'look[s] to you to make counsels of statesmanship and patience prevail on the Israel side.'[79] So, even in Churchill's later (if not more pro-Zionist days) he continued to take into account his allies in the Islamic world. While strategic necessity to keep the Islamic bulwark steady against the Soviets guided Churchill, he also thought it was important to keep his promises to his Arab allies.

Egypt, Iran, and the Middle East

Other sources of concern in the Middle East for Britain in the 1950s were Egypt and Iran. In Egypt, during the Arab–Israeli War of 1948, King Farouk of Egypt grew weary of Abdullah of Jordan's insistence that he head the Arab world. Consequently, Farouk sought to annex part of Palestine to Egypt, so that he might realize his own aspirations of being a major Arab leader. The unrest was compounded by Iraq's desire to bring all the Middle East under an Iraqi-controlled region, while Syria and Lebanon hoped to annex their own parts of Palestine as well. This created an unstable alliance between Arab rulers who distrusted each other.[80] In the aftermath of the Israeli victory in the Arab–Israeli War, Egypt grew increasingly frustrated, partly because of the corrupt and incompetent leadership that resulted in the devastating loss to Israel and partly because of the increased nationalism after the war. This resulted in Egyptians becoming increasingly hostile to the British presence in the Canal Zone. As a result, in the summer of 1952 there was a revolution forcing King Farouk to resign and secede power to Muhammad Neguib and Gamal Abdel Nasser.

After the Conservatives won the 1951 general election, Churchill vented his frustrations with the Egyptian government for shutting down the Suez Canal to any Israeli ships just prior to their own revolution. He argued that the shutdown was 'a complete breach of the armistice' with Israel after the Arab–Israeli War, which he saw as an insult that grew 'more bitter day by day'.

However, for many of the British and certainly for the imperial die-hards, the trouble in Egypt was connected with the situation in Iran, which had traditionally been inside the British Empire's sphere of influence. The newly elected Prime Minister, Mohammad Mossadegh, whom British Intelligence believed to be in league with the Communist Tudeh Party, had nationalized the Anglo-Iranian Oil Company (AIOC, previously the APOC) in March 1951 prior to the general election. Mossadegh, like many Iranians, believed that the incredibly favourable concessions offered to AIOC by the Shah's government in 1933 were immoral, illegal, and were the 'personification of the evils of economic imperialism.'[81] Acting on this notion, Mossadegh expelled the British from their oil refineries at Abadan, which at the time constituted the largest overseas asset held by Britain,[82] causing a crisis for Clement Attlee and the Labour government.

Though Attlee was no imperialist and as Prime Minister oversaw considerable nationalization efforts in Britian, which perhaps gave his government more sympathy with the Iranian nationalization of AIOC, this represented an international crisis with major economic ramifications. Amidst increasing intelligence that accused Mossadegh of irrational behaviour and portrayed him as a madman, Attlee, along with Foreign Secretary Ernest Bevin and his successor Herbert Morrison, began looking into having Mossadegh removed from power by covert means.[83] However, the Truman administration in the United States was very reluctant to give such an operation its blessing and Attlee did not push the matter further. This, of course, remained unknown to the British public and the crisis created a weakness that the Conservatives were happy to exploit in the 1951 general election – and none more so than Winston Churchill.[84]

During his campaign in 1951, Churchill acted the part of an outraged elder statesman who was dismayed at the Attlee government's inability to manage the Abadan Crisis and suggested it could be solved by 'a sputter of musketry'.[85] Moreover, Churchill frequently reminded his audiences that he had played a role in the creation of AIOC while at the Admiralty in 1912. Churchill believed that the faltering British prestige in the Near and Middle East resulted in Egypt and Persia moving away from British authority. He blamed the Attlee government and, specifically, Foreign Secretary Bevin. Though Churchill did not want to 'stick {the Tory Party's} neck out',[86] he still thought that the Abadan matter could have easily been resolved. Churchill argued that 'the loss of India greatly affected our ability to lean on Persia and on the whole region.'[87] He returned to that theme in a speech in Loughton County on 6 October, arguing that the instability 'arose from the decline of British prestige and authority in the Middle East which followed inevitably from the loss of India.'[88] A few days later at a constituency meeting in Woodford, north-east London, Churchill lamented that 'our oriental Empire has been liquidated.'[89]

Though his statements made it easy for the Labour Party to label him a 'warmonger' during the campaign, portions of Churchill's attitude towards the whole of the Middle East and the Islamic world can be glimpsed from these statements. He saw his beloved Empire fading into history, and with it all the strategic positions in India and the Middle East it had commanded. While Churchill was aware, at least in some way, that Britain had to redefine its global role in the postwar world relative to the United States, he was still not happy about seeing the British Empire 'scuttle' from every possession it held. In Egypt, the British position dated from 1882; however, Churchill knew that continued British presence in the Canal Zone owed to the Anglo-Egyptian treaty of 1936, which was due to expire in 1956. This might offer an explanation as to why he fought so hard to keep Egypt and the Suez Canal, a location that he believed 'provided Britain with a commanding bastion in the East despite the irrevocable loss of India.'[90] In Iran, the British position had slowly been built up during the 'Great Game' with Russia and cemented by Churchill himself when he had helped create AIOC while at the Admiralty. But now, for Churchill, both Egypt and Iran were trying to evade the British grasp and go the way of India.

This aspect of Churchill's perception of the Middle East was reinforced by an Eastern Department memorandum written by G.W. Furlonge, head of the Eastern Department in the Foreign Office, on 29 October 1951. In the memorandum, Furlonge warned: 'British withdrawals from India, and particularly Palestine, had diminished the respect and influence Britain had formerly enjoyed throughout the Middle East.' Furthermore, while Jordan, Iraq, and Israel 'still wanted close relations' and 'to cultivate a British connection', Britain's 'predominant position [...] attracted forces of Arab and Iranian nationalism and xenophobia.' Furlonge's memorandum also acknowledged that Islam had helped prevent a 'drift towards communism' owing to its 'patriarchal social structure.'[91] Churchill welcomed this last bit of information as it validated the notion of Islam's incompatibility with communism, a concept Churchill had clung to since the 1920s.

But Churchill's belief in the incompatibility of communism and Islam was not strong enough to alter his belief that a reduced Empire implied weakness. Fuelled by the realites of the shrinking Empire, Churchill projected his anger on to Middle Eastern people, especially the Egyptians. He told the House of Commons on 7 March 1951 that 'it was shocking how little progress there had been among the great masses of the Egyptian *Fellaheen*'.[92] According to Foreign Secretary Anthony Eden's private secretary, Evelyn Shuckburgh, Churchill growled at Eden to tell the Egyptians 'that if we have any more of their cheek we will set the Jews on them and drive them into the gutter, from which they should never have emerged!'[93] After an Egyptian riot in January 1952 in which the Shepheard Hotel was burned down, Churchill wrote to Eden that 'the horrible behaviour of the mob puts them lower than most degraded savages now known.'[94] This was an interesting comment, since in Churchill's cultural hierarchy the Egyptian *fellaheen* were located under the noble Bedouins and Arab merchants but above the wild Islamic frontier tribes. However, in the wake of such terrorism, rioting, and other 'uncivilized' pursuits in Egypt, Churchill thought it reasonable to demote the Egyptian *fellaheen* to the level of the wild tribesmen, or in this case, 'degraded savages'. His contempt for the Egyptian Arabs became similar to that of the Palestinian Arabs, in that they were now resisting British interests and pursuing a nationalist agenda, the same as the Palestinian Arabs had done.

This cultural Islamic hierarchy was another of Churchill's Victorian constructs through which he viewed the Islamic world, and was reminiscent of his Victorian upbringing and had its roots in 19th century hold overs. Churchill's vision of Egypt, was one 'he had known at the turn of the century. He made no secret of the influence of his past experience and indeed took unabashed pleasure in holding what he granted was an old fashioned view.'[95] This was evident in much of Churchill's dealings with Egypt before and after its revolution of 1952 and in the persistent arguments between him and Eden regarding withdrawal from the Suez base. Churchill believed, like Eden and many other British statesmen at the time, that 'Egyptians, like other "Oriental" peoples should be handled with firmness at all times' and that the Egyptians were 'an inferior and essentially cowardly people.'[96] While Churchill had been a progressive Victorian, his views had become almost reactionary and ridiculous in the postwar world.

Nevertheless, Churchill's progressive Victorian fascination with the Islamic world still shone through from time to time. He regularly took holidays in Marrakesh, the city's vistas being among his favourite subjects for painting, as were its Islamic inhabitants.[97]

Churchill also enjoyed the evening feasts with the local pasha, known as T'hami El Glaoui (Lord of the Atlas), who frequently played host to Churchill since 1935 and whom Churchill affectingly greeted as 'My dear Glaoui!'[98] In 1952, while Churchill was on his way to Marrakesh for a holiday, he told his legal secretary, Denis Kelly, that the city was 'the Paris of the Sahara'.[99] For Churchill, Marrakesh represented a gateway to the orient of the past. Though in North Africa, it was still under French colonial rule and was free of the violent nationalism that was brewing in Egypt and elsewhere in the Middle East. However, Churchill and Kelly were 'distressed' by the French administration's lack of respect for the local Islamic inhabitants. When they first arrived, an 'Arab woman [. . .] and a crowd behind her' made an attempt to formally greet Churchill and his entourage, but the French officers escorting Churchill 'swept past them in the dust without a glance, an acknowledgment, or an explanation.'[100] Interestingly, Churchill and Kelly remarked at how the 'landscape' reminded them of 'the Northwest Frontier' but how different the French rule was from the British Raj, because British troops 'learned the local language'[101] and 'respected and interfered as little as possible in local customs and traditions.'[102] Though Churchill had certainly turned from Cairo to Marrakesh as his oriental inspiration, he still held out hope for Egypt.

Shortly after the 1952 revolution in Egypt, Churchill noted in the Cabinet minutes that: 'we should not appear to be defending the landlords and the Pashas against the long overdue reforms for the fellaheen'.[103] This came out of his fundamental belief that 'British influence was good for the Egyptians' and that 'the British had stood for economic progress and had imposed a peace that restrained the ruling class of "Pashas" and landlords from exploiting the peasants.' Other historians have also noted Churchill's Victorian progressivism: 'Churchill consistently demonstrated a concern for the welfare of the common people of Egypt.'[104]

In July 1952 the Free Officers Movement led by Muhammad Neguib and Gamal Abdel Nasser forced King Farouk to resign and set up a new republic. At first, Churchill and others briefly welcomed the change in Egypt's government, believing the Free Officers

Movement to be something like the modernizing Young Turk movement in the Ottoman Empire. Churchill articulated this notion at the Lord Mayor's Banquet on 10 November 1952:

> In July there was a revolution in Egypt rather similar to that of the Young Turks in Turkey many years ago, as a result of which a distinguished Egyptian soldier became [. . .] virtually a military dictator [. . .] I am bound to say I have felt much sympathy with the new hope aroused by General Nequib, that the shocking condition of the Egyptian peasantry under the corrupt rule of former Egyptian Governments would be definitely improved. We are anxious to help the new Government and to negotiate with them on friendly terms. We understand their point of views and we hope they understand ours.[105]

Churchill's hopeful Victorian lens focused on General Neguib and led Churchill to believe that he 'might lead Egypt back to the ranks of the civilized powers' by enacting economic reforms for the *fellaheen* and by working with British interests such as allowing the British troops to stay in the Canal Zone.[106] Churchill noted: 'I am not opposed to a policy of giving Neguib a good chance provided he shows himself to be a friend.'[107]

This, of course, was a short-lived fantasy but was not out of touch with contemporary British thought. Many British officials believed this as well. Robin Hankey, head of British Embassy affairs in Cairo, echoed this idea in a letter to Roger Allen, the under-secretary supervising the Middle East, saying that the Free Officers Movement had a 'standard of integrity [. . .] much higher than anything that has been known in Egypt for years.'[108] Moreover, this notion was reinforced by British perceptions of Nasser's book *The Philosophy of the Revolution* (1955, in English). The British ambassador to Egypt, Sir Ralph Stevenson, wrote that Nasser's book 'has a certain breadth of vision, humanity and idealism which one might be excused for not expecting from a man of his background.'[109] This is a striking contrast with Eden's later comparison of Nasser's book with *Mein Kampf*, and reveals a moment of British optimism in the Egyptian situation.

This moment evaporated quickly into the ether of reality. The new Egyptian government had little desire to work with Britain, wanted the British presence out of the Canal Zone and was determinedly anti-Western. The Egyptian government urged the Arab world to move away from British influence and relied on themes such as 'pan-Arab unity, anti-imperialism, and neutralism'. Such rhetoric weighed heavily on British officials as it 'raised the spectre that Egypt, commanding a union of Arab states, could someday fill the vacuum left by waning British power.'[110] The diplomatic tension was further compounded by the change in the Egyptian stance on Sudan. King Farouk had long 'upheld the traditional Egyptian attitude that sovereignty of the Egyptian crown in the Sudan was vital to Egypt itself.'[111] However, General Neguib was half Sudanese and believed that self-determination for Sudan was paramount for Muslim solidarity in the Middle East, provided its ascension to independence was free of foreign and particularly Western influence. This complete reversal of policy had a twofold effect. The first was that it won tremendous support for the Egyptian regime in Sudan and elsewhere in the Arab world. The second was that it undercut the British rationale for being in Sudan, as they had used Egyptian ambitions to control all the Nile as their reason for continued British presence in Sudan. Since Britain could not 'repudiate their own principle of self determination' Eden and the Cabinet moved to sign a treaty with Neguib in 1953 giving Sudan the choice to either join in union with Egypt or become an independent state.[112]

This was something of a loss for Churchill, who had participated in the 'reconquest' of the Sudan from the Mahdi in 1899. His increasing desperation to cling to any semblance of Empire revealed Churchill's Victorian perception of the Sudan situation. It became clear that 'Churchill was out of sympathy with the devolutionary aspects of post war policy, carrying as they did the demise of older imperial values.'[113] In Churchill's view, the situation 'represented an ignominious surrender of our responsibilities in the Sudan and a serious blow to British prestige throughout the Middle East.'[114] For him, the connection to the larger framework of relations with Egypt was obvious as he was concerned that another scuttle might embolden Egypt or, worse still, the Soviets. In this context, Churchill believed Eden had been too weak in his negotiations with the new Egyptian government and drew parallels with Nazi Germany and Chamberlain's policy of appeasement. Evelyn Shuckburgh recorded that Churchill bellowed to Eden that 'he never knew Munich was situated on the Nile.'[115] In the Cabinet meeting on 30 January 1953, Churchill demonstrated his discontent with the situation, arguing that with regard to Sudan, 'we should not lightly cast away all the benefits which the British administration had conferred on the Sudanese people; nor should we allow the Sudanese to be trapped by Egyptian promises that were unlikely to be fulfilled.' Churchill then argued that Britain should take its stand 'on the argument that it should be left to a properly elected Sudanese Parliament to decide how far the Sudanese people still required the safeguards provided by the special powers of the Governor-General.'[116] This again demonstrated Churchill's steadfast and nostalgic Victorian outlook, as his argument for staying in Sudan was similar to his arguments for continuing British rule in India during the 1930s and 1940s.

In this way, Churchill's understanding of the Sudan situation, and indeed the entire Middle Eastern theatre, brought him into conflict with Foreign Secretary Anthony Eden, who strongly favoured the agreement on Sudan as it represented a 'logical outcome of the long standing promise to confer on the Sudanese people the rights of self government and self determination.'[117] Despite this, Churchill continued to oppose the agreement. He argued that the press would 'sharply criticize' the agreement and would 'involve the Government in serious political difficulties, which would doubtless be exploited by the Opposition.'[118] But Eden and the rest of the Cabinet outmanoeuvred Churchill, who agreed to give Sudan its independence. Though he acquiesced to the Sudan Agreement, he continued to push for firm action against hostile pro-Egyptian elements in Sudan until the free election, which would, according to Churchill, 'offset the damage to our prestige in the Middle East.'[119] He also sought to combat Egyptian, anti-British propaganda in Sudan before the election, by increasing financial aid to Radio Omdurman and reopening the British Council office in Khartoum.[120] It was thought that this action might aid in persuading Sudan to remain in the Commonwealth. This was a vivid representation of Churchill's view of the Islamic world in the postwar period. He realistically understood that the Empire was receding but he did his best to make the change as slow and protective of British interests as possible.

For Churchill, the loss of Sudan and the loss of British prestige in the region made clear the necessity for US involvement in the Middle East as a strategic partner; the deteriorating situation in Iran would prove a useful province on which the United States and the British Empire could unite. Steps had already been taken by the Attlee government to alter the harsh terms of Mossadegh's nationalization of AIOC. In May 1951, the Attlee government took the British case to the International Court at The Hague and then to the UN in September. Once Churchill returned to the office of Prime Minister, he met with Truman in January 1952 and the two agreed to continue the Anglo-American partnership. Consequently, in August 1952, Colville recorded that, 'W has persuaded Truman to join with him in sending a message to to Mossdeq in Tehran', which established 'formal American cooperation' on Iran.[121] Once it became clear, however, that the International Court and the UN were powerless to reverse Mossadegh's nationalization, Churchill and many in the Conservative ranks believed extreme measures were required to solve the situation. This, combined with the election in the United States of the anti-communist Eisenhower in 1952, set the stage for a coup in Iran.

'Operation Boot' or 'Operation TPAjax' as it was known in the United States, essentially arranged for the Shah of Iran to issue a decree dismissing Mossadegh as Prime Minister and replacing him with the much more amenable General Fazlollah Zahedi.[122] This, however, was in violation of the Iranian constitution, which only allowed the parliament to dismiss premiers. The operation was led by Kermit Roosevelt, grandson of President Teddy Roosevelt and cousin to President Franklin D. Roosevelt, and was a success, though not initially. Mossadegh refused the decrees written by the Shah, having been tipped off by the Tudeh Party, and had the messenger arrested. This forced the beleaguered Shah to flee Rome; however, the CIA quickly intervened, synthesizing protests that culminated in the Shah's return and Mossadegh being thrown into prison. By the end of August 1953 it was all over.

Churchill's role in the coup, however, is slightly more complicated. While he jumped at idea of a covert coup and wholeheartedly endorsed Operation Boot, he was not the architect of the plan, as its initial construction began during Attlee's premiership. Churchill merely approved an existing plan and inherited a decision-making structure that was largely the same as it had been under Attlee.[123] Churchill's endorsement for the operation owed partly to Churchill's love 'for dramatic operations' combined with a frustration of 'timid diplomats', partly to his desire to maintain British prestige, and partly to his drive for Anglo-American unity.[124] Colville recorded much of Churchill's sentiments prior to the operation, noting that it would mark 'the first time since 1945 that the Americas have joined with us in taking overt action against a third power.'[125] Moreover, Churchill was able to support the operation in full as both Prime Minister and Foreign Secretary, because the more cautious Eden suffered from ill health and was hospitalized with gallstones in June 1953, leaving Churchill as acting Foreign Secretary. However, just before the operation commenced, Churchill suffered a massive stroke in July 1953, taking him out of action for nearly three months and, with Eden incapacitated, Lord Salisbury became responsible for foreign affairs but 'in clandestine operations he acted in effect as Churchill's lieutenant.'[126]

After the successful conclusion of the coup, Kermit Roosevelt met with Churchill, who was still convalescing from the stroke, to discuss the operation. Roosevelt said that Churchill was 'consumed alternately by curiosity and sleepiness'.[127] He was impressed by Churchill's knowledge of Iranian tribes and geography. He noted that Churchill asked about the Qashqai tribe, an Iranian Bedouin tribe who lived in the south-western part of Iran and whose sympathies were largely anti-British and pro-German. Churchill told Roosevelt that he was wise 'to discourage the Shah from going to Shiraz', a city surrounded by regions controlled by the Qashqai. Churchill went on to say that he 'never could trust those damn Qashqai. They screwed us up in World War One and in World War Two. [They are] a treacherous bunch.'[128] Churchill then turned to the subject of the Shah, saying that 'Mohammed was a smart chap and Mohammed Reza Shah Pahlavi has his smarts too.' Before Churchill sent Roosevelt away, he confirmed that if 'I had been a few years younger I would have loved nothing better than to have served under your command in this great venture.'[129] Churchill was pleased with his discussion and with the result of the operation. The Shah was a happy ally who owed his kingdom to Britain, communism had one less place to make a home, and Britain had held on to some of its former glory. It is important to note that, like Pakistan's entry into CENTO, this too was not a permanent solution and would have effects on Iran's relationship with the West for years to come. But most important of all for Churchill in the new postwar world, Britain and the United States stood together again.

This is evident in Churchill's correspondence all through 1953 with the newly elected US president and wartime colleague General Dwight D. Eisenhower, which demonstrated his increasing desire to share with the United States the British mission of reinforcing the Middle East against communism.[130] To maintain the illusion of greatness, Churchill realized that Britain would require capital and goodwill from the United States. However, his pleas to Eisenhower found the US attitude rather ambivalent as it 'condemned British imperialism in Egypt' but 'supported the British efforts to strengthen the Middle Eastern defence in the containment of possible Soviet penetration.'[131]

Eisenhower continually urged for a more diplomatic approach to negotiations with Neguib, while Churchill believed firm action in Egypt was the only way to ensure security in the region.[132] Eisenhower reiterated that the United States could not become embroiled in a dispute between Britain and Egypt and that he was 'puzzled' by Churchill's repeated attempts to bring in the United States.[133] Eisenhower's diary illustrated that his and Churchill's thinking on the matter was totally out of sync by 1953. Eisenhower recorded that Churchill:

> talks very animatedly about certain [...] international problems, especially Egypt and its future. But so far as I can

see, he has developed an almost childlike faith that all of the answers are to be found merely in the British–American partnership.[134]

Churchill was frustrated with the US approach, partly because he felt the 'special relationship' between the United Kingdom and the United States was slipping away and partly because he, like many British officials, believed the Americans were 'too optimistic about the Egyptian character.'[135] Norman Brook echoed this in a letter to Churchill explaining that Americans 'have less experience than we in negotiation with Eastern peoples.'[136] Churchill deeply agreed with this notion as it harkened back to the Victorian special relationship with the Arabs, while affirming Victorian prejudices. Despite such differences, Churchill and Eisenhower hoped to come to an agreement on the Middle Eastern situation at a summit in Bermuda but, owing to Churchill's stroke, the two were unable to meet. While Eisenhower hoped to stand with Britain as a matter of principle, his position was reinforced by a US arms deal with Egypt (which Churchill hoped to delay until the Canal Zone issue had been concluded) and the desire to keep Egypt out of Soviet hands. This delaying tactic proved ill-conceived, as eventually the Egyptians turned to the Soviets for arms.

Churchill's desire to use heavy-handed tactics drew a lot of criticism, not just from the United States but also from members of the Commonwealth. Muhammad Ali Borgra, the Prime Minister of Pakistan, warned that Britain's quarrel with Egypt might result in the Soviets taking advantage of the situation and gaining influence in the Middle East. Churchill retorted that: 'Her Majesty's Government has nothing but good feelings toward the Arab world and that, indeed, our record supports this.'[137] Churchill continued by citing his own record and Britain's in the region. This statement goes some way in undercutting the notion that 'Churchill did not have the same regard for the Arab states as his predecessors.'[138] While Churchill's Middle Eastern policy aspirations did include Israel as a partner in the region, it did not mean that he treated the Arab nations with disregard. Churchill's desire to secure Arab alliances and his, though reluctant, willingness to fulfil Britain's pledges to Jordan in the event of a Jordan–Israeli war all serves as evidence that Churchill was concerned about the Arab nations.

As tensions between Britain and Egypt continued to grow, in February 1954 word came that Nasser had replaced Neguib as the leader of Egypt. While Eden and others in the Foreign Office saw this change of guard as an opportunity to work towards a settlement on the Canal Zone question, Churchill became excited at the idea of a fight. He confessed to Shuckburgh that he believed Nasser was 'much worse' and that leaving the troops in the Canal Zone would antagonize Nasser, who 'might bring it to a head'. Upon reflection of Churchill's words, Shuckburgh concluded, 'Churchill can only mean attacking our troops, so that we have an excuse for fighting.'[139]

However, Churchill's mindset moved towards a more pragmatic approach when the right economic and strategic elements aligned for another solution. The first thing to change Churchill's thinking was the demand of Rab Butler, the Chancellor of the Exchequer, for £180 million in defence cuts in order to keep the economy solvent early in 1954. Since the primary defensive objective was Soviet containment and NATO membership, the savings could not come from European expenditures; it had to come from the Middle East. The second major change to Churchill's views was Britain's development of its own hydrogen bomb in late 1953, which strategically rendered the Canal Zone useless. These elements, combined with the increased nationalism of Nasser's Egypt, created a situation where the ever-opportunistic politician in Churchill could create a solution and perhaps end his career in a positive light. There were additional factors that contributed to the change on the political scene, including Churchill's stroke, and his (and Eden's) absence on the political stage so that Lord Salisbury in Cairo could negotiate a compromise withdrawal. Whatever the case, the situation had changed and so had Churchill's approach. At the beginning of 1954 he actively sought to quit the Canal Zone, but on terms that would preserve Britain's honour in the Middle East.

By July 1954 the new agreement with Nasser was finalized, and was signed by Nasser himself in October. The new agreement called on Britain to leave the Canal Zone, with permission to return in the event of a major war. British forces redeployed to their new base in Cyprus and, with the hydrogen bomb, order continued to be preserved in the Middle East. Churchill now had to convince the Conservative Party of this new strategy. He had been nervous about the Conservatives' perceptions of his policies since the loss of Sudan, because there were many Conservatives who never wanted to quit Egypt. He explained to the Cabinet the task before him in that there were 'political disadvantages of abandoning the position we have held in Egypt since 1882' but accepted that the British 'strategic needs in the Middle East had been radically changed by the development of thermonuclear weapons.'[140] It was evident that the realistic and pragmatic side of Churchill had won against the romantic imperialist side.

In order to move forward with the policy, Churchill had to convince the right-wing Tories, known as the 'Suez Group', that quitting the Canal Zone was the best option. Julian Amery and the other MPs who shared his outlook on the Empire were far more imperialistic than Churchill on this issue. Amery even lamented that Churchill and the British government were 'sucking up to Ike [Eisenhower]' in their approach to the Middle East.'[141] However, Amery's position was far from that of the pragmatic Churchill who realized that Britain needed the United States. In Parliament, Churchill was able to argue:

> I have not in the slightest degree concealed in public speech how much I have regretted the course of events in Egypt. But I had not held in my mind the tremendous changes that have taken place in the whole strategic position of the world which make the thoughts which were well founded and well knitted together a year ago utterly obsolete, and which has changed the opinions of every competent soldier I have been able to meet.
>
> I should be prepared [. . .] to show how utterly out of all proportion to the Suez Canal and the position which we held in Egypt are the appalling developments and the appalling

> spectacle which imagination raises before us [. . .] I am sure to convince the hon. Gentlemen of the obsolescence of the base and of the sense of proportions.'[142]

This speech turned what might have been a humiliating defeat for Churchill and the Conservatives into a victorious moment. Churchill gave the impression that a 'scuttle' was in fact a strategic redeployment. Perhaps 'it is ironic that Churchill, having objected to the evacuation all along, deserves large credit for the settlement achieved between Britain and Egypt in 1954.'[143] In this way, Churchill's final policy decisions in the Middle East were something of a success. This is especially true because Eden and the Foreign Office helped establish another alliance of the northern tier Islamic states in the Baghdad Pact (1954). The pact established an alliance between Pakistan and Turkey, the most powerful Islamic states with strong ties to Britain and heavy anti-communist outlook. Then in 1955 Britain and Iraq formally entered the pact, creating the Central Treaty Organization (CENTO), thus potentially securing the Middle East from Soviet penetration. This aspect of British foreign policy aided in reducing the need for a British presence in the Canal Zone as well. Churchill was able to hand over the reins of government to Eden, his successor, with a content heart in respect to Middle Eastern affairs.

Unfortunately, this pact further isolated Egypt as it continued to vie with Iraq for a dominant role in the Middle East and was determinedly seeking Soviet assistance. As Egypt became more belligerent, British policy failures in the Middle East became more apparent. Tension was still very high in the Arab world because no real solution had been found to accommodate Israel in the Middle East. CENTO pushed Nasser and the Egyptians further towards the Soviets, who saw the decline of the British in the region as an opportunity to sell arms and to finance the Aswan Dam, as the British and Americans withdrew their pledges to do so. In a final act of retaliation, Nasser nationalized the Suez Canal. This appeared to Eden to leave him with very few options in 1956. He decided to take a hard line against the Egyptians and invade the Suez Canal Zone with the aid of the Israelis but without the support of the United States, resulting in the Suez Crisis.

Publicly, Churchill supported Eden saying that Eden's government was 'restoring peace and order' in the Middle East and that he was confident the United States would come around to seeing that Britain acted for 'the common good'.[144] Eden was grateful for Churchill's support. However, two days later, owing to enormous political pressure from the United States and those in his own Cabinet (Harold Macmillan, Rab Butler, and others) Eden declared a ceasefire. Privately, Churchill was concerned that Eden had mishandled the situation. Churchill confessed to his physician Lord Moran that he wanted to see Harold Macmillan become prime minster and that he could not understand 'why our troops were halted. To go so far and not go on was madness.' Churchill echoed this a month later when he was asked by Moran what he would have done. Churchill replied that he 'wasn't exactly sure' what he would have done but he 'wouldn't have done anything without consulting the Americans.'[145] An additional explanation of Churchill's opinion on Eden's handling of the Suez Crisis was Churchill's belief that 'the unity of Islam is remarkable' and that Eden's policy would lead to hostilities from Jordan and across the Islamic world.[146] Churchill had believed in this unity throughout his entire career, first in terms of pan-Islamism before and after World War I, and then in his battle against Indian independence. He was always careful to craft an approach that (at least in his mind) served to keep the Islamic world unified with Britain, even in his defence of Israel. Churchill no doubt believed Eden to be incapable of such an approach, despite Eden's more affable attitude towards Egypt.

In any case, Churchill's aspirations for the Islamic world fell on the ash heap of history. British relations with the major powers in the Islamic world continued to deteriorate. In 1956, Pakistan left the British Commonwealth. In 1958 a revolution on 14 July in Iraq claimed the lives of several family members of the pro-British Hashemite monarchy as well as the Prime Minister of Iraq, Nuri al-Said, and ultimately placed the socialist Ba'ath Party in power. Dismayed at the events in Iraq, Churchill appealed to the Arab people one last time. Speaking on the death of Nuri al-Said, King Feisal II, and his uncle, Crown Prince 'Abd al-Ilah, Churchill echoed the idea that Israel and the Arab people should work together:

> These three men were the most loyal servants of their country and true friends of their allies. They were swept away in the convulsions of the Arab peoples that is still going on. I trust that counsels of peace and moderation will prevail, and that Arab peoples and Israel will get the long period of prosperity and peaceful development they need.[147]

Despite Churchill's pleas, Iraq made a significant turn away from the West culminating in it leaving CENTO, thus reducing it to a virtually powerless organization. By 1979, with the aid of numerous exploitive policies and concessions for Western powers, one of the seeds that Churchill planted in Iran in the form of a coup in 1953 grew into a full-blown, anti-Western revolution – the effects of which we still feel today. All that remained of Churchill's great Middle Eastern alliance was Jordan, which he refused to abandon in the face of a possible Israeli invasion.

This period of Churchill's career saw him trying to manage the decline of the British Empire in the aftermath of World War II while simultaneously addressing the new challenges of the Cold War. As always for Churchill, British interests were central to his thinking but they were not his only concern. In attending to Indian independence, coping with effects in the Middle East as a result of the new state of Israel, and in dealing with the challenges of a nationalistism in Egypt and Iran, Churchill demonstrated his concern for the Muslim populations, even when he was disagreeing with their leaders.

CONCLUSION

By examining Churchill's entire career, this book has offered a nuanced understanding of his views of the Islamic world. In doing so, it has addressed the questions raised by the gaps in the literature surrounding the topic. With regard to the literature concerning Churchill, this book has contributed to the relatively unexplored dimension of his relationship with the Islamic world by examining his ever-changing ideas, attitudes, and policies towards Islamic regions and peoples. This book complements the extensive literature on British relations with the Orient by placing Churchill in the context of colonial discourse and illustrates the effects that he had on British policy in Islamic regions. Moreover, this book adds to the literature surrounding Churchill and the Middle East by examining the wider context of the larger Islamic world, rather than limiting it to Palestine or Iraq.

Churchill's views of Islamic culture and of Muslims were multidimensional and highly complex. This owed partly to his pragmatic, if not mercurial nature and partly to his willingness to energetically throw his considerable talents at the challenge of whatever project or crisis he was confronted with, whether it was at the Admiralty, the Colonial Office, or as Prime Minister. Churchill's vigorous approach to his career created an intellectual environment in which he could simmer and percolate ideas that were constantly changing and growing. Churchill's nature and energy, combined with the complexity of the Islamic world, has created a multi-layered legacy that is difficult to fully appreciate.

Viewed through a purely strategic lens, Churchill barely had a relationship with the Islamic world at all. Through this life, his policies and approaches were always formulated to advance British interests, with few other considerations. This version of Churchill paints him as an ambitious soldier whose experiences in frontier wars had little effect on him and were merely a prelude to an ambitious and capricious political career. Later, this version paints him as a no-less ambitious minister, who hastily rebuilt the Middle East so that he might move on to more powerful positions and who, in political isolation, barked rabidly imperialist rants about India from the political sidelines. While this version respects his legacy as Prime Minister in the war years, it often condemns his views on Muslims in the postwar world as dangerously anachronistic and one-sided. This aspect of Churchill is undoubtedly true. However, taken alone, it does not reveal the full spectrum of his perceptions of the Islamic world.

There was another side to Churchill; a magnanimous, if not humanitarian side that revealed itself in his personal correspondence and notes, which tell a different story. This version of Churchill became disillusioned with Forward policy, by the horrors of the frontier wars, and even was disgusted with his officers' lack of respect for their defeated adversaries. He was interested in thoughtful debates with the anti-imperialist radical Wilfrid S. Blunt, and as a junior minister tried to find innovative solutions for securing frontier regions that would not alienate the Islamic tribes and would reduce costs. At the Home Office, this version of Churchill tried to lay the groundwork for an alliance with the Ottoman Empire, partially on the grounds that the British and Ottoman Empires were the two largest Muslim powers in the world. Once this proved impossible, this Churchill used his personal friendships with high-ranking Ottoman officers in an attempt to secure Turkish neutrality in World War I, though he was unsuccessful. After World War I, with the help of T.E. Lawrence, this Churchill created two new Arab states that were relatively independent and sought to employ more humane means of policing Middle Eastern regions. He pursued a national home for the Zionists, in part on the basis that it would help invigorate the local Arab population, a notion supported by many leading Arabs at the time. In the 1930s, this Churchill defended the rights of Muslim Indians against the tyranny of a Hindu majority by advocating continued British presence in India. As Prime Minister, this Churchill sanctioned the building of the Central London mosque and continually sought to keep the Islamic world with the Allied powers. He even demanded the independence of Syria from the Free French. In the Cold War era, this Churchill supported the creation of Pakistan, acted as a mediator between Israel and the Arab communities, and only became frustrated with Egypt after it was clear that the nationalist government did not want to co-operate with Britain. However, as with the first version of Churchill, this is not the complete picture.

Both versions of Churchill are correct and both are required in order to fully appreciate Churchill's views of the Islamic world. These versions represent what the Aga Khan called 'interlinking facets' of Churchill's character.[1] He was in love with the concept of the British Empire and what he perceived to be its civilizing mission, but when it fell short of that mission and committed acts of cruelty, such as General Kitchener's aggressive and disrespectful conduct during the Anglo-Dervish War, General Dyer's perpetration of the Amritsar Massacre, or the RAF gunners opening fire on tribesmen in Mesopotamia, Churchill was disdainful. This disdain usually resulted in practical action being taken by Churchill on behalf of the Muslim populations and, at times, led to reformulation of imperial policies.

His struggle to reconcile these conflicting facets of Islamic people culture and politcis can be seen throughout his entire career. At times these 'interlinking facets' could unite. For example, Churchill's support of the Indian Muslims through the 1930s, 1940s, and 1950s. Churchill's magnanimous side was engaged by defending Muslim rights in India and supporting Jinnah in the creation of Pakistan. His strategic, imperial viewpoint was demonstrated by arguing for continued British presence in India so that the Indian Muslims and the British could keep Churchill's perceived threat of Hindu sedition at bay, and by supporting Pakistan to help contain Soviet expansion into Asia and the Middle East. At other times these facets were opposed, such as Churchill's 'violently anti-Turk' attitude once the Ottomans had sided with the Central Powers. Once his magnanimity was exhausted in trying to keep the Ottoman Empire neutral, his need to protect British interests became fully engaged.

In examining Churchill's views of the Islamic world these seemingly contradictory facets of his personality are very evident. On the one hand, he wanted to secure the British Empire from perceived threats, and on the other, he had something of an interest in Islamic culture and people and was genuinely concerned for Muslim populations in the British Empire. Elements of these facets can be traced to his Victorian upbringing. Like many others of his age, he had a romantic notion of the British Empire and was subject to the prejudices of his day. In this light, Churchill's earliest views on Islam and its supposedly political manifestation, pan-islamism, were similar to the correspondent V.C. Fincastle's, which depicted fanatical tribesmen on the north-west frontier who derived inspiration from Ottoman military victories. His faith in the British Empire can also be linked to Churchill's willingness to employ *realpolitik* regarding British strategic interests and Islamic powers. This aspect of his thinking demonstrates a similarity with Benjamin Disraeli, Lord Randolph Churchill, and many other Conservatives who, prior to World War I, favoured an alliance with the Ottoman Empire for strategic reasons.

However, Churchill's experiences on the frontiers of the Empire connected him to the Islamic world by creating shared experiences with Islamic people in oriental places. This ultimately led to sincere interest and a magnanimous view of Islam and it culture, epsically in a British context, which ran deeper than mere strategic interest. This new dimension of Churchill's thinking started evolving early in his political career and was displayed in his critical comments concerning Kitchener, when Churchill left the Conservatives for the Liberals, and in his antagonism towards the arch-imperialist Fredrick Lugard. Compared to Lugard and others of his ilk, Churchill's views were compassionate and thoughtful. For instance, the 'hierarchy of cultural value' he wrote about in *My African Journey*, and then later applied to the broader 'House of Islam', was developed from a mixture of his experiences and ideas he arrived at from the influence of the experts of the day such as Blunt and Lawrence. It is highly doubtful that figures such as Kitchener and Lugard reflected on the Islamic culture and politics in the same way, if at all.

This progressive Victorian outlook stayed with Churchill for the rest of his life, even into the Cold War era when his earlier progressive ideas had become outdated and were even reactionary. This outlook was evident in Churchill's deviation from Lloyd George's policies by his repeated calls for magnanimity towards the defeated Turks after World War I, despite Churchill eventually consenting to Lloyd George's position once he felt British interests were threatened. Churchill's magnanimous view was evident in his testimony to the Peel Commission when he explained why he thought that the Palestinian Arabs were outside the remit of the Hussein–McMahon pledges and that their agricultural techniques were antiquated when compared to the Zionists, and even to other Arabs. This was evident again in Churchill's desire to restructure the Middle East according to the 'Philby Plan' during World War II. This plan clearly echoed back to the ideas of Blunt and Lawrence from the aftermath of World War I. However, fixing such a plan to such a dynamic region in midst of such a major conflict, while hopeful, was clearly an unrealistic strategy. Despite the faults of Churchill's approach to the remnants of the Ottoman Empire in the Levant, it is undeniable that he worked towards solutions for these regions that would be acceptable, at least in Churchill's mind, to Muslim populations even when their leaders did not co-operate with him.

Ultimately, Churchill's legacy in the Islamic world is one of paradoxical camaraderie and shared interests gained through his experiences and personal interactions. It is by exploring his various private correspondence and notes that this legacy becomes most clear. While strategic necessity certainly dictated aspects of Churchill's thinking such as the need for oil, and Russian and later Soviet containment, Churchill often held positions that he believed gave the Muslim subjects of the Crown a good deal. This was evident in his development of nominally independent Arab states, his desire to work with the Hashemites, and his willingness to listen to Muslim concerns through people such as Wilfrid S. Blunt, T.E. Lawrence, Waris Ali, Abdullah of Jordan, M.A. Jinnah, and Ibn Saud. His continued reliance on the Muslim perspective to defend the British presence in India during his speeches in Parliament and elsewhere illustrates this. For if he was unconcerned with the Muslims' plight, his speeches all through the 1930s and 1940s and his explanation to President Roosevelt during World War II would not have contained the dimension of protection of civil rights for the Muslims of India; nor would Churchill have fervently defended Syrian independence to de Gaulle or been willing to defend Jordan against Israel in the early 1950s. These and other facts seen throughout the book demonstrate Churchill's camaraderie with the Islamic world, which was at times motivated more out of political or strategic necessity than friendship.

There were moments, of course, when this alliance did not harmonize. Two major failures of Churchill's career concerned the Isalmic world. First, there was the setback over Gallipoli, and, second, his inflexible attitudes about India in the 1930s. Nevertheless, Churchill gained respect in international affairs for his policies, especially in 1919–22 and after World War II. Despite such respect, there were still instances of dissonance in the relationship between Churchill and the Islamic world, such as his stance regarding the Palestinian Arabs and his views on Egyptian and Iranian nationalism in the 1950s. But in each of these cases Churchill's sympathy with the Islamic interests remained long after his anger. For example, his desire to adopt a pro-Turkish policy after World War I, his desire to give Palestinian Arabs a representative body despite his view that they were outside the pledges of the McMahon–Hussein correspondence, and his eventual willingness to accept the loss of the Suez Canal all represent moments when Churchill's camaraderie with the Islamic world was tested.

Despite these tests, and Churchill's often paradoxical and imperialist goals, it may be said that his alliance did much to advance the Islamic interests. He encouraged the development of two nominally independent Arab states in the Middle East that were based around the concept of the nation, rather than the Ottoman concept of the *vilayet*. Though these means were should be pursued for Churchill's imperialist ends, those nations still exist today and, in Jordan, the direct heir of Abdullah still sits on the throne. Though Churchill sought to keep India confined to the British Empire, he did so by defending Muslim civil rights and, when they chose to break away to create Pakistan, Churchill strongly supported the fledgling state. Though Churchill's view of political and cultural Islam were, to some extent, a Victorian construction that he never fully divorced himself from, and his typical position on matters related to Islamic regions were ultimately imperialistic, he saw British power as a means to advance civilization, which ultimately helps everyone, including Muslims. This approach created a uniquely Churchillian legacy regarding his diplomacy and policies in the developing dymanics of the Middle East, Asia, and North Africa. However, it is worth remembering that Winston Churchill once said he was 'one of the best friends the Arabs ever had.'[2] This might be extrapolated to the entire the entire House of Islam, which during Churchill's lifetime had emerged from Ottoman and British rule to determine its own destiny. It was during these times that the Islamic world needed friends and, at least to some extent, it found one in Winston Churchill.

NOTES

Introduction

1. David Fromkin, *A Peace to End All Peace: The Fall of the Ottoman Empire and the Creation of the Modern Middle East* (New York, 1989), p. 25.
2. David French, 'The Origins of the Dardanelles Campaign Reconsidered' in *History*, Vol. 68, Issue 223 (June 1983), pp. 214, 219.
3. David Fromkin, *A Peace to End all Peace* (New York, 2001), p. 25.
4. Paul Addison, 'Destiny, History, and Providence: The Religion of Winston Churchill', in Michael Bentley (ed.), *Public and Private Doctrine: Essays in British History Presented to Maurice Cowling* (Cambridge, 1994), p. 238.
5. Ibid., pp. 240–1.
6. The quote was popularized by Winston Churchill's grandson, Winston Churchill, who was a journalist who focused on the Middle East. He wrote an account of the Six Day War and was an outspoken advocate of the invasion of Iraq in 2003. See Winston Churchill, 'Churchill on Islamic Fundamentalism' in *Carolina Jounral* 3 March 2006; http://www.carolinajournal.com/exclusives/display_exclusive.html?id=3158, accessed 21 November 2013; Several other examples include, Adrian Morgan, 'Winston Churchill on Islamism', http://www.islam-watch.org/AdrianMorgan/Winston-Churchill-Islamism.htm, accessed 6 April 2011; Anonymous, 'Winston Churchill on Islam and Why he was Right', http://www.articlesbase.com/politics-articles/winston-churchill-on-islam-and-why-he-was-right-293496.html, accessed 6 April 2011; M. Savage, 'Winston Churchill on Islam', http://www.youtube.com/watch?v=gwuduAaWvxU, accessed 6 April 2011; Al Ghurabaa also published an online book entitled *UK at War with Islam* (2006), see P. Risdon, 'Winston Churchill on Islam', http://freebornjohn.blogspot.com/2006/02/winston-churchill-on-islam.html, accessed 6 April 2010.
7. Winston Churchill, *The River War*, first edition, Vol. II (London, 1899) pp. 248–50.

8. Winston Churchill, *A History of the English-Speaking Peoples*, Vol. 4 (London, 1958) {hereafter, *HESP*} pp. 341, 369; for traditional Islamic opinion of the Mahdiyya see Heather Harkey, 'Ahmad Zayni Dahlan's "Al-Futuhat Al-Islamiyya": A Contemporary View of the Sudanese Mahdi', *Sudanic Africa: A Journal of Historical Sources*, Vol. 5 (1994), pp. 67–75.
9. According to tradition, the 'Mahdi' acts as something of a steward for a period of years until the final return of the Messiah and together they rid the world of evil. Belief in the Mahdi is more prevalent in Shia Islam. See Moojan Momen, *An Introduction to Shi'i Islam: The History and Doctrines of Twelver Shi'ism* (New Haven, 1987).
10. Having been stationed in India, Churchill would have been aware of this, not least because he served with British Muslims and Sheiks. Had Churchill been speaking about the entire Muslim faith rather than just the fundamentalist Dervish Empire, he would have undoubtedly mentioned the North West Frontier of India, where he fought Islamic fundamentalists.
11. Churchill to J.E.C. Welldon, 16 December 1896, in Randolph Churchill (ed.), *Winston Churchill Companion*, Vol. 1, Pt 2, pp. 712–13.
12. Winston Churchill, *The River War: An Account of the Reconquest of the Sudan*, second edition (New York, 1964) {hereafter, *RW*}, p. 30.
13. Churchill, *HESP*, Vol. 1, pp. 226, 232.
14. Churchill, *RW*, second edition, pp. 43–44. See also James Muller, 'War on the Nile: Winston Churchill and the Reconquest of the Sudan', in *Political Science Quarterly* No.20 (1991), p. 231.
15. R.F. Foster, *Lord Randolph Churchill: A Political Life* (Oxford, 1981), pp. 111, 120.
16. Churchill's dressing in Arab garments with Blunt was first recorded in a letter from Wilfrid Blunt to Lady Anne Blunt, 5 July 1904, in the British Library Manuscript Collection, Correspondence between Lady Anne and W.S. Blunt (Wentworth Bequest) Vol. CCXC, BL, MSS, Add. 54107. Blunt recorded this type of occasion again in his diary for 19 October 1912 in Wilfrid Blunt, *My Diaries: Being a Personal Narrative of Events, 1888–1914* (London, 1919), p. 812. This was corroborated by Clementine Churchill in Jack Fishman, *My Darling Clementine: The Story of Lady Churchill* (London, 1963), p. 46.
17. Winston Churchill to Lady Lytton, 19 September 1907; Randolph Churchill, (ed.), *Winston S. Churchill Companion*, Vol. 2, Pt 2 (London, 1969) {hereafter all companion volumes will be *WSC,C,*}, pp. 679–80. A 'pasha' was a rank of distinction in the Ottoman Empire.
18. Lady Gwendoline Bertie to Churchill, 27 August 1907, *WSC,C*, Vol. 2, Pt 1, p. 672. Orientalism, as Lady Bertie means it, is not orientalism as Edward Said refers to it. Here, she simply means a fascination with the Orient and with Islam, especially as she feared Blunt's influence on Churchill.

Chapter 1 Early Encounters

1. William Manchester, *The Last Lion: Winston Spencer Churchill: Visions of Glory 1874–1932* (New York, 1983), pp. 251–2.
2. Winston Churchill, *The Story of the Malakand Field Force: An Episode of Frontier War* (Wildside Press Edition, New York, 2006) [hereafter, *MFF*], pp. 247–8.
3. Churchill, *MFF*, p. 41.
4. Numbers taken from Winston Churchill, *MFF*, p. 68.
5. David Edwards, 'Mad Mullahs and Englishmen: Discourse in the Colonial Encounter', in *Comparative Studies in Society and History*, Vol. 31, No. 4 (October 1989), p. 653.
6. Keith Surridge, 'The Ambiguous Amir: Britain, Afghanistan and the 1897 North-West Frontier', in *The Journal of Imperial and Commonwealth History*, Vol. 36, No. 3 (September 2008), p. 420.
7. *WSC,C*, Vol. 1, Pt 2, p. 697.
8. *WSC,C*, Vol. 1, Pt 2, p. 703.
9. *WSC,C*, Vol. 1, Pt 2, p. 753.
10. Edward Said, *Orientalism* (London, 2003), pp. 1–2.
11. Humayun Ansari, *The Infidel Within: Muslims in Britain since 1800* (London, 2004), p. 55.
12. David Jablonsky, 'Churchill: Victorian Man of Action', in David Jablonsky (ed.), *Churchill and Hitler: Essays on the Political-Military Direction of Total War* (London, 1994); WSC, C, Vol.1, Pt 1, pp. 102–3.
13. See Richard Toye, *Churchill's Empire*, pp. 3–61.
14. Jablonsky, 'Man of Action', p. 207.
15. Kirk Emmert, *Winston S. Churchill on Empire* (Chapel Hill, 1986).
16. Churchill, *MFF*, p. 42.
17. Churchill, *My Early Life: A Roving Commission* (London, 1930) [hereafter, *MEL*], p. 180.
18. Churchill, *MFF*, p. 18.
19. See Mehmet Uğur Ekinci, *The Unwanted War: The Diplomatic Background of the Ottoman-Greek War of 1897* (Ankara, 2006).
20. *WSC,C*, Vol. 1, Pt 2, p. 735.
21. Winston Churchill and Lady Randolph Churchill in a series of letters, spring of 1897; *WSC,C*, Vol. 1, Pt 2, pp. 734, 735, 740, 748.
22. Winston Churchill to Lady Randolph Churchill, 6 April 1897; ibid., p. 750.
23. Lady Randolph Churchill to Winston Churchill, 20 April 1897; ibid., p. 754.
24. Winston Churchill to Lady Randolph Churchill, 21 April 1897; ibid., pp. 754–5.
25. Bechhofer Roberts, *Winston Churchill* (London, 1940), pp. 30–1.
26. Churchill, *MEL*, p. 121.
27. Winston Churchill to Lady Randolph Churchill, 26 May 1897; *WSC,C*, Vol. 1, Pt 2, p. 768.
28. Winston Churchill to his brother Jack, 31 August 1897; ibid., pp. 783–4.

29. Dwight E. Lee, 'The Origins of Pan-Islam', in *The American Historical Review*, Vol. 47, No. 2 (January 1942), p. 279, and C.H. Becker, 'Panislamiusmus' in *Vom Werden und Wesen der islamischen Welt: Islamstudien*, Vol. II, p. 242. It is not within the scope of this book to fully explore pan-Islamism. For a list of sources concerning a full discussion of the topic of pan-Islamism, see the first footnote in Dwight E. Lee's 'The Origins of Pan-Islam'.
30. It is remarkable that Sayid Ameer Ali was Waris Ameer Ali's father.
31. See Peter Hopkirk, *The Great Game* (London, 2006) and Rudyard Kipling, *Kim* (London, 1901).
32. Nikki R. Keddie, 'Pan-Islam as Proto-Nationalism', in *The Journal of Modern History*, Vol. 41, No 1 (March 1968), pp. 18–21.
33. Ibid., n. 5, p. 19.
34. Churchill, *MFF*, p. 41.
35. Viscount Fincastle, *A Frontier Campaign: A Narrative of Operations of the Malakand and Buner Field Forces 1897–1898* (London, 1898), pp. 20–1.
36. *WSC,C*, Vol. 1, Pt 2, p. 830.
37. Keith Surridge, 'The Ambiguous Amir', p. 422.
38. Major H.A. Deane, quoted in ibid., p. 424.
39. Lee, 'Pan-Islam', p. 283.
40. Ibid., p. 18.
41. Winston Churchill in a field dispatch from Khar, 7 October 1897, in F.S. Woods (ed.), *Young Winston's Wars: The Original Dispatches of Winston S. Churchill War Correspondent 1897–1900* (Abbot, 1975), p. 9.
42. Churchill, *MEL*, p. 134.
43. Winston Churchill, field dispatch from Khar, 7 October 1897 in Woods, *Young Winston's Wars*, p. 9.
44. Richard Toye, '"The Riddle of the Frontier": Winston Churchill, The Malakand Field Force and the Rhetoric of Imperial Expansion', in *Historical Research*, Vol. 84, No. 225 (August 2011).
45. Churchill, *MFF*, p. 19.
46. Ibid., p. 19.
47. Churchill, *MFF*, p. 42. For more on Ghazis see Bernard Lewis, *The Political Language of Islam* (Chicago, 1991).
48. Churchill, *Malakand Field Force*, p. 40.
49. Fincastle, *A Frontier Campaign*, p. 29.
50. Churchill, *MFF*, p. 40.
51. Winston Churchill, field dispatch from Inayat Kila, 9 November 1897 in Woods, *Young Winston's Wars*, p. 39.
52. Both the 11th Bengal Lancers and the 31st Punjabi Infantry were composed primarily of Punjabi Muslims (as well as Sikhs, Dogras and Gerkhas). See Michael Barthorp and Jeffrey Burn, *Indian Infantry Regiments 1860–1914* (London, 1979). This is notable because this would later influence Churchill's attitudes regarding India during World War II. See Chapter 7.
53. Churchill, *MEL*, pp. 148–9.

54. Douglas Russell, *Winston Churchill: Soldier: The Military Life of a Gentleman at War* (London, 2005), p. 147.
55. Churchill, *MFF*, p. 90.
56. I must thank Churchill Archives Director, Allen Packwood, for bringing this point to my attention.
57. Winston Churchill to Lady Randolph Churchill, 12 November 1896, in *WSC, C*, Vol. 1, Pt 2, p. 701.
58. Churchill, *MEL*, p. 119.
59. Magnus Marsden, 'All-male Sonic Gatherings, Islamic Reform, and Masculinity in Northern Pakistan', in *American Ethnologist*, Vol. 34, No. 3, p. 477.
60. Martin Sökefeld, 'From Colonialism to Postcolonial Colonialism: Changing Modes of Domination in Northern Areas of Pakistan', in *The Journal of Asian Studies*, Vol. 64, No. 4, p. 952.
61. Russell, *Winston Churchill: Soldier*, p. 147.
62. Winston Churchill, field dispatch from Inayat Kila, 9 November 1897, Woods, *Young Winston's Wars*, pp. 52–7.
63. Winston Churchill, field dispatch from Inayat Kila, 16 November 1897, in ibid., p. 52.
64. See Shahin Kuli Khan Khattak, *Islam and the Victorians: Nineteenth Century Perceptions of Muslim Practices and Beliefs* (London, 2008).
65. Churchill, *MFF*, p. 252.
66. Ibid., p. 248.
67. Ibid., pp. 249–50.
68. Winston Churchill to the Duchess of Marlborough, 25 October 1897 in *WSC, C*, Vol. 1, Pt 2, pp. 809–11.
69. Toye, 'Riddle,' pp. 501, 510. Toye rightly references Churchill's letter to Lady Randolph, 21 October 1897 in *WSC,C*, Vol. 1, Pt 2, p. 807; and Winston Churchill, 'The Ethics of Frontier Policy', in *Military Review*, No. 57 (1899).
70. Toye, 'Riddle', pp. 510–11. Some of the examples of Churchill's rhetoric of inevitability are 'This forward movement is beyond recall [...] To retreat is impossible.' Churchill, dispatch 21 September 1897; 'We are in mid stream [...] We must therefore go on.' Churchill, dispatch 16 October 1897.
71. Churchill, *MFF*, p. 249.
72. Ibid. pp. 167, 169.
73. Toye, 'Riddle', p. 504.
74. Churchill, *MFF*, p. 153.
75. Winston Churchill, dispatch from Nowshera, 6 December 1897, in Woods, *Young Winston's Wars* p. 64.
76. Winston Churchill, 'The Ethics of Frontier Policy', in *Military Review*, No. 57 (1899), p. 504.
77. Ibid., pp. 505, 509.
78. Ibid., p. 506.
79. Toye, 'Riddle', p. 502.
80. Churchill to Lady Randolph, *WSC,C*, Vol. 1, Pt 2, p. 807.

81. Said, *Orientalism*, p. 104.
82. Edwards, 'Mad Mullahs', p. 653.
83. *WSC*, *MEL*, p. 129.
84. It is not within the scope of this book to give a full account of the Anglo-Dervish War. See, P.M. Holt, *The Mahdist State in the Sudan 1881–1898: A Study of its Origins, Development and Overthrow*, second edition (London, 1970); David Levering Lewis, *The Race To Fashoda* (Washington, 1986); Winston Churchill, *The River War: An Account of the Reconquest of the Sudan*, first edition (London, 1899), and for a more contemporary view see Richard Berrman, *The Mahdi of Allah* (London, 1931) (Winston Churchill actually wrote the introduction for this book). For a more recent and academic account see Dominic Green, *Armies of God: Islam and Empire on the Nile 1869–1899* (London, 2007).
85. Churchill, *RW*, second edition, p. 26.
86. Robert Rhodes James, *Lord Randolph Churchill* (London, 1959), p. 160.
87. Lewis, *Race*, p. 138.
88. Ibid., p. 139.
89. Ibid., p. 143.
90. Violet Bonham Carter, *Winston Churchill as I knew Him* (London, 1965), p. 42.
91. Winston Churchill, *RW*, first edition, Vol. II (London, 1899), pp. 248–50. For the complete quote see the introduction.
92. For example, Gilbert uses this quote to illustrate that Churchill formed an 'unfavourable' opinion of Islam in general and even extrapolated this notion to Churchill's views of Middle Eastern Arabs. See Gilbert, *Churchill and the Jews*, pp. 52–4.
93. James Muller, 'War on the Nile', in *Political Science Quarterly*, No. 20 (1991), pp. 223–63.
94. *WSC,C*, Vol. 2, Pt 1, p. 445.
95. Another useful source for exploring Churchill's texts in general, especially in this early period, is Manfred Weidhorn, *Sword and Pen: A Survey of the Writing of Winston Churchill* (Albuquerque, 1974).
96. Peter de Mendelssohn, *The Age of Churchill: Heritage and Adventure 1874–1911* (London, 1961), p. 135.
97. Muller, 'War on the Nile', p. 228.
98. Paul Rahe, 'The River War; Nature's provision, man's desire to prevail and prospects for peace', in James W Muller (ed.), *Churchill as a Peace Maker*, (London, 1997), p. 83.
99. Churchill, *RW*, second edition, p. 46.
100. Ibid., pp. 74–5.
101. Winston Churchill in a dispatch from Assiout, 9 September 1898, and Omdurman, 20 September 1898 in Woods, *Young Winston's Wars* pp. 122, 149.
102. Weidhorn, *Sword and Pen*, pp. 28–30.
103. Churchill, *RW*, second edition, p. 21.
104. Ibid., p. 28.

105. Ibid., p. 77. Here Churchill is describing the wars among the various tribes and Islamic factions in Africa.
106. Robert Kaplan, *Warrior Politics: Why Leadership Demands a Pagan Ethos* (New York, 2003), p. 24. This comment is further informed by the fact that Charles Gordon was one of Churchill's heroes.
107. Bonham Carter, *As I Knew Him*, p. 40.
108. Virginia Cowles, *Winston Churchill: The Era and The Man* (London, 1953), p. 54.
109. Bechhofer Roberts, *Winston Churchill* (London, 1940), p. 42.
110. Rahe, '*The River War*; Nature's provision', p. 96, referring to Churchill, *RW*, first edition, p. 56.
111. Muller,'War on the Nile', p. 231, referring to Churchill, *RW*, second edition, pp. 43–4.
112. Lord Riddell, *More Pages from my Diaries 1908–1914* (London, 1934), p. 139.
113. Churchill, *RW*, first edition, Vol. 2, p. 162.
114. Churchill, *RW*, second edition, p. 30. For full quote see introduction.
115. Muller, '*War on the Nile*', p. 230.
116. Churchill, *RW*, first edition, Vol. 2, pp. 221–2.
117. Winston Churchill to Lady Churchill, 26 January 1899, in *WSC,C*, Vol. 1, Pt 2, p. 1004.
118. Bonham Carter, *As I knew Him*, p. 41.
119. Ibid., p. 42.
120. Winston Churchill, 3 June 1899, in Robert Rhodes James (ed.), *Winston S. Churchill: His Complete Speeches*, Vol. 1 (London, 1974) [hereafter, *Speeches*], pp. 31–2.
121. As a supplement to Blunt's extensive diary, see Elizabeth Longford, *A Pilgrimage of Passion: The Life of Wilfrid Scawen Blunt* (London, 1979). Additionally, for a more thorough understanding of Blunt's positions on Islam and the Middle East, see Wilfrid Blunt, *The Future of Islam* (London, 1882) (chapter 5, 'England's Interest in Islam', is especially illuminating).
122. Wilfrid Blunt, *My Diaries: Being a Personal Narrative of Events 1888–1914* (London, 1932), pp. 321–2.
123. Blunt, *Diaries*, p. 683.
124. Randolph Churchill, *Winston S. Churchill: Youth 1874–1900*, Vol. 1 (London, 1966) [hereafter the official biography is *WSC*], p. 340.
125. Churchill, *RW*, first edition, Vol. 2, pp. 211–12.
126. See Violet Bonham Carter, *Winston Churchill: An Intimate Portrait* (London, 1965), pp. 26–7.
127. Margery Perham, *Lugard: The Years of Authority 1898–1945* (London, 1960), p. 237.
128. Micheal Sheldon, Young Titan: The Making of Winston Churchill (London, 2013), p.131.
129. Ibid., p. 248.
130. Ibid., p. 252.
131. Ibid., pp. 254–5.
132. Parliamentary Debates, 27 February 1906, Vol. IV, No. 152, pp. 1022–3.

133. Churchill probably became aware of the *Rubaiyat of Omar Khayyam* when he was playing polo with Muslims and Sikhs during his tour of duty in India. The *Rubaiyat of Omar Khayyam* has several references to polo. For instance, quatrain 50 (as translated by FitzGerald) says: 'The Ball no Question makes of Ayes and Noes / But Right or Left as strikes the Player goes; / AIM! He that toss'd Thee down into the Field, / He knows about it all He -knows HE knows!' FitzGerald footnotes at the bottom of the page, 'Ball- Used in Polo which as a game also originated in the East.' See Edward FitzGerald (trans.), *Rubaiyat of Omar Khayyam* (Jaico book edition, 1948), p. 100.
134. Churchill actually briefly met Aga Khan in 1896 in Poona, where he was described by the Aga Khan as 'eager, irrepressible, and an already enthusiastic, courageous, and promising Polo player'. Aga Khan, *The Memoirs of Aga Khan: World Enough and Time* (London, 1954), p. 85. Aga Khan was the 48th Imam of Shia Ismailism and served as the president of the League of Nations from 1937–8.
135. Winston Churchill to Herbert Samuel, 7 December 1906, in *WSC,C*, Vol. 2, Pt 1 (London, 1969), pp. 604–5.
136. Ronald Hyam, *Elgin and Churchill at the Colonial Office 1905–1908: The Watershed of the Empire-Commonwealth* (London, 1968), p. 349.
137. *WSC*, Vol. 2, p. 227.
138. Ibid., p. 227.
139. Ibid., p. 227. Italics are mine.
140. Winston Churchill in a Colonial Office report, Colonial Office Archives, Kew, CO/883/7/3, pp. 1–2.
141. Ibid., pp. 5–6.
142. Ibid., pp. 6–7.
143. Winston Churchill, *My African Journey* (London, 1972) [hereafter *MAJ*], pp. 27–8. Italics are mine.
144. Robert Kaplan, *Warrior Politics: Why Leadership Demands a Pagan Ethos* (New York, 2001), p. 21.
145. Ronald Hyam, *Britain's Declining Empire: The Road to Decolonisation 1918–1968* (London, 2006), pp. 40–1.
146. This notion of a spectrum of racism and where Churchill would sit within it came from a debate and discussion with Richard Toye at Exeter University, 5 February 2013.
147. Churchill, *MAJ*, p. 38.
148. Manchester, *Last Lion*, p. 388.
149. Churchill, *MAJ*, p. 39.
150. Manchester, *Last Lion*, p. 388.
151. For more information see I.M. Lewis, *The Modern History of Somaliland*, chapter 4, 'The Dervish Fight for Freedom' (London, 1965).
152. Hyam, *Elgin and Churchill*, p. 359.
153. Ibid., p. 359.

154. For a complete examination of Churchill's proposal see his memo on the Somaliland Protectorate, CHAR/10/41.
155. Hyam, *Elgin and Churchill*, p. 361.
156. Blunt, *Diaries*, p. 502. Blunt believed Wyndham might have leverage in the War Department as he had served as Under-Secretary for the State of War from 1898 to 1900.
157. Grey to Lord Elgin, 3 February 1908, The Elgin Papers, Broomhall, Fife 1905–1908.
158. Hyam, *Elgin and Churchill*, p. 363.
159. Ibid., p. 364.
160. Winston Churchill to Lord Crewe on 19 September 1908 in *WSC,C*, Vol. 2, Pt 2 (London, 1969), p. 840.
161. Hyam, *Elgin and Churchill*, p. 366.
162. James Currie to the Colonial Office, 1906, CHAR/10/56/4, p. 3.
163. Ibid., p. 9.
164. All financial numbers taken from Currie's report to the Colonial Office January 1908, CHAR/10/56/4, pp. 28–9.
165. Ansari, *The Infidel Within* p. 29.
166. F.G. Lugard to James Currie, 22 January 1908, CHAR/10/56, pp. 12–14.
167. For a collection of the Indian press's trepidation on Churchill possibly becoming viceroy see Roberts, *Winston Churchill*, p. 137.
168. Blunt, *Diaries*, pp. 688–94.
169. The best biographical work on Enver Pasha is Sevket Sureyya Aydemir, *Enver Pasha*, Vols 1–3 (Istanbul, 1971). Some good sources in English are Glen Swanson, 'Enver Pasha: The formative Years' in *Middle East Studies*, Vol. 16, No. 3 (October 1980), pp. 193–9; Charles Haley, 'The Desperate Ottoman: Enver Pasha and the German Empire I', in *Middle Eastern Studies*, Vol. 30, No. 1 (January 1994), pp. 1–51; Charles Haley, 'The Desperate Ottoman: Enver Pasha and the German Empire II', in *Middle Eastern Studies*, Vol. 30, No. 2 (April 1994), pp. 224–51.
170. Winston Churchill, *The World Crisis Vol. 5: The Aftermath* (London, 1929), p. 356.
171. Winston Churchill, *Thoughts and Adventures* (London, 1932) [hereafter *TNA*], pp. 56–7.
172. Ibid., p. 736.
173. Rene Kraus, *Winston Churchill* (London, 1941), p. 158.
174. Blunt, *Diaries*, pp. 735–6.
175. Ibid., p. 736.
176. Ibid., p. 737.

Chapter 2 Of Oil and Ottomans

1. Winston Churchill in an Admiralty memorandum, 15 June 1912, in *WSC,C*, Vol. 2, Pt 3, p. 1564. See also Paul Kennedy, *The Rise and Fall of British Naval Mastery* (London, 1976), p. 224.
2. Kennedy, *The Rise and Fall of British Naval Mastery*, pp. 224–5.
3. Winston Churchill in a departmental memorandum; *WSC,C*, Vol. 2, Pt 3, p. 1568.
4. Ibid., p. 1567.
5. Lord Roberts in a letter to Churchill, 10 July 1912, in ibid., p. 1593.
6. David French, 'The Dardanelles, Mecca and Kut: Prestige as a factor in British Eastern Strategy, 1914–1916', in *War and Society*, Vol. 5, No. 1 (May 1987) pp. 45–62.
7. Winston Churchill in an Admiralty memorandum in *WSC,C*, Vol. 2, Pt 3, p. 1565.
8. Churchill to Lord Roberts, 12 July 1912, in ibid., pp. 1594–5.
9. For more on the notion of Churchill's concentric circles see, Sara Reguer, 'Persian Oil and the First Lord: A Chapter in the Career of Winston Churchill', in *Military Affairs*, Vol. 46, No. 3 (October 1982), p. 137.
10. Ibid., p. 1946.
11. Winston Churchill in a secret memorandum on 4 July 1913 in *WSC,C*, Vol. 2, Pt 3, p. 1945.
12. Reguer, 'Persian Oil and the First Lord', p. 136.
13. Ibid., pp. 136–7, see 17 June 1914, P.D. Commons, Series 5, Vol. 63.
14. Blunt, *Diaries*, p. 738.
15. Ibid., p. 781.
16. Ibid., p. 791.
17. Martin Gilbert, *WSC*, Vol. 3, Minerva Edition (London, 1990), p. 189.
18. H.C. Seppings Wright to Churchill, 18 December 1911; CHAR 2/53/84
19. Djavid Bey to Winston Churchill, 28 October 1911, in *WSC,C*, Vol. 2, Pt 2, p. 1368. It is remarkable that Churchill and Djavid Bey actually kept a correspondence going since Churchill had visited Constantinople, often congratulating one another on promotions and keeping one another informed about state developments. These letters probably contributed to Churchill's admiration for the CUP and the Young Turk movement in general. For examples of their correspondence see CHAR 2/52.
20. Winston Churchill to Sir Edward Grey, 4 November 1911, in ibid., pp. 1369–70.
21. There were approximately 20 million Muslims in Turkey in 1910. In British India there were approximately 62 million Muslims and 10 million Muslims in Egypt.
22. In *How India Was Won by England Under Clive and Hastings* (London, 1881), the author Rev. Savile quoted Professor Monier Williams (Oxford) who said of British subjects: 'Nearly 41 millions are Mohammedans; so that England is by far the greatest Mohammedan power in the world, so that the Queen reigns

over about double as many Moslems as the Representative of the Khalif himself.' p. viii.

23. See Sabah-ed Din, 'Lords of Islam: Why an Anglo-Turkish Entente may Come', in the Adelaide *Advertiser*, 19 October 1912, *The Singapore Free Press and Mercantile Advertiser*, 1 November 1912. Also see additional editorials in the *Sydney Morning Herald*, 1908; Mohamad Abdalla, *Islam and the Australian News Media* (Sydney, 2010).
24. Lord Grey to Churchill, 9 November 1911, WSC, C Vol.2 pt.2, pp. 1370–1.
25. *WSC*, Vol. 3, p. 190.
26. Winston Churchill to Djavid Bey, 19 November 1911; *WSC,C*, Vol. 2, Pt 2, p. 1321.
27. *WSC*, Vol. 3, p. 188.
28. Ibid., p. 190.
29. French, ' Origins', p. 48.
30. Ibid., p. 49.
31. Walter Reid, *Empire of Sand: How Britain Made the Middle East* (London, 2011), p. 11.
32. Kaiser Wilhelm II quoted in Peter Hopkirk, *On Secret Service East of Constantinople: The Plot to Bring Down the British Empire* (London, 1994), p. 57. There were even rumours that the Kaiser had converted to Islam and had gone on the Haj (the Muslim pilgrimage to Mecca) in disguise. See FO 141/1465 and Lawrence James, *Churchill and Empire: Portrait of an Imperialist* (London 2013), p. 110.
33. Ansari,*The Infidel Within*, p. 85.
34. Ibid., p. 87.
35. Hopkirk, *Secret Service*, p. 54.
36. See chapter 1, p. 32.
37. Winston Churchill, *The World Crisis: 1911–1918*, abridged edition (London, 2005), p. 274.
38. *WSC*, Vol. 3, pp. 188–91.
39. Dan van der Vat, *The Ship that Changed the World: The Escape of the Goeban to the Dardanelles in 1914* (London, 1985), p. 27.
40. See chapter 1, p. 32.
41. Ibid., p. 192.
42. Hopkirk, *Secret Service*, p. 57.
43. *WSC*, Vol. 3, p. 193.
44. Dan van der Vat, The Ship that Changed the World, p. 192.
45. Figure taken from *WSC*, Vol. 3, p. 191.
46. Peter Hopkirk, *Secret Service*, p. 57.
47. Churchill, *The World Crisis*, p. 276.
48. *WSC*, Vol. 3, p. 193.
49. Winston Churchill to Grey in *WSC,C*, Vol. 3, Pt 1, p. 38.
50. Winston Churchill to Enver Pasha in ibid., pp. 38–9. The second paragraph was actually added by Grey before Churchill sent the telegraph.

51. French, 'Origins', p. 48.
52. Herbert Asquith to Venetia Stanley, 17 August 1914, in Michael and Eleanor Brock (eds), *H.H. Asquith Letters to Venetia Stanley* (Oxford, 1985), pp. 170–2; see also Herbert Asquith, *Memories and Reflections: The Earl of Oxford and Asquith*, Vol. 2 (London, 1928), p. 26.
53. Aaron Klieman, ' Britain's War Aims in the Middle East in 1915', in *Journal of Contemporary History*, Vol. 3, No. 3, The Middle East (July 1968), p. 238.
54. French, 'Origins', p. 48.
55. Edward Grey, *Twenty-Five Years 1892–1916*, Vol. 3 (London, 1935), p. 122.
56. Churchill, *The World Crisis Vol. 5*, p. 356.
57. Sir Louis Mallet to Grey, 18 August 1914, in *WSC,C*, Vol. 3, Pt 1, pp. 40–1.
58. Winston Churchill to Vice Admiral Troubridge, 18 August 1914, in *WSC,C*, Vol. 3, Pt 1, p. 41.
59. Sir Louis Mallet to Grey, 18 August 1914, in ibid., p. 42.
60. Winston Churchill to Evner Pasha, 18 August 1914, in *WSC*, Vol. 3, p. 196.
61. Winston Churchill to Admiral Limpus, 18 August 1914, in *WSC,C*, Vol. 3, Pt 1, p. 45.
62. Churchill, *The World Crisis*, p. 277.
63. Herbert Asquith to Venetia Stanley in Brock, *Asquith*, p. 186.
64. *WSC*, Vol. 3, pp. 196–7.
65. Churchill, *World Crisis*, p. 281.
66. Ibid., p. 279.
67. Haley, 'Ottoman I', p. 12.
68. Kaiser Wilhelm II, in Hopkirk, *Secret Service*, p. 53.
69. Ibid., p. 56.
70. Ibid., p. 59. The Sultan remained the Caliph of Islam and could still declare jihad despite losing his governmental powers.
71. See Tan Tai-Yong, 'An Imperial Home-Front: Punjab and the First World War', in *Journal of Military History*, Vol. 64, No. 2 (April 2000), pp. 371–410.
72. See Thomas Hughes, 'The German Mission to Afghanistan, 1915–1916' in *German Studies Review*, Vol. 25, No. 3 (October 2002), pp. 447–76.
73. Lal Baha, 'The North West Frontier in the First World War', in *Asian Affairs*, Vol. 1, Pt 1 (1970), p. 29.
74. French, 'Origins', p. 51.
75. Ibid., p. 47.
76. Lieutenant-Colonel Sir Mark Sykes to Churchill, 24 August 1914, CHAR/13/45/127.
77. *WSC*, Vol. 3, p. 200.
78. French, 'Origins', p. 51.
79. Churchill, *WSC,C*, Vol. 3, Pt 1, p. 278.
80. Gilbert, *The Challenge of War*, p. 221.
81. French, 'Origins', p. 214.
82. Ibid., pp. 215–16.
83. Ibid., p. 219.

84. *WSC*, Vol. 3, p. 359.
85. Arthur Marder, *From Dreadnought to Scapa Flow*, Vol. 2 (London, 1965), p. 199.
86. *WSC*, Vol. 3, p. 222.
87. Winston Churchill, statement for the Dardanelles Commission; *WSC,C*, Vol. 3, Pt 2, pp. 1568–71.
88. *WSC*, Vol. 3, p. 233.
89. Ibid., p. 232.
90. French, 'Origins', p. 212.
91. *WSC*, Vol. 3, p. 234.
92. Admiral Carden to Winston Churchill, *WSC,C*, Vol. 3, Pt 2, p. 380.
93. Asquith to Venetia Stanley, 5 December 1914, in Brock, *Asquith*, p. 327.
94. The siege of Antwerp in 1914 represented a significant loss for the British navy. See Richard Hough, *The Great War at Sea: 1914–18* (Oxford, 1983).
95. James, *Churchill and Empire*, pp. 110–11.
96. See Jonathan Rose, *The Literary Churchill: Author, Reader, Actor* (2014).
97. Winston Churchill, *MEL*, p. 154.
98. Winston Churchill to Admiralty Staff November, 1914; ADM 137/95 p. 114; ADM 137/97 p. 97, 132, 383.
99. James, *Churchill and Empire*, p. 108.
100. Winston Churchill to Clementine Churchill, 28 January 1916, *WSC,C*, Vol. 3, Pt 2, p. 1402.
101. *WSC*, Vol. 3, p. 248.
102. Lord Riddell, *Lord Riddell's War Diary* (London, 1933), pp. 82–3.
103. Ibid., p. 327.
104. Winston Churchill, personal notes, January 1916, CHAR/ 2/71/6-9.
105. *WSC*, Vol. 3, p. 355.
106. Ibid., p. 373.
107. Ibid., p. 355.
108. Winston Churchill, 19 March 1915, War Council Meeting Minutes, in *WSC, C*, Vol. 3, Pt 1, pp. 715–16.
109. *WSC*, Vol. 3, p. 356.
110. Trumbull Higgins, *Winston Churchill and the Dardanelles* (London, 1963), p. 43.
111. French, 'Origins', p. 220.
112. Klieman, 'Britain's War Aims'.
113. Ibid., p. 244.
114. Raymond Callahan, 'What About the Dardanelles?', in *The American Historical Review*, Vol. 78, No. 3 (June 1973), p. 646.
115. Winston Churchill in a War Council meeting, 26 February 1915, in *WSC*, Vol. 3, p. 310.
116. Sir James Meston to Austen Chamberlain, 15 June 1915, Chamberlain papers, Birmingham AC/23/1/7, p. 1.
117. Austen Chamberlain to the War Council, 27 July 1915, CHAR/2/74.
118. Longford, *A Pilgrimage of Passion*, p. 409.

119. Churchill, *The World Crisis*, Vol. 5, p. 356.
120. Longford, *A Pilgrimage of Passion*, p. 409.
121. Ibid., pp. 409–10.
122. Paul Addison, *Churchill: The Unexpected Hero* (London, 2005), p. 83.
123. Stuart Ball, *The Conservative Party and British Politics 1902–1951* (London, 1995).

Chapter 3 Churchill: Minister of War and Air

1. *WSC*, Vol. 4, p. 181.
2. Churchill to Lloyd George September 1918; *WSC*, Vol. 4, p. 195.
3. Ibid., p. 196.
4. Fromkin, *A Peace to End All Peace*, p. 387.
5. 300 Indians killed, 2,000 wounded; *WSC*, Vol. 4, p. 401.
6. Ibid., p. 401.
7. Toye, *Empire*, p. 151.
8. Austen Chamberlain to Ida Chamberlain, 11 July 1920, in Robert Self (ed.), *The Austen Chamberlain Diary Letters: The Correspondence of Sir Austen Chamberlian and His Sisters Hilda and Ida* (London, 1995), p. 138. See also Toye, *Empire*, pp. 149–52.
9. Fromkin, *A Peace to End All Peace*, p. 405.
10. Winston Churchill in a speech to the House of Commons, 8 July 1920; *Speeches*, Vol. 3, p. 3006.
11. Toye, *Empire*, pp. 152–3. For more on the Amritsar Massacre see Alfred Draper, *The Amritsar Massacre: Twilight of the Raj* (London, 1985); Nick Lloyd, *The Amritsar Massacre: The Untold Story of One Fateful Day* (London, 2011); and Dennis Judd, 'The Amritsar Massacre of 1919: Gandhi, the Raj and the Growth of Indian Nationalism, 1915–39', in Dennis Judd (ed.), *Empire: The British Imperial Experience from 1765 to the Present* (London, 1996), pp. 258–72.
12. G.H. Bennett, *British Foreign Policy During The Curzon Period 1919–24* (London, 1995), p. 79.
13. Margaret Macmillan, *Peacemakers: Six Months that Changed the World* (London, 2003), p. 414. One of the local Muslim notables who spoke directly to Lloyd George about the matter of the caliphate was the Aga Khan.
14. *WSC*, Vol. 4, pp. 479–80.
15. This fear was not limited to Churchill, in March 1920 the Foreign Office sent out pamphlets to its officers entitled 'The Incompatibility of Islam and Bolshevism' and also circulated four propaganda pamphlets in the Islamic world which espoused this incompatibility. They were 'The Two Brotherhoods', 'Communism: Failure and Reaction', 'The Watch Tower', and 'Class Distinction'. CO/323/843/f581-597.
16. Fromkin, *A Peace to End All Peace*, p. 387.
17. Fromkin, *A Peace to End All Peace*, p. 494.

18. *WSC*, Vol. 4, p. 472.
19. Churchill to Lloyd George, 22 September 1919; ibid., p. 476.
20. Ibid., p. 473.
21. Ibid., p. 476.
22. James Renton, 'Changing Languages of Empire and the Orient: Britain and the Invention of the Middle East, 1917–1918', in *The Historical Journal*, Vol. 50, No. 3 (2007), p. 648.
23. Churchill, *World Crisis*, Vol. 5, p. 391.
24. Lord Riddell, *Lord Riddell's Intimate Diary of the Peace Conference and After 1918-1923* (London, 1934), p. 208.
25. Macmillan, *Peacemakers*, p. 387.
26. Enver Pasha to Winston Churchill, 3 May 1919; CHAR 16/7.
27. Churchill, *The World Crisis*, Vol. 5, pp. 360–1.
28. Fromkin, *A Peace to End All Peace*, pp. 266–7.
29. Ibid., p. 266.
30. Winston Churchill in a speech to the House of Commons, 16 December 1919; *Speeches*, Vol. 3, p. 2923.
31. *WSC*, Vol. 4, p. 480.
32. Winston Churchill in a speech to the House of Commons, 14 February 1920; *Speeches*, Vol. 3, p. 2936.
33. *WSC*, Vol. 4, p. 479.
34. Churchill to Lloyd George, 24 March 1920; *WSC,C*, Vol. 4, Pt. 2, pp. 1054–5.
35. *WSC*, Vol. 4, p. 482.
36. Ibid, p. 482.
37. Winston Churchill, *World Crisis*, Vol. 5, p. 368.
38. Winston Churcill in a memorandum, 7 June 1920; *WSC,C*, Vol. 4, Pt 2, p. 1116.
39. Churchill, *World Crisis*, Vol. 5, p. 367.
40. *WSC*, Vol. 4, p. 488.
41. Ibid., p. 488.
42. Winston Churchill in Cabinet memorandum, 1 May 1920; *WSC,C*, Vol. 4, Pt 2, p. 1079.
43. Ibid., p. 1082.
44. Macmillan *Peacemakers*, p. 419.
45. Arnold Wilson, *Mesopotamia, 1917–1920: A Clash of Loyalties* (London, 1931), pp. 273–6.
46. Fariq al-Mizhar al-Fir'aun, *al-Haqa'iq al-Nasi' a* (Baghdad, 1952); Amal Vinogradov, 'The 1920 Revolt in Iraq Reconsidered: The Role of Tribes in National Politics', in *International Journal of Middle Eastern Studies*, Vol. 3, No. 2 (April 1972), p. 124.
47. Vinogradov, Ibid., pp. 124–5.
48. A.L. MacFie, 'British Intelligence and the Causes of Unrest in Mesopotamia, 1919–1920', in *Middle Eastern Studies*, Vol. 35, No. 1 (January 1999), pp. 165–77.

49. Churchill to Lloyd George (unsent), 31 August 1920; Gilbert, *WSC,C*, Vol. 4, Pt 2, p. 1199.
50. Winston Churchill in a Cabinet memorandum, 22 November 1920; *WSC,C*, Vol. 4, Pt 2, pp. 1249–50.
51. *WSC*, Vol. 4, p. 498.
52. Aga Khan to Edwin Montagu, 2 December 1920; ibid., p. 498.
53. *The Times of India*, 'One Final Effort', 2 December 1921; CHAR/2/120/37-41.
54. Winston Churchill to Lloyd George, 4 December 1920; *WSC,C*, Vol. 4, Pt 2, pp. 1261–2.
55. *WSC*, Vol. 4, p. 501.
56. Winston Churchill in a Cabinet memorandum, 16 December 1920; *WSC,C*, Vol. 4, Pt. 2, pp. 1267–8.
57. Lord Derby to Churchill, 23 December 1920; Ibid., pp. 1278–9.
58. Henry Wilson in his diary, 17 December 1920; Sir C.E. Callwell (ed.), *Field Marshal Sir Henry Wilson: His Life and Diaries* (London, 1927), pp. 273–5.
59. David E. Omissi, *Air Power and Colonial Control: The Royal Air Force 1919–1939* (London, 1990); Chaz Bowyer, *RAF Operations:1918–1938* (London, 1988); Malcolm Smith, *British Air Strategy Between the Wars* (Oxford, 1984); and Charles Townshend, 'Civilization and "Frightfulness": Air Control in the Middle East Between the Wars' in Chris Wrigley (ed.), *Warfare, Diplomacy and Politics: Essay's in Honour of AJP Taylor* (London, 1986).
60. For more on Trenchard see, Andrew Boyle, *Trenchard: Man of Vision* (London, 1962).
61. Margaret Macmillan, *Peacemakers*; John Keay, *Sowing the Wind: The Mismanagement of the Middle East 1900–1960* (London, 1988); Efraim Karsh, *Empires of the Sand: The Struggle for Mastery in the Middle East, 1789–1923* (Cambridge, Mass, 2003); Elie Kedourie, *England and the Middle East: The Destruction of the Ottoman Empire 1914–1922* (London, 1978).
62. Winston Churchill to John Shuckburgh, 12 November 1921; CHAR/17/15.
63. *WSC*, Vol. 4, p. 197.
64. Interestingly, the two men had trained together as pilots in 1912 and, on occasion, their paths crossed at the naval air bases, Eastchurch and Upavon.
65. Winston Churchill to Walter Long on 8 February 1919; *WSC,C*, Vol. 4, Pt 1, p. 517.
66. Churchill to Battenburg, 6 March 1914; Randolph Churchill, *Churchill Companion*, Vol. 2, Pt 2 (London, 1969), pp. 1911–12.
67. T.E. Lawrence's notes to Liddell Hart 1933; David Garnett, *The Letters of T E Lawrence of Arabia* (London, 1964), p. 323.
68. Garnett, *The Letters of T E Lawrence*, pp. 302, 323.
69. Robert S. Dudney, 'Lawrence of Airpower,' *Air Force Magazine*, Vol. 94, No. 4 (April 2012); Priya Satia, 'The Defence of Inhumanity', *The American Historical Review*, Vol. 111, No. 1, http://www.historycooperative.org/journals/ahr/111.1/satia.html, accessed 4 July 2012. Satia does note that this statement was clearly an overstatement on Lawrence's part.

70. For Churchill's personal experience of the Anglo-Dervish War of 1898, see Winston Churchill, *The River War: An Account of the Reconquest of the Sudan* (London, 1899). For Churchill's personal experience of the north-west frontier see Winston Churchill, *The Story of the Malakand Field Force: An Episode of Frontier War* (London, 1897) and Churchill, 'The Ethics of Frontier Policy', in *Military Review*, No. 57, 1899.
71. See Hyam, *Elgin and Churchill*.
72. See Roy Irons, Churchill and the Mad Mullah of Somaliland: Betrayal and Redemption 1899–1921 (2013).
73. David Omissi, *Air Power and Colonial Control: The Royal Air Force 1919–1939* (London, 1990), p. 14.
74. Lt Col. David J,Dean, 'Air Control in Small Wars', in *Air University Review* (July–August 1983), p. 3.
75. Dean,'Small Wars', p. 3.
76. See chapter 1.
77. Townshend, 'Civilization and Frightfulness', pp. 142–3.
78. Dean 'Small Wars', p. 4.
79. Omissi, *Air Power* p. 14. Also see WC.513 m.3, 24, January 1919, CAB/23/9.
80. Omissi, Ibid., p. 15.
81. Bowyer, *RAF Operations*, p. 62.
82. For an overall account of this dispute see Charles Townshend, 'Civilization and Frightfulness' and Omissi, *Air Power and Colonial Control*.
83. Winston Churchill to Hugh Trenchard, 2 March 1920; *WSC,C*, Vol. 4, Pt 2, pp. 1045–6.
84. This was one of Churchill's favourite sayings regarding the British Empire's relationship with its Islamic subjects. He used it in several letters, Cabinet memorandums and in his book *World Crisis: The Aftermath*, p. 391. Also see *WSC,C*, Vol. 4, Pt 2, pp. 1261–2, 1267–8.
85. For Churchill's belief in the progressive and civilizing effects of the British Empire, see Richard Toye, *Churchill's Empire: The World that Made Him and the World He Made* (London, 2010); Kirk Emmert, *Winston S Churchill on Empire* (Chapel Hill, 1980); Harry William Porter, *The Imperial Policy of Winston L.S. Churchill from 1900 to 1936 as set Forth by his Speeches* (unpublished thesis, 1946).
86. Winston Churchill to Hugh Trenchard, 2 March 1920; *WSC, C*, Vol. 4, Pt 2, pp. 1045–6.
87. Winston Churchill to Hugh Trenchard, 2 March 1920; ibid., pp. 1045–6.
88. Ferguson, *The War of the World*, p. 558.
89. Baker, *Human Smoke*, pp. 7–8.
90. Winston Churchill in War Committee notes on 20 October 1915, CHAR 2/74.
91. Winston Churchill in War Office minutes, 12 May 1919; *WSC,C*, Vol. 4, Pt 1, p. 649. Churchill's position on the use of gas as a convention weapon is a

regular occurrence in his memos. See for instance, Winston Churchill in War Office Minutes, 22 May 1919; ibid., pp. 661–2.

92. Winston Churchill in War Office Minutes, 12 May 1919; ibid., p. 649.
93. Winston Churchill in War Office Minutes, 22 May 1919; ibid., pp. 661–2.
94. Winston Churchill in a letter to Sir Hugh Trenchard, 29 August 1920, CHAR 16/52.
95. Christopher Catherwood, *Churchill's Folly: How Winston Churchill Created Modern Iraq* (New York, 2005), p. 85.
96. Lawrence James, *The Rise and Fall of the British Empire* (London, 1997), p. 398; Ferguson, *The War of the World*, p. 412; R.M. Douglas, 'Did Britain Use Chemical Weapons in Mandatory Iraq?', in *The Journal of Modern History*, No. 81 (December 2009).
97. Douglas, ibid., p. 882.
98. Douglas, ibid., p. 883.
99. Townshend, 'Civilization and Frightfulness', p. 145.
100. Air Staff Memorandum, March 1921, AIR 20/674, pp. 4–5.
101. Andrew Boyle, *Trenchard: Man of Vision* (London, 1962), p. 390.
102. Townshend, 'Civilization and Frightfulness', p. 150.
103. Air Staff Memorandum, March 1921, AIR 20/674, p. 4.
104. Priya Satia, 'Rebellion of Technology', in D. Davis and E. Burk (eds), *Environmental Imaginaries of the Middle East in North Africa* (Athens, 2011), p. 24.
105. Ibid., p. 33.
106. Churchill to Trenchard, 29 February 1920, PRO. AIR 5 224.
107. Priya Satia, *Spies in Arabia: The Great War and the Cultural Foundations of Britain's Covert Empire in the Middle East* (Oxford, 2008), p. 245. For more information on the theory of a panopticon see Jeremy Bentham, *Panopticon* (London, 1791); Michel Foucault, *Discipline and Punish: The Birth of the Prison* (London, 1977).
108. Winston Churchill to Hugh Trenchard, 2 March 1920; Gilbert, *WSC,C*, Vol. 4, Pt 2, pp. 1045–6.
109. Satia, 'The Defence of Inhumanity', p. 7.
110. Churchill to Trenchard, 29 February 1920, PRO. AIR 5 224.
111. Townshend, 'Civilization and Frightfulness,' p. 153.
112. Satia, *Spies in Arabia*, p. 246.
113. Churchill personally sought the use of propaganda in order to prevent unrest. Townshend, 'Civilization and Frightfulness', p. 146; For Air Staff memorandum on use of propaganda pamphlets see AIR 20/674/9, p. 5. On RAF intelligence see Dean, 'Air Control in Small Wars', p. 8, and for a complete overview of British intelligence in the Levant see Satia, *Spies in Arabia*.
114. Townshend, 'Civilization and Frightfulness', p. 144.
115. Dean, 'Air Control in Small Wars', p. 5.
116. Omissi, *Air Power*, pp. 173–4.
117. Gilbert, *Winston S Churchill*, Vol. 4, pp. 796–7.

118. Winston Churchill to Percy Cox, 7 June 1921; Gilbert, *Churchill Companion* Vol. 4, Pt 3, pp. 1497–8. Gilbert noted that this telegram to Cox was drafted by Col. T.E. Lawrence.
119. Cox to Churchill, 24 June 1921; Gilbert, *WSC,C*, Vol. 4, p. 797.
120. Report by OC Mesopotamian Group, 30 May 1921; Trenchard Papers MFC 76/1/139; Omissi, *Air Power*, p. 174.
121. Churchill to Trenchard, 22 July 1921; Gilbert, *WSC,C*, Vol. 4, Pt 3, p. 1561.
122. Thomas Macaulay, 'Essay on Warren Hastings', in *Edinburgh Review* (October 1841). Churchill often cited this passage. See, for instance, Churchill speech on the Amritsar Massacre in the House of Commons, 8 July 1920, in Robert Rhodes James, *Speeches*, Vol. 3 (London, 1974), p. 3006.

Chapter 4 Churchill at the Colonial Office

1. Fromkin, *The Peace to End All Peace*, p. 495.
2. Roger Adelson, *London and the Invention of the Middle East: Money, Power and War, 1902–1922* (London, 1995), p. 25.
3. Ibid., p. 25.
4. Ibid., p. 24. For more on the term 'Middle East' see Rodrick Davison, 'Where is the Middle East', in *Foreign Affairs* Vol. 38, No. 4 (July, 1960), pp. 665–75; Thomas Scheffler, "Fertile Crescent", "Orient", "Middle East": The Changing Mental Maps of South West Asia', in *European Review of History*, Vol. 10, No. 2 (2003); Renton, 'Changing Languages'.
5. For more on the conflict between the India Office, the Colonial Office and the War Office see Timothy Paris, 'British Middle East Policy-Making after the First World War: The Lawrentian and Wilsonian Schools', *The Historical Journal*, Vol. 41, No. 3 (September 1998), pp. 773–93.
6. For more on Churchill and Curzon's adversarial relationship see Bennett, *Curzon Period*, pp. 100–15, 150; and Helmut Mejcher, 'Iraq's External Relations 1921–1926', *Middle Eastern Studies*, Vol. 13, No. 3 (October 1977), pp. 340–58.
7. Percy Cox in Cabinet Meeting minutes, 12 August 1920; *WSC,C*, Vol. 4, Pt 2, pp. 1170–1.
8. Bennett, *Curzon Period*, p. 108.
9. Cabinet minutes, 31 December 1921; *WSC,C*, Vol. 4, Pt 2, pp. 1279–82; CAB/23/23/CC/82.
10. Timothy Paris, *Britain, The Hashemites and Arab Rule 1920-1925: The Sherifian Solution* (London, 2003), p. 119.
11. Fromkin, *The Peace to End All Peace*, pp. 495–6.
12. Paris, *The Sherifan Solution*, pp. 118–19.
13. *WSC*, Vol. 4, p. 509.
14. Ibid., p. 508.
15. 'The Middle Eastern Department,' *Guardian*, 16 February 1921; 'The Air Ministry', *Guardian*, 18 February 1921; 'Case for Frankness: Our Oriental

Empire', *Spectator*, 28 August 1920; 'The Question of the Mandates', *The Times*, 4 March 1921; Satia, *Spies*, pp. 295, 297.

16. Bennett, *Curzon Period*, p. 109.
17. Ibid., p. 109.
18. Churchill to Lord Curzon, 8 January 1921; *WSC,C*, Vol. 4, Pt 2, p. 1296.
19. Edwin Montagu to Churchill, 18 January 1921; ibid., p. 1315.
20. Churchill to George Richie, 23 February 1921; CHAR/5/25.
21. Lord Rawlinson to Churchill, 10 February 1921; *WSC,C*, Vol. 4, Pt 2, pp. 1344–5.
22. Churchill to Sir Percy Cox, 8 January 1921; ibid., p. 1297.
23. The pledge was made in the Hussein–McMahon correspondence (1915–16) in which Henry McMahon urged the Sharif of Mecca, Hussein bin Ali, to revolt against the Ottoman Empire in exchange for an Arab state (it was ambiguous if it was to be an independent state or one under the umbrella of the Empire). The boundaries of this supposed state were also ambiguous, which resulted in much dissention especially as it relates to Jordan, Palestine, and Israel. Additionally, the Sykes–Picot Agreement (1916), which divided the Middle East between France and Britain, and the Balfour Declaration (1917), which made Palestine a home for the Jews, tended to be opposed to one another. For more on the Hussein–McMahon correspondence see Klieman, 'Britain's War Aims', and Elie Kedourie, *In the Anglo-Arab Labyrinth: The McMahon–Husayn Correspondence and Its Interpretations, 1914–1939* (London, 2000).
24. John Fisher, *Curzon and British Imperialism in the Middle East 1916–19* (London, 1999), p. 297.
25. Meinertzhagen is not always a reliable source as he fabricated several elements surrounding his life. For more information see Brian Garfield, *The Meinertzhagen Mystery* (Washington, 2007); N.J. Lockman, *Meinertzhagen's Diary Ruse* (Washington, 1995); P.H. Capstick, *Warrior: The Legend of Colonel Richard Meinertzhagen* (London, 1998).
26. This book will only examine the effect of Lawrence on Churchill's positions and policy. For more on T.E. Lawrence see T.E. Lawrence, *Seven Pillars of Wisdom* (London, 1922); Richard Perceval Graves, *Lawrence of Arabia and His World* (London, 1922); Jeremy Wilson, *Lawrence of Arabia: The Authorized Biography of T.E. Lawrence* (London, 1989); David Garnett, *The Letters of T E Lawrence of Arabia* (London, 1964).
27. *WSC*, Vol. 4, p. 510; Fromkin, *The Peace to End All Peace*, p. 497.
28. Lawrence to Churchill via Eddie Marsh, 17 January 1921, CHAR/17/14.
29. Catherwood, *Churchill's Folly*, p. 102.
30. Paris, *The Sherifian Solution*, p. 130.
31. Richard Meinertzhagen, *Middle East Diary: 1917–1956* (London, 1959), p. 33.
32. Kathryn Tidrick, *Heart Beguiling Araby: The English Romance with Arabia* (London, 1981), p. 181.
33. See CHAR/2/118/96 and Longford, *A Pilgramage of Passion*, p. 418.

34. Churchill originally wanted Hirtzel as the head of the Middle East Department but he refused citing his love of the India Office.
35. Winston Churchill to Arthur Hirtzel, 23 January 1921; *WSC,C*, Vol. 4, Pt 2, pp. 1320–1.
36. Renton, 'Changing Languages', p. 653.
37. Ibid., p. 648
38. Ibid., p. 653.
39. Ibid., p. 653.
40. *WSC*, memorandum, 25 October 1919, *WSC, C* Vol. 4, Pt 2, p. 938.
41. Winston Churchill to Arthur Hirtzel, 23 January 1921; Ibid., pp. 1320–1.
42. Curzon to Churchill, 9 January 1921; ibid., p. 1298.
43. Wahhabism is an ultra-conservative sect of Islam and is primarily practised in modern-day Saudi Arabia. See N. Delong-Bas, *Wahhabi Islam: From Revival and Reform to Global Jihad* (Oxford, 2004); David Holden and Richard Johns, *The House of Saud* (London, 1982).
44. Paris,*The Sharfian Solution*, p. 2.
45. Paris, 'British Middle East Policy', p. 776.
46. Paris, *The Sherifian Solution*, p. 239.
47. Arun Sinha, 'Shia–Sunni Conflict', *Economic and Political Weekly*, Vol. 13, No. 45 (11 November, 1978), p. 1841.
48. Catherwood, *Churchill's Folly*, p. 106.
49. Churchill to Lloyd George, 12 February 1921; *WSC,C*, Vol. 4, Pt 2, pp. 1346–7.
50. Curzon to Lady Grace Hinds, 14 February 1921; *WSC*, Vol. 4, p. 529.
51. Churchill to Lloyd George, 25 January 1921; *WSC,C*, Vol. 4, Pt 2, pp. 1322–3.
52. Churchill to Lloyd George (unsent), 25 January 1921; ibid., p. 1324.
53. *WSC*, Vol. 4, p. 535.
54. Churchill to Lloyd George (unsent), 22 February 1921; *WSC,C*, Vol. 4, Pt 2, pp. 1369–70.
55. *WSC*, Vol. 4, pp. 514–15.
56. Ibid., p. 515.
57. Churchill to Cox, 16 January 1921; *WSC,C*, Vol. 4, Pt 2, pp. 1312–13.
58. Churchill to Worthington-Evans, 25 January 1921; *WSC*, Vol. 4, p. 520.
59. Fromkin, *The Peace to End All Peace*, p. 501.
60. A full exploration of this treaty is beyond the remit of this book. For more on the Skyes–Picot Agreement see Fromkin, *A Peace to End All Peace* and Avi Shlaim, *War and Peace in the Middle East: A Concise History* (New York, 1995).
61. Churchill to Lloyd George, 12 January 1921; *WSC,C*, Vol. 4, Pt 2, pp. 1302–5; CHAR/16/71. Also see Aaron Klieman, *Foundations of British Policy in the Arab World: The Cairo Conference of 1921* (London, 1970), p. 108, n.3.
62. *WSC*, Vol. 4, p. 519.

63. A full exploration of this treaty is beyond the remit of this book. For more on the Hussein–McMahon correspondence see Klieman, 'Britain's War Aims in the Middle East in 1915'; Elie Kedourie, *In the Anglo-Arab Labyrinth*.
64. Fromkin, *The Peace to End All Peace*, p. 499.
65. A full exploration of this pledge is beyond the remit of this book. For more on the Balfour Declaration see Martin Gilbert, *Churchill and the Jews* (London, 2007); Evyatar Friesel, 'British Policy in Palestine: The Churchill Memorandum of 1922', in *Vision and Conflict in the Holy Land* (October 1985).
66. Churchill to Lloyd George, 12 January 1921; *WSC,C*, Vol. 4, Pt 2, pp. 1302–5; CHAR/16/71.
67. Gilbert, *Churchill and the Jews*, pp. 44, 38.
68. Toye, *Empire*, p. 147.
69. Churchill to Cox, 7 February 1921; *WSC,C*, Vol. 4, Pt 2, pp. 1334–5.
70. Churchill to Haldane, 7 February 1921; ibid., p. 1337.
71. Churchill to Hirtzel, 8 February 1921; ibid., p. 1339.
72. Haldane to Churchill, 8 February 1921; ibid., p. 1339.
73. Churchill's Cabinet notes, 10 February 1921; ibid., pp. 1341–2.
74. Churchill to Hirtzel, 23 January and 8 February; ibid., pp. 1322, 1338.
75. *WSC*, Vol. 4, p. 537.
76. Ibid., p. 540.
77. Ibid., p. 537.
78. Churchill to Curzon (unsent), 25 February 1921; *WSC,C*, Vol. 4, Pt 2, p. 1378.
79. Lord Allenby to Curzon, 21 Febuary 1921; ibid., p. 1369.
80. Jack Fishman, *My Darling Clementine: The Story of Lady Churchill* (London, 1963), p. 76.
81. Paris, *The Sharifian Solution*, p. 137. For more on Gertrude Bell see Janet Wallach, *The Desert Queen: The Extraordinary Life of Gertrude Bell* (London, 1996); Gertrude Bell, *The Letters of Gertrude Bell* (London, 1926).
82. Wallach, *The Desert Queen*, p. 296.
83. Ibid., p. 293.
84. Catherwood, *Churchill's Folly*, p. 129.
85. Matthew Spalding, 'Winston S Churchill and the Middle East', in Christopher Harmon and David Tucker (eds), *Statecraft and Power: Essays in Honour of Harold W. Rood* (London, 1994), p. 94.
86. Winston Churchill at the Cairo Conference, 12 March 1921, 'Report on Middle East Conference Held in Cairo and Jerusalem', FO/371/6343.
87. Spalding, 'Winston S Churchill and the Middle East', p. 94.
88. Peter Sluglett, *Britain in Iraq: Contriving King and Country* (London, 2007), p. 41.
89. Churchill to Lloyd George, 18 March 1921; *WSC,C*, Vol. 4, Pt 2, p. 1398. For more on Talib see D.K. Fieldhouse, *Imperialism*, p. 89.
90. Klieman, *Foundations*, p. 107.
91. Churchill to Lloyd George, 18 March 1921; *WSC,C*, Vol. 4, Pt 2, pp. 1398–9.

92. *WSC*, Vol. 4, p. 547. Note: Klieman puts the cost at closer to £31 million, see *Foundations*, p. 111.
93. Lloyd Geroge to Winston Churchill, 16 March 1921; *WSC,C*, Vol. 4, Pt 2, pp. 1395–6.
94. Klieman, *Foundations*, p. 110.
95. Slugget, *Britain in Iraq*, p. 79.
96. Wallach, *Desert Queen*, p. 298; FO/371/6343.
97. Hubert Young and Edward Noel addressing the Political Committee FO/371/6343. Also see Klieman, *Foundations*, p. 110. For more on Major Noel see Edward William Charles Noel, *Diary of Major Noel on Special Duty in Kurdistan* (Baghdad, 1920).
98. Wallach, p. 299. See also R. Bullard, *The Camels Must Go* (London, 1961), pp. 121–2.
99. Winston Churchill to Political Committee, 15 March 1921; FO/371/6343 pp. 60–1.
100. *WSC*, Vol. 4, p. 552.
101. Major Young addressing the Political Committee, FO/371/6343 pp. 189–90.
102. FO/371/6343; *WSC*, Vol. 4, p. 551.
103. Ibid., p. 552; FO/371/6343.
104. Klieman, *Foundations*, p. 117.
105. Winston Churchill to the Joint Political and Military meeting on Palestine, 17 March 1921, FO/371/6343, p. 98; *WSC*, Vol. 4, p. 553.
106. Klieman, *Foundations*, p. 117.
107. T.E. Lawrence to the Political and Military Committee on Palestine, 17 March 1921; FO/371/6343 p. 98; CO/935/1/1.
108. W.H. Deedes addressing the Political and Military Committe on Palestine, 17 March 1921, FO/371/6343.
109. Churchill to Lloyd George, 18 March 1921; *WSC,C*, Vol. 4, Pt 2, pp. 1401–3; CHAR/17/18.
110. Samuel to the Military Committee for Palestine, 17 March 1921, FO/371/6343.
111. Catherwood, *Churchill Folly*, p. 143.
112. Churchill to the Politcal and Military Committee on Palestine, 18 March 1921; *WSC*, Vol. 4, p. 555; FO 371/6343.
113. Catherwood, *Churchill's Folly*, p. 143.
114. Roger Adelson, *London and the Invention of the Middle East: Money, Power, and War 1902–1922* (London, 1995), p. 201.
115. Jessie Raven quoted in *WSC*, Vol. 4, p. 557. Also quoted in Catherwood, *Churchill's Folly*, p. 128.
116. Catherwood, *Churchill's Folly*, p. 128.
117. Wallach, *Desert Queen*, p. 300.
118. Ibid., p. 300.
119. Fishman, *My Darling Clementine* (London, 1966), p. 77.
120. *WSC*, Vol. 4, p. 555.

Chapter 5 The Legacy of the Cairo Conference

1. T.E. Lawrence, *The Seven Pillars of Wisdom* (London, 1992), p. 276, n. 1.
2. Blunt, *The Future of Islam*, p. 204; See also Kathryn Tidrick, *Heart Begiling Araby*, p. 126.
3. Karl Meyer and Shareen Brysac, *King Makers: The Invention of the Modern Middle East* (London, 2008), p. 260. However, this is most likely a misquote from Churchill's speech in the House of Commons on 24 March 1936 when Churchill declared, 'The Emir Abdullah is in TransJordania where I put him one Sunday afternoon at Jerusalem.' Robert Rhodes James, *Winston S Churchill: His Complete Speeches*, Vol. 6, p. 5715.
4. This myth is frequently cited in travel writing and tourism books for Jordan. See Mathew Teller, *Rough Guide to Jordan* (London, 2002), p. 213. and Jenny Walker, *Lonely Planet Guide to Jordan* (London, 2009), p. 165.
5. Mappery.com, http://mappery.com/Jordan-Map, accessed 16 November 2010.
6. Efraim Karsh and Inari Karsh, *Empires of the Sand*, p. 314.
7. Sameul to Curzon, 7 August 1920; *Documents on British Foreign Policy*, Vol. 13, pp. 333–4.
8. *WSC*, Vol. 4, p. 541.
9. Ibid., p. 560.
10. Karsh and Karsh, *Empires*, p. 321.
11. *WSC*, Vol. 4, p. 560.
12. Ibid., p. 560.
13. Mary Wilson, *King Abdullah, Britain and the Making of Jordan* (London, 1987), p. 51.
14. Lloyd George to Churchill, 22 March 1921; *WSC,C*, Vol. 4. Pt 2, pp. 1407–8.
15. *WSC*, Vol. 4, p. 560.
16. Karsh and Karsh, *Empires*, p. 321.
17. Ibid., p. 322.
18. King Abdullah, *The Memoirs of King Abdullah of TransJordan* (London, 1950), p. 203.
19. *WSC*, Vol. 4, p. 561.
20. Ibid., p. 561.
21. Ibid., p. 561.
22. Churchill, House of Commons, 14 June 1921; *Speeches* Vol. 6, pp. 3100–1.
23. Ibid., p. 3095.
24. Ibid., pp. 3100–1
25. *WSC*, Vol. 4, p. 572.
26. Churchill Cabinet Memo, 2 April 1921: *WSC,C*, Vol. 4. Pt 3, pp. 1428–31.
27. Karsh and Karsh, *Empires*, p. 324.
28. Klieman, *Foundations*, p. 117.
29. Churchill to Abdullah, 'First Conversation on Tran-Jordania', held at Government House, Jerusalem FO/371/6343.

30. Ibid., FO/371/6343.
31. Karsh and Karsh, *Empires*, p. 323.
32. King Abdullah, *Memoirs*, p. 204. *WSC*, Vol. 4, p. 561.
33. Churchill, Cabinet memo, 2 April 1921: *WSC,C*, Vol. 4, Pt 3, p. 1430.
34. See Slugett, pp. 4–7; Fromkin, p. 385; Fisk, pp. 177–8; Karsh and Karsh, pp. 296–311.
35. Lawrence, *The Seven Pillars of Wisdom*, pp. 213, 97.
36. Fieldhouse, *Imperialism*, p. 89.
37. Fromkin, *The Peace to End All Peace*, p. 507.
38. Fieldhouse, *Imperialism*, p. 89.
39. Klieman, *Foundations*, pp. 145–6.
40. Fieldhouse, *Imperialism*, p. 91.
41. Winston Churchill to Feisal, 17 August 1922; *WSC,C*, Vol. 4, Pt 3, p. 1960.
42. Winston Churchill to Lloyd George, 24 August 1922; ibid., p. 1966.
43. Winston Churchill, Cabinet meeting minutes, 28 August 1922; ibid., p. 1967.
44. Winston Churchill to Lloyd George, 1 September 1922; ibid., p. 1973.
45. This was true except for the brief period during World War II when the Hashemite throne was deposed during the Revolt of the Golden Square in 1941. This is discussed in chapter 7.
46. Robert Olsen, 'The Second Time Around: British Policy Towards the Kurds (1921–1922)', in *Die Welt des Islams*, Bd. 27, Nr. 1/2 (1987), p. 99.
47. Cairo Conference, 15 March 1921, 'Fourth Meeting of the Political Committee of the Middle East Department'; FO/371/6343.
48. Major Noel, FO/371/6343; see also Robert Olson, 'The Churchill–Cox Correspondence Regarding the Creation of the State of Iraq: Consequences for British Policy Towards the Nationalist Turkish Government, 1921–1923', *International Journal of Turkish Studies*, Vol. 5 (1991), p. 123.
49. Churchill to Cox, 9 June 1921; CO/730/2, No. 148.
50. Olsen, 'The Churchill-Cox Correspondence', p. 124.
51. Cox to Churchill, 20 September 1921; CO/730/2, No. 203.
52. Fieldhouse, *Imperialism*, p. 229.
53. Cox to Churchill, 20 September 1921; CO/730/2, No. 203.
54. Olsen, 'The Churchill-Cox Correspondence', p. 128.
55. Cox to Churchill, 28 October 1921; CO/730/6.
56. Olsen, 'The Churchill-Cox Correspondence', p. 130.
57. Churchill to Cox, 11 November 1921; *WSC,C*, Vol. 4, Pt 3, p. 1668.
58. Olsen, 'The Churchill-Cox Correspondence', p. 132.
59. Hurwitz, 'Churchill and Palestine', p. 6.
60. *WSC*, Vol. 4, pp. 553–5.
61. Cohen, *Churchill and the Jews*, p. 88.
62. See Cabinet meeting minutes, 11 April 1921; CAB/23/25.
63. 'Palestinian Arab Petition', 14 March 1921; *WSC,C*, Pt 2, pp. 1385–6.

64. Isaiah Friedman, 'The McMahon-Hussein Correspondence and the Question of Palestine', *Journal of Contemporary History*, Vol. 5, No. 2 (1970), p. 119.
65. See Major Young's report on the conversation, 20 January 1921; FO/371/6237.
66. Eliezer Tauber, *The Formation of Modern Iraq and Syria* (London, 1994), p. 105; The president of the Palestinian Arab Congress was Musa Kasim al-Husayni, a relative of the future Mufti.
67. For King Hussein's repeated consent to the British government for a Jewish national home see Ormsby-Gore's memorandum on Zionism, 14 April 1917, CAB/24/10/447; and Stein, *Balfour*, pp. 632–3. Hussein's article quoted in Friedman, 'The McMahon-Hussein Correspondence', pp. 117–18. See also The Jewish Agency for Palestine, *Documents*, pp. 161–7. Note that George Antonius believed that the article had even been penned by King Hussein; see George Antonius, *The Arab Awakening* (London, 1938), p. 269.
68. Macmillan, *Peacemakers*, p. 433.
69. Friedman, 'The McMahon-Hussein Correspondence', p. 119.
70. McMahon to John Shuckburgh, 12 March 1922; FO/271/7797.
71. See Renton, 'Changing Languages', p. 655.
72. 'Palestine Royal Commission', Minutes of evidence 12 March 1937; CHAR/2/317/8662-3, p. 503.
73. For an example of Churchill's view of the Palestinians being outside the McMahon–Hussein pledges due to their alliance with the Ottomans see Winston Churchill in a speech at the House of Commons, 23 May 1939; *Speeches*, Vol. 6, p. 6134.
74. See Blunt's Diary, 21 August 1920; MS/459/1975. Blunt Papers, Fitzwilliam Museum, Cambridge. For more on Blunt's dislike of Palestinian Arabs see Tidrick, *Araby*, pp. 108–35.
75. Lawrence, 'Notes on Syria', 25 February 1918, see Wasserstein, *The British in Palestine*, p. 13.
76. Calyton to Bell, 18 June 1918; see Wasserstein, *The British in Palestine*, p. 12.
77. J. Reinharz, *Chaim Weizmann: The making of a Statesman* (New York, 1968), pp. 255–6.
78. Palestine Royal Commission, Minutes of evidence, 12 March 1937; CHAR/2/317/8646; 8666, pp. 502–3.
79. Winston Churchill's remarks to the Palestinian Arabs Delegation; *WSC,C*, Vol. 4, Pt 2, pp. 1419–21.
80. 'Palestine Royal Commission', CHAR/2/317/8646; 8672, pp. 502, 504.
81. Cohen, *Churchill and the Jews*, p. 90.
82. Ibid., p. 91
83. Meinertzhagen minutes, 16 June 1921; CO/733/13.
84. Winston Churchill's remarks to the Palestinian Arabs Delegation; *WSC,C*, Vol. 4, Pt 2, p. 1420.
85. Winston Churchill's remarks to the Zionist Delegation; ibid., pp. 1421–2.

86. Palestine Royal Commission, Minutes of evidence, 12 March 1937; CHAR/2/317/8666, 8728, pp. 503, 507.
87. Gilbert arrived at a similar conclusion regarding Churchill's relationship with Muslims but based this on his experiences during the Anglo-Dervish War and relies on the passage in *RW* (discussed in chapter 1) to make the assertion. See Gilbert, *Churchill and the Jews*, p. 53.
88. Cohen, *Churchill and the Jews*, p. 77.
89. Churchill to Lloyd George, 2 June 1921; *WSC,C*, Vol. 4 Pt 3, pp. 1536–7.
90. Ismar Elbogen (trans. Moses Hades), *A Century of Jewish Life* (Philadelphia, 1960), p. 567.
91. Churchill to Samuel, 3 May 1921; *WSC,C*, Vol. 4, Pt 3, p. 1455.
92. Churchill to Samuel, 14 May 1921; ibid., pp. 1466–77.
93. Departmental minutes, 1 June 1921; CO/733/3; see Cohen, *Churchill and the Jews*, pp. 103–4.
94. Churchill to Samuel, 4 June 1921; *WSC,C*, Vol. 4, Pt 3, p. 1493. Italics are mine.
95. Churchill to Shuckburgh, 15 June 1921; ibid., p. 1508.
96. Weizmann recorded Churchill's position in a letter to Ahad Ha'am, 30 July 1921; quoted in Cohen, *Churchill and the Jews*, p. 115.
97. This was Weizmann's recollection of the conversation at Balfour's house on 22 July 1921. See *WSC,C*, Vol. 4, Pt 3, pp. 1558–61; See also Weizmann's letters to Ahad Ha'am and William Deedes on respectively 30 and 31 July 1921 in Wasserstein (ed.), *The Weizmann Letters*, Vol. 10, No. 227, 228.
98. *WSC*, Vol. 4, p. 625.
99. Churchill's discussion with Shibly Jamal, 15 August 1921; *WSC,C*, Vol. 4, Pt 3, p. 1593.
100. *WSC,C*, Vol. 4, pp. 628–31.
101. Cohen, *Churchill and the Jews*, p. 119.
102. Meinertzhagen, diary entry for 16 November 1921; quoted in Cohen, *Churchill and the Jews*, p. 122.
103. Friesel, 'British Policy in Palestine', p. 199.
104. Cohen, *Churchill and the Jews*, p. 134.
105. Winston Churchill in a speech to the House of Commons, 4 July 1922; *Speeches*, Vol. 4, pp. 3342–52; Also see Cohen, *Churchill and the Jews*, p. 140.

Chapter 6 The Twenties and Thirties

1. See Winston Churchill, *World Crisis*, Vol. 5, p. 396.
2. Stuart Ball, *Winston Churchill* (London, 2003), p. 59.
3. Churchill, *World Crisis*, p. 395. Churchill uses this letter to illustrate his position against Lloyd George's pro-Greek policy and to show that he openly opposed it. However, in Gilbert's *WSC,C*, Vol. 4, Pt 2, p. 1369, the letter is labeled '*not sent*'. This might be one of Churchill's tricks as a historian to illustrate that he was on the 'right side' of history. For another example of this

See David Reynolds, In Command of History: Fighting and Writing the Second World War (London, 2004). Regardless, it does illustrate his views on the subject and echoes several previous sent letters to Lloyd George. Whether or not Churchill made his opinions known in this letter, however, is another matter.

4. Inbal Rose, *Conservatism and Foreign Policy during the Lloyd George Coalition 1918–1922* (London, 1992), p. 230.
5. Churchill, *World Crisis*, p. 392. Churchill's knowledge of Montagu's position comes from a letter Montagu sent to Churchill; see *WSC,C*, Vol. 4, Pt 2, p. 1315; Lord Beaverbrook, *The Decline and Fall of Lloyd George* (London, 1963), pp. 134–5.
6. Churchill, *World Crisis*, pp. 416–17.
7. See *Manchester Guardian*, 1 July 1922 and *The Times*, 27 September 1922.
8. Robert Lloyd George, *David and Winston: How a Friendship Changed History* (London, 2005), pp. 187–8.
9. Churchill to General Harington, 27 September 1922; *WSC,C*, Vol. 4, Pt 3, p. 2043.
10. PRO/CM, 19 September 1922, CAB/23/29, Kew.
11. Churchill in Cabinet Minutes, 7 September 1922; *WSC,C*, Vol. 4, Pt 3, p. 1980.
12. Churchill, quoted in Gilbert, *Churchill: A Life* (London, 1991), p. 452.
13. Churchill in Cabinet Minutes, 15 September 1922; *WSC,C*, Vol. 4, Pt 3, p. 1989.
14. Churchill and Lloyd George in a Press Communiqué, 16 September 1922; *WSC,C*, Vol. 4, Pt 3, pp. 1993–5.
15. *WSC*, Vol. 4, p. 829.
16. Fromkin, *The Peace to End All Peace*, p. 549.
17. Beaverbrook, *The Decline and Fall of Lloyd George*, p. 161.
18. Stephen Roskill, *Hankey: Man of Secrets* (London, 1972), pp. 288–9.
19. Churchill, *World Crisis*, p. 422.
20. Winston Churchill to Archibald Sinclair, 25 September 1922; *WSC,C*, Vol. 4, Pt 3, p. 2029.
21. Roskill, *Hankey*, p. 295.
22. Charles Hardinge to Curzon, 2 October 1922; Hardinge of Penhurst Papers, University Library Cambridge.
23. See David Roessel, 'Live Orientals and Dead Greeks: Forster's Response to the Chanak Crisis', *Twentieth Century Literature*, Vol. 36, No. 1 (Spring, 1990), p. 45.
24. Lord Birkenhead and Austen Chamberlian; Rose, *Conservatism and Foreign Policy*, p. 237.
25. Rose, *Conservatism and Foreign Policy*, p. 237.
26. David Walder, *The Chanak Affair* (London, 1969), pp. 190–1.
27. Ibid., p. 190.

28. Erik Goldstein, 'The British Official Mind and the Lausanne Conference 1922–23', *Diplomacy & Statecraft*, Vol. 14, No. 2 (2003), p. 192.
29. Rumbold to Curzon, 18 September 1922; FO/371/7886/E9444/27/44.
30. Rumbold to Curzon, 17 October 1922; FO/371/7306/E11502/27/44.
31. A.L. MacFie, 'British Intelligence and Turkish Nationalist Movement, 1919–1922', in *Middle Eastern Studies*, Vol. 37, No. 1 (January, 2001), p. 6; for more on intelligence regarding Atatürk and the Turkish national movement see Gotthard Jäschke, 'Mustafa Kemal und England in Neuer Sicht', *Die Welt des Islams*, Vol. 16, Issue 1 (1975), pp. 166–228.
32. MacFie, 'British Intelligence and Turkish Nationalist Movement, 1919-1922', p. 10.
33. Macmillan, *Peacemakers*, p. 381. See Lord Kincross, *Atatürk: Rebirth of a Nation* (London, 1960) and *Atatürk: A Biography of Mustapha Kemal the Father of Modern Turkey* (London, 1965).
34. Churchill, *RW*, second edition, p. 30.
35. Edmund Burke, 'Orientalism and World History: Representing Middle Eastern Nationalism and Islamism in the Twentieth Century,' *Theory and Society*, Vol. 27, No. 4 (August 1998), pp. 493–4.
36. Fromkin, *The Peace to End All Peace*, p. 551.
37. Churchill, *World Crisis*, p. 438.
38. Ibid., pp. 368, 410.
39. T.E. Lawrence (T.E. Shaw) to Churchill, 18 March 1929; *WSC,C*, Vol. 5, Pt 1, p. 1447.
40. Churchill, *World Crisis*, p. 438.
41. Winston Churchill at the Reform Club, Manchester, 17 November 1923; *Speeches*, Vol. 4, p. 3410.
42. Fromkin, *The Peace to End All Peace*, p. 551.
43. Ibid., p. 552.
44. *The Times*, 2 October 1922.
45. Michael Frinefrock, 'Atatürk, Lloyd George and the Megali Idea: Cause and Consequence of the Greek Plan to Seize Constantinople from the Allies, June–August 1922', *The Journal of Modern History*, Vol. 52, No. 1 (March 1980), p. 1048.
46. Keith Middlemas and John Barnes, *Baldwin: A Biography* (London, 1969), p. 113; Robert Blake, 'Baldwin and the Right', in John Raymond (ed.), *The Baldwin Age* (London, 1960), pp. 37–41.
47. Andrew Bonar Law quoted in Gilbert, *Churchill: A Life*, p. 453.
48. Stanley Baldwin in a speech at the Carlton Club, 19 October 1922; Ball, *Conservatives*, pp. 68–9.
49. See Keith Middlemas and John Barnes, *Baldwin*, pp 120–4; Beaverbrook, *The Decline and Fall of Lloyd George* pp. 189–91.
50. To his constituents, Churchill noted that Lord Curzon was 'one of the most obstinate champions of the Treaty of Sèvres' (which Churchill opposed) and argued that 'For the last year he has been in complete control of the Turko-

Greek policy, but apart engrossing the whole business to himself, studiously ignoring Fethi Bey [Atatürk's Minister of the Interior], and preventing any friendly agent being sent to Kemal [. . .] I am not aware of any steps of the slightest effectiveness which Lord Curzon took to remedy matters.' See Churchill to his constituents, November 1922; *WSC,C*, Vol. 4, Pt 3, pp. 2105–6.

51. Winston Churchill quoted in Douglas Hall, 'Churchill's Elections', in *Finest Hour* (No. 101), pp. 49–50.
52. This refers to the Churchill quotation, 'Anyone can rat, but it takes a certain amount of ingenuity to re-rat.'
53. For criticism of Stanley Baldwin's appointment of Churchill to the Exchequer see *WSC*, Vol. 5, p. 61.
54. Stuart Ball, 'Churchill and the Conservative Party', *Transactions of the Royal Historical Society*, Sixth Series, Vol. 11 (2001), p. 312.
55. *WSC*, Vol. 5, p. 62. For Lord Randolph Churchill's tenure at the Exchequer, see Robert Rhodes James, *Randolph Churchill* (London, 1994); Winston Churchill, *Randolph Churchill* (London, 1906).
56. Winston Churchill to the Duke of Devonshire, 7 May 1923; *WSC,C*, Vol. 5, Pt 1, p. 47.
57. Winston Churchill to Sir George Barstow, 2 December 1924; ibid., p. 285.
58. Winston Churchill to Sir George Barstow, 9 December 1924; ibid., p. 285, n. 2.
59. Winston Churchill in a Cabinet memorandum for 30 December 1924; ibid., p. 319.
60. Wilfrid Blunt to Winston Churchill, 5 September 1922; CHAR/2/124B/113.
61. Lord Curzon in Cabinet minutes for 21 April 1921; *WSC,C*, Vol. 4, Pt 3, p. 1444.
62. Winston Churchill in a Cabinet memorandum for 30 December 1924; *WSC, C*, Vol. 4, Pt 1, pp. 318–21.
63. See Winston Churchill to Sir Otto Niemeyer and Sir George Barstow, 23 January 1925; ibid., pp. 351–2.
64. Winston Churchill to Austen Chamberlain, 13 February 1925; ibid., pp. 392–3.
65. See Committee of Imperial Defence minutes, 25 February 1927, and Winston Churchill to Leo Amery, 30 April 1927, ibid., pp. 954–5, 995.
66. Thomas Jones, diary entry for 25 February 1929; Keith Middlemas (ed.), *Thomas Jones: Whitehall Diary*, Vol. 2 (London, 1969), pp. 171–2.
67. Baldwin to Lord Irwin, 25 February 1929; Philip Williamson and Edward Baldwin (eds), *Baldwin Papers: A Conservative Statesmen* (Cambridge, 2004), p. 214.
68. Lord Irwin to Stanley Baldwin, 28 March 1919; *WSC,C*, Vol. 5, Pt 1, p. 1452.
69. Winston Churchill: recollections; ibid., p. 1431.
70. Toye, *Churchill's Empire*, p. 169.

71. Leo Amery to Neville Chamberlain, 4 May 1929; Leo Amery Papers, AMEL 2/3/6 Churchill College, Cambridge.
72. James, *Speeches*, Vol. 4, p. 3523.
73. For more on Churchill and the British Empire see Toye, *Churchill's Empire*; Kirk Emmert, *Winston S Churchill on Empire*; Harry William Porter, *The Imperial Policy of Winston L.S. Churchill from 1900 to 1936 as set Forth by his Speeches* (unpublished thesis, 1946). More specifically on Empire in India see Arthur Herman, *Ganhdi and Churchill* (London, 2008); R. Hyam, *Britain's Declining Empire: The Road to Decolonisation, 1918–1968* (London, 2007); and R. Hyam, *Understanding the British Empire* (London, 2010).
74. James, *Speeches*, Vol. 4, pp. 3526–7.
75. Winston Churchill, *MEL*, p. 103. See James, *Churchill: A Study in Failure 1900–1939* (London, 1981), p. 258.
76. Blunt, *India Under Ripon*, p. 230.
77. Ibid., p. 230.
78. Churchill, *TNA*, p. 32.
79. Lord Randolph Churchill, 'The Primrose League', in *The Times*, 20 April 1885; For Winston Churchill see 'The Scaffolding of Rhetoric' (unpublished) in *WSC,C*, Vol. 1, Pt 2, pp. 816–21.
80. Toye, *Churchill's Empire*, p. 175.
81. Winston Churchill, 'The Palestine Crisis', in *The Sunday Times*, 22 September 1929; Michael Wolff (ed.), *The Collected Essays of Winston Churchill*, Vol. 2 (London, 1976), pp. 168–71.
82. For more on the imperial character of the British people see Peter Cain, 'Empire and the Languages of Character and Virtue in Later Victorian and Edwardian Britain', *Modern Intellectual History*, Vol. 4, No. 2 (August 2007), pp. 249–73.
83. Waris Ali to Winston Churchill, 3 December 1932; CHAR/2/189/126.
84. Winston Churchill to Waris Ali, 6 December 1932; CHAR/2/189/126.
85. Winston Churchill, 'Will the British Empire Last?' in *Answers*, 26 October 1929; Wolff, pp. 172–5.
86. Winston Churchill, 'India and Egypt', Speech at Minster Hall, 20 August 1930, in *Speeches*, Vol. 5. pp. 4912–14.
87. For a full account of Churchill's relationship with Gandhi see Arthur Herman, *Gandhi and Churchill*.
88. Winston Churchill, 'Our Duty in India', Speech at Albert Hall London, 18 March 1931, in *Speeches*, Vol. 5, p. 5007.
89. Winston Churchill, 'A Seditious Middle Temple Lawyer', Speech at Winchester House, 23 Febuary1931, in ibid., pp. 4982–6.
90. Toye, *Churchill's Empire*, p. 177.
91. Ibid., p. 177.
92. See, 'Indian Affairs in London', *Statesmen*, 20 March 1931; 'St George's For England', in *Times of India*, 21 March 1931.
93. Ibid., p. 174.

94. Winston Churchill's recollections; *WSC,C*, Vol. 5, Pt 1, p. 1432.
95. Arthur Herman, *Gandhi and Churchill*, pp. 310–11.
96. Toye, *Churchill's Empire*, p. 173.
97. Katherine Mayo, *Mother India* (London, 1927), pp. 411–12.
98. Mayo, *Mother India*, pp. 108, 168–9. Mayo often linked Christianity and Islam by noting the similarities such as monotheism as juxtaposed to the polytheist nature of Hinduism. See Mayo, p. 327.
99. Ibid., p. 325.
100. Ibid., p. 326.
101. Winston Churchill, 'Our Duty in India', Speech at Albert Hall London, 18 March 1931, in *Speeches*, Vol. 5, p. 5007.
102. Mayo, *Mother India*, p. 342.
103. Mayo, ibid., p. 341.
104. Mayo, *Mother India: Volume 2* (London, 1931); Mayo, *The Face of Mother India* (London, 1935).
105. Sir George Lloyd to Lord Irwin, 25 September 1927; *WSC,C*, Vol. 5, Pt 1 p. 1054.
106. Victor Cazalet diary entry for 10 August 1927; ibid., p. 1042.
107. Winston Churchill to Katharine Mayo, 5 March 1935; *WSC,C*, Vol. 5, Pt 2, p. 1111. It is also notable that Churchill made attempts to help Mayo find photographs for *The Face of Mother India* by writing on her behalf to other members of the Indian Empire Society. See CHAR/2/24A/76.
108. Toye, *Churchill's Empire*, p. 174.
109. Arnold Gyde to Harcourt Butler, 24 August 1931; Harcourt Butler Papers MS Eur.F116/86; Toye, *Churchill's Empire*, p. 179; For Churchill's book review see Michael Wolff (ed.), *The Collected Essays of Winston Churchill*, Vol. 2, pp. 228–32.
110. Winston Churchill to Louis Stuart, 26 October 1933; CHAR/194/61.
111. Winston Churchill, 'Our Duty in India' Speech at Albert Hall London, 18 March 1931, in *Speeches*, Vol. 5, pp. 5007–8.
112. See chapter 1.
113. Winston Churchill in his private notes, 'Note on the importance of fair-dealing with the Moslems of India in connection with the so-called minorities problems.' CHAR/2/189/ 140–142.
114. Toye, *Churchill's Empire*, p. 174.
115. Winston Churchill, 'India: Government Policy', in Kent, 10 June, 1931 in *Speeches*, Vol. 5, pp. 5044–8. Waris Ali wrote to Churchill explaining 'all Muslims and Law abiding people in India thank' Churchill for his speech on Cawnpore. Waris Ali to Winston Churchill, 2 June 1931; CHAR/2/180B/175.
116. Aga Khan, *The Memoirs of Aga Khan: The World Enough and Time* (London, 1954), pp. 89–90.
117. Lord Headley in a statement on 19 March 1931; *WSC,C*, Vol. 5, Pt 2, pp. 305–6.
118. Lord Headley to Winston Churchill, 22 March 1931; ibid., p. 309.

119. Ansari, *The Infidel Within*, p. 130.
120. Though several letters to the press were issued from the Indian Empire Society they were often penned by Mark Hunter, Micheal O'Dwyer, Louis Stuart, or Waris Ali. However, at least twice Churchill critiqued their letters before they went to press. See Winston Churchill to Mark Hunter, 30 June 1931, CHAR/2/180B/181, and Louis Stuart to Winston Churchill, 28 February 1934, CHAR/2/225/45.
121. Winston Churchill, *India: Speeches and Introduction* (London, 1933), p. 5. For Baldwin's criticisms see Parliamentary Debates, House of Commons, 5th Series, Vol. 249, 12 March 1931, pp. 1423–4.
122. Toye, *Churchill's Empire*, p. 172.
123. The Indian Empire Society to the editor of *The Times*, 7 January 1931, p. 8. Italics are mine. The letter was most probably penned by Waris Ameer Ali.
124. Waris Ali to Winston Churchill, 12 April 1931; The *Crescent*, 'The Cawnpore Debate', 12 April 1931; CHAR/2/180B/176.
125. Waris Ali to Winston Churchill, 22 April 1931, CHAR/2/180B/162. The article was 'The Muslim National Conference', in *The Muslim Outlook*, 22 April 1931.
126. Winston Churchill to Waris Ali, 3 June 1931, CHAR/2/180B/180.
127. Waris Ali to Winston Churchill, 24 July 1931, CHAR/2/180B/195; Winston Churchill to J.R. Remer, August 1931, CHAR/2/180B/211.
128. Moului Mahood ul Hasan Kermon asked Churchill to urge the *Morning Post* to publish his article regarding the Muslim's plight in India. Churchill tried but to no avail. See Moului Mahood ul Hasan Kermon to Winston Churchill, 16 June 1933, CHAR/2/193/143.
129. Shujaud din Khan to Winston Churchill, 8 June 1933, CHAR/2/193/137–41.
130. Nawabzeda Muhammad Azim to Winston Churchill, September 1934, CHAR/2/225/10.
131. Winston Churchill to Nawabzeda Muhammad Azim, 30 November 1934, CHAR/2/225/95.
132. Indian Empire Society to Winston Churchill, 8 February 1935, CHAR/2/593/52.
133. P.J. Grigg to Winston Churchill, 1 December 1934, CHAR/2/211/1–7.
134. Though the decision was Churchill's, he was advised by Waris Ali not to join the committee as 'most members will be from the Round Table Conference'. See Waris Ali to Winston Churchill, 3 December 1932, CHAR/2/189/126.
135. Winston Churchill, 'India (Constitutional Reform)' speech in the House of Commons, 29 March 1933, in *Speeches*, Vol. 5, p. 5256. Italics are the authors.
136. James, *Speeches*, Vol. 4, p. 3527.
137. Toye, *Churchill's Empire*, p. 183.
138. See 'Mr. Churchill's Views on India', in *The Times*, 28 October 1933.
139. 'Joint Committee on Indian Constitutional Reform', p. 1843; Toye, *Churchill's Empire*, p. 184.
140. James, *Speeches*, Vol. 4, p. 5627.

Chapter 7 Churchill, the Middle East, and India during World War II

1. Whether or not he was actually a mastermind of the 1929 violence is still debated. Al-Husayni maintained he was not, but an Arab nationalist rival of his, Izzat Darwaza, implicated al-Husayni saying he gave orders for the riots. See Henry Laurens, *La Question de Palestine: L'invention de la Terre sainte*, Vol. 2 (Paris, 1999), pp. 175–6.
2. 'British Policy on Palestine', 17 May 1939, in J.C. Hurewitz (ed.), *Diplomacy in the Near and Middle East: A Documentary Record 1914–1956*, Vol. 2 (New York, 1956), pp. 218–26.
3. Cohen, *Churchill and The Jews*, p. 192.
4. Winston Churchill in a speech at the House of Commons, 24 November 1938, in *Speeches*, Vol. 6, p. 6036.
5. See Gilbert, *Churchill and the Jews*.
6. Cohen explores the concept regarding Churchill's links with Zionism. See Cohen, *Churchill and The Jews.*
7. Churchill's personal minute 20 August 1941.
8. Gilbert, Churchill and the Jews, p.184; In 1950 Churchill told Eliahu Elath that 'he had been a Zionist all his life' See Cohen, *Churchill and the Jews* p. 371.
9. Ibid., pp. 153–4.
10. Ibid., p. 159.
11. Ibid., p. 186.
12. Ibid., p. 186.
13. Winston Churchill in War Cabinet minutes, 19 October 1939, in Martin Gilbert (ed.), *The Churchill War Papers*, Vol. 1 [Hereafter *WSC,WP*], p. 265.
14. War Cabinet minutes CAB/65/5.
15. Lord Halifax quoted in Cohen, *Churchill and The Jews*, p. 206. See War CAB/5/65.
16. Churchill to Lord Lloyd, 28 July 1940; Winston Churchill, *The Second World War*, Vol. 2 (London, 1951) [hereafter *WSC,WW2*], p. 153.
17. Winston Churchill in a speech at the House of Commons, 24 November 1938, in *Speeches*, Vol. 6, p. 6036.
18. Ibid., p. 6307.
19. H.T. Montague-Bell to Winston Churchill, 21 February 1941; CHAR/20/24/46–8.
20. Winston Churchill's notes, 28 February 1941; CHAR/20/24/53.
21. Winston Churchill in War Cabinet minutes, 25 December 1939; *WSC,WP*, Vol. 1, p. 748.
22. For instance, Cohen uses the phrase 'Churchill's utter contempt for the Arabs' repeatedly, see Cohen, *Churchill and the Jews.*

23. Gilbert, *Churchill and the Jews*, p. 180. Also see Telegram from Governor to Churchill, 9 January 1941, CHAR/20/32.
24. Lord Lloyd to Winston Churchill via James Malcolm. It is notable that Churchill wrote his reply in his own pen on Lord Lloyd's letter. The underline is in the original. See CHAR/20/32/22–4.
25. Winston Churchill in a speech at the House of Commons, 23 May 1939, in *Speeches*, Vol. 6, p. 6134. For Maxton's comment see HC Deb, 23 May 1939, Vol. 347, cols 2129–97.
26. Ibid., p. 6134.
27. Cohen, *Churchill and the Jews*, p. 202.
28. Winston Churchill in War Cabinet minutes, 2 December 1940; *WSC,WP*, Vol. 2, p. 1171.
29. For more on the Gold Square Coup see Robert Lyman, *Iraq 1941: The Battles for Basra, Habbaniya, Fallujah and Baghdad* (New York, 2006); and Mohammad Tarbush, *The Role of the Military in Politics: A Case Study of Iraq to 1941* (London, 1982).
30. *WSC,WW2*, Vol. 2, p. 204
31. See R. Melka, 'Nazi Germany and the Palestine Question', *Middle Eastern Studies*, Vol. 5, No. 3 (October 1969), p. 226. Also see Seth Arsenian, 'Wartime Propaganda in the Middle East', *The Middle East Journal*, Vol. 2 (October 1948), pp. 419–21. Also see Lukasz Hirszowicz, *The Third Reich and the Arab East* (Toronto, 1966).
32. See R. Melka, ibid., pp. 224–5.
33. Renate Dietrich, 'Germany's Relations with Iraq and Transjordan from the Weimar Republic to the End of the Second World War', *Middle Eastern Studies*, Vol. 41, No. 4, pp. 464–5.
34. *WSC,WW2*, Vol. 2, p. 214.
35. Francis Nicosia, *The Third Reich and the Palestine Question* (London, 1985), p. 67. Also see H.D. Schmidt, 'The Nazi Party in Palestine and the Levant 1932–1939', *International Affairs*, Vol. 28, No. 4 (October 1952).
36. Dietrich,'Germany's Relations with Iraq and Transjordan', p. 467.
37. Ibid., p. 468.
38. Ibid., p. 474.
39. See Reeva Simon, 'The Teaching of History in Iraq Before the Rashid Ali Coup of 1941', *Middle Eastern Studies*, Vol. 22, No. 1 (January 1986).
40. *WSC*, *WW2*, Vol. 4, p. 460.
41. Roderic Davison, 'Where is the Middle East?', in *Foreign Affairs*, Vol. 38, No. 4 (July 1960), p. 670.
42. *WSC*, *WW2*, Vol. 2, p. 546.
43. Ibid., p. 174.
44. Robin Denniston, *Churchill's Secret War* (London, 1997), p. x.
45. Denniston, *Churchill's Secret War*, p. xi.
46. Ibid., p. 38.
47. Ibid., p. 7.

48. Ibid., p. 7. Also see Harold Macmillan, *War Diaries: Politics and War in the Mediterranean* (London, 1957).
49. Herbert Feis, *Churchill, Roosevelt Stalin: The War They Waged and the Peace They Sought* (Princeton, 1967), pp. 265–7.
50. Metin Heper, *İsmet İnönü: The Making of a Turkish Statesman* (Leiden, 1998), p. 122.
51. Foreign Office registered files, 23 August 1940 and 28 March 1941; Llewellyn Woodward (ed.), *British Foreign Policy in the Second World War*, Vol. 1 (London, 1970), pp. 508–17; 546–51.
52. Foreign Office registered files, 22 November 1940; ibid., pp. 508–17.
53. Churchill to the War Cabinet, 25 January 1943; CHAR 20/127/43-5
54. Churchill to Ismet Inonu, 4 February 1934; CHAR 20/53A/69-71
55. Churchill to the War Cabinet, 31 January 1943; CHAR 20/127/49.
56. Winston Churchill at Cairo, 1 February 1943; Churchill in the House of Commons, 11 Febuary 1943, in *Speeches*, Vol. 6, pp. 6739, 6749.
57. Denniston, *Churchill's Secret War*, p. xi.
58. Winston Churchill at Cairo, 1 February 1943, in *Speeches*, Vol. 6, p. 6739.
59. Denniston, *Churchill's Secret War*, p. 2.
60. Winston Churchill, BBC broadcast, 12 Novemeber 1939; *WSC,WP*, Vol. 1, p. 361.
61. Churchill to Lord Lloyd, 28 July 1940; *WSC,WW2*, Vol. 2, p. 153.
62. See Cabinet Minutes 24 October 1940; CAB 65/9/38. I would like to thank my research assistant, Mr. B. Johnson, for bringing this to my attention.
63. See Lord Lloyd and Lord Halifax, "Proposal that His Majesty's Government Should Provide a Site for a Mosque in London', 18 October 1940 CAB 67/8/68; Colville's notes to Churchill 9 April 1940; PREM 4/32/4.
64. See CAB 67/8/68; Also See the Lloyd Papers GLLD 20/15.
65. J.A. Kensit to Winston Churchill 3 December 1940; PREM 4/32/4.
66. Hansard Oral Answers to Questions, Moslems (Mosque and Cultural Centre, London) HC Deb 09 July 1941 vol 373 cc167-8.
67. See Churchill's quote about the 'sting of the wasp' and 'the horn of the rhinoceros' in RW second edition, p. 30.
68. Winston Churchill to Charles De Gaulle, 6 June 1941, *WSC,WW2*, Vol. 3, p. 266.
69. Charles De Gaulle, *War Memoirs*, Vol. 1 (London, 1955), p. 194.
70. Winston Churchill's notes, 19 May 1941, PREM/3/422/1, *WSC,WP*, Vol. 3, p. 686.
71. See A.B. Gaunson, 'Churchill, de Gualle, Spears and the Levant Affair, 1941', *The Historical Journal*, Vol. 27, No. 3 (September 1984), pp. 702–3; and A.B. Gaunson, 'To End a Mandate: Sir E. L. Spears and the Anglo-French Collusion in the Levant, 1941–1945', unpublished dissertation, University of Hull, 1981. For a defence of de Gaulle's position see Martin Mickelsen, 'Another Fashoda: The Anglo-Free French Conflict over the Levant, May–September 1941', *Revue Francaise d'histoire d'Outre-Mer*, Vol. 63, 1976.

72. Winston Churchill's minutes of the War Cabinet meeting, 19 May 1941; *WSC,WP*, Vol. 3, p. 686.
73. De Gaulle to Churchill, 2 July 1941; F.O.,Spears papers I A; and General Wavell to Churchill, 2 July 1941; PREM/3/422/6.
74. Churchill quoted in A.B. Gaunson, 'Churchill, de Gualle, Spears and the Levant Affair, 1941', p. 709. See also Churchill's minutes, 3 July 1941, PREM/3/422/6.
75. Churchill to Lyttleton at Cairo, 22 July 1941; CHAR/20/36/114. Also see CHAR/20/41/79; FO/371/27302/E4044.
76. See Ibn Saud to Winston Churchill 14 November 1943, CHAR 20/124/76.
77. For the most thorough research on the Philby Plan see Yehoshua Porath, 'Weizmann, Churchill and the "Philby Plan" 1937-1943', *Studies in Zionism* Vol. 5, No. 2, pp. 239–72.
78. Cohen, *Churchill and the Jews*, pp. 227, 231.
79. Cohen, ibid., p. 229. Cohen is referring to the agreement between Weizmann and Emir Feisal that the Jews could return to Palestine, provided the Arabs obtained a kingdom at Damascus. However, once the French drove Feisal from Syria in 1920 the agreement was voided. For Weizmann's feeling of déjà-vous, see Weizmann's minutes from a meeting with the US State Department on 19 January 1943; Chaim Weizmann, *Weizmann Letters*, Vol. 21 (Jerusalem, 1979), p. 2, n. 2.
80. Harry Philby, *Arabian Jubilee* (London, 1952), pp. 211, 215.
81. Winston Churchill from notes of Dr Chaim Weizmann, 12 March 1941; *WSC, WP*, Vol. 3, p. 346.
82. Cohen, *Churchill and the Jews*, p. 230.
83. Porath, 'Weizmann, Churchill and the 'Philby Plan', p. 249.
84. See Weizmann to Sam Rosenman, 4 January 1944; Weizmann, *Weizmann Letters*, Vol. 21, p. 118; Porath, 'Weizmann, Churchill and the "Philby Plan"', p. 249; Cohen, *Churchill and the Jews*, pp. 360–1, n. 156.
85. Winston Churchill's minutes of the War Cabinet meeting, 19 May 1941; *WSC,WP*, Vol. 3, p. 686.
86. Sumner Welles to Policy Advisor Murray, 17 December 1942; United States Department of State, Foreign relations of the United States diplomatic papers, 1942. The Near East and Africa (1942) [FRUS], Vol. 4, pp. 553–5.
87. *WSC,WW2*, Vol. 6, pp. 326–7.
88. A US diplomat named William Eddy paraphrased much of the meeting in a letter to Edward Stettinius, 22 February 1945; FRUS 1945, Vol. 8, pp. 689–90.
89. Gilbert, *Churchill: A Life*, p. 825.
90. Trefor Evens (ed.), *The Killearn Diaries, 1934–1946* (London, 1972), p. 327.
91. William A. Eddy, *F.D.R Meets Ibn Saud* (Washington, 1954), p. 13.
92. Thomas Lippman, 'The Day FDR Met Saudi Arabia's Ibn Saud', in *The Link*, Vol. 38, No. 2 (May 2005), p. 10.
93. Amery to Churchill, 10 September 1941, PREM/4 52/5.
94. Cohen, *Churchill and the Jews*, pp. 232, 241.

95. See Wilfrid Blunt's Diary for 5 June 1921; MSS/467–1975. However, Blunt's opinions on the matter are relatively inconsistent and Churchill would have been most likely influenced by Blunt's earlier ideas. Originally, in *Future of Islam* Blunt argued that an Arab caliphate would 'bring about a full reconciliation of all parties'. This included the Shia, Sunni, and Wahabi sects of Islam. Blunt, *Islam*, pp. 129–31. Blunt only changed his mind in the twilight of his life.
96. Cohen, *Churchill and the Jews*, p. 233.
97. Churchill in War Cabinet minutes, 9 November 1941; PREM/4/52/5.
98. John Keay, *A History of India* (London, 2000), p. 497.
99. Winston Churchill in War Cabinet minutes, 2 February 1940; *WSC,WP*, Vol. 1, pp. 715–16.
100. Winston Churchill to Neville Chamberlain, 20 February 1940, ibid., p. 782.
101. Winston Churchill in War Cabinet minutes, 12 April 1940 in ibid., p. 1038.
102. *WSC,WW2*, Vol. 4, p. 177. Churchill acknowledged that dominion status for India would give all the power to the 'Congress caucus' which was 'far from [his wish]'.
103. Jock Colville, regarding Churchill's mood 12 April 1940; Colville Diary taken from ibid., p. 1038.
104. Note from an interview between Viceroy Linlithgow and M. Jinnah, New Dehli, 4 November 1939; Linlithgow papers MSS Eur. F25/8.
105. Sir Zafrulla Khan to Winston Churchill, 20 June 1940; CHAR/20/5. Interestingly, Khan never mentioned which versus in the Qur'an gave the Head of the Movement the vision.
106. Winston Churchill to Zafrulla Khan, 4 July 1940; CHAR/20/5/86.
107. *WSC,WW2*, Vol. 4, p. 176
108. See Paul Greenough, *Prosperity and Misery in Modern Bengal: The Famine of 1943–1944* (New York, 1982); Amartya Sen, *Poverty and Famines: An Essay on Entitlement and Deprivation* (Oxford, 1981); and Madhusree Mukerjee, *Churchill's Secret War: The British Empire and the Ravaging of India During World War 2* (New York, 2010). For percentages see Christopher Bayly and Tim Harper, *Forgotten Armies: Britain's Asian Empire & the War with Japan* (London, 2004), p. 284.
109. Sen *Poverty and Famines*, pp. 80–3.
110. See R.J. Moore, *Churchill, Cripps and India 1939-1945* (Oxford, 1979).
111. Toye, *Churchill's Empire*, p. 225.
112. Hermann Kulke and Diermar Rothermund, *A History of India* (London, 1992), p. 304.
113. *WSC,WW2*, Vol. 4, p. 179.
114. Ibid., p. 179. On this point Churchill was undoubtedly misinformed; by January 1941 the Indian army's total strength was about 418,000, 37% Muslim and 55% Hindu. See James Lawrence, *Raj: The Making and Unmaking of British India* (London, 1998), p. 542.

115. M. Jinnah to Winston Churchill, 4 March 1942; *WSC,WW2*, Vol. 4, p. 179. See also, CHAR/2/42B.
116. See ibid.
117. *WSC,WW2*, Vol. 4, p. 187.
118. Barnes and Nicholson, *Empire at Bay* (London, 1988), p. 832. This statement would have applied to the polytheist Hindus of India and not the monotheistic Muslims.
119. *WSC,WW2*, Vol. 4, p. 184.
120. Keay, *A History of India*, p. 497
121. Winston Churchill in a speech at the House of Commons, 10 September 1942 in *Speeches*, Vol. 6, p. 6676. See HC Deb, 10 September 1942, Vol. 383, cols 302-10.
122. Herman, *Gandhi and Churchill*, p. 562.
123. Madhusree Mukerjee, *Churchill's Secret War*, p. 244. It is notable that the book heavily favored the Muslim's and displayed a sort of hero worship for M.A. Jinnah. Nichols referred to him as 'the most important man in Asia' and said he was like 'a diplomat of the old school'. See Beverly Nichols, *Verdict on India* (London, 1944), pp. 184, 188–9.
124. Winston Churchill to Clementine Churchill, 1 February 1945; *WSC*, Vol. 7, p. 1166.
125. The term 'Baboos' referred to Hindi clerks who were literate in English. This term was often a racial slur against Hindus but not Muslims.
126. For a complete report of the conversation see R.A. Butler, *The Art of the Possible* (London, 1971), p. 111.

Chapter 8 The Postwar World

1. Toye, *Churchill's Empire*, p. 263.
2. Young, *Last Campaign*, p. 328.
3. Ibid., p. 328; See also J.M. Post and R.S. Robins, *When Illness Strikes the Leader* (New Haven, 1993), p. 122; and B. Park, *The Impact of Illness on World Leaders* (Philadelphia, 1986), pp. 296–303.
4. Winston Churchill to Clement Attlee, 1 May 1946; CHUR/2/4/10.
5. Winston Churchill's speech at the House of Commons, 16 May 1946 in *Speeches*, Vol. 7, p. 7326; see Alex Von Tunzelmann, *Indian Summer: The Secret History of the End of an Empire* (London, 2007), p. 79.
6. Ibid., pp. 7326–7.
7. See Dennis Judd, *The Lion and the Tiger: The Rise and Fall of the British Raj, 1600–1947* (New York, 2004), p. 280.
8. Tunzelmann, *Indian Summer*, p. 146. Also see the Jinnah–Churchill Correspondence CHUR/2/43A-B.
9. M.A. Jinnah to Churchill, 6 July, 1946; Jinnah's statement made 27 June 1946; CHUR/2/42B/258–64.

10. Winston Churchill in a speech at the House of Commons, 18 July 1946, in *Speeches*, Vol. 7, pp .7359–65, HC Deb, 18 July 1946, Vol. 425, cols 1394–448.
11. *WSC*, Vol. 8, p. 248.
12. Winston Churchill to M.A. Jinnah, 3 August 1946, CHUR/2/42B/252. Churchill was actually apt at promoting the 'Depressed Classes' as well. After the leader of the untouchables, Dr Ambedkar, visited Chartwell, he thanked Churchill for 'the sympathy you have envied for the cause of the Untouchables'. Ambedkar to Churchill, 13 November 1946, CHUR/2/52A/41. Also see Toye, p. 272.
13. See Suranjan Das, 'The 1992 Calcutta Riot in Historical Continuum: A Relapse into "Communal Fury"?', *Modern Asian Studies* Vol. 34, No. 2 (May 2000), pp. 281–306; Debjani Sengupta, *A City Feeding on Itself: Testimonies and Histories of 'Direct Action' Day* (London, 2006).
14. M.A. Jinnah to Churchill, 22 August 1946; CHUR/2/42B.
15. Walter Monckton to Winston Churchill, 18 May 1946; CHUR/2/42A/59.
16. Ahmad Said to Monckton, 5 August 1946, (forwarded) to Winston Churchill), CHUR/2/42A/150.
17. Much of their correspondence in the 1940s is kept in CHUR/2/43A–B and CHUR/2/44.
18. Waris Ali to Winston Churchill, 8 December 1946, CHUR/2/42B.
19. Liaquat Ali Khan to Churchill, 11 December 1946, CHUR/2/42B/377.
20. Winston Churchill's speech at the House of Commons, 12 December 1946, in *Speeches*, Vol. 7, p. 7418.
21. The Muslim League to Churchill, March 1947, CHUR/2/43B/151.
22. The Muslim League to Churchill, 18 June 1947, CHUR/2/43B/155.
23. Herman, *Gandhi and Churchill*, p. 567.
24. Ibid., p. 567.
25. Winston Churchill to Jinnah, 11 December 1946, CHUR/2/42B/32.
26. Herman, *Gandhi and Churchill*, p. 567. For experts from the correspondence see CHUR/2/42A-B and CHUR/2/43A-B.
27. Tunzelmann, *Indian Summer* p. 148
28. Winston Churchill's speech at the House of Commons, 12 December 1946, in *Speeches*, Vol. 7, p. 7420. See also *WSC*, Vol. 8 p. 293.
29. Tunzelmann, *Indian Summer*, pp. 163–4.
30. Ibid., p. 168.
31. Churchill to Attlee, 21 May 1946, CHUR/2/43A/107.
32. Churchill to Attlee, July 1947, CHUR/2/43B/128.
33. Julian Amery Diary, 20 July 1952; Julian Amery Papers 4/302.
34. Nicholas Mansergh, *Transfer of Power*, Vol. 10, p. 513.
35. Herman, *Gandhi and Churchill*, p. 568.
36. This last-minute addition for Jinnah was thought by General Ismay (Churchill's wartime adviser and Lord Mountbatten's Chief of Staff) as a bridge too far for Churchill. He was relieved, however, that Churchill was too reticent to the solution of Jinnah as Governor-General of Pakistan. Clearly, General

Ismay did not know of Churchill's relationship with Jinnah. See Alan Campbell-Johnson, diary, 8 July 1947; Alan Campbell-Johnson *Mission with Mountbatten* (London, 1951), p. 132; *WSC*, Vol. 8, p. 335.

37. See Stanley Wolpert, *Jinnah of Pakistan* (Oxford, 2005); Herman, *Gandhi and Churchill*, p. 568.
38. Winston Churchill in a speech at the House of Commons, 30 July 1948, in *Speeches*, Vol. 7, p. 7704.
39. Sir F.K. Noon to Mr Keeling, (forwarded to Churchill) 5 November 1947; CHUR/2/43B/217.
40. Sir F.K. Noon to Churchill, November 1947; CHUR/2/43B/234.
41. Churchill to Mr. Keeling, 24 November 1947; CHUR/2/43B/214.
42. Churchill to Lord Mountbatten, November 1947; CHUR/2/43B/215.
43. Cohen, *Churchill and the Jews*, p. 306.
44. A.J.P. Taylor, review of Bernard Wasserstein, *Britain and the Jews of Europe, 1934–1945* (Oxford, 1979), in *English Historical Review*, Vol. 45, No. 375 (April 1980), pp. 388–92.
45. Cohen, *Churchill and the Jews*, p. 307.
46. Ibid., p. 311.
47. Winston Churchill's speech at the House of Commons, 1 August 1946, in *Speeches*, Vol. 7, p. 7372.
48. Ibid., p. 7374.
49. Cohen, *Churchill and the Jews*, p. 314.
50. Ibid., p. 314.
51. Winston Churchill's speech at the House of Commons, 26 January 1949, in *Speeches*, Vol. 7, pp. 7778–9.
52. Cohen, *Churchill and the Jews*, p. 320.
53. Elath described the interview of 14 September 1950 to Felix Frankfurter. See Elath to Frankfurter, 24 September 1950; The Frankfurter papers, file 00092, C 52. Also See Cohen, *Churchill and the Jews*, p. 371.
54. Cohen, *Churchill and the Jews*, p. 321.
55. Winston Churchill's speech at the House of Commons, 30 December 1948, in *Speeches*, Vol. 7, p. 7767.
56. Intelligence Memorandum, Marcus Sieff, 13 September 1948; CHUR/2/46A/80.
57. Winston Churchill's speech at the House of Commons, 30 December 1948, in *Speeches*, Vol. 7, p. 7766.
58. Ibid., p. 7767.
59. Winston Churchill's speech at the House of Commons, 26 January 1949; *Speeches*, Vol. 7, pp. 7773–82.
60. Ibid., p. 7781.
61. D.K Fieldhouse, *Western Imperialism*, p. 229.
62. See *Avi Shlaim, Collusion Across The Jordan: King Abdullah, the Zionist Movement, and the Partition of Palestine* (Columbia, 1988); Eugene Rogan and Avi Shlaim (eds), *The War for Palestine: Rewriting the History of 1948* (Cambridge, 2001);

Benny Morris, *1948: The History of the First Arab-Israeli War* (New Haven, 2008).

63. Fieldhouse, *Western Imperialism*, p. 229.
64. Winston Churchill's speech at the House of Commons, 26 January 1949, in *Speeches*, Vol. 7, p. 7777.
65. Elath to Frankfurter, 24 September 1950; The Frankfurter papers, file 00092, C 52. Also See Cohen, *Churchill and the Jews*, p. 371.
66. Intelligence Memorandum on stability in the Middle East, 27 August 1951, CHUR/2/46B/201.
67. Winston Churchill's speech at the House of Commons, 23 July 1951, in *Speeches*, Vol. 8, p. 8229.
68. Churchill to Weizmann, quoted in Gilbert, *Churchill and the Jews*, p. 282.
69. Winston Churchill's speech in Washington D.C., 17 January 1952, in *Speeches*, Vol. 8, p. 8327.
70. Aga Khan, *The Memoirs of the Aga Khan*, p. 89.
71. Morris, *Israel's Border Wars*, pp. 258–9.
72. Gilbert, *Churchill and the Jews*, p. 286.
73. Ibid., p. 286
74. Walid Khalidi and Neil Caplan, 'The 1953 Qibya Raid Revisited: Excerpts from Moshe Sharett's Diaries', *Journal of Palestine Studies*, Vol. 31, No. 4 (Summer 2002), p. 90. See Elath to Eytan, 5 November 1953, *Documents on the Foreign Policy of Israel*, Vol. 8, p. 839.
75. Cabinet Minutes, 29 October 1953; CAB/128/26/62nd conclusions, p. 479, CAB/195/11.
76. War Cabinet Meeting, 17 November 1953, CAB/195/11.
77. War Cabinet minutes, 24 March 1954, CAB/128/27, p. 184.
78. War Cabinet minutes, 31 March 1954, CAB/128/27, p. 191.
79. Churchill to Ben-Gurion, 2 April 1954, PREM/11/941.
80. Efraim Karsh, *The Arab-Israeli Conflict: The Palestine War of 1948* (Oxford, 2002), p. 26.
81. Wm Roger Louis, 'Britian and the Overthrow of the Mossaddeq Government'; Mark Gasiorowski and Malcolm Byrne (eds), *Mohammad Mosaddeq and the 1953 Coup in Iran* (New York, 2004), p. 148. For more of Mossadegh's view of economic imperialism see Homa Katouzian, *The Political Economy of Modern Iran* (London, 1981).
82. J.H. Bamberg, *The History of the British Petroleum Company Vol. II: The Anglo-Iranian Years 1928–1954* (Cambridge, 1994), p. 513.
83. Wm Roger Louis, 'Mossaddeq Government', p. 159.
84. For more on the role that the Abadan Crisis played on the 1951 general election see Sue Onslow, 'Battlelines for Suez: The Conservatives and the Abadan crisis, 1950–1951'; *Contemporary British History*, Vol. 17, No. 2 (2003), pp. 1–28.
85. Winston Churchill quoted in Richard Gimblett, 'Sputter of Musketry? The British Military Response to the Anglo-Iranian Oil Dispute, 1951', *Contemporary British History*, Vol. 17, No. 1 (2003), p. 2.

86. Harold Macmillan in Peter Cantrell (ed.), *The MacMillan Diaries* (London, 2003), p. 83.
87. Winston Churchill in a speech at the House of Commons, 30 July 1951, in *Speeches*, Vol. 8, pp. 8232–42.
88. Winston Churchill in a speech at Loughton County High School, 6 October 1951, in ibid., p. 8252.
89. Winston Churchill in a speech at Woodford, 12 October 1951, in ibid., p. 8262; and Toye, *Churchill's Empire*, p. 281.
90. William Roger Louis, 'Churchill and Egypt 1946–1956', in Wm Roger Louis and Robert Blake (eds), *Churchill: A Major New Assessment* (London, 1993), p. 473.
91. G.W. Furlonge Departmental Memorandum, 29 October 1951, FO/371/91200,E1057/8. Also see Ritchie Ovendale, *Britain, The United States and the Transfer of Power in the Middle East 1945–1962* (London, 1996), p. 64.
92. Winston Churchill in a speech at House of Commons, 7 March 1951, in *Speeches*, Vol. 7, p. 7440.
93. Evelyn Shuckburgh, *Descent to the Suez: Foreign Office Diaries 1951–1956* (London, 1987), p. 29. Evelyn Shuckburgh was the son of Churchill's Middle Eastern adviser John Shuckburgh during Churchill's time at the Colonial Office.
94. Churchill to Eden, 30 January 1952, PREM/11/91.
95. Wm Roger Louis, 'Churchill and Egypt 1946–1956', pp. 474–5.
96. Ibid., p. 473. Louis echoes this idea, only illustrating how endemic it was in British official thinking saying, there was a 'recurrent theme that the Egyptians, like other Arabs, respected only force'. See Wm Roger Louis and Roger Owen, *Suez 1956: The Crisis and Its Consequences* (Oxford 1989), p. 47.
97. For examples of Churchill's paitings of Marrakesh and elsewhere in the Middle East see David Combs, *Sir Winston Churchill's Life Through his Paintings* (London, 2003) and Touria El Glaoui (ed), Meetings in Marrakech: The paintings of Hassan El Glaoui and Winston Churchill (Milano 2011). Churchill painted more than 20 artworks of Middle Eastern scenes, including at least seven that specifically focus on the bazaars and markets of Marrakesh.
98. Denis Kelly, 'Unpublished Memoirs', DEKE/2 Kelly papers, Churchill Archives, Cambridge.
99. Ibid., DEKE/2. For more on Churchill's many visits to Marrakesh see Celia Sandys, *Chasing Churchill: The Travels of Winston Churchill* (London, 2003).
100. Ibid., DEKE/2.
101. An interesting comment since Churchill refused to learn Hindi.
102. Ibid., DEKE/2.
103. Winston Churchill, minutes, 26 August 1952, PREM/11/392.
104. Wm Roger Louis, 'Churchill and Egypt 1946-1956', p. 476.
105. Winston Churchill at the Lord Mayor's Banquet, 10 November 1952, in *Speeches*, Vol. 8, p. 8431.
106. Wm Roger Louis, 'Churchill and Egypt 1946–1956', p. 478.

107. Winston Churchill, minutes, 19 August 1952, PREM/11/392.
108. Robin Hankey to Roger Allen, 24 September 1952, FO/371/102706.
109. Stevenson to Eden, 14 September 1954, FO/371/108317.
110. Howard J. Dooley, 'Great Britain's "Last Battle" in the Middle East: Notes on Cabinet planning during the Suez Crisis of 1956', *The International History Review*, Vol. 11, No. 3 (August 1989), p. 488.
111. Wm Roger Louis, 'The Anglo-Egyptian Settlement of 1954', in Wm Roger Louis and Roger Owen, *Suez 1956: The Crisis and Its Consequences*, p. 51.
112. Wm Roger Louis, 'The Anglo-Egyptian Settlement of 1954', p. 51.
113. David Goldsworthy, 'Keeping Changes within Bounds: Aspects of Colonial Policy during the Churchcill and Eden Governments, 1951–1957', *The Journal of Imperial and Commonwealth History*, Vol. 18, No. 1 (1990), p. 83.
114. Winston Churchill Cabinet Minutes, 11 February 1953, CAB/128/26.
115. Evelyn Shuckburgh, *Descent to Suez*, p. 75.
116. Winston Churchill in Cabinet Minutes, 30 January 1953, CAB/130/83.
117. Anthony Eden in Cabinet Minutes, 11 February 1953, CAB/128/26.
118. Winston Churchill in Cabinet Minutes, 11 February 1953, CAB/128/26.
119. Winston Churchill in Cabinet Minutes, 29 April 1953, CAB/131/13.
120. 21 April 1953, CAB/128/26.
121. Colville, *Fringes*, p. 653. Fakhreddin Azimi, 'Unseating Mossadegh: The Configuration and Role of Domestic Forces'; Gasiorowski and Byrne (eds), *Mohammad Mosaddeg*, p. 74.
122. The 'TP' in 'TPAjax' designated that the operation was to be covert.
123. Wm Roger Louis, 'Mossaddeq Government', p. 162.
124. Montague Woodhouse, *Something Ventured* (London, 1982), p. 125.
125. Colville, *Fringes*, p. 654.
126. Wm Roger Louis, 'Mossaddeq Government', p. 167.
127. Kermit Roosevelt, *Counter Coup: The Struggle for Control of Iran* (New York, 1979), p. 207.
128. Ibid., p. 207.
129. Ibid., p. 207.
130. See Peter G. Boyle, *Churchill-Eisenhower Correspondence, 1953–1955* (Chapel Hill, 1990).
131. Ibid., p. 24.
132. See Churchill to Eisenhower, 19 March 1953; and Eisenhower to Churchill, 7 April 1953; ibid., Boyle, pp. 32–3, 38–40.
133. Eisenhower to Churchill, 19 March 1953; *Churchill-Eisenhower*, pp. 33–4.
134. Robert Ferrel, *The Eisenhower Diaries* (New York, 1981), p. 223.
135. Wm Roger Louis, 'The Anglo-Egyptian Settlement of 1954', p. 40. Also see, Robin Hankey to the Foreign Office, 5 July 1953, PREM/11/485.
136. Norman Brooke to Churchill, 14 February 1953, PREM/11/486.
137. Winston Churchill at Prime Minister's meeting 3, 5 June 1953, CAB/133/135.

138. Ovendale, *Britain, The United States and the Transfer of Power in the Middle East 1945–1962*, p. 96.
139. Evelyn Shuckburgh, *Descent to Suez* p. 136.
140. Winston Churchill, Cabinet minutes, 22 June 1954, CAB/128/27.
141. Leo Amery diaries, 15 January 1954, quoted in Wm Roger Louis, 'Churchill and Egypt 1946–1955', p. 487.
142. Churchill in a Speech to the House of Commons, 29 July 1954, HC Deb, 29 July 1954, Vol. 531, cols 724–82.
143. Wm Roger Louis, 'Churchill and Egypt 1946–1955', p. 489.
144. Winston Churchill, 5 November 1956, in the *Manchester Guardian.*
145. Lord Moran, *Churchill: The Struggle for Survival* (London, 1966), pp. 709, 710.
146. Winston Churchill to Clementine Churchill, 11 August 1956, CHUR/1/55.
147. Winston Churchill in a Speech at Kensington Palace Hotel, 6 January 1958, quoted in *WSC*, Vol. 8, p. 1283.

Conclusion

1. See Chapter 8.
2. CHAR/20/32/22–4.

BIBLIOGRAPHY

Primary Sources

A. Unpublished Sources

I. The National Archives, Kew Gardens

Cabinet papers: CAB
Colonial Office papers: CO
Foreign Office papers: FO
Hansard: House of Common Debates
Prime Minister's papers: PREM
Royal Air Force papers: AIR
War Office papers: WAR

II. Personal papers

(Leo) Amery papers, Churchill College, Cambridge
(Julian) Amery papers, Churchill College, Cambridge
Asquith papers, Bodleian Library, Oxford
Balfour Papers, British Library, London
(W.S.) Blunt papers, Fitzwilliam Museum, Cambridge
The Broadwater Collection, Churchill College, Cambridge
(Austen) Chamberlain, Nottingham (microfilm)
(Neville) Chamberlain papers, Birmingham
(Lord Randolph) Churchill papers, Churchill College, Cambridge
(Winston) Churchill papers, Churchill College, Cambridge
Colville papers, Churchill College, Cambridge
Elgin papers, Broomhall, Fife
Felix Frankfurter papers, Library of Congress, Washington D.C.
Hardinge of Penhurst papers, University Library Cambridge

India Office papers: IO, British Library, London
Denis Kelly papers, Churchill College, Cambridge
(T.E.) Lawrence papers, Bodleian Library, Oxford
Linlithgow papers, British Library, London
Lugard papers, Bodleian Library, Oxford
Milner papers, Bodleian Library, Oxford
Trenchard papers, Churchill College, Cambridge
The Wentworth Bequest, British Library, London

B. Published Sources

Note: the place of publication is London, unless otherwise stated.

III. Major works by Winston Churchill

Churchill, Winston, *A History of the English-Speaking* Peoples, Vols I–IV (1956–8)
——— *Amid These Storms: Thoughts and Adventures* (New York, 1932)
——— *Great Contemporaries* (1937)
——— *Ian Hamilton's March* (1900)
——— *India-Speeches* (1931)
——— *London to Ladysmith Via Pretoria* (1900)
——— *Lord Randolph Churchill*, Vols I–II (1906)
——— *Marlborough: His Life and Times*, Vols I–IV (1933–8)
——— *My African Journey* (1908)
——— *My Early Life: A Roving Commission* (1930)
——— *Painting as a Pastime* (1948)
——— *Savrola: A Tale of Revolution in Laurania* (1899)
——— *The River War: An Account of the Reconquest of the Sudan*, Vols I–II (1899)
——— *World War II*, Vols I–VI (1948–53)
——— *The Story of the Malakand Field Force: An Episode of Frontier War* (1898)
——— *The World Crisis* Vols I–V (1923–31)

*IV. The official biography (*WSC and WSC,C*)*

Churchill, Randolph S. *Winston S Churchill Vol. I: Youth 1875–1900* (1966)
Churchill, Randolph S. (ed.), *Companion Vol. I, Parts 1 and 2* (1967)
——— *Winston S Churchill Volume II: Young Statesmen 1901–1914* (1967)
——— (ed.), *Companion Vol. II, Parts 1, 2, and 3* (1969)
Gilbert, Martin, *Winston S Churchill Vol. III: The Challenge of War 1914–1916* (1971)
Gilbert, Martin, (ed.) *Companion Vol. III, Parts 1 and 2* (1972)
——— *Winston S Churchill Vol. IV: The Stricken World 1916–1922* (1975)
——— (ed.), *Companion Vol. IV, Parts 1, 2, and 3* (1977)
——— *Winston S Churchill Vol. V: 1922–1939* (1976)
——— (ed.), *Companion Vol. V, Parts 1, 2, and 3* (1979)
——— *Winston S Churchill Vol. VI: Finest Hour 1939–1941* (1983)
——— (ed.), *Companion Vol. VI: The Churchill War Papers, Parts 1, 2, and 3* (1993, 1995, 2000)
——— *Winston S Churchill Vol. VII: The Road to Victory 1941–1945* (1986)
——— *Winston S Churchill Vol. VIII: Never Despair 1945–1965* (1988)

V. Major collections

Boyle, P. (ed.), *The Churchill–Eisenhower Correspondence, 1953–1955* (Chapel Hill, 1984)

James, Robert R. (ed.), *Winston S. Churchill: His Complete Speeches, 1897–1963, Vols 1–8* (1974)

Kimball, W. (ed.), *Churchill and Roosevelt, the Complete Correspondence Vols 1–3* (Princeton, 1984)

Sand, G. (ed.), *Defending the West: The Truman–Churchill Correspondence, 1945–1960* (Westport, 2004)

Soames, Mary (ed.), *Speaking For Themselves: The Private Letters of Sir Winston and Lady Churchill: The Personal Letters of Winston and Clementine Churchill* (1999)

Wolff, Michael (ed.), *The Collected Essays of Sir Winston Churchill Vols 1–4* (Sydney, 1976)

Woods, F. (ed.), *Young Winston's Wars: The Original Despatches of Winston S. Churchill, War Correspondent, 1897–1900* (1972)

VI. Diaries, memoirs, and monographs

Aga Khan III, *Memoirs of Aga Khan: World Enough and Time* (1954)

Asquith, Herbert, *Memories and Reflections: The Earl of Oxford and Asquith,* Vols I–II (1928)

Barnes, John and Nicholson, David (eds), *The Diaries of Leo Amery Vol. I 1896–1929* (1980)

———*The Empire At Bay: The Leo Amery Diaries Vol. II 1929–1945: The Empire At Bay* (1988)

Beaverbrook, Lord Maxwell, *Politicians and the War* (1928)

———*The Decline and Fall of Lloyd George* (1963)

Bell, Gertrude, *Syria: The Desert and the Sown* (1907)

——— *Gertrude Bell: From Her Personal Papers 1914–1926* (1961)

Berman, Richard, *The Mahdi of Allah* [introduction by Churchill] (London, 1931)

Bonham, Mark and Pottle, Mark (eds), *Lantern Slides: The Diaries and Letters of Violet Bonham Carter, 1904–1914* (Phoenix, 1997)

Bonham Carter, Violet, *Winston Churchill as I Knew Him* (1965)

Blunt, Wilfrid S., *The Future of Islam* (1882)

——— *Atrocities of Justice under the English Rule in Egypt* (1907)

——— *Secret History of the English Occupation of Egypt* (1907)

——— *India under Ripon; A Private Diary* (1909)

——— *Gordon at Khartoum* (1911)

——— *The Land War in Ireland* (1912)

——— *My Diaries,* Vols I–II (1919–21)

Brock, Michael and Eleanor (eds), *H.H., Asquith: Letters to Venetia Stanley* (Oxford, 1982)

Brown, Malcolm (ed.), *The Letters of T.E. Lawrence* (1988)

Buchan, John, *Greenmantle* (1916)

——— *Memory Hold the Door* (1940)

Butler, Sir Harcourt, *India Insistent* (1931)

Butler, R.A., *The Art of the Possible: The Memoirs of Lord Butler* (1979)

Callwell C.E. (ed.), *Field Marshal Sir Henry Wilson: His Life and Diaries* (1927)

Campbell-Johnson, Alan, *Mission with Mountbatten* (1951)

Cantrell, Peter (ed.), *The Macmillan Diaries* (2003)
Colville, Jock, The *Fringes of Power: Downing Street Diaries 1939–1955* (1985)
Curzon, Nathaniel G., *Russia in Central Asia in 1889 and the Anglo-Russian Question* (1889)
——— *Persia and the Persian Question* (1892)
——— *Tales of Travel* (1923)
de Gaulle, Charles, *War Memoirs: Call to Honour, 1940–1942*, Vols I–II (1955)
——— *War Memoirs: Unity, 1942–1944*, Vols I–II (1959)
——— *War Memoirs: Salvation, 1944–1946*, Vols I–II (1960)
Djemal Pasha, Ahmed, *Memories of a Turkish Statesmen: 1913–1919* (New York, 1923)
Doughty, Charles, *Travels in Arabia* (1888)
Ferrel, Robert, *The Eisenhower Diaries* (New York, 1981)
Fincastle, V.C., *A Frontier Campaign: A Narrative of the Operations of the Malakand and Buner Field Forces, 1897–1898* (1898)
Freundlich, Yehoshua (ed.), *Documents on the Foreign Policy of Israel*, Vols VII–VIII (Jerusalem, 1953)
Garnett, David (ed.), *The Letters of T.E. Lawrence* (1938)
Graves, Richard, *Lawrence of Arabia and His World* (1922)
Grey of Falloden, Viscount, *Twenty-Five Years, 1892–1916* (1925)
Haldane, J. Aylmer, *How We Escaped from Pretoria* (Edinburgh, 1900)
——— *A Brigade of the Old Army, 1914, Relating to Operations of 10 Infantry Bde, France, Aug–Nov, 1914* (1920)
——— *The Insurrection in Mesopotamia* (1922)
——— *A Soldier's Story: The Autobiography of General Sir Aylmer Haldane* (Edinburgh, 1948)
Hamilton, Ian, *Gallipolli Diary*, Vols I–II (1920)
Hurewitz, J.C., *Diplomacy in the Near and Middle East: A Documentary Record: 1914–1956*, Vols I–II (Princeton, 1956)
al-Hussein, Abdullah bin (trans. Graves, Philip), *Memoirs of King Abdullah of Transjordan* (1950)
——— (trans. Graves, Philip), *My Memoirs Completed* (1954)
Kipling, Rudyard, *Kim* (1901)
Lawrence, A.W., *Oriental Assembly* (1938)
Lawrence, T.E., *Seven Pillars of Wisdom* (1926)
——— *T.E. Lawrence to His Biographers: Robert Graves and Liddel Hart*, Vols I–II (New York, 1938)
——— *The Home Letters of T.E. Lawrence and His Brothers* (Oxford, 1954)
Lloyd George, David, *Memoirs of the Peace Conference*, Vols I–II (New Haven, 1939)
Lyttleton, Oliver (ed.), *The Memoirs of Lord Chandos* (1962)
Macmillian, Harold, *War Diaries: Politics and War in the Mediterranean* (1975)
——— *Autobiography*, Vols I–VI (1966–73)
Mansergh, Nicholas, *Constitutional Relations between Britain and India: The Transfer of Power, 1942–7*, Vols I–XII (1967–82)
Mayo, Katherine, *Mother India* (1927)
——— *Mother India*, Vol. 2 (1931)
——— *The Face of Mother India* (1935)
Meinertzhagen, Richard, *Middle East Diary, 1917–1956* (1959)

——— *Army Diary 1899–1926* (Edinburgh, 1960)
Middlemas, Keith (ed.), *Thomas Jones: Whitehall Diary*, Vol. 2 (1969)
Moran, Lord, *Winston Churchill: The Struggle for Survival* (1966)
Nichols, Beverly, *Verdict on India* (1944)
Nicolson, Nigel (ed.), *Harold Nicolson: Diaries and Letters 1930–1939* (1966)
——— *Harold Nicolson: Diaries and Letters 1939–1945* (1970)
——— *Harold Nicolson: Diaries and Letters 1945–1962* (1971)
Noel, E.W.C., *Diary of Major Noel on Special Duty in Kurdistan* (Baghdad, 1920)
Philby, H. St John, *The Heart of Arabia: A Record of Travel & Exploration* (1922)
——— *Arabia of the Wahhabis* (1928)
——— *Arabia* (1930)
——— *The Empty Quarter: Being a Description of the Great South Desert of Arabia known as Rub 'al Khali* (1933)
——— *Harun al Rashid* (1933)
——— *Sheba's Daughters: Being a Record of Travel in Southern Arabia* (1939)
——— *A Pilgrim in Arabia* (1943)
——— *Arabian Jubilee* (1954)
Pottle, Mark (ed.), *Champion Redoubtable: Diaries and Letters of Violet Bonham Carter,1914–1945* (1998)
Riddell, Lord George, *Lord Riddell Intimate Diary of the Peace Conference and After 1918–23* (1933)
——— *More Pages from My Diary, 1908–1914* (1934)
Sanders, Otto Limon von, *Five Years in Turkey* (Annapolis, 1927)
Shuckburgh, Evelyn, *Descent to the Suez: Foreign Office Diaries 1951–1956* (1987)
Storrs, Sir Ronald, *The Memoirs of Sir Ronald Storrs* (New York, 1937)
Sykes, Sir Mark, *The Caliphs' Last Heritage: A Short History of the Turkish Empire* (1915)
Thompson, Walter H., *I was Churchill's Shadow* (1951)
——— *Sixty Minutes With Winston Churchill* (1953)
——— *Beside The Bulldog: The Intimate Memoirs of Churchill's Bodyguard* (2003)
Wasserstein, Bernard (ed.), *Letters of Chaim Weizmann*, Vols X and XI (New York, 1977)
Weizmann, Chaim, *Trial and Error: The Autobiography of Chaim Weizmann* (New York, 1949)
Williamson, Philip and Baldwin, Edward (eds), *Baldwin Papers: A Conservative Statesman* (Cambridge, 2004)
Wilson, Arnold, *Mesopotamia, 1917–1920: A Clash of Loyalties* (1931)

Secondary Sources

Note: the place of publication is London, unless otherwise stated.

VII. Selected collections, memoirs, and monographs

Addison, Paul, *Churchill on the Home Front, 1900–1955* (1992)
Adelson, Roger, *London and the Invention of the Middle East: Money, Power, and War 1902–1922* (1995)
Ansari, Humayun, *The Infidel Within: Muslims in Britain Since 1800* (2003)

Antonius, George, *The Arab Awakening* (1938)
Asher, Michael *Khartoum: The Ultimate Imperial Adventure* (2005)
Aydemir, Sevket Sureyya, *Enver Pasha*, Vols I–III (Istanbul, 1971)
Ball, Stuart, *The Conservative Party and British Politics 1902–1951* (1995)
——— *Winston Churchill* (2003)
——— *Parliament and Politics in the Age of Churchill and Attlee: The Headlam Diaries 1935–1951*(2004)
——— (ed., with Anthony Seldon), *Recovering Power: The Conservatives in Opposition Since 1867* (London 2005)
Bayly, C. and Harper, Tim, *Forgotten Armies: Britain's Asian Empire & the War with Japan* (2004)
Bennett, G.H., *British Foreign Policy During The Curzon Period 1919–24* (1995)
Berrman, Richard, *The Mahdi of Allah* (1931)
Bowyer, Chaz, *RAF Operations: 1918–1938* (1988)
Boyle, Andrew, *Trenchard: Man of Vision* (1962)
Bullard, R., *The Camels Must Go* (1961)
Cannadine, David, *Ornamentalism: How the British Saw Their Empire* (Oxford, 2002)
Capstick, P.H., *Warrior: The Legend of Colonel Richard Meinertzhagen* (1998)
Catherwood, Christopher, *Churchill's Folly: How Winston Churchill Created Modern Iraq* (2004)
——— *A Brief History of the Middle East* (2006)
Charmley, John, *Churchill: The End of Glory – A Political Biography* (1994)
Cohen, Michael, *Churchill and the Jews, 1900–1948* (1985)
Colville, Jock, *Action This Day – Working with Churchill* (1968)
——— *The Churchillians* (1981)
Cowles, Virginia, *Winston Churchill: The Era The Man* (1963)
Delong-Bas, N., *Wahhabi Islam: From Revival and Reform to Global Jihad* (Oxford, 2004)
Denniston, Robin, *Churchill's Secret War: Diplomatic Decrypts, the Foreign Office and Turkey 1942–44* (1997)
Ekinci, Mehmet Uğur, *The Unwanted War: The Diplomatic Background of the Ottoman-Greek War of 1897* (Ankara, 2006)
Elbogen, Ismar (trans. Moses Hades), *A Century of Jewish Life* (Philadelphia, 1960)
Emmert, Kirk, *Winston Churchill on Empire* (1980)
Feis, Herbert, *Churchill, Roosevelt Stalin: The War They Wwaged and the Peace They Sought* (Princeton, 1967)
Ferguson, Niall, *The War of the World* (2007)
Fieldhouse, D.K., *Western Imperialism in the Middle East* (Oxford, 2005)
Fisher, John, *Curzon and British Imperialism in the Middle East 1916–19* (1999)
Fishman, Jack, *My Darling Clementine: The Story of Lady Churchill*, (1963)
Fisk, Robert, *The Great War For Civilisation: The Conquest of the Middle East* (2005)
Foster, R.F., *Lord Randolph Churchill: A Political Life* (Oxford, 1981)
Fromkin, David, *A Peace to End All Peace: The Fall of the Ottoman Empire and the Creation of the Modern Middle East* (New York, 1989)
Garfield, Brian, *The Meinertzhagen Mystery* (Washington, 2007)
Germains, Victor W., *The Tragedy of Winston Churchill* (1931)
Gilbert, Martin, *The Jews of Arab Lands: Their History in Maps* (1976)
——— *Churchill's Political Philosophy* (1981)

——— *Winston Churchill: The Wilderness Years* (1981)
——— *World War II* (1989)
——— *In Search of Churchill* (1994)
——— *History of the Twentieth Century* (2001)
——— *Churchill and America* (2005)
——— *Churchill and the Jews* (2007)
Green, Dominic, *Three Empires on the Nile: The Victorian Jihad, 1869–1899* (2007)
Greenough, Paul, *Prosperity and Misery in Modern Bengal: The Famine of 1943–1944* (New York, 1982)
Harmon, Christopher and Tucker, David (eds), *Statecraft and Power: Essays in Honour of Harold W. Rood* (1994)
Heller, Joesph, *British Policy towards the Ottoman Empire 1908–1914* (1983)
Herman, Arthur, *Gandhi and Churchill: The Epic Rivalry that Destroyed an Empire and Forged Our Age* (2008)
Higgins, Trumbull, *Winston Churchill and the Dardanelles* (1963)
Hirszowicz, Lukasz, *The Third Reich and the Arab East* (Toronto, 1966)
Holden, David and Johns, Richard, *The House of Saud* (1982)
Holt, P.M., *The Mahdist State in the Sudan 1881–1898: A Study of its Origins Development and Overthrow* (1970)
Hopkirk, Peter, *Setting the East Ablaze: Lenin's Dream of an Empire in Asia* (1984)
——— *The Great Game: The Struggle for Empire in Central Asia* (1990)
——— *On Secret Service East of Constantinople: The Great Game and the Great War* (1994)
——— *Quest for Kim: In Search of Kipling's Great Game* (1996)
Hough, Richard, *The Great War at Sea: 1914–18* (Oxford, 1983)
Hourani, Albert, *A History of the Arab Peoples* (1991)
Hyam, Ronald, *Elgin and Churchill at the Colonial Office 1905–1908: The Watershed of the Empire–Commonwealth* (1968)
——— *Empire and Sexuality: The British Experience* (1991)
——— *Britain's Imperial Century, 1815–1914: A Study of Empire and Expansion* (2002)
——— *Britain's Declining Empire: The Road to Decolonisation, 1918–1968* (2006)
Irons, Roy, Churchill and the Mad Mullah of Somaliland: Betrayal and Redemption 1899–1921 (2013)
James, Lawrence, *Churchill and Empire: Portrait of an Imperialist* (2013)
James, Robert Rhodes, *Lord Randolph Churchill* (1959)
——— *Gallipoli* (1965)
——— A.J.P. Taylor (eds), *Churchill: Four Faces and the Man* (1969)
——— *Churchill: A Study in Failure, 1900–1939* (1981)
——— *Anthony Eden* (1986)
Jenkins, Roy, *Churchill: A Biography* (New York, 2001)
Judd, Denis, *India: A History* (2000)
——— *The Lion and the Tiger: The Rise and Fall of the British Raj, 1600–1947* (2004)
Kaplan, Robert, *Warrior Politics: Why Leadership Demands a Pagan Ethos* (New York, 2001)
Karsh, Efraim, *Empires of the Sand: The Struggle for Mastery in the Middle East, 1789–1923* (1999)

——— *The Arab–Israeli Conflict. The Palestine 1948 War* (Oxford, 2002)
Keay, John, *Sowing the Wind: The Mismanagement of the Middle East 1900–1960* (1988)
Keddie, Nikki R., *An Islamic Response to Imperialism* (Berkley, 1966)
——— *Sayyid Jamal al-Din 'al-Afghani': A Political Biography* (Berkley, 1972)
Kedourie, Elie, *England and the Middle East: The Destruction of the Ottoman Empire 1914–1921* (1960)
——— *Afghani and 'Abduh: An Essay on Religious Unbelief and Political Activism in Modern Islam* (1966)
——— *The Chatham House Version: And Other Middle Eastern Studies* (1970)
——— *In the Anglo-Arab Labyrinth: The McMahon–Husayn Correspondence and its Interpretations 1914–1939* (1979)
——— (ed., with Sylvia Haim), *Zionism and Arabism in Palestine and Israel* (1982)
——— *Politics in the Middle East* (1992)
Kennedy, Paul, *The Rise and Fall of British Naval Mastery* (London, 1976)
——— *The Rise of the Anglo-German Antagonism 1860–1914* (1980)
——— *The Rise and Fall of the Great Powers: Economic Change and Military Conflict from 1500 to 2000* (1987)
Kincross, Lord, *Atatürk: Rebirth of a Nation* (1960)
Klieman, Aaron, *Atatürk: A Biography of Mustafa Kemal, Father of Modern Turkey* (1965)
——— *Foundations of British Policy in the Arab World: The Cairo Conference of 1921* (1970)
——— *Ottoman Centuries: The Rise and Fall of the Turkish Empire* (1977)
Kramer, Martin, *Arab Awakening and Islamic Revival: The Politics of Ideas in the Middle East* (New Brunswick, 1996)
Kraus, Rene, *Winston Churchill* (1941)
Kulke H. and Rothermund, D., *A History of India* (1992)
Laurens, Henry, *La Question de Palestine: L'invention de la Terre Sainte*, Vol. 2 (Paris, 1999)
Lawrence, James, *Raj: The Making and Unmaking of British India* (1998)
Lewis, Bernard, *The Political Language of Islam* (Chicago 1991)
——— *Islam and the West* (1993)
——— *The Future of the Middle East* (1997)
——— *The Crisis of Islam: Holy War and Unholy Terror* (2003)
——— *From Babel to Dragomans: Interpreting the Middle East* (2004)
Lewis, David L., *The Race To Fashoda* (Washington, 1986)
Lewis, I.M., *The Modern History of Somaliland* (1965)
Lloyd George, Robert, *David and Winston: How a Friendship Changed History* (2005)
Lockman, N.J., *Meinertzhagen's Diary Ruse* (Washington, 1995)
Longford, Elizabeth, *A Pilgrimage of Passion: The Life of Wilfrid Scawen Blunt* (1979)
Louis, Wm Roger, *British Empire in the Middle East, 1945–1951* (1984)
——— (ed., with James Bill), *Musaddiq, Iranian Nationalism, and Oil* (1988)
——— (ed., with Roger Owen), *Suez 1956: The Crisis and Its Consequences* (1989)
——— (ed., with Robert Blake), *Churchill: A Major New Assessment* (1993)
——— *Ends of British Imperialism: The Scramble for Empire, Suez and Decolonization: Collected Essays* (2006)
Lyman, Robert, *Iraq 1941: The Battles for Basra, Habbaniya, Fallujah and Baghdad* (New York, 2006)

Macfie, A.L. (ed.), *Orientalism: A Reader* (2000)
Macmillan, Margaret, *Peacemakers: Six Months that Changed the World* (2002)
Manchester, William, *The Last Lion: Winston Spencer Churchill: Visions of Glory 1874–1932* (New York, 1983)
——— *The Last Lion: Winston Spencer Churchill: Alone 1932–1940* (New York, 1988)
Marder, Arthur, *From Dreadnought to Scapa Flow*, Vols I–IV (1965)
Martin, Hugh, *Battle: The Life Story of the Rt. Hon. Winston Churchill* (1932)
de Mendelssohn, Peter, *The Age of Churchill: Heritage and Adventure, 1874–1911* (1961)
Meyer, Karl and Brysac, Shareen, *King Makers: The Invention of the Modern Middle East* (2008)
Middlemas, Keith and Barnes, John, *Baldwin: A Biography* (1969)
Moore, R.J., *Churchill, Cripps and India 1939–1945* (Oxford, 1979)
Morris, Benny, *Israel's Border Wars, 1949–1956: Arab Infiltration, Israeli Retaliation and the Countdown to the Suez War* (Oxford, 1993)
——— *1948: The History of the First Arab-Israeli War* (New Haven, 2008)
Mukerjee, Madhusree, *Churchill's Secret War: The British Empire and the Ravaging of India during World War II* (2011)
Muller, James (ed.), *Churchill as a Peacemaker* (New York, 1997)
Nicosia, Francis, *The Third Reich and the Palestine Question* (1985)
Omissi, David E., *Air Power and Colonial Control: The Royal Air Force 1919–1939* (1990)
Ovendale, Ritchie, *Britain, The United States and the Transfer of Power in the Middle East 1945–1962* (1996)
——— *Origins of the Arab-Israeli Wars* (2004)
Paris, Timothy, *The Hashemites, and Arab Rule, 1920–1925: The Sherifian Solution* (2003)
Perham, Margery, *Lugard, Volume 1: The Years of Adventure 1858–1898* (1956)
——— *Lugard, Volume 2: The Years of Authority 1898–1945* (1960)
Raymond, John (ed.), *The Baldwin Age* (1960)
Reid, Walter, *Empire of Sand: How Britain Made the Middle East* (2011)
Reinharz, J., *Chaim Weizmann: The Making of a Statesman* (New York, 1968)
Reynolds, David, *In Command of History: Churchill Fighting and Writing World War II* (2004)
——— *From World War to Cold War: Churchill, Roosevelt and the International History of the 1940s* (2006)
Roberts, Bechhofer, *Winston Churchill* (1940)
Rose, Inbal, *Conservatism and Foreign Policy during the Lloyd George Coalition 1918–1922* (1922)
Rose, Jonathan, The Literary Churchill: *Author, Reader, Actor* (2014)
Rose, Norman, *Churchill: An Unruly Life* (1994)
Roskill, Stephen, *Hankey: Man of Secrets* (1972)
Russell, Douglas, *Winston Churchill – Soldier: The Military Life of a Gentleman at War* (2005)
Said, Edward W., *Orientalism: Western Conceptions of the Orient* (1978)
——— *Culture and Imperialism* (1993)
Satia, Priya, *Spies in Arabia: The Great War and the Cultural Foundations of Britain's Covert Empire in the Middle East* (Oxford, 2008)

Scott, A. MacCallum, *Winston Churchill in Peace and War* (1916)
Sen, Amartya, *Poverty and Famines: An Essay on Entitlement and Deprivation* (Oxford, 1981)
Sengupta, Debjani, *A City Feeding on Itself: Testimonies and Histories of 'Direct Action' Day* (2006)
Sheldon, Michael, *Young Titan: The Making of Winston Churchill* (2013)
Shlaim, Avi, *Collusion Across The Jordan: King Abdullah, the Zionist Movement, and the Partition of Palestine* (Columbia, 1988)
——— *War and Peace in the Middle East: A Concise History* (New York, 1995)
——— (ed., with Eugene Rogan), *The War for Palestine: Rewriting the History of 1948* (Cambridge, 2001)
Sluglett, Peter, *Britain in Iraq: Contriving King and Country* (2007)
Smith, Malcolm, *British Air Strategy Between the Wars* (Oxford, 1984)
Tarbush, Mohammad, *The Role of the Military in Politics: A Case Study of Iraq to 1941* (1982)
Tauber, Eliezer, *The Formation of Modern Iraq and Syria* (1994)
Teller, Mathew, *Rough Guide to Jordan* (2002)
Tidrick, Kathryn, *Heart Beguiling Araby: The English Romance with Arabia* (1981)
Toye Richard, *Lloyd George and Churchill: Rivals for Greatness* (2007)
——— *Churchill's Empire: The World that Made Him and the World He Made* (2010)
——— *The Roar of the Lion: The Untold Story of Churchill's World War II Speeches* (2013)
Tunzelmann, Alex von, *Indian Summer: The Secret History of the End of an Empire* (2007)
Vat, Dan van der, *The Ship that Changed the World: The Escape of the Goeban to the Dardanelles in 1914* (1985)
Walder, David, *The Chanak Affair* (1969)
Walker, Jenny, *Lonely Planet Guide to Jordan* (2009)
Wallach, Janet, *The Desert Queen: The Extraordinary Life of Gertrude Bell* (1996)
Wasserstein Bernard, *The British in Palestine: The Mandatory Government and the Arab Jewish Conflict, 1917–1929* (1978)
Weidhorn, Manfred, *Sword and Pen: A Survey of the Writing of Winston Churchill* (Albuquerque, 1974)
Wilson, Jeremy, *Lawrence of Arabia: The Authorized Biography of T.E. Lawrence* (1989)
Wilson, Mary, *King Abdullah, Britain and the Making of Jordan* (1987)
Wolpert, Stanley, *Jinnah of Pakistan* (Oxford, 2005)
Wrigley, Chris (ed.), *Warfare, Diplomacy and Politics: Essay's in Honour of AJP Taylor* (1986)
——— *A.J.P. Taylor: Radical Historian of Europe* (2006)
——— *Churchill* (2006)
Young, John, *Winston Churchill's Last Campaign: Britain and the Cold War 1951–1955* (1996)

VIII. Selected articles

Arsenian, Seth, 'Wartime Propaganda in the Middle East', *The Middle East Journal*, Vol. 2 (October 1948)
Baha, Lal, 'The North West Frontier in World War I', *Asian Affairs*, Vol. 1, Pt 1 (1970)
Ball, Stuart, 'Churchill and the Conservative Party', *Transactions of the Royal Historical Society*, Sixth Series, Vol. 11 (2001)

Becker, C.H., 'Panislamiusmus', *Vom Werden und Wesen der islamischen Welt: Islamstudien*, Vol. II (1932)

Blake, Robert, 'Baldwin and the Right', in John Raymond (ed.), *The Baldwin Age* (1960)

Burke, Edmund, 'Orientalism and World History: Representing Middle Eastern Nationalism and Islamism in the Twentieth Century', *Theory and Society*, Vol. 27, No. 4 (August 1998)

Callahan, Raymond, 'What About the Dardanelles?', *The American Historical Review*, Vol. 78, No. 3 (June 1973)

Das, Suranjan, 'The 1992 Calcutta Riot in Historical Continuum: A Relapse into "Communal Fury"?' *Modern Asian Studies*, Vol. 34, No. 2 (May 2000)

Dean, Lt Col. David J., 'Air Control in Small Wars', *Air University Review* (July–August 1983)

Dietrich, Renate, 'Germany's Relations with Iraq and Transjordan from the Weimar Republic to the End of World War II', *Middle Eastern Studies*, Vol. 41, No. 4, (2005)

Dooley, Howard J., 'Great Britain's "Last Battle," the Middle East: Notes on Cabinet planning during the Suez Crisis of 1956', *The International History Review*, Vol. 11, No. 3 (August 1989)

Douglas, R.M., 'Did Britain Use Chemical Weapons in Mandatory Iraq?', *The Journal of Modern History*, No. 81 (December 2009)

Edwards, David, 'Mad Mullahs and Englishmen: Discourse in the Colonial Encounter', *Comparative Studies in Society and History*, Vol. 31, No. 4 (October 1989), p. 653.

French, David, 'The Origins of the Dardanelles Campaign Reconsidered', *History*, Vol. 68, Issue 223 (June 1983)

——— 'The Dardanelles, Mecca and Kut: Prestige as a Factor in British Eastern Strategy, 1914–1916', *War and Society*, Vol. 5, No. 1 (May 1987)

Friedman, Isaiah, 'The McMahon–Hussein Correspondence and the Question of Palestine', *Journal of Contemporary History*, Vol. 5, No. 2 (1970)

Friesel, Evyatar, 'The "Churchill Memorandum" of 1922', in Richard Cohen (ed.), *Vision and Conflict in the Holy Land* (London, 1985)

Frinefrock, Michael, 'Atatürk, Lloyd George and the Megali Idea: Cause and Consequence of the Greek Plan to Seize Constantinople from the Allies, June–August 1922', *The Journal of Modern History*, Vol. 52, No. 1 (March 1980)

Gaunson, A.B., 'To End a Mandate: Sir E.L. Spears and the Anglo-French Collusion in the Levant, 1941–1945', unpublished dissertation, University of Hull, 1981

——— 'Churchill, de Gaulle, Spears and the Levant Affair, 1941', *The Historical Journal*, Vol. 27 No. 3 (September 1984)

Gimblett, Richard, 'Sputter of musketry? The British Military Response to the Anglo-Iranian Oil Dispute, 1951', *Contemporary British History*, Vol. 17, No. 1 (2003)

Goldstein, Erik, 'The British Official Mind and the Lausanne Conference 1922–23', *Diplomacy & Statecraft*, Vol. 14, No. 2 (2003)

Goldsworthy, David, 'Keeping Changes within Bounds: Aspects of Colonial Policy during the Churchcill and Eden Governments, 1951–1957', *The Journal of Imperial and Commonwealth History*, Vol. 18, No. 1 (1990)

Haley, Charles, 'The Desperate Ottoman: Enver Pasha and the German Empire I', *Middle Eastern Studies*, Vol. 30, No. 1 (January 1994)

——— 'The Desperate Ottoman: Enver Pasha and the German Empire II', *Middle Eastern Studies*, Vol. 30, No. 2 (April 1994)

Hall, Douglas, 'Churchill's Elections', in *Finest Hour* No. 101 (Winter 1998–99)

Hughes, Thomas, 'The German Mission to Afghanistan, 1915–1916', *German Studies Review*, Vol. 25, No. 3 (October 2002)

Hurwitz, David, 'Churchill and Palestine', *Judaism*, Vol. 3, No. 22 (Winter 1995)

Jablonsky, David, 'Churchill: Victorian Man of Action', in David Jablonsky (ed.), *Churchill and Hitler: Essays on the Political-Military Direction of Total War* (London, 1994)

Jäschke, Gotthard, 'Mustafa Kemal und England in Neuer Sicht', *Die Welt des Islams*, Vol. 16, Issue 1 (1975)

Khalidi, Walid and Caplan, Neil, 'The 1953 Qibya Raid Revisited: Excerpts from Moshe Sharett's Diaries', *Journal of Palestine Studies*, Vol. 31, No. 4 (Summer 2002)

Keddie, Nikki R., 'Pan-Islam as Proto-Nationalism', *The Journal of Modern History*, Vol. 41, No. 1 (March 1968)

Klieman, Aaron, 'Britain's War Aims in the Middle East in 1915', *Journal of Contemporary History*, Vol. 3, No. 3, The Middle East (July 1968)

Lee, Dwight E., 'The Origins of Pan-Islam', *The American Historical Review,* Vol. 47, No. 2 (January 1942)

MacFie, A.L. 'British Intelligence and the Causes of Unrest in Mesopotamia, 1919–1920', *Middle Eastern Studies*, Vol. 35. No. 1 (January 1999)

——— 'British Intelligence and Turkish Nationalist Movement, 1919–1922', *Middle Eastern Studies*, Vol. 37, No. 1 (January 2001)

Mejcher, Helmut, 'Iraq's External Relations 1921–1926', *Middle Eastern Studies*, Vol. 13, No. 3 (October 1977)

Melka, R., 'Nazi Germany and the Palestine Question', *Middle Eastern Studies*, Vol. 5, No. 3 (October 1969)

Mickelsen, Martin, 'Another Fashoda: The Anglo-Free French Conflict over the Levant, May-September 1941', *Revue Francaise d'histoire d'Outre-Mer*, Vol. 63, 1976

Motadel, David, 'Islam and the European Empires', *The Historical Journal* Vol.55, No.3 (September, 2012)

Muller, James, 'War on the Nile: Winston Churchill and the Reconquest of the Sudan', *Political Science Quarterly*, No. 20 (1991)

Olsen, Robert, 'The Second Time Around: British Policy Towards the Kurds (1921–1922)', *Die Welt des Islams*, Bd. 27 Nr. 1/2 (1987)

——— 'The Churchill–Cox Correspondence Regarding the Creation of the State of Iraq: Consequences for British Policy Towards the Nationalist Turkish Government, 1921–1923', *International Journal of Turkish Studies*, Vol. 5 (1991)

Paris, Timothy, 'British Middle East Policy-Making after World War I: The Lawrentian and Wilsonian Schools', *The Historical Journal*, Vol. 41, No. 3 (September 1998)

Porter, H.W., 'The Imperial Policy of Winston L.S. Churchill from 1900 to 1936 as set Forth by his Speeches' (unpublished thesis, 1946)

Rahe, Paul A., '*The River War*: Nature's provision, man's desire to prevail and prospects for peace', in James W. Muller (ed.), *Churchill as a Peace Maker* (London, 1997)

Reguer, Sara, 'Persian Oil and the First Lord: A Chapter in the Career of Winston Churchill', *Military Affairs*, Vol. 46, No. 3 (October 1982)

Renton, James, 'Changing Languages of Empire and Orient: Britain and the Invention of the Middle East, 1917–1919', *The Historical Journal*, Vol. 50, No. 3 (2007)

Roessel, David, 'Live Orientals and Dead Greeks: Forster's Response to the Chanak Crisis', *Twentieth Century Literature*, Vol. 36, No. 1 (Spring 1990)

Satia, Priya, 'The Defense of Inhumanity: Air Control in Iraq and the British Idea of Arabia', *American Historical Review 111* (February 2006)

——— 'Air Control and the British Idea of Arabia', in Louis, Wm. Roger (ed.), *Penultimate Adventures with Britannia: Personalities, Politics and Culture in Britain* (2007)

——— 'Developing Iraq: Britain, India, and the Redemption of Empire and Technology in World War I', in *Past and Present* no.197 (November 2007)

Schmidt, H.D., 'The Nazi Party in Palestine and the Levant 1932–1939', *International Affairs*, Vol. 28 No. 4 (October 1952)

Simon, Reeva, 'The Teaching of History in Iraq before the Rashid Ali Coup of 1941', *Middle Eastern Studies*, Vol. 22 No. 1 (January 1986)

Smith C.G., 'The Emergence of the Middle East', *Journal of Contemporary History*, Vol. 3, No. 3 (July 1968)

Spalding, Matthew, 'Winston S Churchill and the Middle East', in Christopher Harmon and David Tucker (eds), *Statecraft and Power: Essays in Honour of Harold W. Rood* (London, 1994)

Surridge, Keith, 'The Ambiguous Amir: Britain, Afghanistan and the 1897 North-West Frontier', *The Journal of Imperial and Commonwealth History*, Vol. 36, No. 3 (September 2008)

Swanson, Glen, 'Enver Pasha: The Formative Years', *Middle East Studies*, Vol. 16, No. 3 (October 1980)

Tai-Yong, Tan, 'An Imperial Home-Front: Punjab and World War I', *Journal of Military History*, Vol. 64, No. 2 (April 2000)

Taylor, A.J.P., Review of Bernard Wasserstein, *Britain and the Jews of Europe, 1934–1945* (Oxford, 1979) in *English Historical Review*, Vol. 45, No. 375 (April 1980)

Townshend, Charles, "Civilization and 'Frightfulness": Air Control in the Middle East Between the Wars', in Chris Wrigley (ed.), *Warfare, Diplomacy and Politics: Essay's in Honour of AJP Taylor* (1986)

Toye, Richard, "The Riddle of the Frontier": Winston Churchill, The Malakand Field Force and the Rhetoric of Imperial Expansion', *Historical Research*, Vol. 84, No. 225 (August 2011)

Viongradov, Amal, 'The 1920 Revolt in Iraq Reconsidered: The Role of Tribes in National Politics', *International Journal of Middle Eastern Studies*, Vol. 3, No. 2 (April 1972)

Wheatcroft, Geoffrey, 'Churchill's Zionism', in William Roger Louis (ed.), *Ultimate Adventures with Britannia* (London, 2009)

Young, John, 'Churchill and the East–West Detente', Transactions of the Royal Historical Society, Vol. 11, No. 6 (2001)

INDEX